Cases and Exercises in
ORGANIZATION DEVELOPMENT & CHANGE

Cases and Exercises in
ORGANIZATION DEVELOPMENT & CHANGE

Editor

Donald L. Anderson
University of Denver

Los Angeles | London | New Delhi
Singapore | Washington DC

Los Angeles | London | New Delhi
Singapore | Washington DC

FOR INFORMATION:

SAGE Publications, Inc.
2455 Teller Road
Thousand Oaks, California 91320
E-mail: order@sagepub.com

SAGE Publications Ltd.
1 Oliver's Yard
55 City Road
London EC1Y 1SP
United Kingdom

SAGE Publications India Pvt. Ltd.
B 1/I 1 Mohan Cooperative Industrial Area
Mathura Road, New Delhi 110 044
India

SAGE Publications Asia-Pacific Pte. Ltd.
33 Pekin Street #02-01
Far East Square
Singapore 048763

Acquisitions Editor: Lisa Cuevas Shaw
Associate Editor: Julie Nemer
Editorial Assistant: MaryAnn Vail
Production Editor: Kelle Schillaci
Copy Editor: Trey Thoelcke
Typesetter: C&M Digitals (P) Ltd.
Proofreader: Eleni-Maria Georgiou
Cover Designer: Gail Buschman
Marketing Manager: Helen Salmon
Permissions Editor: Karen Ehrmann

Printed in the United States of America

Library of Congress Cataloging-in-Publication Data

Cases and exercises in organization development & change / editor, Donald L. Anderson.

p. cm.
Includes bibliographical references.

ISBN 978-1-4129-8773-8 (pbk.)

1. Organizational change—Case studies.
2. Organizational behavior—Case studies.
3. Management—Case studies. I. Anderson, Donald L.
II. Title: Cases and exercises in organization development and change.

HD58.8.C3697 2012
658.4′06—dc22   2011000000

This book is printed on acid-free paper.

11 12 13 14 15 10 9 8 7 6 5 4 3 2 1

CONTENTS

Subject Table of Contents

SUSTAINING CHANGE

EVALUATING AND EXITING ENGAGEMENTS

GLOBAL ISSUES IN OD

INDIVIDUAL INTERVENTIONS

TEAM INTERVENTIONS

WHOLE ORGANIZATION INTERVENTIONS

INTRODUCTION

Organization development (OD) is a process of increasing organizational effectiveness and facilitating personal and organizational change through the use of interventions driven by social and behavioral science knowledge. Organization development is
a practical field that encourages the practitioner to marry the mastery of theory with
the application of it. As an OD practitioner, you will bring your knowledge of a wide
range of research and theories about management practices, organizational change,
motivation, human resource practices, concepts and theories of organization development, and more to bear on real situations with real participants. Your expertise in these
areas will translate into actionable implications for your clients. As a result, the choices
you make as a practitioner have real consequences to the organizations that implement
your proposals.

This book of case studies and exercises in organization development is intended to
allow you to practice practical skills in concert with learning about theories of organizational change and human behavior. The contributors to this book hope that these cases
will help you develop an appreciation for the role of the change agent and OD practitioner. Before we discuss how to use this casebook, analyze the cases, and use the exercises
and activities contained herein, first we will introduce the OD practitioner and OD
process to give you the context for the cases in the book.

THE ROLE AND SKILLS OF AN OD PRACTITIONER

An OD practitioner, or consultant, usually develops a relationship with a client who
invites the practitioner into his or her world for a temporary period to improve some
aspect of the organization, team, or individual. This relationship is "a voluntary relationship between a professional helper (consultant) and a help-needing system (client),
in which the consultant is attempting to give help to the client in the solving of some
current or potential problem and the relationship is perceived as temporary by both
parties" and the consultant's role generally exists as an outsider to the client's system
(Lippitt, 1959, p. 5). However, consider the number of other roles in any organization,
including the OD practitioner, that might be better classified as a *change agent;* that is,
a person who works internally to develop or improve some aspect of the organization's
effectiveness, whether it be through information technology, process improvement,

quality programs, and more. Managers and leaders who restructure organizations, develop teams, and coach individuals also take on many of the responsibilities of the OD role as it is defined here. The field of organization development can apply to this broader range of roles as well to provide a foundation in appropriate practices in leading organizational change.

While there are an increasing number of academic and professional programs that teach organization development concepts and practices, not much has changed since Burke (1993, p. 185) wrote that "there simply is no clear and systematic career path for becoming an OD consultant." There is not yet a single, universally accepted certification or degree that would qualify one to be an organization development consultant. In fact, skills and levels of experience differ greatly among OD practitioners who may specialize in certain intervention types such as coaching, strategic planning, or process design. Bunker, Alban, and Lewicki (2005) note that "knowing that someone is an 'OD practitioner' does not tell you much about the person's training, preparation, background or expertise and skill base" (p. 165). Like our clients, OD practitioners are a diverse community.

Most observers agree that a background in the social and behavioral sciences is a good starting point to expose beginners to introductory OD concepts. Burke (1993) recommends academic training in areas such as organizational psychology, group dynamics, research methods, adult learning, career development, counseling, organization development, and organizational theory. Head, Armstrong, and Preston (1996) recommend courses in business, since most OD work is done in that context, a point echoed by Burke and Bradford (2005), who concur that the OD consultant needs to "understand the language and how profit is made and costs contained according to various business models" (p. 8). Supplementary study in areas such as organizational communication, sociology, public administration, and political science also can provide useful concepts that can add to a practitioner's theoretical and practical knowledge. Participation in groups such as professional associations, conferences, and training courses offered by those associations can be good ways to increase one's knowledge of OD concepts and to expand a professional network. Practical experience, however, is a prerequisite to successful consulting, so shadow consulting with a skilled mentor is among the best ways to gain experience. Those wanting to break in to the field might volunteer to help an internal consultant with a project at work. Assisting an internal consultant with data gathering, data analysis, taking notes during interviews, or simply sitting in on a workshop or facilitated meeting can be excellent ways to watch OD work in action. In addition, a popular way to gain experience is to seek *pro bono* opportunities to work with a nonprofit group. One caveat: Because it is important to present oneself ethically and not to overstate one's level of knowledge, working with an experienced consultant is usually necessary until the beginning consultant gains enough experience to take on the engagement alone.

Individual development and growth is a personal exercise. Different individuals will need and want to develop in different areas of competency and skill. As Varney (1980,

p. 34) put it, "professional development comes through a variety of different kinds of experiences" that are customized to the individual. Participating in a program or activity because it is popular or because it is available may not be the best choice. Reading journals, attending conferences, observing other consultants and obtaining an advanced degree are all possible options, depending on the practitioner. In summary, while there are multiple paths to a career in organization development, there are also many opportunities for those eager and motivated to develop the necessary knowledge, skills, and experience.

THE OD PROCESS

The OD process is based in action research, which "seeks to bring together action and reflection, theory and practice, in participation with others, in the pursuit of practical solutions to issues of pressing concern to people, and more generally the flourishing of individual personas and their communities" (Reason & Bradbury, 2001, p. 1). In its ideal form, the practitioner is actively engaged *with* those experiencing the problem versus conducting research *on* them (Heron & Reason, 2001). Thus participation by organizational members in diagnosing the issues and solving the problem is a key feature of action research. Action research projects generally proceed when an initial problem prompts diagnosis, planning action, taking action, and evaluating results. Once results are evaluated, the cycle begins again.

Traditional action research programs strive to contribute to both theory and practice, bridging the divide between them, and this has been a central objective of organization development throughout its history. The purpose is not just to create new theory, but to create new possibilities for action where theory and action are closely intertwined (Coghlan & Brannick, 2001). The two components of action (practice) and research (theory) are combined in practice as they are in the name. Over time, however, many believe that the gap between theory and practice has widened as practitioners have devoted less attention to contributing to theoretical knowledge (Bunker, Alban, & Lewicki, 2005). Regardless, action research and OD consulting share similar objectives in developing a participative and inclusive process in which practitioners and organizational members jointly explore problems, initiate action, and evaluate outcomes, and where the overall purpose is social or organizational change.

Though OD practitioners today may not necessarily see contributions to theoretical knowledge to be a central objective of every OD project, practitioners have adopted an OD consulting process that generally follows an action research model, borrowing the major tenets of action research. The consulting process diagram pictured in Figure I.1 is generally consistent with what most OD practitioners do. The consulting model looks like a linear process, but most consulting engagements rarely proceed in such a step-by-step manner. The process is more iterative than linear.

Figure I.1 The Organization Development Process

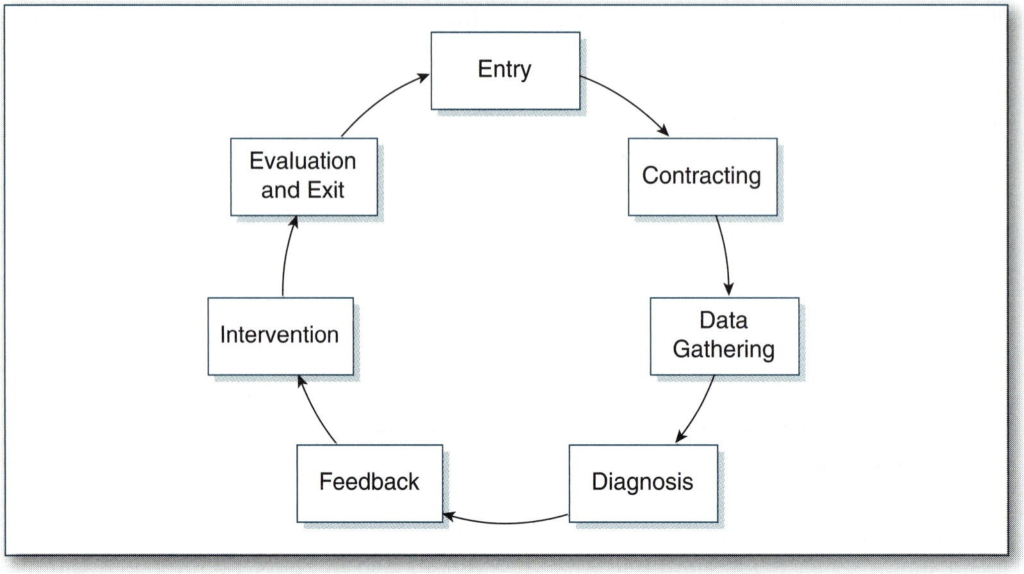

Let's look at each of these stages in turn.

Entry: The first stage of the consulting process is entry, which begins with an initial contact between a consultant and a client.

Contracting: Next, the consultant and client come to agreement on what work will be accomplished. The client makes the request by describing the problem or OD consulting opportunity, and then the client and consultant discuss the engagement and how to create a successful consulting relationship. The consultant responds with a formal or informal proposal about what he or she will do.

Data Gathering: Third, data are generally gathered about the situation, the client, the organization, and other relevant aspects of the problem. This can involve one or more methods or sources of information.

Diagnosis and Feedback: Next, the client and consultant jointly analyze and interpret the data. The consultant presents the client with feedback from the data-gathering stage. The problem may be reevaluated, additional data may be gathered, or an intervention strategy may be proposed.

Intervention: The consultant and client agree on what intervention(s) would best address the problem, and the intervention strategy is carried out.

Evaluation and Exit: The consultant and client evaluate the outcomes of the intervention(s) and whether the intervention(s) have resulted in the desired change. Additional data are gathered at this point and the client and consultant may agree to terminate the engagement or to begin the cycle again (reentry, recontracting, and so on).

THINKING LIKE AN OD PRACTITIONER

Throughout this process, practitioners are confronted with choices at every turn, and these choices are not easy ones to make. Practitioners must make tradeoffs as they decide, among other concerns:

- How to gather the most relevant data when time and access are limited
- Which questions are most germane to ask in an interview or on a survey
- Which model to use in analyzing data, or whether a model is appropriate at all for the situation
- How to prioritize which issues and themes discovered in data gathering are most important to address
- How to frame sensitive concerns in a feedback meeting with a client to encourage action but avoid collusion
- How to genuinely help the client and add value without taking on all of the client's burdens alone
- How to balance concerns of limited time and money in selecting interventions
- Whether to address task or relational interventions first
- How to evaluate the results of the engagement given the many factors involved in personal, team, and organizational change
- When to leave the engagement, staying long enough to leave the client in a satisfactory position for the future but leaving early enough to avoid client dependency

Indeed, any single engagement might confront a practitioner with dozens of difficult decisions such as these. Each decision alternative has its advantages and disadvantages, and each course of action may help to facilitate or hinder the progress of the engagement and likelihood of successful change. An effective choice in one situation might be ineffective in another. Moreover, such decisions usually must be made in imperfect situations, when the ideal approach is impossible for a variety of reasons, whether pragmatic (e.g., half the team is on vacation next week) or idiosyncratic e.g., the culture of this organization discourages surveys). Evidence may point to a variety of conflicting or contradictory actions. Thus the practitioner's best choice is often the answer to the question, "What is the best decision at this point, for this organization and these participants, in this context, given what I know now?"

THE BENEFITS OF CASE STUDIES

The case studies in this book are intended to prompt you to think about answers to that question. Each provides a slice of organizational life, constructed as a brief scene in which you can imagine yourself playing a part. As Ellet (2007) writes, "A case is a text that refuses to explain itself" (p. 19). It requires you to take an active role to interpret it and discover its meaning. Fortunately, unlike the passage of time in real life, in written cases life is momentarily paused to give you the chance to consider a response. While you do not have the opportunity to gather additional data or ask questions of participants, you do have the ability to flip back a few pages, read the situation again, and contemplate. You can carefully consider alternate courses of action, weigh the pros and cons of each, and clarify why you would choose one option over another.

As a result of having to make these choices, you will hone your ability to communicate your rationale for your decisions. Other readers will make different choices, each with their own well-reasoned rationales. Through discussion you will sharpen your ability to solve problems, understanding the principles behind the decisions that you and your classmates have made. You will learn about how your own experiences shape your assumptions and approaches to problems. You will be challenged to develop your skills to provide evidence for your reasoning, defend your analyses, and explain your thinking in clear and concise ways for fellow practitioners and clients alike. You may find that these discussions prompt you to change your mind about the approach you would take, becoming convinced by another reader's well-reasoned proposal, or you may find that your reasoning persuades others that your approach has the greater advantages.

Regardless, you will learn that there is no single right answer at the back of the book or to be shared by the author of the case after you have struggled. For some of the cases in this book, the authors have developed an epilogue that your instructor may share with you (available in the instructor's resources companion to this book) to explain what happened after the case concluded. This information may provide support for the approach you would have taken, or it may make you think that your approach was incorrect. Instead of seeking the right or wrong answer, however, asking yourself if your proposal was well-reasoned given the circumstances is more important than knowing the exact outcome of the case. While you have the opportunity to do so, use the occasion of the case study and the discussion to play with various alternatives. Here, the process may be more important than the outcome.

ANALYZING CASE STUDIES

As you read the cases, take the role of the change agent as you analyze the situation, considering the tradeoffs and choices that professionals experience in real OD situations. Each case is accompanied by discussion questions and resources for further study, should you wish to follow up on the research or theories implicated in the case.

Here are a few tips to get you started with case study analysis.

1. Read the entire case first, and resist the temptation to come to any conclusions the first time you read through it. Allow yourself to linger with the problem, first gathering all of the relevant data about the situation before you propose any solutions or come to any judgment about what's happening or what the client needs to do. Try not to rush to a solution. Maintain a spirit of inquiry, not problem solving, as you read the case again.

2. Use charts to map out organizational structures and underline key phrases and issues. Write questions that come to mind in the margins. Read the case through multiple times to ensure that you have not missed a key detail that would indicate to a client that you had not been paying close attention.

3. Realize that like real life, case studies contain many extra details and describe multiple issues. Organizational life is messy and complex, and not all of these details are helpful or necessary to the consultant or change agent. "A case is a description of a situation, usually a complex one that has multiple meanings, some of which can be contradictory" (Ellet, 2007, p. 90). A consultant helping a team redefine roles and responsibilities may be doing so in an environment in which the company has acquired a competitor or quarterly results were disappointing. Part of the practitioner's role is to sort through and separate the useful primary information from the unnecessary secondary information (or information that is unnecessary for the immediate problem). This is part of the value of these case exercises. Your logic and intuition will develop as your skills and experience grow. Ask yourself what the client is trying to achieve, what he or she has asked of you, and what the core issues and central facts are.

4. Similarly, in any response to a client or reaction to a case, resist the temptation to comment on everything. An OD practitioner can help to prioritize the most pressing issues and help the client sort through the complexities of organizational life. It could be that part of the reason the client has asked for help is that the number of possibilities for action are too overwhelming to decide what to do next.

5. When you are prepared to write a response or an analysis, ask yourself whether you have addressed the central questions asked by the case and whether you have clearly stated the issues to the client. Once your response is written, could you send that, in its present form, to the client described in the case? In that regard, is it professionally written and organized well enough to communicate unambiguously to the client? Will the client understand how and why you reached these conclusions?

6. As you write your analysis, ask yourself how you know any particular fact or interpretation to be true, and whether you have sufficiently justified your interpretation with actual data. Instead of boldly stating that "managers are not trained for their roles," you could write, "only two of ten managers had attended a management training course in the past 5 years, leading me to conclude that management training has not been given a high priority." The latter uses data and makes the interpretation explicit; the former is likely to invite criticism or defensiveness from a client. This does not mean that directness is not appropriate, only that it must follow from the evidence. We will describe the considerations of the feedback process in depth in this book.

7. When you have finished your own thinking and writing about the case, and after you have had the opportunity to discuss the case and options for action with classmates, take the time to write down your reflections from the experience (Ellet, 2007). What did you learn? What principles might apply for the next time you are confronted with these choices?

ABOUT THE BOOK

The case studies in this book will present you with the above issues and more. The authors have included a wide variety of client experiences that address these challenges. These cases reflect real experiences, though some of the details, including client and organization names and significant details, may be changed to ensure anonymity. The organizations included represent a variety of settings in which organization development is practiced, including for-profit businesses, nonprofit organizations, educational institutions, health care settings, and government and public entities.

The book contains three parts. Part I presents cases about the OD process: entry and contracting with clients, gathering data, giving feedback, encountering client resistance, selecting interventions, and evaluating and sustaining change. In some cases, you will read about a client's presenting problem, develop your thinking about possible underlying problems, and form a data-gathering strategy to build on the client's explanation of the presenting problem. Armed with data, in other cases you will need to develop an explanation or diagnosis about what's happening in the organization based on results from interviews, focus groups, or other data-gathering methods. You will have the chance to develop your own skills in giving feedback to clients based on data gathering and diagnosis. You will be confronted with a client's resistance to change that may present a barrier to a practitioner's proposal for action.

Part II addresses interventions in more detail by presenting cases in organizationwide, team, and individual interventions. In this section, cases describe practitioner and client challenges in areas such as organization design and restructuring, leadership coaching, roles in teams, and more. For many of these intervention cases, you will learn about a client's problem and will be challenged to consider which type of intervention would be most useful in this circumstance, to evaluate a practitioner's choices, to design the intervention strategy, or to outline the intervention itself.

Part III presents exercises, simulations, and assessments that you can use on your own or with peers as in-class activities. These activities enhance your knowledge about organizational theory with practical and experiential exercises that provide realistic scenarios that managers and organizational change practitioners regularly experience. Experiential activities included in this section will provide role plays, instruments, and simulations that can help you build practical skills. Some of the exercises contain published assessments or instruments that you will complete on your own, and which you may wish to research more thoroughly by seeking out the references provided. The exercises and activities in Part III are designed to allow you to practice the skills of an OD practitioner in situations that invite you to take a greater responsibility for the interaction. Like the case studies you have read to this point, these exercises will allow you to take on the role of a practitioner and make the real choices and decisions that practitioners must make in their work. Here, however, you will be challenged with less organizational context and more responsibility for live, in-the-moment, dialogue. There will be fewer occasions in which you may pause and reflect, and more opportunities to practice the role of an

OD practitioner in an interactive setting. Some of these experiences and practice exercises may feel uncomfortable at first, as you may be wondering what to say or do in a particular circumstance. Greater confidence will come with practice and feedback from others.

We hope that the cases and exercises in this book leave you with enhanced skills and an appreciation for the complexities and challenges involved in leading organizational change.

ANCILLARIES

Instructor Teaching Site

A password-protected instructor's site is available at **www.sagepub.com/anderson-cases,** offering teaching notes to help instructors plan and teach their courses. These resources have been designed to help instructors make the classes as practical and interesting as possible for students. Teaching notes include:

- Case Summary
- Teaching Points
- Discussion Questions
- Additional Readings
- Exercises
- Case Epilogues

This book can be used as a stand-alone text or as an accompaniment to Donald L. Anderson's textbook *Organization Development: The Process of Leading Organizational Change, Second Edition* (ISBN 978–1–4129–8774–5).

REFERENCES

Bunker, B. B, Alban, B. T., & Lewicki, R. J. (2005). Ideas in currency and OD practice: Has the well gone dry? In D. L. Bradford & W. W. Burke (Eds.), *Reinventing organization development* (pp. 163–194). San Francisco: Pfeiffer.

Burke, W. W. (1993). *Organization development: A process of learning and changing* (2nd ed.). Reading, MA: Addison-Wesley.

Burke, W. W., & Bradford, D. L. (2005). The crisis in OD. In D. L. Bradford & W. W. Burke (Eds.), *Reinventing organization development* (pp. 7–14). San Francisco: Pfeiffer.

Coghlan, D., & Brannick, T. (2001). *Doing action research in your own organization.* London: Sage.

Ellet, W. (2007). *The case study handbook: How to read, discuss, and write persuasively about cases.* Boston: Harvard Business School Press.

Head, T., Armstrong, T., & Preston, J. (1996). The role of graduate education in becoming a competent organization development practitioner. *OD Practitioner, 28*(1/2), 52–60.

Heron, J., & Reason, P. (2001). The practice of co-operative inquiry: Research "with" rather than "on" people. In P. Reason & H. Bradbury (Eds.), *Handbook of action research: Participative inquiry and practice* (pp. 179–188). London: Sage.

Lippitt, R. (1959). Dimensions of the consultant's job. *Journal of Social Issues, 15*(2), 5–12.

Reason, P., & Bradbury, H. (2001). Introduction: Inquiry and participation in search of a world worthy of human aspiration. In P. Reason & H. Bradbury (Eds.), *Handbook of action research: Participative inquiry and practice* (pp. 1–14). London: Sage.

Varney, G. H. (1980). Developing OD competencies. *Training and Development Journal, 34*(4), 30–35.

Part I

CASES IN THE ORGANIZATION DEVELOPMENT PROCESS

CONTRACTING FOR SUCCESS

Scoping Large Organizational Change Efforts

LAURIE K. CURE AND MARILYN SCHOCK

Learning Objectives

- To support your understanding of OD competencies in the entry phase that enhance collaboration and results.
- To assist you in analyzing and organizing complex data and information in the contracting process.
- To identify core interventions, conditions, and deliverables from the engagement that need to be incorporated into the contracting process.

Robert stopped his car and sat quietly in the physician's parking lot located on the north side of the hospital. It was a picturesque August morning. The sun was shining and the summer flowers on the 29-acre campus were in full bloom. Despite the beauty of the day, he couldn't help but take a deep breath and release a long heavy sigh. It had been 6 months since he assumed the CEO position for Valley Medical Center. In that time, he had already encountered some of the biggest challenges of his career.

Valley Medical Center (VMC) was a 135-bed hospital with more than 1,500 employees and 375 practicing physicians. As Robert entered the building, he contemplated his current position and was glad to be meeting with Karen from Results Consulting. He was hopeful that she could assist him in assessing all the critical issues he was experiencing and develop a game plan for moving forward. The gravity of the situation was weighing on him like a 2-ton brick.

"Good morning, Robert," a voice sang as Robert entered his office. Robert's assistant, Terri, dropped several contracts on his desk as she entered. "Your 8:00 appointment is waiting for you in the boardroom."

"Thanks," Robert commented, smiling. Terri had a tremendous history with the organization and brought a wealth of knowledge about the physicians, leaders, and staff. VMC operated in a smaller suburban community of about 55,000 people and many of the employees and physicians had been with the hospital for more than 20 years.

Entering the boardroom, Robert saw Karen admiring the view of the Rocky Mountains. "Hello, it's nice to meet you." He walked toward her with his hand extended. Karen stood and shook his hand firmly. She was excited to be here and brought an array of expertise in organization development. She had worked with many organizations facing challenges similar to VMC and was confident that she could assist Robert in managing this complex situation.

"I'm so pleased to be here. Thank you for the invitation to partner with you." They both took seats at the large conference table, which seemed to dominate the room. Karen proceeded, "I understand from our previous discussion that you are seeking assistance with prioritizing your many challenges and actions. Tell me a little more about what you are facing."

Robert paused briefly and said, "It's difficult to know where to begin. I started here about 6 months ago after a string of short-term, unsuccessful CEOs. In total, there have been five CEOs in the past 24 months, including myself. Prior to that, leadership was highly consistent and secure. Needless to say, these rapid changes in leadership have created instability and gaps in the strategy and direction of the organization. To make matters more complicated, we also have made significant leadership changes in a number of our other executive level positions. Ineffective leadership at that level surfaced and it was essential that we bring in stronger senior leaders to support the organization."

"Wow, I can see where that would be challenging. How are leaders, staff, and physicians reacting to all this change?" Karen asked.

"It's been tough. They have expressed frustration. I think many of them are concerned and unsure about the future. We've heard rumors of staff and physicians feeling afraid and possibly thinking about leaving to work or practice at a competitor hospital. Despite this, however, there is still strong loyalty." Robert stood up. "I would love to take you on a tour of the facility. It would give you a great opportunity to meet different leaders and ask that question of them. It also would be a wonderful way for you to experience the culture and gauge our situation."

Karen and Robert began the tour in the main lobby of the hospital. It was clearly a busy facility with patients and families coming and going frequently. Several sitting areas throughout the space were occupied by people waiting for tests and procedures. Along the rock wall stood a portrait of an older man, looking distinguished and posed. "This might be a good time for me to provide you with some background of our facility." Robert started, "This facility is about 30 years old and was built on land donated by Mr. Thomas, who you see there in the picture. This history had afforded us the benefit of strong community loyalty and commitment. However, our market has become much more competitive. We have always been a sole community provider and the market leader, but recently we have begun to lose market share and patient volumes in critical service lines like surgery, cardiology, and oncology. Our largest competitor is a hospital in Gainesville, just to the north of us. It's a larger city, so they are in a position to offer more comprehensive services. We have recently seen market share declines as a result of their increased presence in our market. To make matters worse, they are building a new hospital just 2 miles from here that is scheduled to open in 9 months."

"It sounds like you have strong commitment to your community and patients. How would you describe your organizational culture?" Karen was curious if the culture of the organization would support their challenges or if it was a pivotal barrier for them.

"From a competitive position, I would say, complacent, and our current market share declines reflect that complacency. I'm seeking to create a culture that is strategic and sustainable over the long term. On the people side, I would add that this facility is very family-oriented. The culture among staff and physicians demonstrates caring, camaraderie, and compassion, which is exactly what you want for a health care facility. On the downside, I would say we struggle with lack of focus and limited accountability. We are operating in a much different environment, a competitive environment. Right now, people are looking out for themselves and we need to be operating as a cohesive team."

Karen found his choice of words interesting. He expressed a sense of urgency, yet characterized several strengths on which the facility could build. She made note and would be certain to bring it up and explore it further at a later time during their tour. They continued down a long, wide hallway from the main lobby to the emergency department. Karen noticed that various smaller hallways guided patients to radiology and the laboratory. Robert greeted patients and families kindly as they walked, "Good morning. Can I help you find something?" His caring was evident and the patients responded warmly.

Along the walls, Karen saw a large collage of photos recognizing various employees for their contributions to patient care. Next to the pictures was a placard on the wall that hosted the company's mission, vision, and values. "Share with me how you live your mission. What do those statements mean to the employees here?" she asked.

Robert said, "Well, VMC is owned and operated by a large nonprofit health system with hospitals throughout the country. As part of a system, we share in the mission, vision, and values of our parent company to ensure integration of purpose across all of the hospitals. Our mission is to provide excellent patient care. This is supported by a vision to be the market leader in clinical quality, patient satisfaction, and operational excellence. As you know, delivering on a mission requires focusing on what matters most." Robert paused. At that moment, they passed a woman wearing a white lab coat embroidered with the hospital's blue and red logo and the words *Operating Room* below.

Robert smiled to her. "Hello, Patricia. Do you have a moment?" She nodded and stopped next to Karen. "How is your son? He was preparing to go out of state for college last we talked." Karen continued to be impressed by the genuineness that she saw him exhibit with people around him.

"Thanks for remembering. We drove him out there this weekend. It was exciting to see him start a new chapter in his life," Patricia said. "I'm meeting Sam shortly about expanding hours in the cath lab, but I am happy to chat with you." She smiled at Karen and shook her hand.

"This is Karen. We have engaged her services as we seek to improve performance and relationships here at VMC." Robert engaged the two in dialogue. "Patricia is our Director of Surgical Services. Karen was just asking about how we live our values here at Valley. What are your thoughts in response to that question? I thought it would be better for her to hear from one of our leaders."

"Definitely." Patricia spoke with confidence and friendliness. "When Robert came on board, Valley's leadership developed five priorities. We recognized that to be successful we had to focus on a few important things. For us, these are strong employee engagement, high patient satisfaction, quality patient care, being physician friendly, and achieving financial strength."

Karen listened intently. "That sounds great, but I still wonder how your people live those values. So often, companies have wonderful visions and strategies that live on the wall," she pointed to the plaques, "or in a three-ring binder on the shelves of leaders." Karen smiled as both Robert and Patricia laughed. They had several of those binders in their office from previous attempts to build strategy.

Patricia continued, "We have adopted six ground rules that mold the organization's behaviors to support the culture. They are nonnegotiable and all leaders and employees within the organization adhere to them in order to be successful within the culture. Prior to these, we felt a little lost. We were running around doing a lot of things, but none of it felt like it mattered. We also had the mentality that if you were a great clinical provider, that was enough. We now realize that attitude and behavior are equally, if not more, important."

"So, what are your ground rules and how do they support this culture change you are undergoing?" Karen asked

"The ground rules are: no excuses, we are a team—sink or swim we do it together, bring up your good ideas, poor performance will be addressed, the phrase 'that's not my job' is not acceptable, and support and manage up other team members." Patricia was excited as she explained. "The ability to identify basic rules that everyone accepts enhanced the transformation of the culture and ability to provide quality care. It also provides leadership with the building blocks so we can have conversations with employees and physicians who are not practicing our values."

Karen was beginning to put the pieces together. She looked toward Robert who began walking them slowly toward the elevators. "Clearly, when you arrived, it seemed the facility was not in a position to achieve its objectives with the existing structure and ways of thinking. So, the priorities and ground rules served as a foundation for building a new focus."

Robert nodded. "You asked about culture earlier. The ground rules create an environment of accountability, which was lacking prior to my arrival. Concentrating on the priorities with the ground rules as behavioral guidelines allows everyone in the organization to focus on delivering excellent patient care by creating mutual trust, individual motivation, and teamwork."

Karen said, "The real work then involves developing processes and support mechanisms to hardwire desired behaviors. That's where I can come in."

Patricia agreed wholeheartedly. "Our new leadership team has made tremendous strides in creating the base. What's difficult now is holding people accountable to these standards in a respectful, yet firm way. We have undergone a great amount of change recently. When you speak to living our values, every employee must do this in every interaction with our patients. Achieving this consistency is a challenge for us. We also struggle with elements of teamwork."

Patricia needed to be at her next meeting, so she left the two. Karen was grateful for the time with Patricia. Robert stopped just outside the elevator doors and pushed the up arrow. "The five priorities might be a good way for me to discuss our successes and challenges with you. Let's start with employee engagement." At that moment, a small beep signaled the arrival of the elevator and the doors opened.

Robert leaned over and pushed the button for the fifth floor, the top floor of the hospital. "VMC seeks to select the best people to deliver high-quality care. Our ground rules help to define behavioral expectations and support employee accountability."

Karen was inquisitive. "You've done a great job selling me on many of your new changes." She laughed nervously. "Where are you experiencing the most significant challenges when it comes to your people?"

They exited the elevator on the fifth floor and across the hall was the human resources office. "Perfect timing." Robert opened the large glass door and was greeted by Dawn, the chief human resources officer. After a friendly introduction, Dawn proceeded to tell Karen about the significant employee challenges VMC was confronting. Like other health care providers, VMC faced strategic challenges in relation to shortages of health care workers, including nurses and physicians.

Dawn said, "We must remake our workplace to attract and retain staff. We want to be in the top 10% of the country with employee engagement scores. We measure this using an annual survey. All our employees took the survey just before Robert arrived. We had 95% participation, which is great, but only scored in the 50th percentile nationwide for engagement. We were so disappointed in our results." She proceeded to explain that as VMC works to change its culture, they were tackling a couple of critical employee issues. Their philosophy is to have the "right people on the bus." This means they must recruit and retain individuals who match the culture. With a new competitor hospital opening soon, many of their best employees are considering leaving. They fear that with all the changes at VMC, it might not be a good place to stay.

In addition, VMC has a large percentage of employees who are no longer the right fit for the culture. Dawn continued, "Many of our employees have behavior and attitudes that are negative and we have not addressed them in the past. Our leaders are struggling to conduct these difficult, yet important conversations. They also may not have the skills to establish the changes necessary to lead our new direction. We are committed to supporting them in enhancing their leadership abilities."

"You hit on a key point," Karen said. "Often, our leaders are not well equipped to lead. We take people who are great at their jobs and promote them to management without the proper training and skills development to lead people." Both Robert and Dawn agreed.

Dawn was passionate at this point. "I couldn't agree more. We are working hard to understand and respond to employee needs. We are 100% committed to retaining and hiring highly skilled staff and leaders who bring excitement and positive attitudes. We also need to address those employees who are actively disengaged."

The time with Dawn was helpful. Karen was beginning to get a better sense of the core issues that Robert was dealing with at VMC. As they left Dawn's office, they encountered additional staff moving in and out of patient rooms providing care. "Patient satisfaction is a second priority for us," Robert explained. "We have to remain connected and responsive to patients' desires if we are going to be successful. Patients have increasing expectations for their care and continuously striving to improve is important. Sometimes our staff gets stuck thinking they can continue to do things the way they always have." Robert paused. "When I first arrived, our patient satisfaction scores were in the 30th percentile. I have a goal that we will be in 90th. I want to be among the best. Our patients deserve that and I need staff and leaders who can get us there." Karen saw a bit of desperation in his eyes.

They proceeded to the staircase and headed down to the fourth floor, where they encountered a petite woman. "Good morning, Dr. Jacobs. It's good to see you." said Robert.

"Hi, Robert. What are you up to this morning? Moving and shaking as always?" Dr. Jacobs had a boisterous laugh. She grinned at Karen and introduced herself as one of VMC's hospitalists. She couldn't stay long because she had patients to attend to, but she shared with Karen the importance of strong physician relationships to the hospital's success. "As physicians, we work in partnership with the hospital. They need us and we need them."

She left and Robert explained, "Our hospitalists provide care to all our patients while they are in the hospital. Our third priority is to be physician friendly. This requires us to think like a doctor and help make our facility easy for them to practice in. Sometimes, we have to change how we work in order to do this."

"We talked earlier about all the changes you have going on," Karen said. "I think change management and culture might be areas we can focus on. Dawn mentioned shortages of health care workers and physicians. Do you have enough physicians practicing in your community?" Karen was linking the critical pieces of the puzzle together.

"Good catch," Robert said. "We're actually actively recruiting for many specialties, including orthopedic surgery and OB/GYN. We're also finding that many new doctors want to be employed by the hospital instead of owning their own practice. From an organization development perspective, this changes the rules of the game a bit."

Karen inquired further and Robert proceeded. "Previously, we worked in partnership with our physicians. Sometimes, we think we have more control with people who are employed, but instead I want us to consider how to maintain loyalty by involving physicians in decision making. This is something we don't do very well. We often make changes and implement new process without asking our key stakeholders: physicians and staff."

Karen was collecting some great information and already formulating some thoughts and recommendations for Robert. It seemed he needed ways to hardwire cultural change that supported the facility's success factors. She was anxious to hear about the last two priorities.

"You've shared with me the first three priorities. Expand on the final two if you would?"

Robert headed toward the new tower, which was recently constructed. As they walked, he introduced Karen to the fourth priority; high-quality patient care. "As a health care provider, we have an obligation to provide quality care. People expect that from us. If you come to the hospital for surgery or any kind of treatment, you expect to get quality care that fixes your problem. Our quality is actually very good. We have great patient outcomes that are supported by data that we submit to federal programs. We are also surveyed regularly by several agencies and score well."

"That sounds positive, but somehow, I suspect there is more to the story," Karen joked lightly.

"You're catching on. Again, our challenges with this priority lie in our people. Everyone does really well within their workgroups. The only problem is our patients don't just experience one part of the hospital. They touch many departments and see many different people throughout the course of their visit. If our various departments are not working together, we risk looking disjointed. If we are to increase our quality and patient satisfaction, our different departments need to come together and work more cohesively with one another."

"Many of your concerns and challenges are people focused," Karen noted. "This is often a concern for senior leaders. The 'softer' side of the business can be more challenging, because it is not a black-and-white solution. Tell me what you've done so far."

"You're correct there. I consider myself to be an inspirational leader. I have painted the vision and begun seeking many of the hard solutions, like restructuring and bringing on new senior leadership. We are changing our physician strategies and enhancing our market strategies, but sometimes, I'm at a loss with how to move the people side forward."

Karen could feel her heart light up. This was so common and she brought such talent in this arena. "I think I can help," she stated confidently. "First, let's finish with your final priority.

Robert knew just how to wrap up. "Our final priority is ensuring we remain financially stable. I believe strongly that if we do everything else well, finances will follow. However, I must admit, I get nervous when I see our patient volumes and market share declining. We have always had strong financial performance, and still do, but our recent challenges in the market have me a little on edge. Our payor mix is changing. More patients are entering our facility without insurance or the means to pay. As a not-for-profit hospital, we believe we have a community obligation to serve, but we must balance that with financial sustainability."

They entered a beautiful new part of the building. "This must be the new tower you referred to earlier," Karen said.

"Indeed. This was completed about 2 years ago. Our community is growing rapidly and we were running out of space. We built this addition to accommodate a new OB floor for births, an intensive care unit, as well as support services space. We also have expanded radiology and the laboratory."

"This all seems exciting." Karen was wondering about the expansion in light of their market position. "How does this all play out with your current environmental challenges?"

Robert cleared his throat. "That continues to be the issue. We must sustain and grow patient volumes. We're in a turnaround situation. Our financial operating margins are at risk as we start to absorb interest and depreciation expenses for the new building. With these financial pressures, we must be the best. We need to enhance team-based decision making, maintain consistent and focused leadership, and prioritize opportunities. We can't be all things to all people. I have so many things that need my attention; some days, I don't even know where to begin."

"The tour was wonderful." Karen had a million items floating through her mind. "I have some immediate thoughts that I would like to share with you and then I will create a proposal that outlines my additional recommendations. Can we return to the boardroom and conclude our discussion?"

"I welcome your input," Robert said with relief and comfort.

Discussion Questions

1. How would you initiate your engagement with Valley Medical Center? What are the steps you would take as you begin the entry and contracting phase?

2. In considering the case above, where does Valley Medical Center have strengths? Where do they have challenges? What are the critical success factors for the hospital?

3. As an OD practitioner, what recommendations would you make to support Robert in achieving his goals? How would you ensure these are included in the contracting process?

4. Valley Medical Center is experiencing a great deal of change. What recommendation would you make to help them more effectively handle the change they are experiencing?

FOR FURTHER READING

Lusthaus, C., Adrein, M.-H., Anderson, G., Carden, F., & Montalvan, G. P. (2002). *Organizational assessment: A framework for improving performance.* Ottawa, Canada: International Research Center.

Senge, P. M. (1990). *The fifth discipline: The art and practice of the learning Organization.* New York: Doubleday.

Senge, P. M., Kleiner, A., Roberts, C., Ross, R., Roth, G., & Smith, B. (1999). *The dance of change: The challenges to sustaining momentum in learning organizations.* New York: Doubleday.

THE DISCIPLINE DILEMMA IN RAINBOW HIGH SCHOOL

LIZE A. E. BOOYSEN AND STELLA M. NKOMO

Learning Objectives

- To help you understand the steps involved in the consulting contract.
- To make you aware of the ethical issues involved in the entry and contracting stage of a consulting project.
- To help you identify clients, or client subsystems in a consulting project, and to clarify client and consultant roles.

Annette Duval, the Principal of Rainbow High School, was driving home after yet another difficult day at school. She thought about that day's staff meeting regarding the rising frequency of race-based conflict and violence at her school and the different perceptions among her staff on these issues. She could not understand why the staff failed to reach consensus on how to deal with these issues at school, nor why everyone was so emotional about it. It was really a difficult meeting for her to control. On top of that, another educator handed in her resignation, the fourth resignation this year. She had to admit, teaching at Rainbow High School was no joke and very stressful, and she pondered: "To be quite honest, if I were not so much invested in the school, and if I were not as resilient—or maybe so proud—I would have taken up that other principal's position the Department of Education offered me 2 months ago. But no, I want to finish my work here at Rainbow High School. I will not give up; I am a good principal. I will stay on and get my 15-years-long service award."

Annette's mind slipped to when she started as principal at Rainbow High School in January 1994, just before the first democratic elections in South Africa and official end of apartheid.[1] She had to relocate from a rural town, Ficksburg, near Bloemfontein in the Orange Free State, to Gauteng, Johannesburg. It was a huge change.

She was the deputy principal of a prestigious private girls' school in the small town and got promoted to this well-known public high school in the large cosmopolitan, world-class city, Johannesburg. Annette smiled as she thought about the enormous change the school had undergone since the start of her tenure, and she was pleased to be pivotal in affecting the change. Before the elections in 1994, Rainbow High School had been an Afrikaans medium school, named after a former apartheid prime minister, with exclusively White learners and teachers. It was located in the heart of a White, working-class neighbourhood. But by 2000, the school had been renamed Rainbow High School[2] and the demographics and culture of the school had changed dramatically. Now, it was an English medium school, more than 80% of the learners were people of color (African, Coloured,[3] or Indian), and many learners were being transported from less privileged communities, as far as 30 miles per day.

The teachers' demographics also changed from exclusively White to almost 40% people of color, and 51% of the teachers were now female. Annette chuckled when she remembered how astonished everybody was when it was announced that she, an Afrikaner White woman, was going to be the next principal of one of the model schools in South Africa. She also could recall the resistance she had to deal with from her all-White male management and extended management team at Rainbow High School. Both the deputy principals and all four department heads were White males. Now, at least one of the two deputy principals was a White female, the other deputy principal was still a White male from the original team, and very near retirement. Also, three of the four department heads were women, of which one was a person of color.

Annette thought, "Yes, I can really be proud of the transformation I effected in Rainbow High School." She smiled wryly when she recalled the morning's difficult staff meeting, and said to herself, "Rainbow High School is not without its problems at the moment. Our teachers are not really committed. They do not want to go that extra mile anymore. We are losing teachers almost every term. Six in the past year and a half, four of them people of color, who all in their exit interviews indicated one way or another that work stress and difficult interpersonal relations were part of the reasons why they resigned. Although we have come such a long way in this school, and we changed so much over the past 11 years, why do we still have these kinds of problems?" To Annette it was very clear—discipline. The students merely need to be disciplined more thoroughly and effectively. "The problem is," she concluded, "all teachers do not see discipline in the same light. There are different standards—and that confuses the children. How can it be that the teachers cannot agree on how to discipline the students? This is really strange. These problems with differences of opinion on discipline didn't exist when I first started at Rainbow High School. Might this be a cultural thing?"

While she negotiated the Johannesburg peak traffic, she tuned in on FM Radio 809 and heard that after the commercial break there would be an interview with a diversity management expert, Dr. du Pont, a leadership professor at one of the leading South African business schools and also a management consultant. The topic was "How to effectively manage diversity in South African organizations."

She said to herself, "Good timing, maybe this will give me some insight!" After listening to the interview, she made a mental note to phone Dr. du Pont to ask for help with the issues at Rainbow High School. For the first time that day, she felt relieved—now she had a plan!

ENTRY AND CONTRACTING: FIRST CONTACT TELEPHONE CONVERSATION

Dr. du Pont had a busy day. A few hours ago she had a radio interview on her diversity work in the Johannesburg studios of FM Radio 809, and this had gobbled up most of her day. She returned to her office at the business school and was going through her e-mails when her phone rang.

Annette: Hello. Is this Dr. du Pont?

Dr. du Pont: Yes, this is she.

Annette: My name is Annette Duval, the Principal of Rainbow High School. I listened to your radio interview earlier today and I really believe you might be able to help me with some diversity issues we have at the school.

Dr. du Pont: Well, I certainly will try. Can you give me some background and idea of what you perceive to be the problem?

Annette: Well, it's a broad range of issues. We have a high turnover, and the educators and learners are uncommitted. They experience real racism in some instances and in others they are perceived as racist. We have even had instances of conflict and violence among the learners!

Dr. du Pont: Why, Mrs. Duval, do you think these problems are occurring now? When did you first realize this was happening?

Annette: These issues have been cropping up persistently over the past 4 years, but now it is really starting to escalate.

Dr. du Pont: How have you dealt with this in the past, and have you ever approached any consultants to deal with the issues at hand?

Annette: I have never sought any help until now. Actually, the radio interview really motivated me to take action. Nothing I have tried so far at school seems to work.

Dr. du Pont: Can you tell me more about your school's demography: the management team, the educators, and children?

Annette provided a thorough breakdown but made the following promise: "You know, Dr. du Pont, I will fax you an organizational chart of the school's management and educators." (See Figure 2.1.)

Figure 2.1   Rainbow High School Organizational Chart

		Principal Annette Duval	

Deputy Principal Marinda Williams	Deputy Principal Kobus Verster

Head of Department Languages Erna Mills	Head of Department Natural Sciences Angus Bothma	Head of Department Life Sciences Susan Smith	Head of Department Management Sciences Mike Williams
Solomon January	Peter Strauss	Sonja van Wyk	Lindiwe Khumalo
Jackie le Roux	Julius Vundla	Johan Scott	Nandi Sithole
Melinda Meyer	Leratho Mohapi	Pete Mills	Martin Nelson
Thembi Dube	Stefan Els	Ntombi Segwale	Nhlanhla Maponya
Tshepo Phosa	Graham Scotness	Latoya Briel	Albert Pienaar
Ben Engelbrecht	Danny de Bruyn	Tumi Mapetla	Lebogang Nkosi

Dr. du Pont: Can you give me information about other recent important events, changes, the children's pass rates, and the possible disciplinary cases to which you referred?

Annette: I think the annual report will give you all the information you need. I also will get this to you promptly.

The phone conversation had been a long one. After numerous questions, replies, and follow-ups Annette asked: "Now that you have a clearer picture of what I'm up against, are you still willing to help me with the problems I am experiencing at school?" To make sure she understood what is expected, Dr. du Pont inquired: "Mrs. Duval, what exactly do you want me to do at Rainbow High School?"

Annette answered: "I am now at my wit's end and do not know what to do anymore. I have tried everything and the problems do not stop. What bothers me most is the high staff turnover and low commitment of educators, and also the current lack of discipline in the school. I am wondering also if there might be some cultural differences I do not know how to deal with? I want you to please come and have a look at whatever is going on at my school and help us so that we can deal with it, to make it better. My staff and I will do our best to help where we can, and we will give you open access."

Dr. du Pont replied: "Mrs. Duval, I understand that this is very important to you. I am also very glad that you are not asking me to just fix everything, but that you do want to be part of the process, and that you also see the importance of involving all the educators. That is good. Together we will see what needs to be done. I think our next step must be a meeting with you and your management team to explore the issues further and to get their input on how the issues can be resolved. How do you feel about this?" Dr. du Pont also suggested this meeting so that she might observe the dynamics in the management team and to hear how the other members formulate and talk about the problems at the school. She thought this information was imperative in order to get consensus view of the issues at hand.

Annette agreed to the meeting and added: "I also suggest that we invite a Department of Education representative as they will be funding the consulting project." Dr. du Pont replied, "That's great and I would like to add Dr. Ella Magema to my team. She is a colleague of mine and she, too, is a leadership professor and management consultant. Dr. Magema also specializes in diversity issues in organizations and I think it would be wise to invite her to this meeting. We both are firm believers that working as a cross-cultural team models cross-cultural relationships and this gives us the ability to deal with issues from multiple perspectives."

Annette liked Dr. du Pont's suggestion and they both decided on possible dates for the next meeting. "Let's have the meeting at the business school," Annette suggested. "Are you sure? We can do it at your school." Dr. du Pont replied. "No, it would be better for me if we get together at the business school," Annette insisted. Dr. du Pont agreed.

MEETING WITH MANAGEMENT TEAM AND OTHER STAKEHOLDERS

After the initial introductions from Dr. du Pont, and a prompt to Annette to explain why she called this meeting, Annette dominated the discussion. "Good day all, thank you for being here. I would like to introduce Mr. Singh, the representative from the Department of Education. This is the first time that I have approached professionals to consult with on our problems at the school, and I have decided that our experts should be Drs. du Pont and Magema. Let me go ahead and sketch the trigger events leading to us having this meeting today." Annette laid out the problems at Rainbow High School. Marinda and Kobus, the two deputy principals also present at the meeting, reaffirmed what Annette said. They literally used the same language and phrases that Annette had used to describe the problems, and were constantly deferring to her. Drs. du Pont and Magema made extensive notes during the meeting on the perceived issues and only asked questions for clarification. They deliberately steered away from probing into sensitive management-staff interpersonal issues, since the relationship between Mr. Singh and the management of Rainbow High School was rather formal.

Annette concluded the meeting by saying: "Mr. Singh, Dr. Magema, and Dr. du Pont, I appreciate your time and attention. In conclusion then, I think it is now agreed that Drs. du Pont and Magema will proceed working with Rainbow High School on the issues at hand. However, I will need you to submit a proposal to me as soon as possible and then I will, as a final step, need approval from the Department of Education to continue. Thank you again, and let's get the ball rolling!"

Afterward, Drs. du Pont and Magema discussed the meeting that had just taken place. Dr. du Pont said: "Ella, I really found it a pity Mr. Singh was present today. His presence made it rather difficult to ask more sensitive and probing questions. Everyone was very aware of him being from the Department. What do you think?" "Yes," replied Dr. Magema, "they have a very formal relationship. I think it would be a good idea to include another 'fact finding' meeting as part of our proposed contract. Then at that meeting the extended management team should be the only ones present, even without Mrs. Duval. This way I'm sure we'll get more detailed information." They both agreed and continued their drive home, discussing how they would proceed with the Rainbow High School project.

CONSULTING CONTRACT

Drs. du Pont and Magema sent the following proposal to Annette a week after their meeting at the business school.

Dear Mrs. Duval,

Ella and I have had a chance to discuss and reflect on our discussion last week with you, your deputy principals, and the representative from the Department. Given our experiences with diversity and transformation[4] work, we are convinced that the first step is to develop a shared vision among management and staff regarding the best strategies for transformation and instilling a culture of valuing diversity in Rainbow High School. Hence, we propose the following:

- *A strategic planning and training workshop session with all staff members. We would like to conduct individual interviews with nine selected members of staff, as well as focus groups with all staff, (same gender, same race groups) prior to the workshop. The interviews would be between 45 minutes to an hour and the focus groups an hour and a half. The purpose of these interviews and focus groups will be to assess individual and group perspectives of staff members on the transformation challenges as well as views about the way forward. The data will be treated as anonymous and only aggregated data will be reported in the report and workshop.*

This kind of prework will assist us in identifying the pertinent transformation issues and designing the workshop. The workshop should be scheduled for one full day. The outcomes of the workshop would be:

- A transformation and diversity vision for Rainbow High School connected to your strategic vision and plan;
- An accurate gauge of the level of commitment to transformation and valuing diversity;
- Perceptions of the barriers to transformation; and
- Higher levels of knowledge and competency in dealing with diversity issues.

The workshop will be highly interactive, with the goal of reaching consensus on the issues and creating an awareness and understanding for diversity issues in the workplace. We also will provide input on current thinking and good practices for transformation and valuing diversity in organizations. The workshop slides and a report on the outcomes of the workshop will be made available to all involved in the interviews and focus groups.

If the workshop achieves its goals, the next step would be to establish a working committee to lead and implement an internal process of transformation in Rainbow High School.

Subsequent to the acceptance of this contract and prior to us starting with the interviews and focus groups, we would like to schedule a 2-hour meeting at the school with you and your extended management team in order to clarify our roles and the process with them. We also want to get a better understanding of how they perceive the issues.

Our fees are $90 per hour per consultant and include travelling costs. The costs will be:

- Extended management meeting (2 × $90 × 2), $360
- Individual interviews (9 × $90), $810
- Focus groups (4 × $135), $540
- Interviews and focus group analysis,
- Workshop design and report (18 × $90), $1,620
- Conduct workshop (8 × $90 × 2), $1,440
- Total costs: $4,770

If this proposal meets your and Department of Education's approval, we would like to move ahead and schedule the extended management meeting, interviews, and focus groups as soon as possible and also set a date for the workshop session. We also can discuss the proposal over the phone in more detail. Lastly, we attach our abbreviated CVs for your perusal.

We look forward to hearing from you.

Sincerely,

Drs. Anne du Pont and Ella Magema

Annette discussed the proposal with her deputy principals and with Mr. Singh. The proposal was accepted, the Department of Education made the funds available, and the project was scheduled to start early in February, just after the December holidays and after the hectic time of the start of a new year had subsided. When Annette phoned Dr. du Pont to tell her that the proposal was accepted and that they wanted to move forward with the project, Dr. du Pont inquired how the rest of the teachers felt about the project. Annette answered: "Oh, I have not discussed it with them, but they will all be perfectly OK with it. They know I will make decisions that are only in the best interests of Rainbow High School." Dr. du Pont urged Annette to share the content of the proposal and the gist of their conversations with all the teachers as soon as possible. She also urged Annette to have a series of conversations with the department heads, as well as with the rest of the teachers in their work teams, to make sure they understood what this project entailed, why it was necessary, and how it would help to solve the issues at the school.

At the last staff meeting before the end of the school term, Annette informed the department heads, as well as the rest of the staff, about the upcoming project. After the meeting, Annette sent out the following memo to all staff about the project and the planned data gathering.

Dear Teachers:

As you know, we have engaged external consultants to assist us with identifying the best strategies for instilling a culture of valuing diversity and learning excellence at our school.

Professors Anne du Pont and Ella Magema are experts in change management, leadership, and diversity. A summary of their backgrounds is attached. They have met with myself, Mrs. Marinda Williams, and Mr. Kobus Verster to discuss the challenges and issues confronting the school. On 8 February, they will have a meeting with the extended management team, and on 17 February and 24 February, they will be at the school to conduct interviews and focus groups with all the educators. The purpose of these sessions is to get your views on challenges facing the school, as well as the way forward. The interviews and focus groups are anonymous and no individual responses will be reported. All of the information gathered will be aggregated as part of a diagnosis of the key issues that need to be addressed in formulating a strategy.

I ask that you cooperate in this process because we need your full participation and input. Working together, I believe we can develop a plan of action to realize our goals.

Please find attached the schedule for the interviews and focus groups.

Kind Regards

Mrs. Annette Duval

CONCLUSION

That afternoon, after Rainbow High School closed for the December holidays, Annette was driving home in the usual congested Friday afternoon Johannesburg traffic and said to herself: "I am so glad I got consultants to deal with the discipline and conflict issues at Rainbow High School. Now I can go on with managing the teachers and get them to do their work."

Discussion Questions

1. "The contracting conversation is a time to explore some of the initial issues that have prompted the client to call, but also to clarify how the consulting process will work, from negotiating expectations to discussing roles and outcomes." (Anderson, 2010, p. 106). Critically analyze the process Drs. du Pont and Magema followed in the entry and contracting phases of this consulting project.

2. Did they succeed in the purposes of the contracting phase? Give a thorough discussion in which areas they succeeded, and those in which they were less successful. Substantiate your discussion with facts from the case and OD theory and literature.

3. Do you think there was a mutual and clear understanding of expectations, roles, and responsibilities? Why or why not?

4. Critically analyze the contract that Drs. du Pont and Magema sent to their client, Annette Duval.

5. Does the contract include all the necessary elements that are supposed to be included in a consulting contract? Explain.

6. If you were the consultant, what would you have done similarly or differently in preparing the contract?

7. What possible ethical issues can you identify in this contracting phase, and how would you as consultant deal with the issues?

8. While the contracting phase does not include formal data gathering like interviews or surveys, a lot of data has already been gathered during contracting that can be instructive as the consultant approaches the data-gathering process and the rest of the project. Based on the case information, give a description of the following and discuss how this can inform the rest of the project.

9. Describe the primary client in this consulting project.

10. Identify and discuss possible other clients or client subsystems in this consulting project.

11. Describe the organizational culture of Rainbow High School.

12. What is your gut feeling about the client(s), how the problem has been presented, and how the process/project will play out in the organizational culture?

NOTES

1. Apartheid was based on a system of legislated racial categorization and separation dividing the population into Whites, which include Afrikaners and the English, and Africans, Asians, and "Coloureds." It maintained the system of inclusion and privileging of Whites as a group, and excluded not only the indigenous African people but also other groups who were classified as non-White. This separation governed every sphere of life, from education to employment, and resulted in legislating discriminatory practices by minority Whites toward the Black majority.

2. The school changed its name to Rainbow High School to reflect South Africa's vision of creating a rainbow nation united in its diversity.

3. "Coloureds" are the descendants of Black and Indian slaves, the indigenous Khoisan people, and White settlers in South Africa.

4. *Transformation* in South Africa has a very specific meaning linked to the implementation of legislation toward transforming the workplace, and the economic and social landscape in the country. While statutorily based racial discrimination has systematically been abolished in South Africa since 1980, a number of significant law reform efforts have been initiated since its first democratic elections in 1994. This legislation is geared toward achieving greater social justice and equality and to redress past unfair discrimination, as well as to achieve proportional representation reflective of the national demographics.

REFERENCE

Anderson, D. L. (2010). *Organization development. The process of leading organizational change.* Thousand Oaks, CA: Sage.

FOR FURTHER READING

Booysen, L. (2007). Societal power shifts and changing social identities in South Africa: Workplace implications. *Southern African Journal of Economic and Management Sciences, 10*(1), 1–20.

Booysen, L. A. E., & Nkomo, S. M. (2010). Employment equity and diversity management in South Africa. In A. Klarsfeld (Ed.), *International handbook on diversity management at work: Country perspectives on diversity and equal treatment* (pp. 218–243). Cheltenham, UK: Edward Elgar.

Hannum, K., McFeeters, B., & Booysen, L. (Eds.). (2010). *Understanding and leading across differences: Cases and perspectives.* New York: Pfeiffer.

Nkomo, M., & Vandeyar, S. (Eds.). (2009). *Thinking diversity, building cohesion: A transnational dialogue.* Amsterdam: Rozenburg and UNISA Press.

A CASE OF WINE

Assessing the Organizational Culture at Resolute Winery

FRANZISKA MACUR AND KENNETH M. MACUR

Learning Objectives

- To recognize and analyze simple but subtle clues of an organization's culture.
- To engage a client and develop a data-gathering strategy.
- To analyze data and make recommendations to a client.

FIRST IMPRESSIONS

Dr. Marlena Michaels was hired as a consultant by Conrad Main, the president of Resolute Winery. Sales had been sluggish in recent years, even though production had been good. Mr. Main had tried different strategies to find a solution himself, but so far none of them had worked. An outside consultant seemed to be the most promising strategy.

Dr. Michaels looked forward to this job. Traveling through wine country was one of her favorite vacation activities. Partly because of this hobby, she decided to make one additional stop at a neighboring vineyard before meeting her new client. The winery advertised free wine tastings. Because her trip was in the off-season, customer traffic was likely to be sparse.

Sure enough, at the River Creek Winery, three people were working the store and she was one of four patrons. The room was open and the three employees could converse with each other and with any of the customers. They were friendly and helpful. She watched as the three employees seemed to rotate responsibilities; running the cash register, pouring wine, getting something from the back room, or answering questions about the products.

She sampled four locally produced reds. The winery did not appear to have any limit to how many she could have tried, but four (approximately one-ounce) glasses seemed plenty. She purchased several bottles of wine and a special bottle of sherry.

There was a little more customer traffic at the Resolute Winery. The room was a bit smaller than at the River Creek and the five employees were busy. Here, she paid $6 for a souvenir glass that was required to enjoy a limit of four "free" samples. She made her first selection, a pinot noir, and told Mary, the employee who was chatting to her. Mary then called another employee, Diane, who came over to pour the wine.

Dr. Michaels must have had a confused look on her face, because when Diane left to pour for someone else, Mary explained.

"They told me that I would overpour, so now I have to get Diane to pour for me," she said, obviously embarrassed as she also rolled her eyes and shook her head.

"Oh," Dr. Michaels replied with a little surprise.

The routine continued for each of the four samples she requested. She asked Mary for a taste of something, Mary would call Diane, who would come over and pour one ounce or less of wine, and ask, in a tone that was intended to demonstrate interest, how Dr. Michaels liked the last variety.

ENGAGING A CLIENT AND DEVELOPING A DATA-GATHERING STRATEGY

It was close to three o'clock when Dr. Michaels finished her last sample. She asked where she might find Mr. Main. The clerk at the cash register looked at her with a suspicious look and asked, "What do you want to talk to Mr. Main about?"

"We are having a business meeting." Dr. Michaels wondered about the interest but even more about the mistrust of the employee.

Mr. Main was an older-looking guy with little hair and a tired face but good-hearted expression. He seemed relieved to see her. "Did you find it okay?" he asked.

"Yes, the signs on the road are excellent," Dr. Michaels responded. "You should get a good crowd in here just from those."

"We do," he said. "People seem to respond to this kind of advertisement. All the wineries in the area get about 50% of their visitors just through those."

"What about the other 50%?"

"Well, those find us either through travel guides or through word of mouth. Those customers are more likely to come back, buy more wine, and order more on an ongoing basis."

"And those seem to be your problem?" Dr. Michaels asked while starting to jot down notes.

"You could say that, I guess," Mr. Main said and paused for a moment. "We still have enough one-time customers—we just have less and less who come back."

"Could it be the wine?"

"No, the wine should actually bring more people in. We won two important prizes just last year."

"Interesting. So, tell me why I am here."

"When my grandparents started the business three generations ago, we were a real family business. I grew up here. I love this place. I am worried, though. My family worked hard to build this place, but now it seems like it's just a job to almost everyone here. We never had dreams to be Gallo or Mondavi. We did, however, dream of a vineyard where everyone would feel like family: customers, employees, even our suppliers. This dream seems to be fading. I cannot put my finger on it, but things could be better. . . . Business just doesn't feel right anymore."

He sighed, pausing long enough for Dr. Michaels to ask, "Could you give me some specific examples where your dream and your reality don't match?"

"Well, we do have quite a bit of personnel turnover. Personnel in the higher positions seem to stay, but the entry level staff, mostly younger people, leave shortly after they start. This is very hard on the managers. You start to train somebody and when they are given some responsibility they take off. I guess it has to do with the new generation. They just work differently. . . . Another example for this is our last annual Christmas party. Half of the employees didn't show up and the excuses they had were disappointing. It was sad."

"You mentioned 'higher positions.' How are roles and responsibilities assigned?"

"Here, let me give you a copy of our org chart."

Dr. Michaels couldn't help sounding surprised, "Not many organizations your size have an org chart!"

"I do believe it adds some professionalism," Mr. Main said proudly.

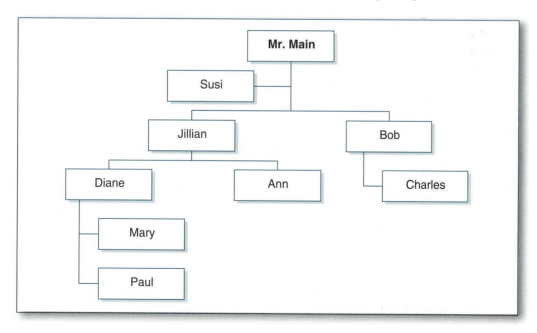

Dr. Michaels scanned the chart and asked, "How has the structure changed over the years?"

"Well, everybody knew the first org chart without writing it down—it was the family tree!" Mr. Main chuckled. "But when my dad started to turn the business over to me almost 10 years ago, we hired an HR consultant who helped us create this structure. There were fewer family members and more outsiders then. The consultant felt that it was a good time to put in some structure. It took folks a while to get used to the new policies and procedures, but eventually, things settled in. In the 'old days' everybody did just about everything. It was chaos at times. I'm not sure how we were able to be so successful and grow the business like we did. I think we were successful in spite of ourselves. Now, everybody on the team knows exactly what they're responsible for." He paused.

"I remember watching my grandfather 'train' somebody new. They would walk in; ask if there was a job. Grandpa would ask one or two questions; tell them all of the company's 'policies' . . . 'show up on time, work hard and do what you're asked to do.' If they said, 'yes,' they were hired and then he would point and say, 'Go help that guy.' When it was time to harvest, everyone would pick. Now, there is only one member of the family left . . . me. We have eight outsiders, plus seasonal workers, of course."

Mr. Main sighed and Dr. Michaels jumped in, "Tell me, what problem do you think you are trying to solve?"

"Hmm. Well, I really can't put my finger on it. Things just don't seem to be going right. For the first time in my life, coming to the vineyard feels like coming to work. I tried a few different things to see if I could find out what was wrong and change the mood of the place, but nothing seems to work."

"We installed a complaint/suggestion box. We got exactly one complaint, and that was worthless. We created a customer satisfaction survey. That told us that we were doing great: 8.9 average on a 10-point scale. But it doesn't seem that we are getting the referrals we used to get. To try to motivate employees, I started an Employee of the Month program. Randomly, I pick one of the employees and put their picture on a plaque. You might have seen it when you walked in. We tried a couple of different customer service programs; you know, like the FISH! Philosophy. Everything seems to work for about 2 weeks, and then we're back to the beginning. I just don't get it.

Dr. Michaels asked, "I know that your time is limited today. Could you give me a copy of your customer service survey? And could you tell me about the one complaint you received and why you felt it was worthless?"

Mr. Main opened a file drawer and pulled out a blank survey. As they walked out, he explained the one complaint. "Jennifer Bent was its author. It was 'technically' anonymous, but everyone knew. She started here thinking that she should be the president . . . at least that's what her supervisor told me. She wrote something along the line of, 'You should encourage people to go above and beyond instead of training people to say, 'That's not your job' or 'That's not how we do things around here.' I was told that this was a family business. But this never felt like family.'

"She quit about a week later. She wasn't ready to put in enough time and work her way up to the position she felt qualified for. She never admitted to her own limitations."

"Do you have a mission statement, Mr. Main?" Dr. Michaels asked.

Mr. Main laughed. "My grandfather never understood the point of a mission statement. But whenever anybody asked him about making wine, he always said this," and Mr. Main pointed at a sign that read:

> In wine, there is truth.
> In good wine, there is hard work.
> But family makes wine come to life.

Dr. Michaels committed those words to memory and turned to say good-bye. "I'll see you tomorrow, Mr. Main."

Dr. Michaels went back to her hotel. Before she opened her notebook to start planning her approach, she replayed her first impressions in her mind:

She was astonished to witness the delegation of wine pouring responsibility. Dr. Michaels knew that the employees had no idea that they were communicating the organizations' culture in so simple a task as to pour a sample of wine. She also replayed the comparison of Resolute and River Creek.

Mr. Main was an interesting guy. He knew everything there was to know about wine, yet his strong family ties to the winery didn't allow him to step back and look at the organization objectively. Based on how he handled the one complaint in his complaint box, he also seemed to be afraid of or unwilling to listen to feedback, even though he asked for it. Dr. Michaels wondered how he would respond to her measures and suggestions, especially if it would be in line with the complaint box.

While it seemed obvious that culture was the culprit, she also knew there was no data to support her hypothesis that family left the family business. She also knew that systems, processes, and a family atmosphere are not mutually exclusive. But in this case, the system worked against family.

Mr. Main had used the term *team,* which made her wonder. Was it too early to suspect that there was very little "team" here? Even less team spirit? The org chart showed an overly layered hierarchical structure that allowed for little team work and even less personal growth and individual input. The job descriptions were army clear. In her opinion it was not surprising that employees didn't feel any kind of ownership or family share toward the winery.

DATA GATHERING, ANALYSIS, AND RECOMMENDATIONS

Dr. Michaels sent a proposal to Mr. Main outlining the following actions for determining the key issues at Resolute Winery.

- Data Gathering
  - Observations of Daily Happenings
  - Observations of Company Meetings
  - Individual Interviews
  - Revised Customer Survey
- Analysis
- Recommendations and Next Steps

On her first day at the winery, Dr. Michaels parked in the customer parking lot and noticed that three spots were specifically reserved for Mr. Main and the two managers, Jillian and Bob. The rest of the parking lot was labeled "customer parking." As the winery was not yet open, she concluded that the other cars belonged to the other employees.

She decided to start her research by observing daily routines. When she entered the winery, none of the clerks knew who she was and what she was hired to do. Only the two managers greeted her and welcomed her to the company. All of the work through the day was channeled through Jillian and Bob.

She watched the wine pouring ritual reoccur time after time. She also noticed that when Diane needed a new case of wine she was required to get Jillian's authorization. In one instance, when Jillian had left the winery and one type of wine ran out, Mary took it off the list of offerings for the day.

Jillian spent most of her day observing Mary and Ann. When she was not wandering around the store, she was in her office looking at sales reports for the previous months. Dr. Michaels also noticed that when Jillian was in the store and the clerks had a hard time serving all the customers, she never joined in and helped at the counter. The same was true for Ann, the cashier. Ann seemed to be rather bored and played with her BlackBerry most of the time. In contrast to Jillian's constant appearances, Mr. Main didn't enter the store once.

The store had a small area where they sold wine accessories. In the afternoon, Jillian brought in a big box of wine bottle decorations and ordered Ann to put them on display. After watching her do this for a few minutes, she left for her office. Ann turned around to Dr. Michaels:" I really don't understand why she orders those. . . . They will never sell. She should order more of the napkins. We are always out of those. But nobody asks me," she added with a mixture of frustration and disinterest.

Every month, the employees were supposed to gather for a company meeting. Frequently, the meeting was cancelled for lack of an agenda, according to Mr. Main. Dr. Michaels was early for this month's meeting and chose a seat at the corner of a long board table. When Bob arrived next, he sat opposite her and pointed out that she was sitting in Jillian's chair and that maybe she would want to move to another seat. Bob suggested a seat for her at the other end of the table. Sure enough, when Jillian entered, she went right to the chair that Dr. Michaels had vacated. There was one chair between Bob and Jillian—clearly the head of the table. It became obvious that that seat was reserved for Mr. Main. When the remaining workers entered the room, each one targeted one specific chair. Dr. Michaels wondered if only by coincidence the seating order reflected the organizational chart.

The meeting only took 25 minutes. Mr. Main welcomed everybody and started right away to talk about a new blend they were going to offer this season. He described the taste of the wine and showed everybody the bottle with the new label. Bob commented on the blend and said he, also, thought that the taste of this particular wine would be a bestseller. While Bob talked a little bit more about the wine tasting that he and Jillian attended, Ann checked her messages on her BlackBerry. Diane was drawing on her note pad. Dr. Michaels noticed that Diane was the only one besides Mr. Main who brought something to write on.

Mr. Main looked around and said, "Well, if there are no other questions, I guess we can all resume with our daily work." Mary cleared her throat. She looked to Dr. Michaels like she was hoping to get support from her. "I was just wondering if it might be possible for us to taste the wine before we serve it? It is really hard to describe a flavor without experiencing it for yourself." Her face was dark red. She looked on the table.

"Oh," Mr. Main looked surprised. "Well, I guess we can arrange that. Jillian, could you pour a sample tomorrow after work?" Jillian nodded. Mr. Main closed the meeting.

Dr. Michaels went to her hotel and reviewed her notes. She looked forward to the individual interviews that were scheduled for the rest of the week. She tried to clear her head to conduct them as objectively as possible. But she still couldn't help having certain expectations about the outcome of those interviews.

The interview consisted of a handful of questions that could be answered on an 11-point (+5 to −5) Likert scale. Based on the employee's response, Dr. Michaels posed two to four follow-up questions. She responded to the numeric score, as well as various verbal and nonverbal responses. Additionally, Dr. Michaels led each employee through a values exercise that assessed their perceptions about critical values.

In this exercise, each employee was presented with a list of 50 words that described values; for example, honesty and profitability. Employees were asked to select the ten most important values to them in the list. Once the ten were selected, they were asked to narrow the list to five, then to three, then to one.

After doing this exercise with each employee and Mr. Main, Dr. Michaels's hypothesis was supported even further. The focus on family, highlighted in her initial interview with Mr. Main, was only his focus. Bob mentioned something about family and group feeling, but none of the others did. Ann even laughed when she saw the word *family* in the list. "Family is at home," she said.

When it was Mary's turn, she thought about it a little bit longer. "You know, I some-times hear Mr. Main talk about the old times, when it was a real family business. It always sounds like fun. I wish I would have been around for those times. He surely misses them."

Dr. Michaels felt that she could go on forever with her observations yet get the same results over and over. Because of this, she decided to move on to the customer survey. It seemed to her that this kind of data would be important to Mr. Main and might help convince him of her recommendations for the organization and its employees.

In the original survey Mr. Main had created, the customers were faced with a simple Likert scale asking them how they would rate the customer service. The majority of the responses targeted a 7, 8, or 9 out of 10. Mr. Main saw this as proof that the customer service was overall satisfactory. Dr. Michaels opted for an add-on. She added an open-ended question to the survey, asking customers what they really liked or disliked about their experience at the winery. She hired two college students to hand those surveys out for a week and combine the results. Not surprisingly, for many customers this one was one of several wineries in the area they visited. Therefore, many responses included comparisons between Resolute and its neighbors. Most of the time, Resolute seems to be rated lower than River Creek or Wine Wonderland. And often customers referred to intangibles, like "friendlier," "better atmosphere." or "over there, they seem to have more fun."

Discussion Questions

1. Reflect on Dr. Michaels's first impressions of these two wineries. What do these brief snippets tell you about each organization's culture?

2. After her initial interaction with Mr. Main, what data do you think Dr. Michaels should gather? Why? How would you propose gathering that data?

3. What was wrong with Mr. Main's approach to data gathering?

4. Evaluate the different data-gathering strategies Dr. Michaels used. Create an analysis of each data set.
   a. Daily Observation
   b. Company Meeting
   c. Employee Survey or Interview
   d. Values Exercise
   e. Customer Survey

5. Create a summary report and a list of recommendations for Mr. Main. How would you define and measure the success of those recommendations?

FOR FURTHER READING

Denzin, N. K., & Lincoln, Y. S. (2000). *Handbook of qualitative research.* Thousand Oaks, CA: Sage.

Hilburt-Davis, J., & Dyer, W. G. (2002). *Consulting to family businesses: Contracting, assessment, and implementation.* San Francisco: Josey-Bass/Pfeifer.

Levinson, H. (2002). *Organizational assessment: A step-by-step guide to effective consulting.* Washington, DC: American Psychological Association.

Utilizing Exploratory Qualitative Data Collection in Small Organizations

Consulting for the Multicultural Community Connections

Cerise L. Glenn and Shawn D. Long

Learning Objectives

- To help you understand how to gather and use exploratory qualitative methods.
- To help you understand how to incorporate people's cultural worldviews into case study analyses.
- To practice addressing numerous stakeholders' perspectives when preparing recommendations for a client.

Olivia Johansen is the current program director of a nonprofit agency called The Multicultural Community Connections, or what is affectionately referred to as the MCC by students, employees, parents, and community members. As a first-generation immigrant, Olivia is committed to making sure newly located immigrant individuals are adequately socialized in the community of Lakeland, but more importantly, they become aware of the resources and opportunities that are available to their families during their stay in Lakeland. As a highly touted program innovator, Olivia is excited to debut her latest project, Bridges—a summer camp to help build ties between children, teachers, and community members of diverse backgrounds. Bridges helps the Lakeland community in three tangible ways. First, it provides a fun, safe environment for children in the summer.

Next, it promotes awareness of diversity for teachers while helping them fulfill their continuing education requirements, and finally, the camp provides local college students with "hands-on" experiences as they work with teachers and children.

Although Olivia is competent and heavily involved in the daily operations of MCC, she is growing frustrated with her employees working at Bridges. The employees have difficulty working together and cannot agree on how to properly run the camp. Worse yet, some students have begun to tell their parents about the lack of organization at the camp. Since Bridges is relatively new, Olivia believes she has time to turn things around. She does not have time to oversee the regular operations at both MCC and Bridges, but she is committed to the success of the program because she strongly believes in the intent of the camp. In light of this commitment, Olivia hires a small consulting team from Integrated Solutions (IS), a local consulting firm, to diagnose and fix the problem immediately.

MULTICULTURAL COMMUNITY CONNECTIONS

The Multicultural Community Connections is a nonprofit organization working to foster community building among diverse populations in Lakeland, a large metropolitan area in the southeastern region of the United States. The primary goal of MCC is to help diverse immigrant populations adjust to the culture of the United States, but mainly southern culture. MCC primarily works with Latino populations, but assists members of other migrant populations as well. MCC's current initiative, Bridges, seeks to improve the educational experiences of migrant elementary school students. MCC strategically attempts to build positive relationships with the students, their families, their elementary school teachers, and other members of their local community. MCC is comprised of a small number of bilingual Latin American staff members who oversee the daily operations of the agency. Throughout the building, MCC's mission is posted on bulletin boards in the break room, above the time sheet, and in the bathrooms, as if to remind the staff of the goals of the organization and why MCC exists. The agency's mission is as follows:

1. Understand and influence students' and teachers' perceptions, tolerance, knowledge, and empathy about diverse populations to help increase students' successful integration into American educational settings;

2. Help teachers develop and implement tools and strategies in the classroom that encourage effective communication and understanding of and between members of diverse cultural backgrounds;

3. Build and maintain collaborations between students, families, teachers, and other community members to assist diverse populations.

The staff often comments on their wish that the organization actually "lived up" to the ever-present bulletin boards.

BRIDGES SUMMER CAMP

Bridges Purpose and Overview

In light of the current initiative of working with elementary schools, MCC developed a summer camp named Bridges for elementary school-aged children to help achieve its broad mission and goals. Bridges is a 6-week summer program to help build connections between local school teachers and the children that reside in the neighborhoods surrounding these schools. Bridges has four objectives: (1) help teachers understand the cultural backgrounds of their students, (2) help teachers develop teaching strategies for diverse groups of students, (3) help students build connections and trust with their teachers, and (4) help build stronger connections between families, schools, and surrounding communities. The camp operates at a local community center in Lakeland from Monday to Thursday. It also exposes the children to resources and activities in the area outside of their neighborhoods on "Friday Fun Days."

Bridges teaches neighborhood children, primarily African American and Latino, pride in their cultures and respect for other cultures. Although this is the summer camp's first year, MCC has been pleasantly surprised to have 45 students enroll in the program. They believe that the families are interested in helping their children be more successful at school, but some of the staff members also believe the large response is due to their success in raising funds to make the camp free for the students. The students come from a variety of nations, including Guatemala, Mexico, Nigeria, and Peru, and have various religious and cultural backgrounds.

Bridges Personnel

To build continuity and institutional success, two MCC staff members, Laura and Isabel, are assigned to the Bridges summer camp full time. The other staff members visit the summer camp to check in and help the children adjust to the teachers on an "as needed" basis. The camp moderators are full-time teachers in the local area who receive continuing education credit for participating in the program. Five elementary school teachers from local communities have been hired to moderate the summer camp. Although the teachers bring an average of 8 years of teaching experience to the Bridges program, they are having instructional and relational difficulties with the migrant children and members of their families. The experienced teachers want to learn strategies to assist the students to perform better in the classroom and they believe that learning more about their students' backgrounds will help the students feel more included in the classroom to become successful students. The teachers self-identify as socioeconomically middle class. There are four female teachers and one male teacher. Three of them are European American (including the male) and the other two are African American women. The teachers will receive continuing education credit and a stipend for their participation. Undergraduate students also have been hired as teaching assistants for the teachers to help them oversee activities and supervise the students. They were hired because they plan to become elementary school teachers after completing college or are fluent in Spanish.

Bridges Summer Camp Training

The five teachers and teaching assistants participate in a week-long orientation and training program prior to the 6-week summer camp. The training program primarily focuses on cultural dynamics associated with teaching a diverse group of students. The students are diverse in their race/ethnicity, gender, class/socioeconomic status, age, nationality, and religion. The main reading text for the week is about language barriers and poverty for migrant populations. Additionally, the faculty members and their assistants are required to attend interactive workshops with speakers from Latin American and African nations.

MCC'S PROGRAM DIRECTOR HIRES INTEGRATED SOLUTIONS

The Bridges camp has been running for a week and is having several problems. The problems range from inexperienced staff running the program, lack of organizational structure for the children, translation problems between the Latino and American staff and students, lack of administrative processes to achieve summer camps goals, lack of day-to-day operational plans for staff and students, poor communication between the Bridges staff and the main MCC office, lack of a point of contact for the summer camp, among a number of other issues. In light of these problems, the program director, Olivia Johansen, decides to contact Integrated Solutions (IS), a local consultant firm with expertise in nonprofit organization development, to see if they could offer guidance to her on these emerging issues. Olivia met the executive director of IS, Gloria Stephens, a year prior at a local chamber luncheon and remembers she still has Gloria's card in her Rolodex. Gloria is happy to hear from Olivia and about the project. She assigns four dedicated, experienced IS members to meet with Olivia to discuss the project.

The four-member team is excited to offer Olivia useable solutions to her organizational problems. Two of the team members, Brock and Jessica, have backgrounds in organizational and intercultural communication. The other two, Jamie and Nicole, have backgrounds in educational leadership and curriculum development. All of the team members are fluent or at least conversational in Spanish. Quite an impressive group! During the initial phone interview, Olivia expresses the need for the agency to have "fresh eyes" on the Bridges program to better understand the communication and teamwork problems occurring with the program. She candidly explains that she needs the IS team to "fix the damn problem." The 3:15 conference call with Olivia and the IS team proceeds as follows.

Olivia: I'm so pleased that you are interested in this project. I am at my wit's end trying to manage two offices and the problems arising are fixable, but I prefer to have another set of eyes on this.

Brock: We are happy to help. Gloria spoke highly about your energy and the things that you are doing at MCC, so we're thrilled that you called us and we will certainly see what we can do. First, what do you see as the problems?

Olivia: Oh my gosh, where do I begin? [*laughing, with a sigh*] The teachers and their assistants are not getting along. The two full-time paid staff members are not doing a good job of overseeing the Bridge program, even after I found extra money to help them out to run this program; I'm feeling pulled in a million different directions. My main job is at MCC. Bridges was supposed to be an easy and impactful program, but things are not working out. I would just cancel the whole thing and start from scratch with new people, but we have lots of donors who support this program. Plus, I love the idea of this program. It's greatly needed. We need to keep our kids off the street and make them success-ful. It just seems that I'm the only one around here who cares. I need help now and fast! I cannot run this program by myself, and you would think that expe-rienced teachers would take a leadership role. I'm starting to think that they are just here for a check too. I need help . . . fast!

Brock: Olivia, we are here to help you! We love your program and we will see what we can do!

Olivia: I'm glad to hear that. Gloria sent me the rates and the terms. Send over a con-tract now and I'll sign it and we can meet tomorrow.

Jessica: Wow, Olivia, you do mean business. I'll send you an electronic copy in an hour and you can send it back this evening. We will meet you tomorrow. We would love to see your space.

After accepting the challenge and contract, Integrated Solutions agrees to meet with Olivia again the next day to begin the process. After brief introductions, Olivia begins by telling the "real" story about the Bridges summer camp. To test the team in their Spanish, Olivia tells parts of the story in English and others in Spanish, her native language.

Olivia: I don't understand what's going on with the program. The teachers aren't doing what they are supposed to do. They keep calling me for every little thing. I have to manage this office and cannot fix every little problem. They refuse to work together as a team. I've heard from parents of the children that their kids are noticing how disorganized the program is. The teachers complain that they don't have clear instructions and the assistants aren't as helpful as they can be either. When I come to the camp, the assistants seem to be watching the kids, but they don't look happy. My staff has a hard time communicating with the teachers. One of them is learning English, but since Spanish is her native lan-guage she has a hard time interacting with them. When she tries to communi-cate, they get frustrated and send her to an assistant or try to translate through one of the kids who speak Spanish. At first I thought these problems would work themselves out over time, but after a week, and now with the parents' complaints. . . I don't know. This is turning into a messy situation and I need your help to fix it right now. You will have complete access to the entire Bridges program. Talk to whomever you want and let me know what information you will need. Oh, by the way, I need a report by next Friday. We don't have all summer to fix this program; it is a summer program!

This is all the information provided to the team. Olivia does not provide any more concrete directions. The team can start working on this immediately. Jessica requests that Olivia inform the Bridges staff that the IS team will be around regularly over the next week and needs their cooperation. Olivia readily agrees and the IS team plans to start visiting the camp the following day.

DATA-COLLECTION OPTIONS FOR QUALITATIVE EVALUATION

Due to the quick starting date, the exploratory nature of this project, and the small staff at Bridges, IS decides to use qualitative methods of data collection and organizational evaluation of the summer camp. Ideally, the team would take a multimethodological approach to this type of work, but given the short time window for their report, Brock believes that eliminating the quantitative component is necessary and will not impact the final results. Brock explains, "Look, there are a number of reasons to eliminate quantitative assessments. First, all of our quantitative instruments are in English and many members of the Bridges community are not fluent in English. Second, we really don't have time to translate and pilot the new survey in a week. Finally, it can help us build a little rapport with the folks at the summer camp by interviewing and talking with them."

The IS team agrees that analyzing program documents, observing interactions at Bridges, and interviewing staff, students, and parents would give the client a robust picture of the organizational issues at hand without compromising the quality of the data and eliminating the quantitative component that the IS organization generally uses. Each team member takes the lead on one or more aspects of the qualitative data collection.

Program Documents—Nicole and Brock

To obtain background information about Bridges, the team decides to start by collecting and reading existing program documents, such as staff job descriptions and policy manuals. Nicole and Brock are in charge of this aspect of the project. Document analysis is a critical component of understanding the story of an organization and its members. The way in which an organization documents its activities leaves an important "paper trail" that reflects the ways in which it produces, certifies, and codifies information for its personnel (Lindlof & Taylor, 2002). By closely examining the organizational documents, Nicole and Brock will understand how key roles are defined and evaluated at MCC.

Nicole: Let's start by looking at all the personnel files, recruitment materials sent to parents, as well as materials used to recruit the teachers.

Brock: Great idea. This will help us understand how the end users of these documents perceive Bridges, as well as the implicit and explicit expectations communicated throughout the documents.

In addition to examining the job announcements and recruitment materials sent to parents, Nicole also asks Olivia for the training manual for the teachers, their evaluations of the training session, the job descriptions for all personnel, and a schedule of daily operations for the summer camp. After reviewing the documents, Nicole and Brock discuss their preliminary assessments.

Brock: So, Nicole, what do you think?

Nicole: From reading the documents I conclude that: (1) the teachers have clear job descriptions, (2) the teachers go through training prior to the summer camp, and (3) MCC staff assigned to work for the summer camp do not have details for their duties related to the summer camp. What do you see, Brock?

Brock: The position description for the assistants is very loosely defined as "helping the teachers" and "overseeing the children as necessary." MCC staff participated in the training at times, especially when visitors came to the office. Only Olivia and her assistant met with the assistants prior to their first day on the job, and the external hires received the mission statement for the summer camp, but may not have seen MCC's mission statement (although it is online) and may not have the same understanding of MCC's purpose as the small, permanent staff.

Nicole: Very nice, Brock.

Brock: Back at you, Nikki. We make a great team.

Nicole and Brock also notice that not all of the external materials are written in both English and Spanish. Although Olivia believes in allowing the staff access to all nonconfidential information, some of the internal nonconfidential documentation is not translated into both languages.

Collecting and analyzing program documents allows researchers to obtain a more holistic view of how the summer camp was designed and how the personnel were prepared for the camp. This initial research information helps the IS consulting team frame areas needing more detailed information for making recommendations with a short reporting time. Additionally, analyzing the daily schedule (see below) helps Brock and Nicole understand how the summer camp runs on a daily basis and helps the team devise a plan for the next step of data collection—direct observation.

Bridges Daily Schedule	
8:30–9:00 a.m.	Breakfast
9:00–10:30 a.m.	Session I
10:30–11:00 a.m.	Break and Snack
11:00 a.m.–12:30 p.m.	Session II
12:30–1:00 p.m.	Lunch
1:00–2:15 p.m.	Afternoon Activity
2:15–2:30 p.m.	Prepare Kids to Go Home (Report to bus or parent pick-up area)
2:30–3:30 p.m.	Afternoon Debriefing and Planning Session with Teachers and MCC Staff
Friday Fundays	
8:30–9:00 a.m.	Breakfast
9:00 a.m.–2:15 p.m.	TBA (Make sure kids get lunch.)
2:15 p.m.	Return to Camp
2:30 p.m.	Kids Depart for the Day

Direct Observation—Jamie and Jessica

While Nicole and Brock analyze MCC's documents, Jamie and Jessica engage in direct observation for 2 days. Direct observation, also referred to as participant observation, allows consulting teams to understand ordinary, day-to-day events in their natural environment (Lindlof & Taylor, 2002; Patton, 2002). It takes place "in the field" with direct contact with the people at work. This allows the IS team to understand the context in which people interact and helps gather additional data to get a more complete understanding of how the summer camp runs from the perspective of the personnel, students, and parents. Direct observation entails taking extensive notes while observing daily activities as they naturally occur. It further helps the team get a more holistic view of how the summer camp works to help the IS team determine what additional data collection may be needed for specific recommendations for the program director.

Thursday Observation—Jamie and Jessica

Jamie and Jessica arrive early, around 8:00 a.m., to observe the camp, which starts at 8:30. Isabel, one of the Bridges staff members, greets them warmly in Spanish and invites them to have breakfast with her and the students.

Isabel proceeds to hug Jamie, Jessica, and several of the students as they come into the cafeteria. Isabel also talks to the parents as they drop off their children.

First Parent: Good morning, Isabel. Who is in charge of programming and sending permission slips home to parents? I would appreciate more notice about the Friday Field Day trips.

Second Parent: [*overhearing the first parent's comments*] Permission slips? I didn't know we needed to sign those for the Friday trips. Isn't that covered in the Bridges application and enrollment process? Why do we need to sign separate permission slips for each activity our kids do?

Isabel continues to smile warmly, but does not directly address either of the parents' comments. She changes the subject by talking about the students' eagerness to participate in the summer camp. As the two parents leave, they discuss the situation.

Second Parent: They need to get their stuff together here.

First Parent: [*nodding in agreement*] But at least it's someplace nice and safe for the kids in the summer.

The students are quite active during breakfast. They often get up from their tables to stand outside or talk and play with other children. A couple of the assistants wander in and interact with the students. One of the students sees Jamie taking notes and asks:

Student: Why are you doing homework?

Jamie: I'm not doing homework, but taking notes.

Student: Why are you taking notes?

Jamie: [*unsure of how to respond*] You're right, honey. I am doing my homework.

Two African American teachers also come to talk to the students during breakfast. None of the other teachers eats breakfast with the students. Jamie makes a note to ask about the teachers' responsibilities during this time, as well as the assistants, since not all of them came to breakfast either. Jessica glances down at her watch and notices that it is 9:05 a.m. The Bridges staff members do not seem to notice the time and let the students finish eating. Over breakfast, the staff members and two teachers visit each table to talk with the children and ask about what they did for fun last evening. Everyone seems to be enjoying themselves.

After briefly jotting down notes, Jessica and Jamie decide to separate and observe different Session I activities. Jessica watches the first- and second-grade children who are being taught by one of the female, White teachers. There is an assistant in the room to help her.

Teacher: [*whispering to her assistant*] Why do the students constantly show up late? I cannot stay with my lesson plans due to their late breakfast. Plus they have to settle down.

Exasperated, the teacher sighs and begins the lesson of the day.

Jessica notices that the teacher has written the agenda for the session on the dry erase board in English. The students are instructed to draw pictures of their homes. Later they will draw pictures of their family members. They have large sheets of paper on their tables and boxes of crayons, markers, and colored pencils at the center of the tables.

When the teacher asks students to begin drawing their houses, the assistant repeats these directions in Spanish. The students begin going through the boxes to get the supplies they want to begin drawing. Some of the students, who have read the board, start labeling their spaces in the home, such as their bedrooms and play area. One of the bilingual students explains the instructions to another student who only speaks Spanish. The student begins adding her family to the drawing as well.

"Work on your own pictures, please," the teacher says. "And make sure to follow directions. You're only drawing your home right now."

The assistant rolls her eyes in Jessica's direction and smiles. She makes a comment in Spanish about sticking to the directions and only the directions. Jessica tries not to laugh, especially because she does not want to be rude since she knows the teacher does not understand her comment. The teacher continues with the activity and ends the session promptly at 10:30 so the kids can go to break. The assistant takes the kids outside for snacks and juice. As Jessica leaves the room, she meets with Jamie. As she glances in the room where he left, Jessica notices this assistant is staying behind to clean up the room while the teacher takes the students to snack time.

Jamie observes another session. Toward the end of the session, the teacher distributes permission slips to the students for the Friday activity off-site.

"You cannot go to the park this Friday if you do not have your parents sign this form."

One of the students hands Jamie a permission slip, saying, "So you can come tomorrow, too." As Jamie smiles and takes the slip, he notices it is only in English.

Olivia enters the room. "How is it going, my IS team?" she asks.

Jamie, concerned about the English-only note, asks, "Are all of the parents fluent in English?"

"They are not. Why?" Olivia says.

Jamie shows Olivia the permission slip.

Olivia sighs. "Oh my, my, my. Every document should be in English *and* Spanish. Thank you for catching this. This is why you guys get paid the big bucks!"

Olivia leaves to call all of the assistants out of their rooms to begin writing handwritten translations for the students to take home this evening. After Olivia leaves, the teacher glares at Jamie as she says: "I really wished you would have run this by me first before talking to Olivia."

NOTES COMPARISON MEETING WITH THE IS TEAM

During the IS team debriefing meeting, the explicit cultural differences appear as a common theme.

"One of the core conflicts may be based on tensions between monochromic and poly-chromic orientations to time at Bridges," Jessica says.

Time orientations are important factors to consider when working in intercultural organizational settings. Monochromic people or cultures typically schedule one thing at a time (Hall, 1959, 1976; Hall & Hall, 1987). Time is compartmentalized and there is a time for everything (Devito, 2007). Monochromic cultures include Germany, Scandinavia, Switzerland, and the United States. Polychromic-oriented cultures or people schedule multiple tasks at the same time. These may include conducting business with different people, eating, working on other projects, and helping family members. Latin Americans and Mediterranean cultures, for instance, are considered polychromic cultures. Members of cultural groups socialized in both time orientations, such as African Americans and Latinos in the United States, may choose one over the other or use both depending on the context.

Jessica: The teachers are using organizational structures from their schools to punctu-ate their days. For example, they expect to have planning time to themselves. Here it is in the morning. They also expect clear directions from their supervi-sor regarding curriculum and content, and they often complain about their assistants.

Jamie: The roles of the assistants are not clearly defined or enacted. For example, some of the assistants came to breakfast, some didn't. Some take the students to snack while others remain behind to clean up the classroom and prepare it for the next session. The Bridges staff and teachers have much more developed job descrip-tions that outline the schedule of the day.

The IS team members report their findings to Olivia after the planning meeting ends at 3:30 p.m. Olivia is very impressed with the work IS has completed so far and asks for suggestions for implementing their findings.

Discussion Questions

1. What should the IS team recommend to Olivia? Should IS collect additional data before making specific suggestions? Why or why not?

2. What are the benefits of using program documents from MCC to begin collecting data for the Bridges summer camp? What are the potential drawbacks of this method? In addition to the documents the IS team collected, what other docu-ments would be helpful to see before visiting the summer camp? What would the team learn from these documents?

(Continued)

(Continued)

3. You may have noticed that Jamie and Jessica could not remain passive observers during their direct observations and at times became an active part of the organization. How do you think their interaction with the personnel and students impacted their ability to make key observations? How should they balance observing with participating in the daily activities of Bridges in the future?

4. This case also illustrates how people's worldviews, ways in which they perceive and understand societal norms, become embedded in organizational culture in ways that may not be apparent to an organizational insider. Jessica's observation regarding how different cultures regard and use time in the workplace reflects aspects of different worldviews. What recommendations should the IS team make to Olivia about the organizational culture of Bridges? How should Bridges modify its daily operations in ways that respect cultural differences, yet help the summer camp function more cohesively?

REFERENCES

DeVito, J. A. (2007). *The interpersonal communication book* (11th ed.). Boston: Allyn & Bacon.

Hall, E. T. (1959). *The silent language.* Garden City, NY: Doubleday.

Hall, E. T. (1976). *Beyond culture.* Garden City, NY: Anchor Press.

Hall, E. T., & Hall, M. R. (1987). *Hidden differences: Doing business with the Japanese.* New York: Anchor Books.

Lindlof, T. R., & Taylor, B. C. (2002). *Qualitative communication research methods* (2nd ed.). Thousand Oaks, CA: Sage.

Patton, M. Q. (2002). *Qualitative research methods and evaluation methods* (3rd ed.). Thousand Oaks, CA: Sage.

FOR FURTHER READING

Allen, B. J. (1995). "Diversity" and organizational communication. *Journal of Applied Communication Research, 23*(2), 143–155.

Chen, G. M., & Starosta, W. J. (2005). *Foundations of intercultural communication.* Lanham, MD: University Press of America.

Given, L. M., (Ed.). (2008). *The Sage encyclopedia of qualitative research methods.* Thousand Oaks, CA: Sage.

Case 5

Identifying the Scope of Work at Dixie Weaving, Inc.

Brian J. O'Leary and Christopher J. L. Cunningham

Learning Objectives

- To understand the challenges of developing a comprehensive data-collection strategy.
- To recognize the importance of identifying key data sources and appropriate data-collection methodologies.

"**Y**ou say your turnover rate is close to 40%? You're right, that is serious, and yes, I think we probably could help you resolve the problem. Let me discuss this briefly with a colleague and get back to you," Joe said, ending his call with Bill, the director of human resources at Dixie Weaving, Inc. They had spent the past 20 minutes discussing an ongoing cycle of challenges faced by Dixie Weaving with its production employees that was making it impossible for the organization to keep well-trained personnel on the manufacturing floor at all times.

Dixie Weaving is a fabric weaving company based in the southeastern United States that operates facilities throughout the country. Their Piedmont plant was experiencing unacceptably high levels of turnover, which prompted Bill Johnson, Dixie's corporate human resources (HR) manager, to contact the faculty in the Masters of Industrial Organizational (I-O) psychology program at Southern Metropolitan University for help. The parties had worked successfully together in the past on other projects. An exploratory meeting at Dixie's Piedmont plant initiated discussions about the situation and management's belief that the solution was to be found in revamping the training program.

"Hey, Ian!" Joe yelled across the office suite to his colleague. "Any chance you've got time to work on a consulting job with me over the next few months?"

"Sure—who's it with this time?" Ian asked.

"Dixie Weaving."

"Oh, good. What's the challenge?"

Joe relayed his chat with Bill, and he and Ian agreed that it was time to schedule a visit with Dixie's HR and management team to figure out what was really going on with this high rate of turnover.

"Great to see you both! It's been awhile." Bill greeted Joe and Ian at Dixie's main head-quarters. "I'd like to introduce you to the folks who manage the departments we were discussing last week." The team they greeted included Mike Payne, the plant manager and subject matter experts (SMEs) from the two departments—Winding and Weaving—most affected by the turnover bug, including the two floor supervisors, Hector Ramirez from Winding, and Sam Smith from Weaving; a senior operator from each department, Bubba Jones and T. J. Spratt; as well as the lead training coordinators for the Piedmont plant, Steve Troutman and Cindy Lee.

After the introductions, Joe initiated the discussion: "Before we get started, could you tell us a little about your operations and how you fit in Dixie's grand scheme?"

"Sure," said Mike. "I'm not sure exactly what you want to know, but I'll give you an overview. The Piedmont Plant employs 1,500 nonunion employees in a 24-hour opera-tion running two, 12-hour shifts, 7 days a week. We have two major manufacturing processes—winding and weaving. The Winding department is responsible for creating the nylon yarn used in the weaving process. The Weaving department creates the fabric that is used in our commercial products. We are dependent on our Chattanooga plant for raw materials, while several other plants are dependent on us for the fabric we produce."

Joe said, "Now, tell us a little more about this turnover problem you're having." He and Ian then assumed the role of "sponges," listening and absorbing all the details that this panel of experts could convey, including their ideas about possible causes and poten-tial solutions. The team provided a bevy of good ideas and observations, each providing a unique perspective.

Providing the "big picture" perspective, plant manager Mike pointed out that "the cur-rent level of turnover is unsustainable and needs to be reduced quickly before it impacts our competitive position. I don't care who's responsible; we just need to do *something* before it affects the bottom line. If we can't meet our production goals, it's going to slow down other plants. If that happens, Corporate's going to have my head!"

Bill expressed his frustration with HR's inability to attract and hire qualified workers. "While these jobs don't require a college degree, they do pay well and Dixie is a great company to work for. Our biggest problem is that we're getting dangerously close to exhausting our local labor pool. Where are we going to find better people?"

Hector and Sam, the floor supervisors, expressed concern about day-to-day opera-tions. Sam noted, "Under the current conditions, we simply can't meet our departmental quotas." Hector chimed in, "yeah, and it takes a while for new workers to learn how to do these jobs effectively and safely. We just don't have the bench strength to keep up.

There are also a lot of rules that need to become second nature to all our workers to keep this place safe, but many of them are still focusing on the basics of their jobs. Someone's going to get hurt . . . or worse. Just last week we had a guy turned into a pancake by a rolling machine. It was ugly."

"And another thing," Sam added, "I can't even understand a lot of 'em, especially on the night shift, because they're a bunch of foreigners. They barely speak English."

Bubba and T. J., the most experienced workers on the floor, were rather quiet during most of the discussion, but Joe and Ian sensed they had something to say. When prompted, Bubba huffed, "Well, whatever happens, I'm tired of babysitting. You send these people into my area before they can even tie their shoes, let alone a weaver's knot. And then you expect me to teach them the ropes while still meeting my quota." T. J. nodded emphatically in agreement.

Somewhat defensively, Cindy, the training coordinator, stated with some surprise, "Bubba's comments are interesting considering that we put all new hires through a rigorous 12-week training program before they ever hit the floor. If you've got a better idea, we'd love to hear it."

Sensing a heightening of tensions, Ian shot Joe a look that suggested it was time to redirect the conversation. "Hey Mike, this input is really helpful to us as we start to get our bearings on this project. Before we leave today, do you think we could take a quick plant tour? I think that'd really help us put things in perspective as we organize a proposal for you all to consider."

Mike agreed. "We just need to get you some PPE (personal protection equipment) and have you sign a waiver."

With that, Bill took Joe and Ian to get outfitted with a safety vest, protective goggles, and earplugs. They also had to remove their watches and rings. They entered one of the largest enclosed spaces they'd ever seen. "How big is this place?" Ian asked.

"We've got over 40 acres under roof with over 1,000 winders and weaving looms. Our first stop will be the Winding department," Bill said in a loud voice that Joe and Ian still had to strain to hear over the din. As they continued to follow Bill along the yellow-taped path, they noticed several large machines with freshly painted orange zones on the floors surrounding them. "What's with the paint job?" Joe inquired.

"Remember that 'pancake' incident Hector mentioned? Well, that's supposed to help prevent that from happening again—by the way, don't go in the orange zone without a buddy," Bill added with a concerned expression.

As they turned the corner, narrowly avoiding being run over by a forklift, Bill exclaimed, "Watch your step! You've gotta keep your eyes open around here. Anyway, the Winding department is where we produce the nylon yarn used in Weaving. It takes two people to operate a winder: one to load the raw materials and the other to remove the finished product. Operators are also responsible for monitoring the machine to ensure that it doesn't break. We've had problems keeping these machines running lately."

Ian asked, "So what happens when a machine goes down?"

"First," Bill said, "the operators hit the emergency stop button and report the problem to their floor supervisor. The floor supervisor then makes an announcement over the

PA requesting help from any available workers. Typically, these are people who are on break or eating lunch."

"How often does that happen?" Joe asked.

"About every other day, generally on the night shift," said Bill.

After meandering through the vast complex, they finally arrived in the Weaving department. Joe and Ian were impressed by the size and complexity of the looms. Hundreds of spools of yarn were loaded on long racks of spindles that fed like a huge spider web into the weaving mechanism. Bill continued. "Each of these looms produces more than 50 yards of fabric a minute. A senior weaver and an associate weaver are responsible for monitoring the operation to remove empty spools and 'tie-on' new spools, all while the machine runs continuously. If they exceed a certain number of line breaks at any given time, the machine has to be shutdown and yarn has to be rethreaded, which can take 20 minutes or more."

Joe noticed a rather forlorn-looking individual who appeared to be using something that looked like an anvil to scrape excess yarn off of the used spools. "What's she doing over there?" he inquired.

"Oh, that's one of our newbies, Harriet. She was hired about 6 weeks ago. It looks like this week she's been assigned to work with Jimmy James, one of our best weavers, so he can bring her up to speed. We could use a dozen more just like him," Bill thought aloud. "Anyway, she's doing what's called the 'burn off.' All of the used spools have to be free of yarn before they're put on the spindle cart and shipped back to the Winding department for reuse. That bar is a like a hot iron that melts through the remaining yarn, which is then tossed in the recycle bin."

"So is that all Harriet does for her whole shift?" asked Joe.

"Actually, that's normally something they save for the last few minutes before their breaks and the end of their shifts to clean up the area. I'm not exactly sure why she's doing it now." Bill said somewhat puzzled.

Having been in the facility now for almost half an hour, Joe and Ian were feeling the effects of the oppressive heat. "Phew, it has to be 90 degrees in here," Ian complained as he wiped the sweat off his forehead.

"I'd put it closer to 95," Joe said. "I can't imagine working in here on my feet for 12 hours at night during the winter, let alone during the day in the summer. No wonder I haven't seen a smiling face since we left that air-conditioned meeting room. In fact, I think I'm about ready to head back." Bill and Ian did not argue with him.

Having completed their tour, Joe and Ian did indeed have a better understanding of the operation and had identified some additional things to ponder. "Thanks for your assistance today, Bill," Ian said. "I think we've got a much better sense of some of the factors likely to be connected to the turnover challenges your organization is facing. At this point, I think it would be very beneficial for us to take some time to perform a more comprehensive evaluation. Why don't Joe and I put together a summary of today's meeting, identify some possible directions for us to go, and get back to you in a couple days?"

"Sounds like a plan," Bill agreed. "What do you need from us?"

Joe replied, "Access, more than anything else. Let us formulate a plan with more detailed needs and we'll discuss them at our next meeting. See you soon."

On the drive back, Ian was thinking that one of the many benefits of being a professor of industrial-organizational psychology was the opportunity to climb down out of the "ivory tower" to apply the theories and research that he taught in the classroom and find out just what does and doesn't work in the real world. Each client presented a unique set of challenges that often required Joe and him to stray far from the beaten path to find truly creative solutions. Dixie was no exception. "Hey, Joe, do you think they have any idea of just how many issues are probably underlying this turnover problem of theirs?"

"Well, it sure doesn't take a PhD to see that we've got plenty of paths to explore," Joe replied. "You can't spit without hitting something that could be contributing to their turnover problem. I'm really looking forward to seeing what else we can find out."

They returned to their offices and immediately began working on their plan for a more complete diagnosis of Dixie's current challenges. After reviewing their experience, they felt confident in their conclusion that turnover was just one symptom of much deeper problems existing in the organization. Both Ian and Joe felt that this organization development (OD) challenge would most definitely require an integrated systems perspective. All of the issues raised by the client SMEs were valid and Ian and Joe needed to figure out a way to reconcile them and to understand how they were all connected to turnover. No input-process-output (IPO) focus, or strengths-weaknesses-opportunities-threats (SWOT) analysis would suffice given the complex web of factors and the prevailing cultural norms that were clearly influencing the safety, morale, and behavioral issues that they observed during their plant tour. What they needed to do was to develop a work plan for a comprehensive diagnosis that Ian and Joe could use to help Dixie understand and help itself deal with its underlying process and procedure issues.

One of their biggest challenges now was for Ian and Joe to strike the appropriate balance in presenting their approach. It was obvious from their discussions and observations at the plant that morale at the plant was low and communication among the various constituencies was inadequate at best. They also had to guard against coming across as "egghead know-it-alls" sent down from on high to save the ignorant savages. Ideally they could adopt some sort of process consultative approach. Dixie management and employees had to see this as a collaborative effort or Ian and Joe were never going to get the level of cooperation they needed to complete this project.

To this end, they decided that the best approach would be to sketch out a rough summary of the areas they'd like to explore and propose to meet with the project team to hash out the details. This approach would provide them with additional perspectives and build trust that would be vital throughout the process.

Joe called Bill the next day with their proposal. "I'm sending you an outline of where we'd like to go from here based on what we learned in yesterday's meeting. I'd like to review this with you briefly and, if it looks OK to you, I'd like to present it to your team tomorrow." Joe felt confident that he and Ian had taken a good approach with this project and he was eager to move forward with defining the scope of what lay ahead.

When he received the e-mail from Joe, Bill was most interested in seeing what types of resources would be required to support this project. He was curious also about the scope of what the consultants were proposing to do. The e-mail read as follows.

Bill,

Based on yesterday's meeting and plant tour, we feel that the turnover issue you iden-tified is more complex than it appears on the surface. We are confident we can help you and Dixie resolve this issue, but we need to gain a more complete picture of your operations. We think the best approach is the following multipronged process:

- *Informational Interviews*
- *A series of interviews with employees at multiple levels throughout the affected departments, from both the day and night shifts. The topics that we will be dis-cussing in these interviews include the following:*
  - o *Hiring Process*
  - o *Training*
  - o *Experiences on the Plant Floor*
  - o *Supervision and Performance Management*
  - o *Communication*
- *Documentation Review*
- *An examination of the job descriptions and training materials related to the positions in question (because many of the issues raised in yesterday's meeting involve HR-related practices and policies).*
- *In-Depth Job Observation and Analysis*
- *Conducting an extended period of observation of the workers in the Winding and Weaving departments. The purpose of these observations is to better under-stand the day-to-day knowledge, skills, abilities, and other personal characteris-tics required for safe and effective job performance.*

With your support, and using our full team of two primary consultants and four graduate student associates, we anticipate that the data-collection process will take no more than 2 weeks, and we would like to begin as soon as possible. Data analysis and development of our proposed solution should be ready for presentation to you 2 weeks after data collection is complete.

All data we collect during these interviews will be managed by us to protect the anonymity of the interviewees, but we will provide a summary report along with our recommendations. We recognize that this will cause some disruption to the normal daily operations and we will do everything we can to minimize the inconvenience. We would appreciate it if you would emphasize to all employees, and particularly supervisors, the importance of their participation in this process to addressing the turnover problems you are currently experiencing.

Best regards,

Joe and Ian

Bill saw nothing in the e-mail that placed any particularly onerous burdens on him or his staff, although he was somewhat surprised at the scope of the information that was being requested. And, of course, he was a bit concerned that this "simple" issue was much more complicated than he had initially envisioned. He replied with his willingness to move ahead with the proposed plan and set up the following day's meeting. There was a lot of work to be done, but he was excited to have Joe and Ian as partners in this process.

Discussion Questions

1. What important business details regarding data gathering and facilities access need to be addressed upon entering into this project?

2. Why might Dixie Weaving employees choose not to cooperate with the consultants at this stage in the project?

3. Do you agree with the multipronged diagnostic strategy outlined by Joe and Ian in their e-mail to Bill? How would you carry out each of the prongs they describe?

4. Do you agree or disagree with Joe and Ian's time estimates for this diagnostic phase of the project? Why or why not? What factors would you consider in developing an estimate?

5. What are some creative and empirically sound ways to conduct in-depth observations within the plant without causing too much concern on the part of employees?

FOR FURTHER READING

Block, P. (2000). *Flawless consulting* (2nd ed.). San Francisco: Pfeiffer.

Burke, W. W. (1987). *Organization development: A normative view.* Upper Saddle River, NJ: Pearson Education.

Howard, A. (1994). *Diagnosis for organizational change: Methods and models.* New York: Guilford Press.

Lundberg, C. C. (2008). Organization development diagnosis. In T. G. Cummings (Ed.), *Handbook of organization development* (pp. 137–150). Los Angeles: Sage.

Nadler, D. A., & Tushman, M. L. (1977). A diagnostic model for organizational behavior. In J. R. Hackman, E. E. Lawler, & L W. Porter (Eds.), *Perspectives in behavior in organizations* (pp. 85–100). New York: McGraw-Hill.

Schein, E. H. (1999). *Process consulting revisited: Building the helping relationship.* Reading, MA: Addison-Wesley.

Case 6

A MANUFACTURING CRISIS IN BAYRISCHER SILICON PRODUCTS

BRUCE O. MABEE

Learning Objectives

- To strengthen your confidence and realism in negotiating with a client group (or consultant team) who may have predetermined actions that they want to take.
- To sharpen your resolve to build client-consultant consensus about the diagnosis even in an anxiety-producing situation, and to pull stakeholders who are significantly affected by the situation into building the diagnosis.
- To stretch your readiness to adapt the diagnosis as unexpected data emerge, and patience to continue adapting the diagnosis as intervention actions are taken.

Barry Kravich recognized the voice on the phone as Irene Lorraine, a human resources (HR) manager he had met in California.[1] "I am working in Germany now," Irene said, "but let me just get to the point. We're facing a situation that happened suddenly, and I thought of you as someone who may be able to help."

Irene had been a participant in Barry's consulting skills workshop, and she had been using the skills for over a year in her new HR manager role. She had an energetic and positive style, seemingly unafraid of any challenge, so when she was asking for help, Barry was honored to get the call.

"Karl, our plant manager, asked me to facilitate strategic planning for our plant's management team in an off-site retreat," Irene said. "But I feel that there is more to this than just an analytical planning session. The plant just fell into a major crisis. If you are willing, I'd like to have you talk with Karl." Irene briefly described the technical problem as she understood it, but she preferred to have the manager explain.

INITIAL AGREEMENTS BETWEEN
CLIENT AND CONSULTANTS

Karl Arnstadt, the plant manager, contacted Barry, asking about his experience with strategic planning. Karl saw a need for his management team to be thinking strategically.

When Barry asked Karl to describe the situation that led him to want strategic planning, Karl described a sudden, major "scrap situation" in which the machines that produced computer memory modules had "plopped" more than a million euros worth of useless modules within a few minutes.

Confused, and a bit shocked at Karl's reasoning, Barry asked, "Why would you want strategic planning when you have a major problem that you need to solve immediately?"

"This is the only time we may ever be open to real strategic thinking." Karl described several times when they had tried to be creative and strategic, yet always, in his opinion, they had come to similar "in-the-box" answers about the route that the plant would take to the future.

Irene and Barry agreed to facilitate the retreat Karl had requested on the condition that the management team would quickly test whatever plans they created. Barry insisted, "If you are willing to look at your early results very soon, and you are committed to change the plans quickly if a new need is seen, this session may allow you to begin building out-of-the-box alternatives."

The consultants proposed that a second retreat occur several weeks after the initial one. In this "revisit," all parties would learn soon what seems to work and then hone or adjust the plans in response to the real-time data, which the early actions would reveal. A third "Follow-Up Day" would be scheduled several months later.

Karl reacted positively to the idea of revisiting and revising. "You're right, we won't solve all this in one meeting, and there is much more we need to take on after this." Yet, Karl pushed the quickness of the early tests even quicker; because of Barry's travel from the United States to Germany to facilitate, all agreed that it was more practical to hold the first two sessions within several *days* of each other rather than several weeks apart.

Barry got off the phone and immediately booked the flight to Germany.

The venue chosen was a large cabin in a hilly, woodsy resort, not fancy or heavily equipped electronically. Although the site was within 15 kilometers (10 miles) of the plant, the rustic atmosphere was very far from the manufacturing buzz of the plant.

THE FIRST MANAGEMENT MEETING

On the first day of the retreat, Irene and Barry presented a wide variety of strategic variables, seeking management team consensus on topics such as markets, trends in computer memory technology, engineering expertise, and the role of the plant within the company. With each variable, the consultants asked the managers to review what they believed was going on and what was most important to improve, for both the immediate crisis and for the long-term development of the plant.

The management group quickly and strongly reached a consensus that made the external consultant uncomfortable. The group dismissed many strategic variables, including market and technology trends, yet they had very strong interest in a single issue: chronically poor communication between the management and the supervisory level who reported to the managers. One of the managers, Dierdre Reddig, spoke what the others clearly felt: "With our current level of trust, nothing else we solve will ever get implemented effectively. Many supervisors who report to us do not believe we care about them."

Barry was uncomfortable with the sense that this "communication" diagnosis was too "soft" for the nature of the technical issues that had to be addressed to get the machines not only repaired but also constantly upgraded. "Irene and I have been raising the kinds of issues that are normally important in strategic planning, yet one issue is dominating your attention. You know your plant better than I do, so I have to ask you to consider this carefully: Is the communication with the supervisors so important that you want to stake your future on it as well as your recovery from this crisis?"

The group was quiet. The leader did not speak. After several uncomfortable minutes ticked by, one of the newer managers spoke up. "I believe that if we do not deal with the supervisors, we will be unable to solve the problems. I frankly do not understand how the machines work well enough to know what to fix. My supervisors who report to me are the ones who know. I am not happy about this, but it's true."

A senior manager spoke. "Gustav is right. I also should better understand our processes, but I do not."

After several other managers added similar thoughts, Karl clinched the choice to make communication the main strategic priority. "We have been in our ivory towers, and now we are feeling the pain of that. We need the supervisors, and that is what we need to fix—as management, we cannot fix the technical problems that brought us here today."

> **Reflection Stop 1.** Imagine you are Barry right now. What are you thinking and feeling in the consulting role? What would you do here? Please take a minute to reflect before you continue reading.

SUPERVISORS HEAR THAT "MANAGEMENT WANTS INPUT"

Before noon on that first day of the management meeting, someone must have "leaked" what was going on. Supervisors back at the plant had learned that the management team was interested in their "input." The supervisors responded, unsolicited, within 2 hours, delivering by phone just before 2 p.m. a list of 14 demands of management.

Several managers' anger flared at the audacity, yet while still behind the closed doors of the retreat, other managers in the group calmed them down. "Let's listen to these supervisors for once and show enough respect to seriously consider what they propose."

Figure 6.1 Issues from Supervisors Presented by Phone to Management Meeting

1. Some managers show low respect for supervisors in front of employees.

2. Problems with vending machines in the lunchroom get lost in management priorities.

3. Some managers frequently miss meetings scheduled with supervisors.

4. Software projects get signed off by managers who do not know the requirements.

5. Managers meet, then tell the supervisors conclusions. Supervisors' knowledge is missed.

6. Supervisors are not included in weekly plant reviews. They cannot learn or add to their knowledge.

7. Pay differentials between shifts are handled poorly.

8. Managers order projects on short notice that require complex shift changes.

9. Some managers talk behind the backs of others, hurting employee morale.

10. Managers who do not know the current production embarrass specialists (and themselves) with customers.

11. Customers call the floor directly and make demands, and managers do not intervene.

12. We need new windows. They still leak!

13. Managers need to learn all employee names, in their own area at least.

14. No one has followed through on the noise levels in Area 5.

By the end of the first day, the managers accepted several supervisory proposals, and a meeting was arranged for the following day with all 80 supervisors to discuss further changes.

LARGE MEETINGS WITH ALL SUPERVISORS FROM ALL SHIFTS

Actually, two meetings were held to accommodate all three shifts of supervisors in this 24/7 operation.

The majority of supervisors, approximately 60, could attend the 14.00 (2 p.m.) meeting in the last hour of the day shift, an hour prior to the beginning of the evening shift. The other meeting was scheduled at 22.00 (10 p.m.), so evening shift supervisors could attend at the end of their shift, and night shift supervisors could come in before their shift began.

Reflection Stop 2. Now, as if you were Barry, what are you thinking and feeling? What would you do now? Please take a minute to reflect before you continue reading.

MEETINGS WITH SUPERVISORS, PLANS FOR CHANGE

Most supervisors did attend the all-supervisor meetings. A skeleton crew of supervisors remained on the manufacturing lines, and several supervisors did not attend for undetermined reasons.

Each meeting was co-led by one senior manager and one "junior" manager who had been chosen by the management team for having trusted relationships with supervisors. Irene and Barry attended, but did not facilitate; the choice was made that the regular managers would have more credibility by facing the angry supervisors rather than by passing that task to professional facilitators. The managers started each meeting with a 5-minute introduction of the "bad news" that the management had assessed in the previous day at the retreat. They further presented the management conclusion that "supervisors are critical in the plant leadership," and added that the management group felt, "We have been ineffective in two-way communication with supervisors." The two managers presented the purpose of these emergency meetings as "an exchange of what we all know, and a commitment to what we must do next."

Indeed, the tone of the supervisors was skeptical. Barry could see eyes rolling and looks of hardened disinterest among some of the supervisors. One supervisor openly asked, "Why should we believe that this will be any different than previous meetings with us?" The senior manager replied, "There is no reason to believe this will be different. Only time will tell whether we are sincere. You must be the judge of that."

The managers did not at first present the 14 demands that had come the previous day, instead letting the issues arise from the large groups. As each issue was raised, one manager wrote it on a flipchart. These were prioritized by the whole group later in the meeting.

As facilitator, one manager did ask about an item from the 14 demands when no one brought it up: "Someone suggested earlier that we include an appointed supervisor in the weekly plant status review. Does anyone here believe this is worth trying?" Several supervisors agreed with the suggestion, Ms. Reddig adding, "That poor supervisor should not have to face all of you managers alone. Two supervisors should come." By the following week, two supervisors began attending weekly reviews.

After the first large meeting, Irene heard grumbling among supervisors that the manger had misinterpreted some issues raised by supervisors. She asked the complaining supervisors why they did not speak up at the meeting; several of them then went to the top manager who had facilitated and told him about the complaints. He pulled out the flipcharts and corrected the misstatements as they watched.

Several times in the meeting, a supervisor shouted, "That's not what he meant!" to correct the manager's notes. The manager learned to write more accurately, or to ask, "Does this capture what you meant?"

The meetings each lasted about 90 minutes, longer than the hour planned for each. Supervisors gladly continued to assert additional issues, and time became tight when the

Figure 6.2   Plant Issues and Plans—Top 10 Priorities—Supervisory Meetings

Issue	Plan	Leaders
Weak communication between 2nd/3rd shifts.	Begin daily log, so next shift can read it.	JS, TS
Software code testing often misses key problems.	Whoever writes code must not be the tester!	RT, JP
The cooling apparatus has broken down at least once every year.	Replace the entire mechanism with a new generation.	GR, KL, JP
Some managers never listen to supervisors. There is no recourse.	Survey supervisors. Use employee survey format.	JS, MP
Management offices are "hidden"—it's not neutral turf.	Move management offices to cubicles in center of plant.	MN, TG
Repeated schedule changes affect employee families.	Create centralized database for schedules.	TS, JS
Suppliers of chemicals often slow in delivery.	Track order/delivery times; give feedback.	DD, SF
Lunchroom vending machines offer no healthy choices.	Negotiate with vendor.	FR, DR
Engineering creates delays in upgrades.	Form teams of engineers/techs.	DF, KL
Resentment for manager parking spots.	Special slots for anyone in a meeting.	JS, RF

managers pushed to have the group nominate and vote on the most pressing issues. When priorities were determined this way, the managers then sought volunteers to take the lead on each issue. Whispering began in the room about the extra time this was taking from supervisors who had to get home or begin their shift.

THE VISIBLE CHANGE

One proposal that emerged in the large meetings was stated with some humor. Jon Reinhardt suggested a major change in the layout of the management offices, which were located in the secluded corners of the building, a several minute walk from the main floor. Supervisors who proposed the change said that many employees and supervisors were intimidated to enter the "ivory tower" of management offices. This brought quiet smiles to the faces of many supervisors. The managers did not smile.

The proposal advocated an "open-plan," with management offices in cubicles at the center of the plant. The point was open communication, so supervisors could discuss needs immediately on "neutral turf."

Approximately 25 ideas were approved from the supervisory meetings. The change in the office arrangement was the largest-budget item approved by the top managers. Managers Marna Newmann and Thomas Grande volunteered to lead this project, which they took directly to Karl Arnstadt for his budget-approval signature. The management offices were changed to the newly proposed cubicle layout within a month.

CONSULTANT CLOSING—AFTER THE ACTION PLANNING, BEFORE THE IMPLEMENTATION

When the two meetings were completed, Irene and Barry met with Karl for a summary meeting. "Tell us how it went," Barry started.

"Much better than I expected," Karl replied. "Thank you for helping us get moving on an issue we have needed to address for years."

"You are not done yet, are you?" Barry asked. "I want to stay in touch with you and Irene, to find out what works and what does not work. I want to keep up phone calls with you, and also with a few of your managers and supervisors, to see what they see succeeding and failing. Does that work for you?"

Karl and Barry parted on positive terms. Barry and Irene took a couple of hours to debrief what they each saw, giving feedback to each other about the specific actions each took through this period.

Barry felt that Irene had been instrumental, not only in briefing him on the culture and the personalities, but in her quick, "friendly-but-deadly" confrontations of managers and supervisors. His main suggestion to Irene was, "Take advantage of the positive influence you have achieved. If you ever get tired or discouraged, call me to give you a boost!"

Irene felt that Barry's flexibility enabled the managers to pursue what they believed was required, rather than doggedly pursuing his initial menu of strategic planning issues. "They are used to taking orders, but you let them *give* the orders, which led to a very different scenario than had ever happened here before." Irene suggested that Barry consider looking at his style when among Germans: "You could gain more respect by showing you can take a hard stand. Then, you do not have to continue taking a stand!"

In their final moments of this trip, Barry said to Irene, "Thank you for pulling me into this. Of course, it has just begun. They have quite a few action plans to implement—as planned, or not!

"I wish I could be here to see these actions take place, but you will be here, Irene. I want to stay in touch about how you are influencing these interventions as they unfold— so I hear the early results. The real data, about what can work and what cannot work around here, will be emerging in the next few weeks."

Irene committed to Barry that she would be "constantly pushing" the managers to implement what they had planned, "and I plan to keep them acting with their eyes open!"

Life in the plant for the next few weeks went very differently than it had in the past. Life in the plant also did not go on exactly as planned in the meetings. Intervention rarely occurs as planned.

Discussion Questions

1. The client manager, Karl, had requested strategic planning, yet when Barry asked why that would serve the "scrap situation," Karl gave an unusual answer: "It's the only time we may ever be open to real strategic thinking." At this point, what preliminary diagnosis do you see occurring, and what further diagnostic processes might lead to the most effective actions?

2. This is a question of when the real diagnosis and intervention occur: When Barry facilitated the first strategic planning meeting of the managers, was that an intervention, or was it merely preparation for a *diagnostic* meeting that would occur with the supervisors? What data do you see in this first management meeting that suggested immediately scheduling the two supervisory meetings?

3. The two consultants, Irene and Barry, did not lead the large diagnostic/action planning meetings with the supervisors. Instead, managers led those sessions. What conditions made it a good idea or a bad idea for the clients, not the consultants, to lead the meetings?

4. List the steps of the action research process as you have learned them. Compare the process in this case to the process as you have learned it, for the gathering of data, diagnosis, and action planning. How can a consultant maintain the integrity of connecting diagnosis to action when the process unfolds quickly and in an unplanned order, such as this crisis situation?

5. When the client and consultant together clarify the diagnosis and connect the action plans to it ("What's really going on now, and how will our plans make that better?"), this builds relationships that allow continued questioning after implementation. What next steps do you suggest to Barry as he sets the stage for the follow-up meeting 3 months from now?

NOTE

1. Is this story real? Yes, the story is presented as it actually happened. Names and details were changed to maintain anonymity.

FOR FURTHER READING

Anderson, D. L. (2010). *Organization development: The process of leading organizational change.* Thousand Oaks, CA: Sage.

Burke, W. W. (2008). *Organization change: Theory and practice* (2nd ed.). Thousand Oaks, CA: Sage.

Kets De Vries, M. (2009). *Leadership coaching and organizational transformation: Effectiveness in a world of paradoxes* (INSEAD working paper series). Fontainebleu, France: INSEAD. Retrieved from http://www.ila-net.org/Publications/CDROM/pdfs/Leadership_Coaching_IGLC_2009.pdf

THE IVORY TOWER OPENS UP

ALEXANDRA MICHEL AND KATRIN NOEFER

Learning Objectives

- To help you understand the complex structures underlying change initiatives in higher education.
- To interpret survey data in a meaningful way.
- To take a consultant's perspective and brainstorm your ideas for improving change projects.

MEETING BETWEEN UNIVERSITY MANAGEMENT MEMBER AND ORGANIZATION DEVELOPMENT (OD) CONSULTANT TO CLARIFY THE CONSULTANCIES' OFFER

Ms. Darborough[1] knocked at her boss's office door. "Sorry for the interruption, Peter, but Jennifer McSullivan from Free Way consultancy is here for you. Can I bring her in?" Peter Murphy looked up. "Oh, thank you, Sandra, I was so busy reading our change strategy proposal, that I almost forgot the appointment. Yes, of course, please bring her in."

When she arrived, Peter stood and welcomed the woman from Free Way consultancy, a small woman. Had he not talked to his friend and former colleague Martin Sprigg from Milton University, who had recommended Jennifer as a very competent consultant, Peter might not have believed it. But Martin told him that Jennifer managed a very difficult project at Milton University in which the communication process between leaders and their subordinates needed to be improved. There was a lot of resistance in the project, but

Jennifer managed to successfully implement that communication strategy. Martin had told Jennifer about a possible new job at Harpers University, so she had called Peter in his office the previous week and he gave her a short overview. She sounded quite optimistic that she could be of help. Peter stepped toward her and thought that if she could work those miracles here at Harpers, too, then she was just the person he needed. "This might get interesting," he thought.

"Hello, Mrs. McSullivan, it's good to see you. I'm so busy preparing the university's change initiative that I don't really know where to get started, but I am being impolite, please take a seat first."

"Thank you, Mr. Murphy. From the conversation with Martin last week, I got the impression that it's a very challenging project you're going through. As far as I understood, there is a big change initiative planned to raise the university's competitiveness in the international field of higher education. I also think you mentioned being faced with organizational structures and processes that are quite different from for-profit organizations. Our consultancy specializes in working with public administration, but as every organization has its own peculiarities, would you mind telling me more about your present situation?"

"Of course not," Peter said. "I'll be glad to outline the project details for you. I agree that every organization is different, especially universities. They seem to be huge sleeping beauties that need to be awakened for the challenges every competitive organization has to face nowadays. It all started a month ago, when the executive board, academic senate, and supervisory board here at Harpers published a change strategy. Its aim is to raise the university's competitiveness with different change projects. I think change is good, and more than necessary at our university, but there are so many different areas that should undergo change."

Jennifer interrupted. "Can you give me an example?"

He replied, "We would like to enhance the study conditions by restructuring departments and improving existing curricula. That means introducing new bachelor's, master's, and PhD student programs so that our university also attracts students from all over the world and study results are comparable on an international level. There also needs to be an improvement in service facilities."

"Are you referring to work and family balance, especially for young researchers?" she asked.

"Yes, exactly, that's just one of the many other change projects. We want to give talented researchers a better chance to combine family and work practices. In addition, we want to improve our personnel development to promote our academic staff managing their diverse tasks in teaching, research, fund-raising, and leadership. Speaking of research, there is a huge need to improve national and international cooperation between universities and to link research activities with practice. We want to enlarge our cooperation with different organizations, because our research needs to offer solutions to existing, real problems. So, you see, there's not just one area; there are many."

"When are the executive board and all the other groups involved planning to get the projects started?" Jennifer asked.

"You see, people planning the change initiative are quite aware about the specifics of a university structure."

"Sorry, but what are you referring to exactly?" Jennifer said.

Peter explained. "We have ten different faculties[2] here at Harpers: Humanities with psychology, philosophy, theology, then law, the medical department, sciences with physics, math, or for example economics and engineering. We have 5,000 members of academic, technical, and administrative staff and approximately 16,000 students."

"That's quite a lot," she said.

"Yes it is. It's not only that we have diversity in research interests; universities also have quite specific traits. Leadership and decision processes are quite different than in other profit and nonprofit organizations. The values and incentives systems here at Harpers also vary hugely from other organizations."

"What does that mean?" Jennifer asked.

"Characteristic of our university is the decentralized structure. The faculties and departments within one faculty are not really connected. Those decentralized structures might make it very difficult to organize a holistic change approach."

"But what about the leaders in the different faculties? Can they promote the change processes?"

Peter thought for a moment before he replied. "Well, you see, the strategic development of a university is set by the executive board, supervisory board, and academic senate. University management and deans usually have limited decision making opportunities concerning their employees. It all really depends on governmental regulation and deregulation. For example, professors are employed by the state and not by the university itself."

"What about the employees?" she asked.

"Well, they are usually elected for certain decision groups, but only for a limited time."

"Okay, I see," Jennifer said. "They have those responsibilities on top of their normal work load."

Peter agreed. "Yes, and so there's a certain continuity lacking."

Jennifer said, "I find that when talking about change initiatives, it also depends a lot on people's value systems and how they get involved."

"I agree, but a university culture places a lot of emphasis on critical thinking to boost research freedom. Employees want to develop knowledge, and they like their autonomy to be flexible and creative," Peter replied.

"So, employees want to have an opinion and make up their own mind?"

"Yes, but that also means that they question strategic change initiatives and don't deliberately take over those aims."

"In other consultancy projects I have been involved with," she said, "incentives are a huge motivator. What about that at Harpers?"

Peter looked for the right words. "To be honest, they are almost nonexistent so far. A faculty can have an increase in funding for projects, but this money will not get to the employees. Instead, the incentives focus on every employee's intrinsic motivation is to finish their dissertation, to push their own career, and maybe to be good or lucky enough to have their own research department. It's then more their recognition as experts in their research community, proofed by publications in peer-reviewed journals, citations, or invitations to give conference keynotes, but that's not measurable in terms of money. Academic's self-development is necessary, but it's not exactly seen as a huge incentive."

"That means the motivation to work on leadership issues or strategic development is rather small?" Jennifer asked.

"Yes, exactly," Peter replied. "And mind you, because of those decentralized structures, staff is often faced with limited working contracts. This is a problem because people might not be willing to participate in change projects."

She looked for confirmation. "Okay, you're saying that people are too busy getting their research and doctorates done and don't have enough time to identify with the university."

Peter tried to make his point clear. "Yes, sort of, and you know, people might not appreciate those change projects. In fact I am rather worried that they see it as an extra burden to their already demanding working conditions. They don't really see what's in it for them. So, do you think you now have an understanding of the university's structures and functions?"

"Yes, thank you. I believe I understand the special situation at Harpers and the challenges you face getting people involved in the change projects. What I think might be our first task is to find out how informed and involved students and staff feel since the change strategy was published."

He agreed. "You're right. Give me time to inform the steering committee for the change initiative about our plans and maybe that can be the starting point for our next meeting?"

Jennifer nodded. "Good idea. Are 2 weeks enough?"

"Certainly. I will see you then," Peter said.

MEETING TO PLAN THE DATA-COLLECTION PROCEDURE (2 WEEKS LATER)

Jennifer entered Peter's office. "Hello, Peter. Last time we met, you had a lot on your plate concerning the change projects. How are you doing so far?"

Peter rose from his chair. "Hello, Jennifer. It was good talking with you about the change projects. It really straightened things out for me. But to be honest, I still had a lot of thinking to do on how to proceed."

"Well, good, let's take your ideas as a starting point, shall we?" she said.

Peter led the consultant to a table to sit down. "Okay, what I thought was this: We need to talk to a lot of people from different research areas to involve them more in ongoing projects, but I also want to know whether academic staff and students are informed about and committed to our change strategy. We have planned to successfully finish all our change initiative within 3 years."

Jennifer nodded in agreement. "Okay, that means you want to do cross-sectional and longitudinal evaluations."

Peter looked at her and nodded. "Yes, I guess so. I would like to ask participants now at the beginning of the change initiative, as a starting point, but I would also like their opinion in between and at the end of the whole initiative."

She said, "That is a good idea, because you can then improve the change procedures while the initiative is still going on, but at the same time, you can have a final evaluation to check whether the intervention was really successful. Who should participate?"

It seemed that Peter had waited for just this question. "Okay, first of all, the research assistants. They don't participate as much in boards as professors do. Therefore, they don't have the same amount of autonomy for decision processes. And I would like to ask the students, as well. They are true members of this university and contribute immensely to its success."

"Okay, fair enough. Concerning how you want to proceed, may I suggest something?" Jennifer asked.

"Of course, please fire away."

"I think it would be good to have a convenience sample. And it also saves you a lot of time if you can distribute the questionnaire online instead of paper-pencil."

Peter was quite surprised. "Online? Well that could work, but how do we contact them? A lot of students have a university mailing address, but seldom use it."

"What about lectures?" she suggested. "You could address the different projects there and heighten students' awareness."

He thought for a moment. "True, I guess you're right. And the employees already have a university mailing account, so there should be no problems."

Jennifer nodded. "Good. Let's come to the tricky part now. What variables should be included in the questionnaire? Research on change processes identifies process variables like information, participation, or procedural justice. Change characteristics, for example the perception of benefit of change, also play an important role for positive employees' reactions."

Peter replied, "Okay. Information is very important. The questionnaire should include questions about the communication strategy. Does the management make the aims and results of this change initiative transparent for everybody?"

She reflected on past consultancy projects. "Okay—talking about being informed. My experience with different change projects in the past demonstrated that people not only like to be informed about what is going on, they also like to actively participate and feel that they have control about what's going on."

He agreed. "So participation should be included as well. From my own experience I can see that people are feeling that they're being treated unfairly if they don't see the opportunity to participate. What do we do about that?"

"You should ask certain questions concerning procedural justice, meaning the fairness of decision processes made by university management."

Peter said, "Okay, but if we are asking about procedural justice, we also should include whether the change is evaluated as beneficial and useful."

Jennifer agreed. "Yes, it's very important that employees can answer the following question for themselves: Was the change project useful for their work unit or rather a big hindrance? We can call that benefit or consequences of change."

He looked out of the window for a moment before he replied. "Yes, people's reactions to the change process are crucial for every change initiative, because it's them living those ideas day by day."

Jennifer jumped to the next variable she wanted to be included in the questionnaire. "Therefore, I would suggest that you ask about commitment."

"Commitment?"

She explained. "It's usually committed employees who believe in the value of the change and then promote it. You see, if people have a positive attitude and emotional attachment toward change and believe in the aims and goals of the organization, then they are more willing to follow."

"Does it also mean that employees who have a positive attitude support the changes more easily?" Peter asked.

"Yes, you can include that aspect in your questionnaire study and name it change support."

He suddenly realized that they were just brainstorming their ideas, "Okay, before we continue, let me get something to write and jot it all down here. So, we had information and participation, procedural justice, and value of change?"

"Well, it was *benefit* of change," Jennifer said.

"Sorry. You're right. And the last two were commitment to change and change support. Okay, that should be it," he concluded.

She said, "I think you could include two more variables. We talked about values and that they are important for supporting change. If people feel that their values are very similar to those here at Harpers, then they are more willing to support change."

"Okay, so how would you label this?" Peter asked.

"Let's call it values-congruence fit. And let's include job satisfaction for academic staff, as well as study satisfaction for students. You mentioned that a lot of employees only have part-time jobs that are often restricted."

"Yes, that's right," he said. "Some only get contracts for 2 years, and if they are very lucky, for 3 or 5 years."

"Those employees might not be satisfied with their work and therefore less willing to support change, so, I definitely think you should include this one, too," Jennifer said. "It's getting quite complex, but research on change shows that benefit of change, information, participation, and procedural justice are positively related to commitment to change, values-congruence fit, change support, and job satisfaction."

Peter pondered that for a minute and then said, "Let me write it all down. Or even better: I think I should draw it, so I get a clearer picture."

Jennifer waited for him to write it all down. "So, now that we identified all the important variables, you can get your questionnaire together," Jennifer said.

Peter's thoughts raced ahead. "Yes, I will talk to our IT expert to get it all online."

"Great! How long do you think he will need?" she said.

Figure 7.1 Study Variables and Hypothesized Relations

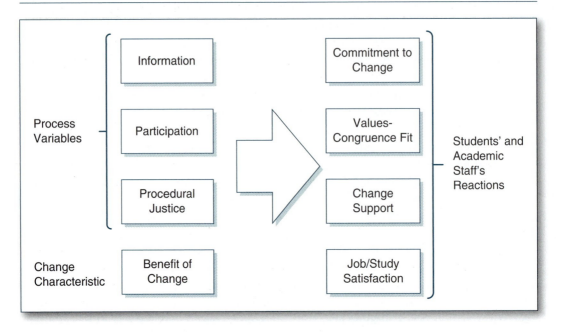

Peter thought for a moment. "Well, it all needs to be carefully planned, and we need three points in time: the beginning, middle, and the end of the change. So, I think, we should get started in about 2 weeks. Thank you for your support, Jennifer."

She smiled at him. "You're welcome. There's one more important point that I would like to mention, Peter."

"Yes?" he asked.

"As you have three points in time for your surveys, you should evaluate the data after the first round and check how well university members are informed about the change."

Peter thought that this was a very good idea.

She continued, "You can then see whether your communication strategy worked so far. If not, you can still improve the process. And if you need any help in doing so, please don't hesitate to contact me."

Peter thanked Jennifer for her offer. "I will keep this in mind."

PRESENTING RESULTS AT THE CHANGE INITIATIVE STEERING COMMITTEE AT HARPERS UNIVERSITY (2 MONTHS LATER)

Peter Murphy waited before the steering committee of the change initiative. The committee consisted of selected members of different decision boards (the executive board, supervisory board, academic senate) of Harpers University. He was ready to give a short introduction about the ongoing processes before Jennifer McSullivan took over and presented the survey results. He recognized Karen Paddington, whom he had worked with in the past. Two or three other familiar faces looked expectantly at him.

Finally, Michael Surrington, the university president, spoke. "Dear ladies and gentlemen, I am glad that you could all make it for the meeting. Peter Murphy has been in charge of conducting the change initiative. There are a lot of different projects to consider, and it's no easy task. Students and university staff fill out online questionnaires three times. The first survey round is finished now, and we are all very curious about your results, Peter, so please go ahead."

Peter stood and hoped that they would not be too disappointed. The results were not encouraging, and it was his and Jennifer's task now to deliver this message. *Well,* he thought, *that's just the way it is, so the truth better be told.* "Thank you for that introduction, Michael. I would like to give you a short summary on what has happened. As you all know, the change strategy was announced and published on the university homepage 4 months ago, and its aim was to raise Harpers University's competitiveness. So the starting point was to inform students and staff about the projects and get them involved. We worked with Free Way consultancy, which specializes in public administration, to evaluate our work. We carefully planned which variables we wanted to include in the survey, thereby taking Harpers University's specifics into account. So, Jennifer McSullivan here and I included the following variables in the questionnaire study. We wanted to know how informed students and staff felt about the projects, how they estimated their possibilities to get involved, and how fair they perceived the decision processes concerning the change projects. We also wanted to know whether they perceived the change as beneficial and if they were committed. Other important variables on the part of employees and students were the fit between personal and organizational values, change support, and of course job and study satisfaction. So, after we figured out those variables, Free Way administered the online survey. With this first survey, at the beginning, we want to find out whether the projects are going well or whether we need to intervene. The second survey is planned after one-and-a-half years, and the third when the projects are over. This way we may rate the overall effectiveness of the change initiative. We have a chart here, but I would like to hand things over to Jennifer now."

Jennifer stood. "Thank you, Peter. Ladies and gentlemen, I am pleased to present the first results to you. This first chart shows how participants rated the information they received, their possibilities to actively participate, their evaluation of the fairness of decision processes, and how they saw the benefit and usefulness of the changes."

After a short pause, Jennifer continued. "Those tables and figures[3] make it very clear that the information about the change projects did not reach university members. The overall participation rate was only 29%. More precisely 4,600 students (16,000 were addressed by e-mail) and 748 members of academic staff (3,100 were addressed by e-mail) participated in the survey. Respondents had the impression that the changes

Figure 7.2   Student and Academic Staff Ratings of Process Variables and Change
Characteristics of the Change Initiative at Harpers University

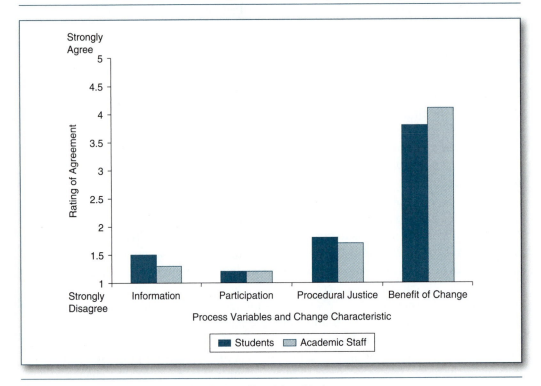

Note. 4,600 students and 748 members of academic staff participated in the survey.

were useful indeed, but on the contrary they did not feel well involved and informed. In addition, the perception of procedural justice was rather low. Concerning the other variables, I would like to mention that values-congruence fit. Job and study satisfaction were in the middle range, but commitment to change and change support were rather low. The chart shows that those last variables ranged between 1 and 2.5, with 1 indicating very low agreement and 5 very high agreement."

"The last chart I would like to present to you today shows why it is so important to invest work and time in a systematic information and participation strategy."

"As you can see, both process variables and perceived benefit of change play a major role in predicting how employees are committed to and support ongoing changes at Harpers University.

"Ladies and gentlemen, I come to the conclusion that although we planned the change initiatives very carefully, employees were not satisfied with the proceedings and therefore did not support the projects very well so far."

Now it was said. Jennifer and Peter looked at each other, before looking around and at the astonished and disbelieving faces.

"But how can that be?" Karen asked. "We informed deans of all faculties and asked them to distribute the information of the change strategy in their faculties. In addition, we

Figure 7.3   Students and Academic Staff Ratings of Their Reaction Toward the Change
Initiative at Harpers University

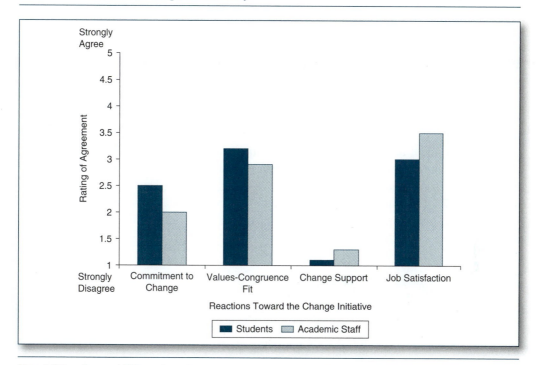

Note. 4,600 students and 748 members of academic staff participated in the survey.

Figure 7.4   Results of Regression Analysis

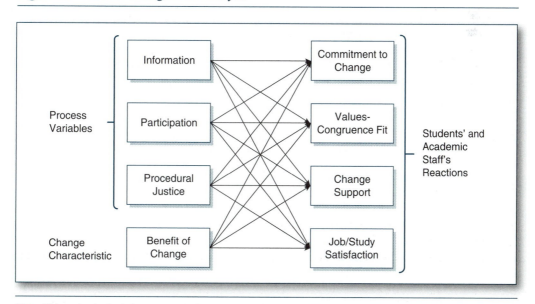

Note. All hypothesized relations were significant with p < .001; N = 5,348.

informed all members of the university on our homepage. How can staff and students all feel left out?"

There was a long pause.

"That's what we need to find out, I think," Peter said. "Maybe we from the university thought it was all well-prepared and crystal clear, but those data speak for themselves. We were obviously wrong and we need to find out how we can improve our information and participation strategy, don't you think?"

President Surrington said, "Jennifer, Peter has told us that you have successfully managed a change project at Milton University. Do you have any fresh ideas for improvement?"

Jennifer nodded, as she had expected that question. "Certainly, I thought about the reasons, too. And I think it would be a wise starting point to have a closer look at the data and gather as many ideas as possible on how to improve. I have several ideas in my head and, if you like, I can work out a proposal and present my ideas to you."

President Surrington said, "That sounds like a good idea. Please go ahead and do so."

Discussion Questions

1. Why do you think university students and staff did not feel well-informed or feel they lacked the opportunity to participate?

2. What elements should a systematic communication and participation strategy at Harpers University include? What actions can be taken on an individual, team, and organizational level to improve the flow of information and participation?

3. Please take over the perspective of the consultant: What creative methods would you suggest to get fresh ideas to improve the communication process?

4. Considering the low feedback rate, how can employees' participation and cooperation in the change projects be raised?

NOTES

1. The case is based on an actual organization and real organizational experiences. Names, facts, data, and situations have been changed to protect the privacy of individuals and the organization.

2. Numbers presented here are fictitious and for anonymity reasons do not correspond to the real project data.

3. All presented results are fictitious and, for anonymity reasons, do not correspond to the real project data.

FOR FURTHER READING

Caldwell, S. D., Herold, D. M., & Fedor, D. B. (2004). Toward an understanding of the relationships among organizational change, individual differences, and changes in person-environment fit: A cross-level study. *Journal of Applied Psychology, 89*(5), 868–882.

Cunningham, G. B. (2006). The relationships among commitment to change, coping with change, and turnover intentions. *European Journal of Work and Organizational Psychology, 15*(1), 29–45.

Herold, D. M., Fedor, D. B., & Caldwell, S. D. (2007). Beyond change management: A multilevel investigation of contextual and personal influences on employees' commitment to change. *Journal of Applied Psychology, 92*(4), 942–951.

Herscovitch, L., & Meyer, J. P. (2002). Commitment to organizational change: Extension of a three-component model. *Journal of Applied Psychology, 87*(3), 474–487.

Kernan, M. C., & Hanges, P. J. (2002). Survivor reactions to reorganization: Antecedents and consequences of procedural, interpersonal, and informational justice. *Journal of Applied Psychology, 87*(5), 916–928.

Michel, A., Stegmaier, R., & Sonntag, K. (2010). I scratch your back—you scratch mine. Do procedural justice and organizational identification matter for employees' cooperation during change? *Journal of Change Management, 10*(1), 41–59.

Wanberg, C. R., & Banas, J. T. (2000). Predictors and outcomes of openness to change in reorganizing workplace. *Journal of Applied Psychology, 85*(1), 132–142.

Engineering Culture Change With Strategic Initiatives

Nicole M. Laster

Learning Objectives

- To understand the sense-making process involved in qualitative research.
- To analyze and interpret qualitative data by developing major themes from interview data.
- To understand how to transform themes into arguments or conclusions, supporting them with data.
- To begin the process of turning conclusions into practitioner advice.

Interviewing is a common method of data collection for consulting. The following case details an organizational consulting context, a consulting goal, an interview instrument, and three interview data samples in an effort to provide an experience with the data collection and data analysis steps associated with this method. Ultimately, the goal of this case study is to begin the data analysis stages of interview data. To do so, the consultant needs to determine if the interview guide is working or if it needs to be revised, as well as to begin determining what themes are beginning to emerge. Consultants will practice the art of open coding, high level sense making, and instrument revision.

BACKGROUND

Ingredients International is a leading manufacturer and supplier of the finest quality bakery and food ingredients, specialty chemicals, polymer additives, and specialty blending equipment. For 100 years it has supplied a variety of breads, gourmet sweets, industrial ingredients, processed food ingredients, polymer additives, and specialty blending equipment—all supported by unrivaled technical service. Over the past 3 years, the company has undergone a number of changes to include a merger and an acquisition, new leadership, and the adoption and discontinuance of a number of products, procedures, and initiatives. Essentially, Ingredients International is experiencing a major strategic cultural change.

Since 2009, Ingredients International has worked to overcome the challenges of merging two disparate cultures that spent years competing for market share to create a culture emphasizing both alignment within and empowerment among the organization and its members. To support this vision, the company launched a new mission and a new set of core values soon after consolidation in an effort to create functional and principle consistency. In particular, two key initiatives—*Quality* and *Innovation*—fuel the company's current systems. Ingredients International understands that any decrease in product or people quality could harm the company's reputation. Moreover, innovation is also necessary to continue to evolve, expand, and respond to environmental needs. As you might imagine, each of the two previous legacies emphasized different cultural values. In spite of the merger and perhaps because of it, shareholders expect the company to continue to be pioneers in the field to maintain market strength. Because both initiatives are important, new programs and processes have been launched in support of quality and innovation. The Agility team and the InnoVantage program were introduced as key drivers of these key initiatives. *Agility* is an important characteristic that suggests employees be quick and smart about adapting to unexpected internal and external needs. In addition, *InnoVantage,* a program intended to capitalize on individual and collaborative innovations between several key departments, has been instituted as a vehicle for submitting new ideas to support organizational evolution. The company's cultural nucleus focuses on its ability to both adapt and grow, while maintaining the product quality and high service standards making Ingredients International a market leader. However, it is unclear if the initiatives are working in tandem with the cultural emphases of alignment and empowerment. Company leaders are interested in determining if the initiative programs are effectively supporting to their culture.

PROGRAM GOAL

Ingredients International has asked your firm to determine the impact and effectiveness of its cultural initiatives. Strong cultures translate into greater financial success. In an effort to understand the communication amidst the program initiatives, the primary goal of this project is to contribute to the company's own self-study aimed at improving both programs and communication surrounding cultural initiative integration, and possibly adjust its current approach to address any and all deficits. Since they are unsure if employees are shedding old legacy practices and more concerned that the company does not yet have a single culture, your client has asked you to determine what, if any disparities exist in the cultural initiatives program, and advise on an intervention to strategically realign the organization.

DATA COLLECTION

The first month of evaluation was spent surveying multiple organizational documents, including the company newsletters since January 2009, the Town Hall meeting notes, specific initiative flyers (e.g., Quality, Innovation), and e-mails introducing the more specific programs of those initiatives (e.g., Agility, InnoVantage). After reviewing these documents multiple times and meeting with the human resource director, an interview guide was developed (see the Appendix).

Questions were developed to gather three levels of information about the initiatives from employees: awareness, understanding, and engagement. Employees were asked if they had heard of the initiative or program (if they had not heard of it, the second and third level questions were irrelevant, but this information was still helpful). Employees were asked to explain what they knew about a particular initiative or program (this would indicate the degree to which an employee understood the objectives of the program or initiative). Employees then were asked if this program or initiative made sense for their work, and if so, how did they engage in it (this would not only reveal whether the programs and initiatives were being understood and employed correctly, but might also reveal in what ways a supervisor might be supporting that program or initiative in a particular department). In addition to the assessment on these three levels, employees also were asked how well these programs or initiatives were working and if they thought they had been communicated and implemented effectively.

Sample excerpts from three interviews are included in the pages that follow. The transcripts are taken from the portion of the interviews involving the Quality initiative and Agility program only and do not include data about the Innovation initiative and InnoVantage strategy. All three of these interviewees work at one of the plants. After you review the interviews, you will be asked to make a preliminary diagnosis, to evaluate your instrument, and to think about what possible intervention(s) might be needed—at least at this point.

INTERVIEW 1

Interviewer: Are you familiar with the Quality initiative?

Material Handler: It sounds familiar. So, I'm sure I've heard it before.

Interviewer: What, if anything can you tell me about it? Is there anything you could recall about it?

Material Handler: The Quality initiative? Aren't we like striving to be the best or innovative or . . . something? I don't know. I'm sorry.

Interviewer:	No need to be sorry. I am just trying to understand how well this information has been communicated to the employees and what they know about it. Is there anything in particular that you can recall about the Quality initiative?
Material Handler:	Well, you hear about it once, and that's it. They act like we are going to get it and remember the one and only time they tell us. My manager probably got this memo, and was told to make sure you mention this stuff. And they do it and that's . . .
Interviewer:	Okay, so how much would you say you know about the Quality initiative? Let's say you had to quantify it?
Material Handler:	Not too much. Heard about it, I suppose. Not sure what it's supposed to do, or what we're supposed to do. Maybe work hard . . . be good workers . . .
Interviewer:	Would you be able to explain any ways are you involved with the Quality initiative?
Material Handler:	Well, if product doesn't make it out of my plant the right way, then it's messed up all the way around. Quality starts in our plant. So, yeah, everything's supposed to be stainless steel and we're supposed to be safe and have all guards and stuff like that. And if we don't make it right, if it doesn't get packaged right, or it doesn't get packaged at all, the takedown time, we have to redo it, or they have to figure out what's wrong with the process in the first place.
Interviewer:	So, it sounds like the Quality initiative is about having product leave your plant without any problems?
Material Handler:	Sure, yeah, definitely. That's quality to me.
Interviewer:	Do you think that Ingredients International could do anything so the Quality initiative makes more sense to you? How could they communicate it better to you, or to people that you work with, so that they get it?
Material Handler:	I think people understand the fact that they are dealing with food. If we get a customer complaint or something like that, then they trace it back to whomever, you get a pretty strong slap on the hand for that. So, I think they understand that quality is very important here. Plus, in our monthly meetings, they tell us about the customer complaints. When it's something really major, they'll put it on the TVs and stuff, so everybody can see it, and what not to do.
Interviewer:	Oh, really? TVs?

Material Handler: Yeah. In the break room.

Interviewer: Can you give me an example of something that could be considered a quality issue shared on a TV?

Material Handler: A customer found these [*pulls an item out of his pocket*]. We sometimes tie the bag with red clips. A customer found a bunch of red clips in the box, so they put that error on the TV. Oh, and another thing, some of the guys were putting the floor mats on the conveyers, and that was a big deal because the conveyors hold the cartons that hold the food. That's on the TVs now too. Anything that just seems terrible. They put it on the TVs. And sometimes, old stuff gets sent out to customers. I remember when we were having a problem with a particular customer, like it was going overseas and somehow, in the transit, it was getting messed up in the boxes and the boxes were getting torn, and they were trying to blame it on us and our trailers or whatever. So, that was a big deal. Everybody in the plant knew about it, because they kept talking about it in the meetings, like I said, and it was all over the TV. One of the supervisors came up with the new system with the QA people to check the product so it's not old and the customer doesn't leave us.

Interviewer: So do you think the TVs help maintain quality in the plants?

Material Handler: Everybody looks at the TV because they're in the break room. There's nothing else to do in there anyway, so the TV's great, I think.

Interviewer: And then you all talk about it?

Material Handler: Well, like I said, they'll talk about it in the meetings. Depending on if it has to do with your department, then yeah, everybody talks about it, because nobody wants to get in trouble. They like to put communication on the TVs. If they don't have to talk to you, then they're not going to talk to you.

Interviewer: You mentioned that a couple of the employees, you mentioned the supervisor and the Quality Assurance people came up with a new system to prevent old material from shipping out. Is that correct?

Material Handler: Yeah.

Interviewer: Are you familiar with the Agility program?

Material Handler: Yeah. Actually, I was awarded second place.

Interviewer: Really? What was your idea?

Material Handler: Yeah. Me and Justin Green and Bob Martin for this quarter.

Interviewer:	What did you and Justin develop?
Material Handler:	We were having problems with the two-bundle in one of our stills.
Interviewer:	What's the two-bundle?
Material Handler:	A two-bundle; it's just a ring of tubes inside the still that hold cold water to help the vapor turn back into a liquid. Well, our stills are under vacuum, the tube under is leaking water, and water and a vacuum don't mix well at all. So, we took the water out of the two-bundle and put glycerin in there, and it lasted for like 6 months. Then, finally, we got it taken apart and fixed. But at the time, we really needed that still going, so we had to come up with something to get it going, and that's what we did.
Interviewer:	So, it was a good Band-Aid?
Material Handler:	Yeah, a Band-Aid, that's basically what it was.
Interviewer:	And it sounds like it helped to keep the plant processes moving?
Material Handler:	Yeah, it saved us a lot of money at the time, because we were in the process of putting in another still, so that bought us some more time, until we got the other still going, then we were able to take it down and fix it the right way. But at the time, they were in dire need of that still, so we had to do something. It was cool that they appreciated what we did.
Interviewer:	How would you explain the Agility program? What would you say it is?
Material Handler:	I would say it's when a group of people gets together and tries to find a better way of doing things, or a smarter way of doing things, a quicker way of doing things, something like that.
Interviewer:	What about the process you mentioned earlier about the manager and the QA person who solved the issue of sending out old product overseas? Would you classify that at part of the Agility program?
Material Handler:	I guess . . . they didn't get an award, so maybe it's not really agility? I suppose it could be.
Interviewer:	What do you think about the Agility program? Do you think it's important? Do you think it's working?
Material Handler:	I don't know. I was surprised to even have my name mentioned on it, because there's been times I'll come up with something, me and my partner, and it'll fix something, or make it better, then 2 or 3 weeks later you hear in the meeting, oh, yeah, such and such came up with this, and it's a gray hardhat, and our name's not even

mentioned. So, you're like, okay, well, that's the last time I'm going to do that.

Interviewer: Because you don't get credit for it?

Material Handler: Exactly. It's not like I want the credit or anything like that, but I definitely don't want someone else taking the credit for something I did. I don't know. I've been here 5 years. I've seen these programs come and go. I know the guys on the floor don't take them all too serious, because they've seen the same things. So there's an award, so what? It seems like every year they've got a new program or something like that. Then, like I said, we got it for this quarter, and supposedly the president was supposed to come give you some certificate or something, or shake your hand or something. I ain't seen him. I haven't seen him since the summer. No phone call, no memo, nothing. I'm not going to hold my breath. So, it's like okay, it's just another program. I got my name on a little piece of paper in front of my desk, and that's about it. Honestly, I think we've always been trying to come up with an easier and a better way to do what we do. To me, the Agility program is nothing new, we always try to improve things.

Interviewer: Do you think it's just a name for something you've always been doing?

Material Handler: Yeah. These guys must need to feel important. They might put something on the TVs about something that happened in some other plant, but it has nothing to do with us. It's like we don't really even see it until they give you the little yellow coffee cup with the "Agility" on it for Christmas, or something. I don't know.

Interviewer: Of all the strategy and initiatives that are going on here at Ingredients International, which ones make the most sense to you and to your job?

Material Handler: Well, I guess the Agility program makes a lot of sense to my job, because we're constantly having problems, and we've got to be quick with a solution, because we supply like three different plants, so we've got a lot of people depending on us.

Interviewer: What are some suggestions for how they could be better communicated?

Material Handler: I don't know. Maybe the person that's talking about it should act like they're halfway excited about what they're talking about, instead of just reading it and going to the next one. If they're not excited about it, then why the hell should I be excited about it?

Like I said, it just seems like somebody sent them a memo, "Make sure you talk about . . . " Yeah, it doesn't seem like they're excited about it, so you take it as like one of those things that's just going to pass on through again.

INTERVIEW 2

Interviewer: Are you familiar with the Quality initiative?

Blender: Oh, yes. Our quality has been very good. We haven't had any complaints here lately at all. I think we produce good quality. We work hard to have quality products and do quality work.

Interviewer: Are you familiar with the actual initiative? In particular, what Ingredients International is doing to promote a quality platform. Does this sound familiar?

Blender: I'm not real familiar with that. Maybe, I've heard them talk about it. . . . Yeah, they talked about something like that in a meeting. I guess. But, you know, I'm not really sure. . . . Okay, I don't really know what it is.

Interviewer: Is there anything that you do in your work to ensure quality in your job as a blender?

Blender: Well, make sure the shop orders what we need, make sure everything is right with amounts of what we do. Just got to make sure you read everything on there right and make sure when you blend it, that everything is like what it says on the shop order. And if you go by that, there's no other way, you shouldn't be able to mess things up. It's just like it's right there in front of you.

Interviewer: Do you think that quality is important enough to make it part of the cultural values?

Blender: I think it is very important.

Interviewer: Can you give me an example?

Blender: Well, if you was to put the wrong ingredient into a product and then they go and send it across America and it ends up being wrong, they can lose money by sending all of it back to us and then we've got to rework things, so if you do it right the first time it will be right. That's what we work on too. First time needs to be right, so make sure everything is right the first time so we won't have no issues after that.

Interviewer: Certainly. How informed do you feel about the Quality initiative as a program? Are you aware that it is a formal program at the company?

You mentioned that it may have been mentioned in a meeting but it was not very clear . . .

Blender: Right. Well, it's not clear, well . . . to me. I guess I didn't know it was a program.

Interviewer: Do you think there is anything management can do to improve that?

Blender: Maybe by putting it on paper and handing it out to everybody, like a worksheet. Well, . . . not a worksheet, not like homework, but an information sheet and has it, that plus when they tell us, we come here for a meeting, they tell us. If they would do a handout for everybody, I think that would be good.

Interviewer: That's a really good suggestion. Have you heard about the Agility program?

Blender: Oh yes. They talk about agility all the time. I guess it's a big deal right now.

Interviewer: Who talks about the Agility program? Your supervisors?

Blender: The guys in the plant are always talking about who won.

Interviewer: Have you ever won?

Blender: No.

Interviewer: Have you ever submitted an idea to be considered for an award?

Blender: I guess I didn't know I could. Doesn't your manager have to submit your name? The newsletter always shows who won. I think our plant has won a couple of times. People make a big deal about it if someone in the plant wins. I think they win money. Don't they?

Interviewer: Is that the way you understand it? That your manager submits your name and if you win you win money and it's featured in the newsletter?

Blender: That sounds good to me. I'll go with that [*smiling*]. Look, truth is I really couldn't tell you. I suppose if I won one I might know.

Interviewer: That's fine. But you have heard of the Agility program right?

Blender: Sure.

Interviewer: Are you aware of how it is connected to the Quality initiative?

Blender: Nope.

Interviewer: Do you think this Agility program adds value to your jobs?

Blender: Well, if you win, it has a value. I think people like competition, so for that, it's good. Some people get mad when they don't win because they think they had a good idea and should win.

Interviewer: All right, sure. Of the initiatives we've discussed, which ones are the most familiar to you, or which ones seem the most important to you? Which ones relate to you in your job here or seem important to you?

Blender: Probably Quality.

Interviewer: Quality? What about Agility? You seemed to know quite a bit about Agility.

Blender: Well, quality is always important. I think having awards for new ideas is fine, but we still need to do quality work.

Interviewer: Do you think that the initiatives have been communicated well? Could they improve the communication about the initiatives so that it makes more sense to y'all?

Blender: Well, yeah, I think so, but they should have more meetings besides once every 3 or 6 months. I think they should have maybe, maybe once a month, you know, to keep it in your head. We have a planning meeting once a month but it's not about these things. And a handout maybe and maybe more than one handout a month, know what I'm saying? Maybe once a week . . .

INTERVIEW 3

Interviewer: Are you familiar with the Quality initiative?

Mixer: I'd say I was somewhat familiar. I've heard of it. From what I understand, part of the Quality initiative, you know, is to make sure that the products are delivered in the right quantity and in a timely manner to the customer without defects.

Interviewer: Umm . . . hmmm . . .

Mixer: Part of this initiative, for example, for me, is to make sure that one of my lines of products is completely separated from another line. This means from the raw materials to the finished product.

Interviewer: Okay . . .

Mixer: So they are not stuck together like before. Sometimes they are not mixed well, so a customer complains about the product quality, you know? And sometimes certain customers have special requests. They might want certain allergens separated from the typical mixed product.

Interviewer: So is it fair to say that one way you engage in the Quality initiative is by making sure raw materials are separate and allergens are separate.

Mixer: Yes. Sure, that's one way. Yeah, it's part of what we call the Quality Assurance program because it supports our vision and direction. That's from the raw material that you sell. You separate the materials from one another so they are not contaminated or they meet the customers' specs.

Interviewer: Uh huh.

Mixer: That's the first one. The second thing I follow is . . .

Interviewer: Are you a manager here?

Mixer: No. I'm just a mixer. A mix engineer, I like to say. Been a mixer for 5 years.

Interviewer: You seem to know a lot about this stuff.

Mixer: Yeah, well, I'm just doing my job.

Interviewer: But how do you know so much about the Quality initiative?

Mixer: Management tells us.

Interviewer: When and how do they share this information with you? I guess I am most curious about the way they tell you about initiatives and programs.

Mixer: They talk about them in the meetings. Not every meeting. We have a meeting every day at the beginning of the shift. Most of the time those meetings are about our daily goals or any problems that may have happened. It depends if they have something new to tell us about something. Some shift leaders think these things are important. Ronnie is really good about telling us new stuff.

Interviewer: That's interesting. Did you say you have another example of a task related to the Quality initiative?

Mixer: The second example is with the production process itself. It is about how you keep the material, making sure that every material escapes together. Everything must be cleaned. The scoop must be kept clean to ensure quality. And no food must be in contact with you, direct contact. You must use gloves. Then the bin clean out must be proper. The clean must meet a standard and it is cleaned on two levels.

Interviewer: Right.

Mixer: So people on that they call it A clean, B clean.

Interviewer: Right. So you see that as engaging in the Quality initiative?

Mixer: Yes, of course. And then apart from being cleaned by the blender, the supervisor, the team leader also ensures that it is clean and then the third level is the lab must inspect it. So, really there are three layers. Three layers and then the lab tests them. And if it doesn't conform, you know, it is reworked if possible. If not, then it's discarded. So as much as possible, you want to make sure that anything leaving the premises conforms to the customer's specs.

Interviewer:	Okay. Have you heard of Agility? The Agility program?
Mixer:	Oh sure, the Agility program.
Interviewer:	What can you tell me about this program?
Mixer:	I think agility is actually a part of performance, performance activity, you know? This means that people must be oriented in such a way that they move in response to needs. A way to deliver effectively to our customers. So that is the response, you know to, mainly to customers' needs. It is basically a quick response. It must be fast and timely.
Interviewer:	Right. Do you think you engage in the Agility initiative with your job?
Mixer:	Of course.
Interviewer:	How so?
Mixer:	It's part of the response. Agility isn't our job, but in many cases, we have to respond with agility. I have to respond in a timely manner, you know, to what the, I mean, the response is a platform indicator.
Interviewer:	What do you mean by that?
Mixer:	A platform indicator? Well, I guess I see that as a component of quality. If we are responding in a timely manner to make things better then quality improves. Also you want to make sure to utilize your machines productively. But the idea is not too much. If it were too much, then the cost of production would be exceeding our profit. But I have no idea of the actual numbers.
Interviewer:	Right.
Mixer:	So there's that part of the Agility program. It varies from one section to another. We all do different things.
Interviewer:	Are you aware of an incentive program for agility ideas?
Mixer:	Of course. I see this as a carrot and stick motivation for people to do their jobs. I guess they have to do something. But why not just do your job? Why not make your job better if it is not working well? Maybe I'm just cynical about rewarding people for doing their job. For some people it probably works. And maybe it creates a feel-good culture.
Interviewer:	Do you think your coworkers understand all of these initiatives?
Mixer:	I would think they would, but I know they don't. We all get the same information. We're all told the same thing and you can always catch information on the TV and in the newsletter.

Interviewer: Of the initiatives we've discussed, which ones are the most familiar to you, or which ones seem the most important to you? Which ones relate to you in your job here or seem important to you?

Mixer: I'd have to say that they are all important. I'd like to think management would only include things that make our jobs better. But honestly we are overworked. Most people pull overtime hours because they need the money or we are shorthanded. Some people work 7 days a week. When you're tired, or angry that you don't get to spend time with your family, it might be harder to see the value.

Interviewer: That makes sense. Is there one that relates to your job more than others?

Mixer: Not really. I guess I really don't do much for InnoVantage, but it doesn't seem very relevant to my job. I can see that it is important to the company, but to me personally, probably not unless I have to learn how to mix a new product.

Interviewer: How would you rate or characterize the communication about the initiatives?

Mixer: Enough for me.

Discussion Questions

1. After reading excerpts from three interview transcripts, describe what you think is happening. In other words, what is your initial reaction to how well the Quality initiative and the Agility program are working? Is one working better than the other?

2. Ingredients International wants to know if employees are aware of, understand, and are engaging in these initiatives. Based on this sample, what can you tell them about the Quality initiative and the Agility program? What specific evidence from the transcripts supports these conclusions?

3. Interview guides are often modified after the first few interviews to adjust to information that surfaced in the interviews. Adjustments are made when participants do not have a useful response to certain questions or when certain questions need to be added to account for information employees shared unexpectedly. What modifications do you think need to be made to the interview protocol to improve the experience?

4. Based on what you know about the Quality initiative and the Agility program, what advice would you give to Ingredients International about its cultural initiatives program?

APPENDIX

General Assessment of Understanding

I understand Ingredients International has been rolling out a cultural platform for sustainability and growth. What do you know about the company's plan to ensure long-term growth? (e.g., Quality, Innovation, Agility, InnoVantage).

Platform Initiatives: Quality (and Agility) and Innovation (and InnoVantage)

1. Are you familiar with the Quality initiative?

2. What can you tell me about this program?

3. In what ways are you involved with the Quality initiative?

4. How do you integrate the Quality initiative into your work?

5. Is Quality initiative relevant to your job?

6. How does it affect your job? In what ways, or why not?

7. What do you think about the Quality initiative?

8. Do you think this is important? Why or why not? Is it working? In what ways, or why not?

9. What would make the Quality initiative make more sense to you or be more relevant to your work?

10. Are you familiar with the Agility team?

11. What can you tell me about this program?

12. In what ways are you involved with the Agility team/component?

13. How do you integrate Agility into your work?

14. Is the Agility team/component relevant to your job?

15. How does it affect your job? In what ways, or why not?

16. What do you think about the Agility component?

17. Do you think this is important? Why or why not? Is it working? In what ways, or why not?

18. What would make the Agility initiative make more sense to you or be more relevant to your work?

19. Are you familiar with the Innovation initiative?

20. What can you tell me about this program?

21. In what ways are you involved with the Innovation initiative?

22. How do you integrate Innovation into your work?

23. Is the Innovation initiative relevant to your job?

24. How does it affect your job? In what ways, or why not?

25. What do you think about the Innovation initiative?

26. Do you think this is important? Why or why not? Is it working? In what ways, or why not?

27. What would make the Innovation initiative make more sense to you or be more relevant to your work?

28. What can you say about the InnoVantage program?

29. What can you tell me about this program?

30. In what ways are you involved with the InnoVantage program?

31. How do you integrate the InnoVantage program into your work?

32. Is the InnoVantage program relevant to your job?

33. How does it affect your job? In what ways, or why not?

34. What do you think about the InnoVantage initiative?

35. Do you think this is important? Why or why not? Is it working? In what ways, or why not?

36. What would make the InnoVantage program make more sense to you or be more relevant to your work?

Big Picture

1. What is your general reaction to these initiatives?

2. Do you think the initiatives are making a difference? In what ways?

3. Which initiative or program makes the most sense to you and your job? Why? Or can you name one initiative you think has made a difference in your job or this company?

4. Do you think the initiatives have been communicated well to you?

5. Is any of what I've asked you today unclear to you?

6. What, if anything, would make it better?

7. Do you have any questions for me?

ORGANIZATION CULTURE— DIAGNOSIS AND FEEDBACK

MARY K. FOSTER AND VICKI F. TAYLOR

Learning Objectives

- To practice analyzing and synthesizing quantitative and qualitative data to understand organizational culture and to identify underlying causes of organizational issues.
- To recognize the strengths and weakness of quantitative and qualitative methods of data collection related to organizational culture.
- To practice summarizing data in a manner that enables client understanding and action.

Dr. Vivian Metger, an experienced human resources consultant, sat at her desk pouring over the results from the organizational culture survey she had just finished administering. Next to her sat pages of notes from the personal interviews she also had conducted with employees from RMC, a privately owned, boutique, engineering consulting firm. This was her first look at the survey data and she wondered how the results would compare with her findings from the 23 personal interviews she had conducted over the past 2 weeks. Soon she would be meeting with Dr. Joe Keller, the president and chief executive officer of RMC, to discuss her assessment of the firm's organizational culture. Dr. Keller and the other principals of the firm had asked Dr. Metger to present her findings to the management board and eventually to the entire organization.

For several years the organization had struggled to reconcile differences in values and expectations among the leaders of the firm. These differences tended to fall along generational lines. The organizational culture assessment was designed to engage the leaders of the firm in a process of joint discovery through which their differences in values and expectations could be examined. The plan was to collect information about perceptions related to the organizational culture, analyze the information, summarize findings, and then share the information with the company's leadership in order to jointly determine whether the culture needed to be realigned. Based on their review and discussion of the findings, interventions would then be developed and implemented.

BACKGROUND

RMC was a small, privately owned company that employed about 250 people in six offices in the United States (three in the Northeast and three in the South). The largest office and company headquarters was in New York. The company specialized in design, inspection, and rehabilitation services for all types of bridges and related transportation projects. Martin Reichard, a Russian immigrant and aspiring concert violinist, founded the company in 1893. He became one of the 20th century's most famous bridge designers. He built the firm on his reputation for engineering excellence, imagination, and innovative design. Over the years the nature and philosophy of the firm's business had changed little. The organization had a sense of pride in their heritage and accomplishments. The principal owners of the firm were revered for their expertise and achievement. The founder's field notes were enshrined on the wall in the main office. Referring to the founder, it wasn't unusual to hear employees ponder aloud, "What would the old man think about this?" Most of the principals had joined the firm as staff engineers, worked their way up in the organization, and eventually become partners. Dr. Keller had started with the firm 35 years ago as a staff engineer and subsequently held positions as partner, chief engineer, and president before becoming chief executive officer (CEO). Like Dr. Keller, aspiring engineers often joined the firm because of its reputation and opportunities for advancement. RMC was a place to spend one's entire career and "becoming a partner" was an achievable goal for talented, committed engineers.

Dr. Metger had had a decade-long relationship with the firm. She had completed a number of human resource consulting projects for RMC over the years, so she knew many of the partners and employees and a bit about their organization. She was often called in when the company faced a personnel or human resource crisis. Over the years, she and Dr. Keller had talked about how differences in values and management styles among the firm's leaders had led to conflicts and tension within the firm. Some of the leaders were perceived as autocratic, privileged, and out of touch with contemporary technology and modern management practices. Others were respected for their skill and competence, yet they were slow to embrace the latest technology or management practices. Still others were perceived as more democratic, egalitarian, and fully embracing technology and modern management practices. Often the differences among the leaders of the firm fell along generational lines with the younger leaders being technically savvy and embracing a more participative leadership style. This generation of leaders often chafed at the lack of clear standards of accountability and wanted to create a meritocracy.

Dr. Keller was frustrated by the ongoing conflict and tension. As CEO he felt torn between his comfort with the "ways we've always done things" and his responsibility to ensure the ongoing success of the organization. He felt the firm risked losing some of its best young talent if he did nothing; yet it was hard to get agreement among the leaders as to what should be done. Dr. Metger had suggested that an organizational culture assessment could engage the leaders of the firm in a process of joint discovery through which the situation in the organization could be examined. She explained that once information about the organizational culture was collected and then shared with the company's leadership, it would help everyone see if there was alignment or lack of alignment in perceptions about the company culture. If there were issues of alignment, this assessment would provide an evidence-based approach to thinking about what should be done to help resolve any differences in values and expectations.

Dr. Keller felt that Dr. Metger's experience with the firm would allow her to quickly and credibly assess the company's culture. After Dr. Keller and Dr. Metger had agreed on the terms of the project, he sent an e-mail to everyone in the organization, explaining that Dr. Metger would be surveying all of the employees and conducting interviews with members of management and the staff in order to assess the organizational culture. He assured them that their responses would be anonymous. Dr. Metger had promised to ensure that no individually identifiable information would be shared with management or included in her report. He closed his e-mail by stating:

> We look forward to seeing the results of this work. We like to think that we create a work environment that reflects the societal and professional responsibilities espoused in our Vision. With your help, Dr. Metger's report will provide us with insight about how well we are "walking the walk" compared to "talking the talk."

RECENT EVENTS AT THE FIRM

Prior to starting the cultural assessment, Dr. Metger met with Dr. Keller to discuss his perceptions of the organization. During their meeting, Dr. Keller mentioned that he had noticed two trends at RMC that bothered him. One trend was a sense of complacency or entitlement among some of the staff. In fact, he had recently overheard a project manager say, "There's a joke around here that the reason why the office is so quiet is because we don't want to wake up the people who are sleeping." Dr. Keller was surprised and chagrined by the comment. The company had always focused on treating employees like family and doing what was best for the employee even if it wasn't best for the business. There was a hesitancy to enact consequences for underperformers. Rarely had someone been fired or demoted, and there was a tendency to have less stringent performance standards for some of the more senior employees. Dr. Keller said that he now wondered if these practices and approaches served the best interests of the company. Perhaps it was time to transition from a tenure-based culture to a performance-based culture.

Dr. Keller explained that another trend of concern to him was perceptions about what the firm valued. The company had always emphasized engineering excellence versus profitability. Managing project profitability had a lower priority than satisfying the client.

Dr. Keller wondered if these attitudes and practices still served the company well. He wondered if they could change the company culture to respond to the realities of business today without losing the things that had made the company successful in the past.

APPROACH TO DATA COLLECTION

With this background in mind, Dr. Metger began to design the cultural assessment. All employees would be invited to complete a questionnaire either electronically or via hard copy, and all nine of the principals and at least two people from each of the six offices would be personally interviewed. For the questionnaire, Dr. Metger used a modified version of the Organizational Culture Profile (Detert, Schroeder, & Mauriel, 2000; Enz, 1988; O'Reilly, Chatman, & Caldwell, 1991) to assess culture; a three-item scale to measure perceived organizational fit (Cable & DeRue, 2002); a 13-item scale to measure employee job satisfaction (Hackman & Oldham, 1975); and a six-item scale to measure affective commitment (Meyer, Allen, & Smith, 1993). Finally, she included some control variables (e.g., gender, marital status, education, tenure, location, and position). See Tables 9.1 to 9.6 for a summary of the measures and data collected via the questionnaire.

For the interviews, which were conducted either in person or over the phone, Dr. Metger developed a list of open-ended questions regarding the organization and the office

Table 9.1   Derived Organizational Culture Value Dimensions

Dimension	Items	Dimension	Items
Detail Oriented (alpha = .86)	Precise Detail oriented Analytical Careful Consultative Quality orientated	Team Oriented (alpha = .85)	People oriented Team oriented Collaborative
Trustworthy (alpha = .93)	Fairness Honesty Integrity Promise keeping Trustworthiness	Authoritarian (alpha = .72)	Authoritarian Controlling
Stable (alpha = .63)	Rules oriented Job security Stability Predictability	Innovative (alpha = .84)	Innovation Takes advantage of opportunities Experimental Risk taking

Dimension	Items	Dimension	Items
Outcome Oriented (alpha = .88)	Achievement oriented Action oriented High performance expectations Results oriented Aggressive Competitive		

Source: Derived from measures by Detert et al. (2000), Enz (1988), and O'Reilly et al. (1991).

Note. Respondents rated the value items using a 7-point scale: 1= very uncharacteristic to 7 = extremely characteristic; to deal with the social desirability effect, the scale had increased graduation at the upper end (i.e., 2 = uncharacteristic; 3 = neutral; 4 = slightly characteristic; 5 = characteristic; 6 = very characteristic).

Table 9.2   Perceived Person-Organizational Fit (Cable & DeRue, 2002)

Factor	Item
Perceived P-O Fit (alpha = .93)	The things that I value in life are very similar to the things that my organization values. My personal values match my organization's values and culture I feel a strong sense of belonging to my organization. My organization's values and culture provide a good fit with the things that I value in life.

Note. Respondents rated these items using a 7-point scale: 1= strongly disagree to 7 = strongly agree (4 = neutral).

Table 9.3   Commitment and Satisfaction

Factor	Item
Affective Commitment (Meyer et al. 1993) (alpha = .93)	I would be very happy to spend the rest of my career with this organization. I really feel as if this organization's problems are my own. I feel a strong sense of belonging to my organization. I feel emotionally attached to this organization. I feel like "part of the family" at my organization. This organization has a great deal of personal meaning for me.

(Continued)

Table 9.3 (Continued)

Factor	Item
Job Satisfaction (adapted from Hackman & Oldham, 1975) (alpha = .91)	Current level of job security
	Fringe benefits
	Number of personal growth options
	Coworkers
	The degree of respect and fair treatment received from supervisor
	The feeling of worthwhile accomplishment
	The chance to get to know other people while on the job
	The amount of support and guidance received from your supervisor
	Salary
	Ability to contribute to the organization
	The amount of independent thought and action you can exercise in your job
	Future job security
	The challenge in your job

Note. Respondents rated these items using a 7-point scale: 1= strongly disagree to 7 = strongly agree (4 = neutral).

Table 9.4 Descriptive Statistics

Variable	Mean	Std. Dev.
Organization Values		
Detail Oriented	5.60	0.83
Trustworthy	5.56	1.02
Stability	5.01	0.82
Outcome Oriented	4.89	1.01
Team Oriented	4.62	1.22
Authoritarian	4.14	1.33
Innovative	3.91	1.17
Other Key Variables		
Perceived P-O Fit	5.18	1.20
Affective Commitment	5.25	1.22
Job Satisfaction	5.37	0.93

Table 9.5 Correlations Among Control and Study Variables

Study Variables	Control Variables					
	Gender	Marital Status	Job	Education	Location	Tenure
Organization Values						
Detail Oriented	−.05	.02	.06	.06	−.02	.05
Trustworthy	.03	.11	.12	.07	−.03	.20*
Stability	.10	−.05	.00	.07	.06	−.03
Outcome Oriented	−.05	.09	−.09	−.15	−.06	.13
Team Oriented	−.13	.14	−.16	−.12	−.01	.04
Authoritarian	.07	.03	.09	−.05	.01	.19*
Innovative	−.11	.06	−.10	−.26**	−.11	.18
Other Key Variables						
Job Satisfaction	−.04	.10	.17	−.01	−.03	.28**
Affective Commitment	−.01	.23*	.15	−.10	−.06	.45**
Perceived P-O Fit	.02	.17	.00	.22*	−.02	.28**

Note. * p < .05; ** p < .01; *** p < .001.

Table 9.6 Correlations among Study Variables

	Individual Outcome Variables		
	Satisfaction	Affective Commitment	Person-Organization Fit
Organizational Values			
Detail Oriented	.34**	−.01	−.10
Trustworthy	.29*	.34**	.32**
Stability	.21*	−.07	.036
Outcome Oriented	.22	.16	.17
Team Oriented	.36**	.21*	.38**
Authoritarian	−.11	−.22*	−.07
Innovative	−.02	.09	−.03
Person-Organization Fit	.55**	.58**	

Note. * p < .05; ** p < .01; *** p < .001.

cultures. She asked people about perceived company values, rituals, stories, incidents, practices, rules, procedures, physical arrangements, inside jokes, significant events, contradictory behaviors, inconsistencies between formal and informal practices and policies, perceived differences in culture, and perceived fit with the culture. See Table 9.7 for a sample of verbatim responses to those questions.

Table 9.7　Employee Verbatim Responses to Personal Interview Questions

- "We tell our employees and customers the truth—even if that means admitting we're wrong."
- "There have been times when we returned money to our clients."
- "We are consistently honest, and if there's an error made we will come clean."
- "If we can save the client money, we do so and don't just bill the project for the allowed amount."
- "We've had clients tell us to add money to our proposals because they know we won't spend it just because it's there."
- "We don't accept anything less than ethical behavior toward our clients and staff."
- "As a rule we charge only for the work we do versus the amount of time estimated to do the work."
- "We adhere to our ethics, even if our competitors aren't playing fairly."
- "If there's a possibility for a conflict of interest we bring it to the attention of our clients."
- "We risked losing a job with a contractor in order to deal ethically with a client."
- "There's a level of expectation and a process in place that ensures quality, plus an ongoing dialogue among team members."
- "The CEO imposes more stringent criteria than what is required by our clients."
- "We've always insisted that our basic practice and procedure is to do the best job possible."
- "When we discuss projects with the staff, we ask for proficiency. We expect them to do a really fine job and to think things through."
- "Nothing gets completed without having it checked in detail by a PE (professional engineer), project manager, a principal, or a peer that's adequately informed on the subject."
- "We do what's best for the employee, even if it's not best for the business."
- "We have a reluctance to let people go—whether it is for lack of work or poor performance."
- "I made a design error and I was told not to worry about it. The company was very loyal and supportive."
- "We celebrate people's milestones, both personal and professional."
- "We encourage our engineers to obtain additional education and we pay for it."
- "I feel a great amount of loyalty to the firm and feel that I have always been treated fairly."
- "Some companies would have unloaded people during a slack time like we're currently in, but we are trying to keep full employment even if it means that the owners won't make money."
- "We give our employees year-end bonuses, even if we're not performing well financially."
- "When I was hired, I was told that I'd be joining a family, and that's what it feels like."
- "I don't see an organizational culture. I see us as being a collection of satellite offices that resist being systematic and corporate."
- "The operating committee may vote on a decision, but Florida does what it wants."
- "We're a bunch of different companies with the same name."

- "My local office is most important to me. We operate separately from the rest of the organization."
- "I feel like we are a bunch of stepchildren. We all have a different mother and Dad doesn't come around much."
- "Our core values are relatively consistent throughout the organization, but there are differences that reflect our size and location."
- "Our organization is a collection of six different fiefdoms; however, three overarching values are present in every office: loyalty to the employee, commitment to the client, and being trustworthy."
- "Ohio is more formal due mostly to the size, and the other offices tend to be more liberal and closer knit."
- "The comment has been made that what's in the staff manual only pertains to Ohio."
- "We have some general overarching cultural values but we are more of a collection of subcultures."
- "I don't agree with the idea that the culture of the Ohio office is the default organizational culture."
- "Some offices appear to be exempt from standard operating procedures."
- "Employees are not treated fairly or equally. Expectations for employees differ vastly but without compensation."
- "We're less stringent with our older employees than we are with our younger employees."
- "Sometimes we're too demanding, too focused, too crisp with employees and that may impinge on their feeling of being respected."
- "We have a performance appraisal process in place but we don't hold supervisors responsible for completing the appraisals."
- "We don't really have a metric for measuring performance."
- "They (management) don't seem interested in my professional development, just my skill set."
- "We promote from within to maintain a good fit, but maybe we need to bring some fresh people into management."
- "There's a tendency to establish rules, but not willingness to follow up and confront rule breakers."
- "We don't see our work being handled with the same level of priority as the work generated in Ohio."
- "A lot of people complain about the pay and about the management."
- "I think the people out front (top management) are unaware of what's going on."
- "Here we go into a lot more analysis and detail than what a lot of firms do and I don't know if that's to our betterment or our detriment"
- "When they promoted me they broke the rules. It demonstrated that they were willing to make exceptions for people based on performance versus tenure."
- "Authoritarian, the way decisions are made and sent down the organization without any input or feedback from those low on the chart; that ties in with the carefulness . . . review by associates and senior associates."
- "It's the absence of those procedures that makes the implementation of those values difficult. It's split between what we're supposed to do and what actually happens . . . the way I understand it's suppose to work was . . . EIT work is reviewed by a PE under the review of the project manager . . . similarly if a PE does something then he'll show it to the EIT for developmental

(Continued)

Table 9.7 (Continued)

purposes . . . but the way it really works is . . . the PE is helping the EIT along so the PE has already checked the work because he's basically done it . . . the work doesn't get checked thoroughly. It should be reviewed by the project managers but they don't. What happens is that the work goes out and we end up back checking. There's also a lot of high-quality people working here who do something right the first time . . . if someone isn't good it's known and their work gets checked twice and other people get stuck fixing other people's work."

- "I think we live up to it in terms of due diligence but in terms of the tools to do the job we are really lacking. . . . I don't think that we are keeping up with the current engineering technology. . . . I think the number one thing is software and how to use it. . .we're not totally aware of all that the software can do for us . . . we need training and we don't have time for the training because we are always under a time crunch."

- "Sometimes we're not as thorough as we should be, but that doesn't dilute the honesty; it's just that the work gets ahead of us."

- "At times when we get into a situation where we are losing a lot of money, we may look for ways to see if we can get any extra money . . . but that's not a contradiction because its not a lie . . . we may look very closely to see if there is anything that we can bill for . . . we wouldn't do that if we were making money."

- "At times we overengineer a problem in cases where the client expects and is willing to accept (and pay for) something less than what we would like to provide."

- "Our ability to retain the best is limited by our willingness to retain all employees; it results in inflated salaries when you compare us to others in the industry and a less motivated staff and younger employees will seek out better pay and perceived working conditions . . . "

- "There's a fine line between overengineering and doing excellent work. We cross that line too often."

- "Sometimes we fail to give people the feedback they need to make improvements."

Discussion Questions

1. Critique Dr. Metger's approach to learning about RMC's organization culture. If you were in her shoes, what would you do differently? The same? Why?

2. Use the data from the case to assess the culture at RMC. What are the key issues? How do the findings from the quantitative data differ from the findings of the qualitative data? How are the findings similar?

3. If you were in Dr. Metger's position, what recommendations would you give Dr. Keller? Why? Write a two-page report summarizing your findings and making specific recommendations for any interventions needed.

4. Role-play the conversation between Dr. Metger and Dr. Keller in which she shares her findings and makes recommendations.

REFERENCES

Cable, D. M., & DeRue, D. S. (2002). The convergent and discriminant validity of subjective fit perceptions. *Journal of Applied Psychology, 87*(5), 875–884.

Detert, J. R., Schroeder, R. G., & Mauriel, J. J. (2000). A framework for linking culture and improvement initatives in organizations. *Academy of Management Review, 25*(4), 850–863.

Enz, C. A. (1988). The role of value congruity in intraorganizational power. *Administrative Science Quarterly, 33*(2), 284–304.

Hackman, R., & Oldham, G. (1975). Development of the job diagnostic survey. *Journal of Applied Psychology, 60*(2), 159–170.

Meyer, J. P., Allen, N. J., & Smith, C. A. (1993). Commitment to organization and occupations: Extension and test of a three-component conceptualization. *Journal of Applied Psychology, 78*(4), 538–551.

O'Reilly, C. A., Chatman, J. A., & Caldwell, D. F. (1991). People and organizational culture: A profile comparison approach to assessing person-organization fit. *Academy of Management Journal, 34*(3), 487–516.

FOR FURTHER READING

Cameron, K. S., & Quinn, R. E. (2005). *Diagnosing and changing organizational culture: Based on the competing values framework.* San Francisco: Jossey-Bass.

Harrison, R., & Stokes, H. (1992). *Diagnosing organizational culture instrument.* San Francisco: Pfeiffer.

Harvard Business Review. (2002). *Harvard Business Review on culture and change.* Boston: Harvard Business Press.

Hofstede, G., Neuijen, B., Ohayv, D. D., & Sanders, G. (1990). Measuring organizational cultures: A qualitative and quantitative study across twenty cases. *Administrative Science Quarterly, 35*(2), 286–316.

Schein, E. H. (1984). Coming to a new awareness of organizational culture. *Sloan Management Review, 25*(2), 3–16.

Wagner, S., Martin, N., & Hammond, C. (2002). A brief primer on quantitative measurement for the OD professional. *OD Practitioner, 34*(3), 53–57.

Engaging Broader Leaders in the Strategic Planning of Lincoln Women's Services

Bruce O. Mabee

Learning Objectives

- To sharpen your negotiation for effective feedback on the first contact with a client.
- To encourage you to promote safe, early tests that provide empirical feedback—quickly confirming, refuting, or expanding perception data from surveys or interviews.
- To keep your eye on whatever continues after the intervention—in the situations and actions that are usually much more important than the intervention or its direct results.

Maria Worthington was looking for a strategic planning facilitator for the Lincoln Women's Services Center, a not-for-profit organization that focuses on the career progress of young women with moderate to severe medical conditions in an eastern U.S. city.[1] Maria, the executive director, and John Balmore, the board chair, were referred to Barry Kravich, an OD consultant with many years of strategic planning experience in a wide variety of institutions, yet who had no background in the center's professional specialty.

INITIAL AGREEMENTS ABOUT THE PRIORITIES AND APPROACH

In the first meeting, when Barry asked Maria for an overview of the situation, she emphasized that the center was growing steadily. "We have been enjoying success because we make a difference in the lives of women who often face a difficult time at work yet have strong career abilities. We have the funding, and we have the support."

However, there was a very physical obstacle to their growth: "Our offices share this building with another state-sponsored program, and they also need the space." Their landlord, a progressive state government, was not in a position to initiate new construction on the architectural-landmark structure, located in a densely built, urban neighborhood. "There is no easy place to expand, and our reputation depends on maintaining the continuity we have achieved in this unified space." Maria foresaw a potentially difficult competition with the other program.

Barry inquired about the interests of various people associated with the center, and Maria saw value in Barry's proposal to form a strategy team that could represent stakeholders beyond the board and staff. This temporary team would interview a broad array of groups affected by the center's programs, including spouses of clients, medical professionals, the businesses they served, the state, and respected leaders in their professional field. Getting input from a full range of stakeholders would create opportunities to consider a full range of strategic issues—including issues that may have unexpected bearing on the space squeeze.

The strategy team would be advisory. They would not determine strategy, but would communicate about it and help identify options appropriate for the center. Strategy would remain the board's responsibility, informed by Maria as executive director as well as the strategy team's results.

The center had received acceptance for a government grant supporting strategic planning, and the government agency would require updates on the progress.

Barry probed to identify as wide a range of stakeholders as possible. He applied a "circle" model of stakeholders, to draw out "who affects us and who do we affect?"

Maria easily identified a breadth of stakeholders, including experts from the professional field on which the center was based, serving medically disadvantaged women.

Maria believed that the field experts likely would be interested in adding their perspective in the center's planning and would also be served themselves by the involvement with this institution.

Barry offered two questions for recruiting a team that could initiate sustainable strategic planning. (1) Can leaders be chosen who together will have enough influence to get the strategy executed? (2) Would some try to control the direction to their own biases instead of working as a team?

Maria conferred with John for the board perspective, and key board members agreed that Maria had the professional relationships that could enable her to recruit a team with sufficient stature and interest in the cause.

Barry suggested a starting template: two spouses of clients, two employees (representing professionals and staff) and two medical leaders from outside the center. This group would need to include at least one active board member and one person well-connected to the businesses that they served.

Maria recruited an appropriate mix. In fact, nine staff and volunteer leaders committed to serve on the strategy team.

Figure 10.1 Stakeholder Map Template

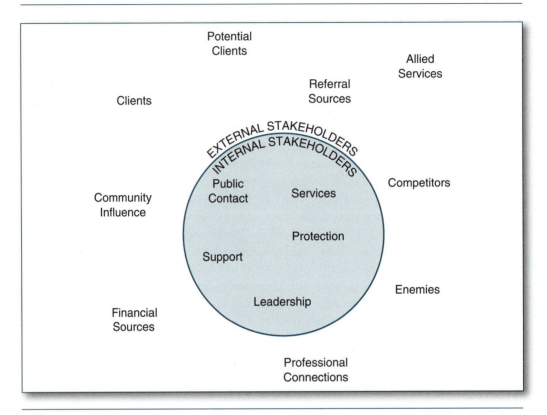

Note. From Bruce O. Mabee's Strategic Action System. Copyright Bruce O. Mabee. Reprinted with permission.

AGREEMENTS WITH THE STRATEGY TEAM

Barry asked Maria to arrange a kickoff meeting with the strategy team. With the scheduling difficulties of busy professionals, two were unable to attend the evening options she offered. For practicality, they set a date that those two had to miss.

In the kickoff meeting, Barry offered a template for the interviews of the center's stakeholders and a general outline for the first "vision meeting," in which the feedback from the interviews would be reviewed. The vision meeting also would have the goal of drafting an initial vision for the strategic plan.

"I'd like you to critique the questions for the interviews and also the agenda for the larger meeting. This hopefully will help pull you together as a team—and besides, you will be the ones conducting the interviews." Barry suggested that even more important than the data, the most critical purpose of the interviews was to *strengthen relationships with the key stakeholders* of the center. This approach also saved significant consulting fees, which they all approved!

Barry introduced a potential set of questions for the interviews.

Figure 10.2   Vision Meeting—Tentative Agenda

PURPOSE. To pool the vision of friends and colleagues.

Goal: To identify several strategic actions that we can test.

AGENDA.

4:00 Opening. Purpose and issues. Plan for evening.

4:15 Stakeholders.
- Who is here, and why are you interested?
- Who are other stakeholders, and what are their interests?

5:00 Time Line.
- Strategy team reviews draft. Group adds comments.

5:30 Visions & Common Ground.
- What visions have we heard from stakeholders?
- What other visions ought to be considered?

6:30 Forces & Priorities.
- What issues drive or restrain achievement of the vision?

7:15 Reality Tests—Before We Commit in June.
- Brainstorm ideas that could jump-start Lincoln.
- Your role. Is there any "test" that you'd want to join?

7:50 Final Comments. Parting advice for Lincoln.

Figure 10.3   Interview Questions

Introduction. Lincoln Women's Services is undertaking "strategic action." You have been valuable to Lincoln, and we want Lincoln to get the most from you! We also want you to gain the most from your association with Lincoln.
  Please tell me what to keep anonymous.

1. **Involvement.** What have been your most significant interactions with Lincoln?

2. **Perceptions.** What stands out to you about Lincoln? What have you heard from others?

3. **Gains.** What do you gain from Lincoln—and hope to gain?

4. **Pains/Costs to You.** What needs to improve in the future?

5. **Vision.** Do you have a view of how Lincoln should change, and not change, in the future?

6. **Impact.** How do you hope Lincoln will be better because of your involvement?

7. **Follow-Up.** How can Lincoln best stay in touch with you?

One of the members found the question about perceptions, "What stands out to you?" to be confusing; the group agreed that rewording it to read, "What seems to be the center's reputation?" would clarify it. Two other questions were reworded for clarity by the group, and Question 3, "What do you hope to gain from Lincoln?" was removed as redundant to Question 2. Each member committed to conduct three to five interviews, in-person or by phone, depending on who they were trying to reach.

> **Reflection Stop 1.** *Imagine you are Barry right now. What are you thinking and feeling in the consultant role? What would you do now? Please take a minute to reflect before you continue reading.*

STRATEGY TEAM INTERVIEWS AND PREPARATION FOR THE VISION DAY MEETING

Barry received data over a 5-day period, some in e-mails, some through the U.S. mail, and some obtained by his telephoning the interviewers.

Figure 10.4 Interview Data

Comments turned in by interviewers.

- Any change in direction at the center must be sure to keep the clients as the top priority.
- Our main task is the transition of our current clients back to mainstream work.
- Many of the spouses I speak with comment about how inaccessible the center's location is.
- It matters most how we create a path for them to get into mainstream work.
- Teamwork among our counselors and medical professionals makes or breaks our clients.
- My own wife has had nothing but the most interested and committed doctors and counselors.
- We have to beware of any expansion. It has the potential for dilution of our effectiveness.
- Our professionals know this field, yet there is no research with the depth and specificity we need to get the women into real work. We simply need to learn much more about this.
- We need to look more at the long-term career paths of our clients, beyond their previous jobs.
- The roles of these well-trained staff need to be known and used more.
- Our clients are often prominent in the community. Their bosses sometimes do not recognize this!
- Not all public and private employers are equally ready for our clients. Some are resistant.

- We cannot serve all women. We have a specialty that we must honor or we will serve no one.
- We need to learn more about the businesses to which we send our clients, and they need to know more about what we do here. Coordination must be a priority.
- The spouse's role is critical. Our best professionals also work amazingly well with husbands.
- This building is too "artsy." It is too costly to make changes, especially with new technologies.
- Nationally, our center is in the forefront. It can and should be teaching other institutions.
- The center is worth the drive. My wife gets attention that has made the difference in her outlook.
- I have no quarrel with the business leaders. They are just not trained for our clients.
- Often the counselors and medical professionals do not communicate about our clients. We need to get involved before and after the transitions from our center to the work world.
- It takes so much constant effort to prepare our clients! We cannot let anything weaken this.

Observations by consultant after the strategy team interview results.

> *The executive director was able to recruit high-powered leaders, who actively participated.*
> *The state is an environment of intertwined politics, likely to be difficult to influence.*
> *The strategy team followed through effectively and the board seems flexible and responsive.*
> *No group or issue has appeared likely to undercut the directions these people are taking.*

FINAL PREPARATION FOR THE VISION MEETING

Barry compiled the notes and themes that appeared across the interviews.

He was relieved that the original plan for the vision meeting still seemed appropriate. He had previous experiences where last-minute changes in a meeting plan had thrown off the planning team. Also he had seen planning groups get cynical and lose interest when executives or consultants overrode their input. Barry knew that long-term follow-through would depend very much on the commitment levels of groups who had helped shape the plan.

Reflection Stop 2. Now, as Barry, what are you thinking and feeling? What would you do now to be prepared for the feedback meeting? Please take a minute to reflect again before you continue reading.

VISION DAY—THE FEEDBACK MEETING

Twenty-four people attended the vision day meeting. Three who were invited had said they could not attend because they would be out of town. The broad stakeholders of the center were well represented.

Maria opened the meeting by introducing John as board president, the strategy team, and Barry. Strategy team members introduced each of the stakeholders she or he had interviewed. Maria then presented a short overview of "why we are here" and how this meeting was a first step. Barry presented the goals and the planned agenda.

Barry led the whole group in identifying "who is not here," drawing a map of stakeholders of the center and adding names to the map as individuals identified. Stakeholders included clients, the professionals who served them, families of clients, government regulators, and more than 15 other groups who affected, or were affected by, Lincoln. Barry asked for brief statements of the feedback—the priorities of each stakeholder: "What do they care about in their own lives, and what do they care about most regarding Lincoln Services?"

The whole group constructed a time line across a long wall of paper, projecting key points in the center's development from its start, to the present, to the future. Stakeholder interests, from the feedback and from other knowledge about each stakeholder group, were noted on the time line.

Barry next asked what different kinds of visions, portraying what the center could become, the interviewers had heard from the stakeholders. This evolved into a group discussion about the possible futures of the *field* of women's medical support—and in each scenario, what effective role the center could play. A single model took shape as this discussion evolved, which Barry drew on a flipchart: a three-dimensional pyramid showed five key groups in the corners—the women clients (at the top), their friends, their families, the medical professionals, and (of course) Lincoln support professionals. Barry asked each interviewer whether they believed the stakeholders they had interviewed would recognize the value of their role in this model. The consensus of all present said, "Yes!"

The group divided into subgroups to draft concrete action plans. The priority was to "apply this model and make the best progress on that time line." Barry asked the groups to seek at least one idea that could jump-start the process, and several ideas were planned as tests in the coming weeks. Fifteen members of the group volunteered for various task forces to carry out the tests and plans in the next few weeks. The first key action was asserted by John: "Our board needs to be 'on board' with this, and I will convene them within a week and let all of you know the board's specific commitments about what we have started here." A "commitment day" was scheduled in 6 weeks, (1) to capture early feedback from the actions that were being tested, and (2) to commit (or revise and commit) the new strategy of the center.

Discussion Questions

1. What risks and what advantages do you see in asking this strategy team to critique the questions, do the interviews, and present the feedback at the meeting? What questions and guidance might you bring as a consultant in Barry's position to maximize the advantages and minimize the risks?

2. To whom do you believe feedback should be presented? What advantages and disadvantages do you see in presenting this feedback to staff only, to the board (or a board committee), or to a group larger than the 24 who were there?

3. What is implied by the data you see? How would you organize it for presentation to the vision meeting? Would you present it to anyone else first?

4. Does the interview data (or other data you see here) suggest any changes in the meeting agenda that might set up more effective follow-through?

5. Two main sources of data are gathered and fed back in this design: first, the interviews of stakeholders, and then, the early results of the action tests. In traditional "plan the work and work the plan," the feedback is completed, then the plan is detailed before being implemented. Compare the cycles of learning and action in this case with the traditional approach. What are the advantages and disadvantages of each approach?

NOTE

1. Is this story real? Yes. The story is presented as it actually happened. Names and details were changed to maintain anonymity.

FOR FURTHER READING

Anderson, D. L. (2010). *Organization development: The process of leading organizational change.* Thousand Oaks, CA: Sage.

Marshak, R. J. (2006). Emerging directions: Is there a new OD? In J. V. Gallos (Ed.), *Organization development: A Jossey-Bass reader* (pp. 833–841). San Francisco: Jossey-Bass.

Case 11

RESISTANCE TO CHANGE

Technology Implementation in the Public Sector

MARIA VAKOLA

Learning Objectives

- To help you understand causes of resistance to organizational change.
- To realize differences among cultures, especially in a change context.
- To evaluate the role of unions in change.

A publicly owned company decided to implement a technology project to make its services more effective. Changes were related to a new information technology system implementation that would enable a number of major organizational changes, such as changing work processes and practices. This effort faced many hurdles, especially resistance from employees. Resistance to change, which means lack of support to a change project, is a very well-known cause of failure in change projects. This case study aims to analyze change recipients' reactions to a technology change and their impact on change success. The researcher was given access to a vast array of documents detailing the rationale for this change initiative. Archival data were available also, and these included consultancy reports, memoranda of this and previous changes, and copies of staff attitude surveys. A number of interviews were conducted as well.[1]

SETTING UP THE SCENE

This European organization employs 500 employees and its aim is to process public employees' retirement applications. The average age of employees is 48 years and their level of education is as follows: 10% hold a postgraduate degree, 25% are university graduates, 60% have completed upper secondary education, and 5% completed a 6-year basic education. This organization is characterized by bureaucracy, predictability, stability, and control. The structure is rigid and promotions are based on seniority and years of service, and there is secure employment and predictability. This organization's problem is low productivity. In some cases citizens' requests are processed with a delay of 10 months to 2 years, while the same requests in other European countries are processed in 2 to 3 months. Apart from these delays, citizens/customers report other problems, such as mistakes, rudeness, and long queues. Low productivity and daily arguments between citizens/customers and employees has attracted media attention.

Employees feel that their contributions are not valued and they are not paid well. Julie, who is the only employee in the human resources (HR) department, commented, "Management teams come and go. But we stay here and we make the effort. Every time the government changes, we have a new management team with good intentions. Intentions are not enough. They have never invested in training and development. They only ask for things—they never give." Interview results showed that promotions are based not on performance results but on seniority combined with who you know. It is not the good performers who succeed in this organization but the networkers or the members of a very strong union. Another finding was a shared feeling among employees that nothing can be changed and every time there is a change project nothing will happen in the end.

On the contrary, the management team believes that employees enjoy a very good work environment free of stress. Employees have jobs for life and there is no pressure for results or a goal-setting process. The management team agrees that salaries are quite low, representing limited job requirements and workload. They blame employees and the union for the failing of change projects suggested in the past.

The management team has decided to update their services by implementing a technology system, transforming all their files and archives into electronic ones, and training their people how to use it. This decision was supported by the government, as it had to be aligned with European legislation, and the management team was informed that they had to implement this project following a very strict timetable.

DESCRIPTION OF THE CHANGE

Top management's decision to invest in technology was followed by a bureaucratic process of an open call for proposals to identify the most suitable consultants and technology providers to implement the project. Then the top management team invited all managers to a meeting to inform them about the aims and objectives of this project and to celebrate the positive impact that they believe this project will have on the organization's future.

During the meeting, managers expressed concerns about the tight timetable of the implementation. Several commented that "it isn't how we do things around here." Some employees have computers on their desks but they are not used to dealing with citizens' applications electronically. John, who manages the biggest team of administrators, said

"It isn't only that they aren't using technology, it's that they don't trust technology. I heard many times that if you don't keep a hard copy you are lost." Julie, the HR person, informed the top management team that IT competencies were quite limited in this organization; only 30% of them know how to use basic applications such as Word. She also suggested to start investing in training early enough to avoid negative reactions to technology use because employees would need to learn a new software program developed to meet the organization's needs.

The top management team sent out a written invitation to gather all employees in an open meeting where the change project was officially announced. The purpose of this meeting was to celebrate the change project launch and focus on its anticipated positive impact on daily operations. However, employees started asking tough questions and complained about general people management issues and salaries, which led to tensions, arguments, and a negative atmosphere. This meeting added to the existing climate of suspicion and lack of trust between employees and the top management team.

Three months later, the consulting company and the provider who undertook the project came to map the processes and ask for specific requirements. The consultants called a meeting and invited people to participate in order to get insight about how their systems work and exchange views on their real needs and specific user requirements. These visits and frequent meetings brought some negative comments and rumors in the corridors arose that didn't help the implementation of this change. Initial comments from people participating in these meetings included:

- "There is no chance that I'm going to use this system. I'm happy as it is now."
- "Never mind, we have seen this over and over again. People get a huge amount of money for consulting services and nothing is implemented at the end. So I'm not worrying."
- "I am very close to retirement so it's not for me."
- "It isn't a bad idea but I cannot stay overtime to learn how to use it."

The top management team for the first time called supervisors to inform them about the decisions they made and to ask for cooperation. Supervisors commented that since the training hadn't been started yet, it was very difficult for them to persuade their people to start using these computers.

RESISTANCE TO CHANGE

During the next 2 months, the consultants realized that they had to deal with two main problems. First, they encountered huge delays because the union had started blocking their way in collecting vital information and data, and, second, resistance to change, which was seen as direct or indirect refusal for cooperation.

The consultants concluded that resistance to change was starting to block the project. They informed the top management team that people resisted for a number of reasons.

First, they noted, technology will facilitate goal setting and performance management. There were a number of employees who didn't perform well and caused delays in dealing with citizens' applications. These people justified their behaviors by blaming other departments' inefficiencies and delays. Up to then it was impossible to check and track down the progress of an application. As a result, it was impossible to measure the efficiency of an employee in dealing with an application. The ability to measure the quantity of daily process of an application would create problems for those who choose not to perform. Jackie, a newcomer with a postgraduate qualification and experience from a private bank, commented:

> When I came here, I had nothing to do. I didn't even have an office. Two weeks later my supervisor left me some applications to examine and make a recommendation. I studied this subject but I didn't have the experience so I asked my colleagues. I was very surprised to see how knowledgeable they were. They knew what they were talking about and they were really willing to cooperate with me. I completed my cases in a month and went to my supervisor's office to make a presentation. I remember that my colleagues were really angry about this because, as they informed me, this number of cases usually takes 6 months to be completed. They made explicitly clear that they didn't want me to go there again in less than 6 months and we can easily blame other departments, etc., for these delays.

Second, the new system created confusion and stress. Some employees seemed to understand its benefits but they were reluctant to start using it because either they didn't have the competencies and didn't believe in themselves enough to start learning them, or they couldn't accept the idea of using technology to support their daily functions. Stress and confusion were more apparent in older employees. For example, some older employees admitted in a private conversation that they were afraid of "losing face" in front of younger employees who were more competent in technology use. As one of them said, "I have 30 years of service here and a young boy comes along who could be my son or my grandson and arrogantly tells me, 'this is useful to play CDs and not as a tea or coffee holder, if you know what I mean.'"

Third, the role of the union didn't facilitate the implementation process. They decided to campaign against the change and organized group meetings and face-to-face communication to persuade people not to participate. Their main argument was that technology implementation may be beneficial but its use should be rewarded, and an extra allowance for technology use should be added to their main salary. So they decided to negotiate and asked for a small pay raise because employees had to learn new competencies that they would use for the organization. This wasn't possible and was rejected by the top management team because the change project was an expensive one. As a result, the union decided to call for nonparticipation.

Finally, there was lack of trust between the management and the employees. The organization was characterized by poor change history, which means that many change initiatives were started but they weren't implemented or were half implemented by the end.

In the past, the top management paid expensive consultants to implement a series of improvements in the organization and persuaded people to invest in time and effort. But in the end, management was replaced and those who came didn't build on the existing change but preferred to start new ones. As a result, the majority of the people didn't believe in change.

However, some people welcomed this new change and started supporting it. They were a minority but they had strong arguments and were involved in discussions among colleagues in which they expressed their opinions. Nick, who works in logistics, said, "It was about time to see this positive change. We suffered enough from not having a fast and reliable electronic system. I'm really happy and ready to start the training."

Suddenly the top management team decided not to approve a training budget and suggested organizing on-the-job training. Some employees were competent in using the new system and they could show it to the rest of the employees. The management team believed that this was not only a cheap way of training the workforce but also an effective one.

WHAT HAPPENED IN THE END

Eighteen months later the system was ready to be used. It was decided to keep the old system in parallel to avoid major disruptions. The use of the new system wasn't easy for the following reasons. First, in some departments younger employees had to show their supervisors how to use the new system, and the older employees didn't feel comfortable asking questions and sorting out problems. Second, some people thought that only those who knew how to use the technology had to be involved in change, which led to some arguments and tensions among employees. Supervisors had to support their employees in using the new system, but this didn't always happen because they also needed support. The top management team decided to pay overtime to those people who wanted to stay beyond their normal work hours, but the union prevented the majority of people from participating. Again there were many delays, citizens were really frustrated, and yet again this organization found itself in the news media for offering poor services. So the management team decided to stop the old system to put pressure on the employees to start using the new one.

Nearly 3 years from the first announcement, this change was finally fully implemented in this organization. However, it cost more than initially planned and there were many tensions and arguments during the implementation, which had a negative impact on employees' morale. During the first months of the implementation, queues were longer and citizens' complaints more frequent. Still, a number of people, a minority, faced problems using the technology. Overall, while the change was implemented, it cost more, it was more time consuming, and key users talked about many mistakes in system planning and implementation.

Discussion Questions

1. What were the major sources of resistance to change in this organization?

2. What strategies would you suggest to deal with this resistance?

3. What was the role of leadership in this case?

4. Please read the paper "Lufthansa's Transformation Marathon: Process of Liberating and Focusing Change Energy" by H. Bruch and T. Sattelberger, 2001, *Human Resource Management, 40*(3), 249–259.

   a. Analyze the role of human resources management and the union in transforming Lufthansa.

   b. Make a comparison between the Lufthansa case and this one regarding the role of human resources management and unions in change implementation.

   c. Identify success and failure factors related to change implementation in both cases.

5. Evaluate the role of consultants in this case. What would you have done differently?

NOTE

1. The real name of the company is confidential and the names of interviewees remain anonymous.

FOR FURTHER READING

Armenakis, A., & Bedeian, A. (1999). Organizational change: A review of theory and research in the 1990s. *Journal of Management, 25*(3), 293–315.

Judge, T. A., Thoresen, C. J., Pucik, V., & Welbourne, T. M. (1999). Managerial coping with organizational change: A dispositional perspective. *Journal of Applied Psychology, 84*(1), 107–122.

Oreg, S. (2006). Personality, context, and resistance to organizational change. *European Journal of Work and Organizational Psychology, 15*(1), 73–101.

Piderit, S. K. (2000). Rethinking resistance and recognizing ambivalence: A multidimensional view of attitudes toward and organizational change. *Academy of Management Review, 25*(4), 783–794.

Wanberg, C. R., & Banas, J. T. (2000). Predictors and outcomes of openness to changes in a reorganizing workplace. *Journal of Applied Psychology, 85*(1), 132–142.

Case 12

RESISTANCE TO CHANGE

Assessing Readiness for the Implementation of an Enterprise Resource Planning (ERP) System at MedDev, Inc.

PRAVIN A. RODRIGUES AND ARUNA FERNANDES RODRIGUES

Learning Objectives

- To help you understand the variety of factors that influence the implementation of an enterprise resource planning project.
- To introduce you to some of the challenges and complexities related to the job of a change agent.
- To help you understand the significance of history and organizational structure in change projects.

Anita Campos's office phone buzzed. It was Tom, the chief information officer (CIO) of MedDev, Inc., a medical supplies company. "Hi, Anita, this is Tom. I just left Gary Franz's office and I need to meet with you to discuss some concerns he and I have regarding the successful implementation of our project. Would it be possible to meet some time this afternoon? I have asked Gloria to set up some time for us to meet. You should be seeing an Outlook meeting request come through shortly."

Anita was expecting this call. Tom had told her that he would be in an audit committee meeting with Gary Franz, the chief financial officer (CFO) of the organization. "Sure, I'll look for the meeting request. Is there anything in particular I should be reviewing prior to our meeting?"

Tom had recently hired her as an internal organization development consultant to support a multimillion dollar enterprise resource planning (ERP) project. The scope of the project included all global operations across Europe and North America.

"Well," Tom said, "It might be helpful to provide you with some background information right now. As you are aware, this project is the largest capital investment project the company has undertaken in its long history. As the CIO and project director, I feel a tremendous pressure to ensure we position the project for success this time around. I just left the monthly audit committee meeting with representatives of our external audit firm. As we discussed previously, the audit firm has been tasked by Gary to ensure we are on track for project success. In their most recent update, they highlighted an area of organizational risk and have recommended an area for change management focus. I would like to share the document with you and bring you up to speed on their recommendation."

"Oh, good." Anita said. "Can you tell me a little more about the change management focus area, perhaps provide me with some context?"

"The auditors have recommended that we implement a change readiness assessment for the organization," Tom said. That, Anita thought, should not be a problem. She had conducted similar assessments for former clients; however, she still wasn't sure of the context for the recommendation in this situation.

Tom added, "Gary has requested that we provide a high-level plan, approach, and timeline for execution for the change readiness assessment at our next steering committee meeting. I thought we should meet at the earliest possible."

The steering committee was comprised of vice presidents (VPs) from different functional areas, including information technology, finance, legal, marketing, research and development, customer service/e-commerce, sales, operations, product development, and supply chain management. The role of the steering committee was to provide approval on project strategy and procedures, including timing and budget.

"Sure," Anita said, "I'll look forward to our meeting."

To prepare for the meeting, Anita began reviewing some of the documents that defined the organizational structure of the company. She also thought through the historical background of the company.

Tom had spent his entire career rotating through various positions in operations and information technology (IT) at MedDev. Prior to taking on his recent assignment within IT, including a move from operational to IT roles, he had witnessed extensive changes in IT systems. He survived through various cycles of boom and decline that the company had experienced over the years.

Within the past year, he was named project director for the ERP project, the largest capital project undertaken within the organization to date. Within the organizational structure of MedDev, Tom reported directly to the CFO, Gary Franz. Anita had recently been hired as the change management leader (organization development) dedicated to supporting the project. MedDev had never had anyone dedicated in the role of "internal OD consultant" for any projects prior to her coming on board for this project. Anita's role was created based on the advice of XL Infotech, a well-reputed technology and global IT management consulting firm. Both MedDev as well as XL Infotech had a stake in the success of this project. For XL Infotech, it was the first time a component of their technology was being implemented in the medical devices industry.

In her internal role, Anita reported directly to the CIO. However, indirectly she was responsible for advising multiple levels of the executive leadership team on all human capital and workforce transition issues. The levels assigned to her included the steering committee, the project management office (PMO), the project team, and all management and staff impacted by the project.

MedDev was the global leader in the medical devices industry. It had grown rapidly via acquisitions, resulting in the use of many disparate systems across the supply chain. Various technologies were in place from order entry to areas of procurement, planning, demand forecasting, planning, customer service, and inventory management.

The 5-year growth projections for the organization were extremely promising, but the company was facing pricing pressures from global competitors and new entrants to the market.

The world headquarters for MedDev were located in a suburban location in northern Nebraska. Housed alongside the corporate headquarters were also the operations facility, where products were assembled, packaged, and shipped. Customer service, product development, research and development, quality, and sales and marketing departments were all located in an adjacent facility.

The headquarters had been built in 1977 and it was a simple nonassuming structure. The corporate campus was set in a small town and was completely invisible from the main intersection closest to the campus. Unless you grew up in the area or were directly involved in business transactions with the organization, you would never know that this global company was even located in this small community.

MedDev had a long and distinguished history of having been a major supplier to world renowned hospitals, leading medical centers, acute care, and long-term care facilities. The chief executive officer (CEO), Michael Zucker, started the business out of his garage while completing high school. Innovative products, smart marketing strategies, and a large market for the products allowed the company to grow rapidly. In many ways, it exemplified the often touted American business success story.

Michael Zucker is a key decision maker and influencer of policy, not only in the industry but also in many ancillary industries. The company's chief operating officer (COO) also has seen the organization through its various stages of growth. The chief technology officer (CTO) has been the person responsible for delivering and receiving several patents for many of the products, which have delivered a competitive advantage to MedDev over the years. The remainder of the senior leadership team is varied in its tenure. Gary Franz had recently been hired to provide a focus on cost efficiencies. The senior vice president (SVP) of operations had come on board from a global automotive industry organization and was tasked with optimization and delivering value.

When Anita had joined the organization, the director of organization development, who had only recently been hired into a full-time capacity in the organization, had interviewed her. The senior vice president of human resources (HR) also had been recently hired. Anita had developed good relationships with the entire HR leadership team during her interview processes and within the first few weeks of being on site.

Anita was still in the process of assessing the factors that would influence and help drive the change management strategy. She had yet to meet with most of the key senior executives and leaders that she was supposed to advise and coach through the change process.

Having had solid experience in both internal and external consulting roles for multi-million dollar business transformation projects, she was well aware of many of the challenges presented by leadership, as well as the organizational politics that could undermine effective implementation of large-scale change initiatives. She had successfully delivered business results and productivity enhancements to global Fortune 100 companies, so she was confident in her capabilities of working effectively in global, matrixed, and complex organizational structures. She felt she was well-positioned for success in the role. The project management committee that interviewed her had emphasized that they were seeking someone with an easygoing management and leadership style who could quickly build rapport with leaders across all levels in an organization. It was communicated clearly to her that the competencies of developing trust, fostering creativity and innovation, and establishing a sense of teamwork were essential to achieve success on the ERP project.

MedDev had recently begun to diversify into other areas for which there were higher demands and some of these new business segments had become very successful enterprises. Unfortunately, the IT systems of the organization had languished: many of the applications being used were custom developed in the 1970s; it had become very expensive to maintain multiple disparate systems as the company had grown via acquisitions in the recent years; MedDev could not deliver the information leaders required to make informed business decisions or plan for future business growth.

The company had hired a VP of sales, customer service, and e-commerce to further develop the Web marketing and e-commerce strategy. With the successful business models of e-commerce companies such as eBay, Amazon.com, and Overstock.com, MedDev was keen on diversifying and growing the business via a multichannel marketing strategy.

A ping from her e-mail system brought Anita's attention back to her computer screen.

Tom was requesting a meeting in an hour. A meeting at such short notice was unusual. This must be important, thought Anita.

An hour later Anita walked into Tom's office. She had been to his office for meetings before. As always, the top of his wooden desk was littered with documents. She quickly glanced at the family picture clearly visible behind Tom's seat. She had enjoyed meeting his family at one of the company picnics.

Tom greeted Anita. "Thanks for coming in at such short notice."

"Oh, that's fine," Anita responded. "I wasn't locked into any other meetings this afternoon." She took a seat on the other side of Tom's desk.

Tom began, "I would like to reiterate on behalf of the PMO and the steering committee how pleased we are to have you on board."

Anita acknowledged the compliment with a smile. "Thank you. I am really keen on hearing more about your meeting with Gary and the audit committee."

"Sure, let me print you a copy of the audit firm report." Tom opened documents on his PC and sent them to the printer located in his office. He picked up the pages and handed them over to Anita. "Here's the most recent audit firm risk assessment. Go ahead and take a few minutes to review these documents. While you're doing that, I'll check my e-mail and voice messages." Tom smiled, then added, "I have been in meetings all day and this is the first opportunity I have had to check my messages."

Anita quickly reviewed the documents she had been handed. As she read through the document, she circled the areas titled "Organization Risk" toward the end of the second page and underlined the areas of risk, action items, and watch items listed. In her role as an OD consultant, she had reviewed similar documents several times before. She had developed the skill to quickly focus on the most important elements related to her role. More than 10 minutes had passed before Tom turned away from his computer and addressed Anita.

"I wondered if you had any questions before I share observations from the meetings."

Anita was glad for the opportunity Tom presented. "Actually, yes, I was wondering what you were referring to in our earlier phone conversation when you said that we should ensure that we position the project for success this time around. What did you mean by 'this time around'?"

"Oh, yes, yes," Tom said. "I guess I made the mistake of assuming that you know the history related to this project. See, MedDev had launched this project with limited success a few years ago. At that time, the organization had allocated insufficient resources to get the project accomplished and after implementing a few modules of the software in operations, the project stalled and was then put on hold due to lack of resources in terms of both time and money. I was leading up the European IT organization and there was another CIO leading the project efforts at the time. Many of the steering committee executives and middle level managers who are on our project team as business process owners (BPO) and technical leads went through the previous deployment. They have either been on the previous project team or have been in operations, customer service, and finance, or as end clients using the partial software system that is currently in place."

With a grim face Tom said, "To put it lightly, that rollout was a fiasco. Anyway, coming back to the present project," Tom paused, then continued, "After having conducted interviews with members of the executive and steering committee, the audit firm has identified multiple areas of organizational risk. There appears to be some confusion among members of the steering committee regarding the scope of the ERP project and its relationship to other current or potential business process improvement projects at MedDev. In order to address this, the change management team will need to look at the initial business case and compile a summary distinguishing the planned benefits of the ERP project from the other process improvement initiatives underway."

"That is extremely useful information that I did not gather from the documents. Can you elaborate further?"

Tom added, "When we announced the launch of the project this time around, many managers voiced concerns to their leaders directly that they didn't think the project would succeed this time around either."

Anita was intrigued. "Why do you feel they are voicing their concerns to their leaders?"

Tom explained, "I sense they are bitter at their perceived loss of control once we put this new system entirely in place. During the last project, they were not included in the planning and definition efforts and were just told what to do. Here's what helped me focus on this problem: I was in a meeting the other day and Bob, the manager of supply chain operations, asked if we would be repeating the last fiasco again. He tends to be a wild cannon when it comes to comments. However, in this case, I would consider his comments to be representative of the feeling across the operations team right now."

"How did you respond?" Anita asked.

"Well, I informed him that this time around we had hired you to ensure that we place a primary focus on people during this rollout."

"How did he react to that?"

"Well, he just smirked and made a wise comment about the effect of some more management layers on the project team."

Anita made a few notes and said, "You have shared very useful information with me. There are a couple of methods we could use for the readiness assessment that come to mind so we can identify areas of resistance. I will review all the information I have gathered from you and consult with my team too. You and I can regroup after that to review my proposal."

Anita stood up to leave, and then realized she needed one more piece of information. "Before I go, any idea when the next steering committee meeting is?"

"In 2 weeks," Tom responded.

"Great, I will aim for a review of the proposal early next week. That will give us sufficient time to modify, if required, and develop the slides for presentation at the steering committee meeting," Anita said as she picked up her planner and other documents off Tom's desk.

"Good. That should work. I look forward to our next meeting," Tom said.

Discussion Questions

1. How resistant are you to change? Do you think that change should always be welcomed? If you were the CEO of a company, what would you expect from the senior leadership in responding to change initiatives?

2. Who is the change agent in this case? What are the potential challenges the change agent is likely to encounter at MedDev?

3. If you were the change agent at MedDev, what process would you suggest to ensure success of the ERP project?

FOR FURTHER READING

Aiken, C., & Keller, S. (2009). The irrational side of change management. *McKinsey Quarterly, 2,* 100–109.

Cady, S. H. & Dannemiller, K. D. (2005). Whole system transformation: The five truths of change. In W. J. Rothwell, R. L. Sullivan & G. N. McLean (Eds.), *Practicing organization development: A guide for consultants* (pp. 440–455). San Francisco: Jossey-Bass.

Jones, B. B., & Brazzel, M. (Eds.). (2006). *The NTL handbook of organization development and change: Principles, practices, and perspectives.* San Francisco: Pfeiffer.

Kee-Young, K., & Hee-Wong, K. (2008). Managing readiness in enterprise systems-driven organizational change. *Behavior and Information Technology, 27*(1), 79–87.

Van Dam, K., Oreg, S., & Schyns, B. (2008). Daily work contexts and resistance to organisational change: The role of leader-member exchange, development climate, and change process characteristics. *Applied Psychology: An International Review, 57*(2), 313–334.

WHERE DO WE BEGIN?

Selecting an Intervention at the Springfield County Office of Economic Development

DONALD L. ANDERSON

Learning Objectives

- To help you evaluate the issues involved in selecting an intervention.
- To help you prioritize issues and interventions when multiple areas of change exist.

The Springfield County Office of Economic Development (OED) is responsible for attracting businesses to Springfield County and establishing a friendly climate for new and existing business owners. The OED advocates for out-of-state businesses to establish satellite offices in the county and thereby grow local employment opportunities. The management team consists of 12 managers who supervise regional departments in offices located throughout the county. The regional department staff works with potential client businesses to help them with land-use planning, site selection, local tax incentives, and more. The management team reports to Maria, the division director.

Christina and Gilbert, organization development (OD) consultants from the county's human resources division, have been asked by Maria to work on a team development intervention. In their initial meeting, Maria gave an overview of the organization and described the presenting problem to Christina and Gilbert. She had some concerns about the performance of her management team, and she wanted their help in developing an OD intervention to address her concerns. Specifically, she noticed that:

- Team members were highly intelligent, experienced, and competent in their jobs. Most had tenure with the division of more than 10 years.
- Team meetings had become awkward, with only a few members speaking. Some team members did not participate at all.
- Team members on multiple occasions had made commitments that they did not keep. When confronted about this behavior, team members became resistant and dogmatic. Maria used the words "passive-aggressive" to describe the team.
- Maria had one-on-one meetings weekly with each of her managers, and these meetings were very pleasant, even enjoyable.

According to Maria, the team's past performance had been quite good on an individual basis, with each region "doing just fine," as she put it. However, Maria explained her concern that in the future, team members would need to work more closely together than they had to this point, and she questioned their ability to do so effectively. In the past, economic development managers would work on projects in their own regional area, but increasingly this was becoming a challenge. More projects were crossing geographic boundaries, and were thus involving two, three, or even four different regional jurisdictions, causing confusion as to which manager was responsible for the project. There had been instances of managers making conflicting decisions on a project, resulting in delays and frustration to the client businesses. Maria had proposed to the team several months ago that they reorganize, with members holding responsibility for a portfolio of companies to target by size and industry, independent of region or geography. She reported that the team's reaction was unambiguous—they did not like the idea of organizing differently and saw no need to disrupt the current structure of the team. Maria told Christina and Gilbert that she dropped the issue after that, but was still considering it. She was anxious to get Christina's and Gilbert's help in improving the performance of the team.

THE DATA-GATHERING PLAN

After their initial meeting, Christina and Gilbert proposed conducting hour-long individual interviews with each member of the management team. In their interview guide, they developed the following questions based on Maria's description of the team. They sent this in advance to Maria, who enthusiastically agreed to both the data-gathering plan and interview questions.

1. Tell us about your role and responsibility on this team.
2. What is the team's purpose? What are the goals of this team? Do you think everyone on this team shares an understanding of the team goals and purpose?
3. What are the team's strengths?

4. In what areas do you think this team could improve?

5. How well does this team currently perform? Is the team meeting its goals?

6. How well do team members work together?

INTERVIEW RESULTS

Over a 10-day period, the two consultants shared responsibility for conducting the interviews. They each attended every session—one would ask questions and continue the conversation while the other was responsible for taking notes. They captured verbatim quotes where they could, and combined their notes into a document that resulted in almost 80 pages of single-spaced notes for the 12 interviewees. Next came the challenge of trying to sort through the mountain of quotes to find the themes that came across consistently in the interviews.

They organized the data by creating four categories that appeared in the majority of the participants' statements. These four issues directly addressed the concerns that Maria had shared with them, they were specific enough to take action on issues the client could influence, and they were selective (Christina and Gilbert quickly realized that they could not include everything, particularly themes that appeared only once or twice). They prepared a document that listed the following themes followed by exact quotes from interviewees. As they had committed, interviewee names remained anonymous in written reports, with sources of the quotes known only to them.

Feedback on OED Team Performance

1. Past team conflicts and the inability to engage in conflict effectively causes team members to hold back.

   - *"We had some shouting matches in the past. Now we just avoid it."*
   - *"The larger the group the more dysfunctional it becomes. If we bring everyone together we get passive agreement—people say one thing but then go off and do their own thing."*
   - *"When there's conflict, sometimes people shut down because of the disagreement."*

2. Generally team members do not describe their work as highly interdependent on others (i.e., one cannot succeed unless a peer also succeeds).

   - *"What we've struggled with is that we've never had a common vision, goals, or set of objectives for the larger team. We've been very free in allowing the teams to set their goals and objectives."*
   - *"Around here, the feeling seems to be that we're a bunch of people doing the same thing so let's be a team."*

3. Team members frequently mention distrust of team members as a problem in team dynamics.
   - *"I think trust is an issue. I feel that I can trust [team member A] and [B], but I take everything [C] says with a grain of salt."*
   - *"I think there are two or three people I could never trust. I think they would stab me in the back without a second thought."*

4. Team members appear to collaborate when needed but on an as-needed, ad hoc basis.
   - *"We collaborate when there is a crisis or urgent need for action, but there has to be something that instigates it."*
   - *"We don't generally need to coordinate our work very often. I have my own region and that's it. But when the opportunity arises, sure, we collaborate."*
   - *"When we need to get two or three people together, we collaborate very well."*

Christina and Gilbert agreed that prior to the meeting with Maria where they would present the data, they would first meet together to decide what interventions might be appropriate for this team and agree on a recommendation.

THE CONSULTANTS MEET

Christina: I felt that the interviews went well. I was really surprised that team members were forthright, honest, and not hesitant about sharing their opinions.

Gilbert: I agree. I had assumed, based on Maria's comments, that the group might be a bit inhibited about speaking up, but that didn't seem to be the case at all.

Christina: And often I run into at least one interviewee who either puts off the interview or cuts it short, but everyone seemed to genuinely want to be interviewed.

Gilbert: I think our experience echoes what Maria was saying about how easy it is to talk to the team one on one, but when they get together, things seem different. We certainly heard that from them directly as well. Overall, I think Maria's explanation of the team dynamics was fairly accurate.

Christina: Yes, there are clearly some close relationships among participants, but some awkward and distrusting feelings among some of them. It's not that they don't know each other well, but no one wants to be the dissenting voice, so they just don't say anything.

Gilbert: Now based on all that we know, I'm wondering what we should propose in terms of interventions. Based on what we've learned, I think this team will never come together as a team unless they understand how they are interdependent in their roles.

Christina: I don't get the impression that this team is really feeling like they are a team. They don't feel a responsibility to one another.

Gilbert: They don't seem to share a team vision, either. And without a shared team purpose, vision, and goals, I don't think they have the foundations of being a team.

Christina: I feel the problem is that they don't know enough about how to interact effectively to make any vision a reality. I don't sense that they respect each other as peers. I think we should start by using an instrument such as the Myers-Briggs Type Indicator, where they could learn more about themselves and their own assumptions and approaches, and truly learn how to engage with their peers as individuals with their own unique talents, skills, and styles. Then I would use a conflict instrument so they could start to identify their own individual patterns in conflict and learn how they can more effectively "storm" when conflict occurs.

Gilbert: I don't agree. I would never start with an individual instrument with this team. They already have plenty of experience as individuals. This is already a collection of individuals. It's barely even a group. They need to learn to stop acting as individuals and become a team. If we start with an individual instrument, we reinforce the idea of being solitary at the expense of the collective.

Christina: But they can't change as a team until they change as individuals. I would always start with some kind of individual learning or development first so they can bring that knowledge of themselves and their own style to the team intervention. Then they can approach the team mentality with confidence about their own contributions.

Gilbert: I would work with this team on team issues first. Define a team vision, clarify the team purpose, and set team goals. The team goals should involve everyone, and the goals would be phrased in a way that they can't be met unless everyone contributes. They would have metrics to check the team's progress, and they would learn that they can't act as individuals but have to help each other out to accomplish the team goal.

Christina: Eventually they need goals, but if they can't work together and deal with conflicts when they inevitably occur, wouldn't we just be setting them up for failure? They would have goals they can't meet because they don't have effective working relationships. It would just feed the distrust and frustration they all feel.

Gilbert: I can see what you're saying, but overall, I have bigger questions. Will this team be able to make progress on converging as a team and becoming interdependent if they think Maria is going to reorganize them soon? Will they make progress on trust and conflict if they think this team is a temporary endeavor?

Christina: This is a tough one. Where do we begin?

Discussion Questions

1. Based on what you know about the early stages of the organization development process (contracting, data gathering, diagnosis, and feedback), how would you evaluate the work that Christina and Gilbert have done to this point? What would you have done differently, if anything?

2. Summarize Christina's and Gilbert's proposed courses of action. How does each explain the rationale for his or her approach? List the advantages and the drawbacks of each course of action.

3. Do you find yourself agreeing more with Christina, or do you agree more with Gilbert? Why? Is there a different course of action you would propose?

4. How would you propose structuring the feedback meeting with Maria?

5. In your view, how do individual and team interventions relate? When do you think an intervention should be directed at the individual level, and when should it begin at the team level?

FOR FURTHER READING

Argyris, C. (1970). *Intervention theory and method: A behavioral science view.* Reading, MA: Addison-Wesley.

Beckhard, R., & Harris, R. (1987). *Organizational transitions* (2nd ed.). Reading, MA: Addison-Wesley.

Harrison, R. (1970). Choosing the depth of organizational intervention. *Journal of Applied Behavioral Science, 6*(2), 181–202.

Reddy, W. B. (1994). *Intervention skills: Process consultation for small groups and teams.* San Francisco: Jossey-Bass.

TO CHANGE WITHOUT APPEARING TO CHANGE

Creating Stability in a Multichange/Multiresolution Government Agency

MATTHEW G. ISBELL

Learning Objectives

- To understand the problems that exist in a multichange environment.
- To address process and ethical issues confronted by external consultants.
- To apply theoretical concepts to a resistant audience.

SETTING

Nutrition Education for Client Care (NECC) (a pseudonym) is a state government agency that addresses health and nutrition education needs for low-income clients. It has more than 50 local offices (LOs) across the state that deal directly with clients. The LOs are all coordinated by a state office (called "the state" by most staffers). Most of the state office staff are not from LOs and consequently have very little understanding of what happens, in a practical sense, at those offices.

BACKGROUND

NECC is a large statewide agency operating with a mission to address nutrition education needs and reduce the dramatic increase in weight gain seen within the state. For years this program has been working with low-income parents and their children to instill good eating habits while also promoting a strong sense of self-efficacy among clients to take control of their dietary lives.

The agency has a long history working on nutrition topics. Employees are dedicated to the mission and organization, and generally they have a long tenure with NECC— turnover in most LOs is low (especially in the rural LOs). While a dedicated and passionate staff can be an asset to a company, it also can make a change initiative difficult. At NECC, three issues have emerged recently, which have created a roadblock to change. First, in the past 5 years NECC has gone through immense developmental change, so much so that staff members frequently speak of these successive changes as the cultural norm rather than the exception. These changes have taken a toll on LO staffers, and there have been recent failures in the implementation of new programs.

Second, adding to the current climate of change, are the discrepancies between LOs in terms of funding. LOs in larger urban areas are dealing with more clients but have limited resources (e.g., funding, time, space). As a result, employee turnover has increased and burnout is more prevalent. Rural LOs have more flexibility with funds and resources but deal with a more dispersed population. The different clientele and resource issues across the LOs make it difficult to roll out a "one program fits all" type change.

Finally, a shift in the leadership and direction of NECC is beginning to surface, with consequences to employee morale and agency productivity. While there is still a large percentage of "lifers," many new staffers have climbed the ranks and earned management positions in some of the LOs. The "young bloods" are more open to changing and updating the processes within NECC to modernize the delivery of education to the clients. Many of the lifers, however, have met the process changes with resistance. The young bloods see this as an entrenchment issue where lifers have become set in their ways and refuse to make changes.

In January, NECC brought in an organizational implementation consultant to help roll out a new program statewide. The new program—called participant-centered learning environment (PCLE)—creates a major change in the way nutrition education is conducted at LOs. With this change the LO staffer's role becomes more of a coach and less of an instructor, and clients are encouraged to participate and even lead discussions.

PROBLEM

State-level management wants to institute the PCLE without making it "feel" like another change. Management is aware of the change-weary morale of the staff and is concerned that employees will not accept another change. Consequently, management is attempting to implement a new process without awareness of the implementation.

To address the state's problem, the consultant goes to three different LOs to get a sense of the morale. Below are the reports from these LO visits and meetings with the state. The reports are first person narratives of the consultant's experiences.

Local Office 26, Okemos County, Mid-March

"Please don't tell me this is facilitated discussion again," Beth says as we sit in her office.

Beth is the LO director and has been for 5 years. In those 5 years, NECC has seen four major organizational changes—the most recent just last fall when the entire state switched to a new online computer tracking system for clients.

"I mean seriously, isn't this just facilitated discussion with a new title? We did this already; we went to the meetings, the trainings, and the online in-services. We did everything the state asked and what happened? The state pushed a bunch of new material in our lap, gave us a pat on the back and said 'go do it.' Guess what? Nobody did it! The project failed. There was no support for it beyond those few trainings that I just mentioned."

Beth exhales, stares at me for a moment and just shakes her head. The frustration is palpable. She is tired. Her local office had a hard time with the technology change and is already fretting the upcoming change to the breastfeeding program slated for next year.

"It's one thing to make the needed changes. You should have seen the computer system we were using before last fall. It was from the Stone Age. The computers could barely play Frogger, let alone keep track of our clients and scheduling. Before that change, we had to create a new nutrition education package based on the new food pyramid—and that took forever. For decades we have been telling our clients about how to eat well using the old pyramid, and now we have a new one that says something else. Prior to that change we had the dreaded facilitated discussion fiasco. Sometimes I wonder if the state even thinks before they tell us about the 'the next best thing.' Now here we are, back to facilitated discussion, except you are calling it participant-centered learning. If there is a difference, I don't see it. And, unless the state comes up with some better support and policies behind this program, it will go the way of the dodo."

She turns around and shows me the bookcase behind her. In it are more than 50 binders. She tells me they are all different plans and programs the state has proposed over the years. I ask her how many of those programs she is currently using.

"That's the point. I am not using any of them. It is kind of an ongoing joke here at our office. This is our very own State Hall of Shame. But, every time the state issues a new binder, we have to train on it and try to implement it here in our LO. So much time has been wasted in useless trainings, and every training just adds to the growing frustration here at the LO. The state has no idea how time-consuming it is to ramp up for a new program. It's stressful; it's a commitment of time and resources, and both are in short supply around here."

Local Office 51, Grandville County, Early April

I walk into the Grandville LO and the first thing to hit me is how busy it is. LO 51 is one of the largest urban office in the state. LO 51 accounts for almost 20% of the entire client load in the state. The office is crammed with people when I arrive, and it's only 8:30 a.m. The staffer at the front desk informs me I will have to wait because Rita has to fill in for a staffer who called in sick. At 9:15, Rita finally emerges from her office to greet me.

"I am so sorry; I apologize for the wait. We are just swamped today. This is the third day in a row one of our staffers has called in sick. On a good day, with a full staff, we MIGHT be able to stay on schedule, but when we are down a person or two, forget it. You might as well throw the schedule out the window."

Rita's office is tiny, with one small window looking out onto a parking lot. Papers are piled everywhere and there is barely enough room for two people to talk. We start talking only to be interrupted twice by phone calls.

"This is the problem, right here. I can barely get started talking with you before someone calls or a staffer comes in. I know the state is interested in this new program, but unless there are more resources involved with participating, I just don't see how I can manage it. There is only so much time. Yesterday I was supposed to teach a class on eating with whole grains. By the time class came around we were running behind by almost 2 hours on the schedule. Some clients had been sitting in our wait room for 2 hours to receive individual counseling! I just ended up putting in a DVD about healthy eating and had the class watch it while I helped out with our waiting clients. I had to leave them in there alone to watch a DVD. And that's not the first time; it's the norm around here. Some of those clients have seen that DVD three or more times."

Rita takes me to where they hold nutrition classes. It's a narrow room with a path going down the middle. On the left side are a few rows of chairs and a TV. Rita explains that there's a major shortage of space in the building so she has to share the classroom with another agency.

"There is no room in here to teach the kind of classes the state wants us to teach. I would LOVE to teach a participant-centered class, but show me where I can do that. I can't put the chairs in a circle, it would block the path and there would be a pole in the middle of the circle. Plus it's difficult to get clients to talk when people are walking through the room to get to the other agency. This is what I have to work with. I have no resources to get another room and new furniture. My first priority is getting more staff here, and even that is difficult to do. The state allocated funds in a way that does not account for client load. Some rural agencies are getting almost the same budget we are but serving a fraction of the client load we have. Tell me how I can make this work, and I will listen, but unless you can find funding for more staff it will always be a DVD for our nutrition education classes."

Local Office 33, Wayne County, Mid-April

"Don't even think about talking to her." That was the response I got when I inquired about whom I should talk to at LO 33. It seemed to be an inside joke to which I was not privy. The state staffer chuckled and rolled his eyes before telling me about Janet.

"She has been here for a hundred years! It will be the quickest conversation you have; she never does any of the new programs."

Armed with this information, I truck out to Wayne County to meet Janet. At 64, she is a pleasant lady who is proud to show off her 40-years-of-service plaque, which is now 3 years old.

"I just don't care. I have seen more hair-brained ideas come out of that state office than I would care to remember, and I have probably forgotten half of them. (laughs) When you have been around as long as I have, you just see things differently. Those state people think they know what's best. They graduate with some fancy degree from some big state school and come here determined to change NECC. All these young bloods mean well, but none of them spend anytime at the LOs. They don't know what it is like to actually *do* the programs they create. So I don't bother to do them."

I ask her how she can avoid all these changes, and she laughs.

"Avoid? I don't avoid them; I just don't do them. I have been 'round here long enough no one says anything to me. I have a plan for my LO, and I execute that plan. Sure I tweak it every now and then, but do we really need to change the way we teach so our clients can sit in a circle to talk? No! The clients don't even want to be here. Half of them show up for class late and spend the entire class sending messages on those damn cell phones. The other half of the class has children in tow that are running around making a ruckus. The less we have to 'engage' the clients, the better. They don't want to be engaged. They just want their benefits. Pure and simple."

State Office, Lansing, Early May

Based on the visits I conducted with the three LOs, I created a summary report of my findings and a preliminary implementation plan. I based the plan around the three main obstacles that emerged from my conversations with LO members—successive change fatigue, funding disparities, and staffer resistance.

The plan was a simple four-phase approach to implementation that would address the obstacles while trying to make it appear as if NECC was not making any changes at all. In the plan I explained why each of the four phases was important:

Phase 1: Awareness Cultivation (Approximate Time of Phase: 1–3 Months)

Working with the consultant, a state implementation team should start bringing the staff up to date about the features and benefits of participant-centered nutrition environments. During this phase, the consultant can help guide discussions on what the LO is already doing that is participant centered and what can be done to enhance nutrition education further. The awareness cultivation phase is important for "priming the pump." The staff becomes familiar with the enhancement long before the adoption occurs. This will help reduce change fatigue and minimize the appearance of sudden change.

Phase 2: Preadoption (Approximate Time of Phase: 1 Month)

The second phase of the nutrition education adoption is a logistical one. In this phase, LO directors assess the office's readiness to implement PCLE or new enhancements to the current participant-centered approaches. A key component of this phase is choosing a program champion to build bonds with reticent staffers. Based on material designed by the consultant, LO directors can identify employees that would champion the new program and help build good will among coworkers. Another component of this phase is a needs assessment. LOs should conduct a budget analysis and staffing assessment to see what needs exist in order to implement PCLE at their local offices. LO directors can work with the consultant to develop assessment material that will help identify areas in need of resources.

Phase 3: Adoption (Approximate Time of Phase: 2–8 Months)

Once the first two phases are completed, the LOs can work on adoption or enhancement of participant-centered approaches to nutrition education. This phase starts with a statewide training on PCLE. Once completed, the LOs can continue to adopt new elements of PCLE. At the state level, the needs assessments for each LO can be prioritized and common needs across LOs should be addressed. The consultant should assist in the development of training materials and train-the-trainer programs to ensure consistent implementation across state agencies.

Phase 4: Maintenance (Approximate Time of Phase: Ongoing)

The final phase of the adoption is maintenance. This phase is ongoing and ensures that all staff has a system in place to mentor and monitor the PCLE program. The maintenance phase is imperative to the success of the adoption or enhancement as it allows staff to address issues and concerns with PCLE. This phase also emphasizes the need for ongoing training updates for all staff, and an adapted training program LOs can conduct as new staff joins the NECC family. At the state level, assessment of the program at regular intervals is required to monitor consistent use. On a yearly basis, new LO budgets should be reviewed and prioritized. The consultant should provide guidance on possible assessment and assurance tools to continue the maintenance of the program.

In addition to the summary, I created a sample plan (Appendix 1) based on my findings. I also provided a blank plan (Appendix 2) so state staff members could start preparing for the implementation of PCLE.

At the state meeting everyone was excited about the proposal. The state asked if a coaching guide could be created on how to implement the change. In the guide, they wanted to have more information about addressing staff concerns and choosing a champion. The state also wanted a needs assessment form that would be easy for a nonaccountant to use.

By the end of the meeting we were all discussing potential next steps. The statewide conference was coming up in August, and state staffers were hoping to unveil some of these new ideas. The state also asked if I could start producing some material to "kick-start phase one."

I left the meeting with one final suggestion: "If you want to minimize the change, you should try to reduce the jargon you are using. I have heard many of you talking about how PCLE is just 'how education will be at NECC.' If that is the case, maybe you should reduce the use of 'PCLE' and just talk about nutrition education as you normally would, but include more PCLE ideas."

Everyone agreed.

Statewide Conference, Detroit, August

In the 3 months leading up to the statewide conference, I created the requested material for the state. A new "coaching guide" to LO implementation was created with numerous forms and summaries. It was a toolkit-type guide with documents intended for use by LO directors. In addition, several internal newsletters were created and a new nutrition-focused blog began to help increase awareness. Finally, we removed all wording about PCLE to focus on this program as just a part of "what we already do here at NECC."

The conference was supposed to highlight the information in the guide and discuss ways to build awareness for the new nutrition education program. Every LO director was asked to attend. Just prior to the beginning of the conference I was pulled aside by a state staffer.

"I wanted to let you know that we have decided to make a few changes to the documents you have written up. We decided it was best to give the program a name so we are keeping PCLE. We still want you to make it feel like this is not a change, but the people who created the program wanted there to be a distinction. Also, we love your articles and the blog you have created, but the state is not sure what the legal issues are around posting a blog with this information and the NECC name attached to it. So we are going to have to wait a little before launching the site. You know as they say here, NECC is on the information dirt road."

Soon after, the conference titled, "Changing the Way We Do Nutrition Education: Participant-Centered Learning Environments" began. What followed was a 3-hour presentation on all the changes that were going to occur at the NECC LOs to support PCLE: meetings, trainings, and online in-services.

Back to the drawing board. PCLE has launched, and somehow I need to make it seem like NECC is not changing nutrition education while acknowledging that we are "changing the way we do nutrition education."

As I scanned the room to see people's response to the presentation, I caught Beth's eye. She looked at me, smiled, and sighed. Another dodo for the collection.

Discussion Questions

1. What would you do next? How would you roll out the plan with a staff weary from multiple changes?

2. How can the plan be tailored in a way that agencies with few resources and various clienteles (urban LOs versus rural LOs) feel as if they can implement PCLE?

3. In what ways can the plan be implemented so lifers and young bloods both accept it? What might be their responses, and how will you react to these?

4. What would you have done differently? Would your proposal have looked different when you met with that state in early May?

5. What material and resources would you produce for phase one of the implementation plan knowing that NECC is an "information dirt road"?

FOR FURTHER READING

Lewis, L. K. (1999). Disseminating information and soliciting input during planned organizational change: Implementers' targets, sources and channels for communicating. *Management Communication Quarterly, 13*(1), 43–75.

Lewis, L. K. (2000). "Blindsided by that one" and "I saw that one coming": The relative anticipation and occurrence of communication problems and other problems in implementers' hindsight. *Journal of Applied Communication Research, 28*(1), 44–67.

Lewis, L. K. (2007). An organizational stakeholder model of change implementation communication. *Communication Theory, 17*(2), 176–204.

Miller, V. D., Johnson, J. R., & Grau, J. (1994). Antecedents to willingness to participate in a planned organizational change. *Journal of Applied Communication Research, 22*(1), 59–80.

Zorn, T. E., Christensen, L. T., & Cheney, G. (1999). *Do we really want constant change?* San Francisco: Berrett-Koehler.

APPENDIX 1

PCLE Sample Timeline

Phases	July	Aug	Sept	Oct	Nov	Dec	Jan	Feb	Mar	Apr	May	June
Phase 1: Building Awareness												
Email bi-weekly class "sneak peak"												
Informally discuss participant-centered classes with staff												
Phase 2: Preparation												
Assess staff readiness												
Make training and materials budget												
Select program champion(s)												
Give training resource toolkit to champion												
Phase 3: Adoption												
Conduct agency-wide training on PCLE												
Purchase material and classroom furniture for positive learning environment												
Adopt new classes on NE schedule												
Send ongoing communication about PCLE												
Publish success stories for all staff												
Phase 4: Maintenance												
Provide refresher trainings												
Implement mentoring program for consistent quality of classes												
Assess feedback to adjust classes and schedule trainings												

APPENDIX 2

PCLE Blank Timeline

Phases	July	Aug	Sept	Oct	Nov	Dec	Jan	Feb	Mar	Apr	May	June
Phase 1: Building Awareness												
Phase 2: Preparation												
Phase 3: Adoption												
Phase 4: Maintenance												

WHEN A CONTRACT IS NOT ENOUGH

MARGARET DICOCCO AND MATTHEW J. BORNEMAN

Learning Objectives

- To recognize the importance of creating a clear and comprehensive contract that is equitable to both the client and the consulting firm.
- To recognize the need to evaluate and define both the consulting firm's and potential client's organization value structure prior to contracting.
- To recognize the value of good communication practices throughout a project including the potential of changing contractual obligations based on changing organization needs.

CONSULTING ORGANIZATION OVERVIEW

The Consulting Organization

Deep within America's heartland resides a small, private consulting firm housed within a graduate psychology program. Designed to act as a practicum for graduate students pursuing doctoral degrees in applied psychology, the firm functions as an independent entity within the university. Organization members include a program faculty member as the director and program students as associates. Students are required to participate in the consulting firm for a minimum of two full academic years. Student members are termed junior associates during their first year, achieving the status of senior associate based on completing the first year and independently leading a consulting project.

This organization is unique in that it is managed primarily by the associates, with the director acting only as an overseer and advisor. Total associate numbers over the years have ranged from 4 to 12 members and are generally dependent on the number of students accepted for each class, along with the speed at which students move through program requirements.

Most client interest in the firm is generated through word of mouth, but the firm does conduct specific and directed advertising as well. Consulting projects since the firm's inception in 1982 have included such tasks as conducting and analyzing focus groups, performing program evaluations, and facilitating a private educational organization in reconstructing its identity to incorporate a research focused agenda, among many others. Project choice is based on a combination of associate interest, skill level of the associates, and educational value of the project. Project teams consist of a project leader and team members. Consulting projects are generated from clients both inside and outside the university setting.

Consulting Organization Values

Considering the fundamental purpose of the consulting firm is educational growth for its members, one may assume a lack of flexibility within the value framework of the organization. However, because the membership within the firm is transient and the "employment" compulsory for all members, there is a certain degree of fluctuation that can occur within the firm's value structure from project to project and semester to semester. The standard values that do not change are:

1. All decisions pertaining to the consulting aspects of the firm are made by the associates within a democratic framework.

2. The quantity of projects should not interfere with the normal matriculation of members through the hosting academic program.

3. All projects using a research framework will adhere to the ethical standards of research practice.

Negotiating a Contract

One of the benefits to clients in hiring this particular firm for consulting work is the significantly reduced rates charged by the firm. For instance, firm fees at the time of this project consisted of associate hourly billing at $40 an hour and staff hourly billing at $10 an hour. At the time, these fees represented about half of the going rates for independent consultants at the low end. Hourly rates were kept low to ensure a steady stream of clients for the students' development, as well as being indicative of the nonprofit nature of the firm. However, these savings came with drawbacks in the form of the firm associates' weekly availability, clients' receipt of exclusive attention, and the speed of project completion. Being students, all firm members had other pressing responsibilities to the program and were required to provide only 20 hours per week to the firm. Furthermore, associates often work on at least three different projects at any given time of the year, meaning that most associates are minimally team members on multiple projects throughout their membership with the firm.

During the negotiation stage of the relationship with a client, project leaders fully disclose the student status of the firm's associates and explain in great detail the time constraints associated with this type of organization structure.

OVERVIEW OF THE PROJECT

The Consulting Team

For this particular project, the team consisted of a project leader with senior associate status and three team members with junior associate status. The firm's personnel size at the time was nine members; six senior associates and three junior associates.

The Client

This client was a member of the university community. The client heard of the firm via a conversation with the firm's founder and professor emeritus of the program, and worked for a large state agency housed within the university. The client's primary goal for seeking the firm's assistance was to explore the volunteering behaviors of her constituents in an effort to increase volunteer activity within the state.

The Contract

Contracts for this firm follow a very specific template that includes a brief explanation of the primary goals of the project, a detailed description of the firm's role, a detailed description of the client's role, a tentative timeline, and the fee structure. After a few meetings with the client to establish the parameters of the project (entry stage), a memorandum of agreement (MOA) or contract was developed and signed (contracting stage). For this project, the firm's responsibilities included the following.

1. Scholarly literature in various fields pertaining to the assessment of volunteer behavior will be reviewed. Information gained from this search will facilitate the formulation of survey items as well as the creation of a focus group protocol.

2. The focus group protocol will consist of a detailed outline of questions to be discussed within the focus group and moderator scripts to be followed for the conducting of focus groups. Furthermore, a procedural model will be provided, supplying a step-by-step procedure for conducting the focus groups.

3. The survey will focus questions on volunteer intent and attempt to quantify and qualify specific barriers to engaging in volunteer behaviors. Survey items will be constructed based on information gained from the literature reviews as well as specific

information supplied via the focus groups. The survey will be designed to not exceed four pages and will be formatted for scanning responses directly into a database.

4. The parameters will be provided to the client for stratifying the sample. Once demographic proportions are provided, the formula for implementing a stratified proportional random sample also will be provided to the client.

5. Once completed surveys are provided, they will be scanned, data will be cleaned, and analyses will be conducted based on the demographic variables provided for stratification purposes.

6. Analysis results will be compiled into a report consisting of an executive summary followed by tabular and graphical representations of the quantitative data. Responses to qualitative data will be appended to the report.

The client's responsibilities included the following.

1. Client will provide demographic frequency estimations of constituents for the configuration of the stratified proportional random sample.

2. Client will conduct all focus groups and provide the firm with a written summary of the focus groups' proceedings.

3. Client will consult with the firm on the development of the survey.

4. Client will print all surveys and will secure an outside agency to provide the capability for mailing surveys and reminder cards to constituents.

The timeline illustrated completion times for the firm based on the client's timeliness in providing the necessary information. Thus, no specific dates were provided, rather wording was structured as such: "Survey development will be completed 2 weeks post receipt of the summaries from the focus groups, contingent on the timely input from the client." The total value of the contract was estimated at $3,700.

THE CONSULTANT/CLIENT INTERACTIONS

Researching the Survey

Team members followed a standard directed literature search protocol, with each team member seeking applicable literature within different discipline databases (e.g., business, psychology, sociology, education). Team members chose their top five articles, provided annotated bibliographies, highlighted the questions in the studies that would fit best with the survey to be constructed and forwarded them to the project leader. The project leader chose 10 from the entire set to act as the guidelines for survey development. The primary inclusion criteria for this review process included access to the actual survey items, precise scoring instructions, and generalizability of study to the intended population. In addition to the articles found by the team, the project leader also evaluated the articles suggested by the client. The end product identified four themes pervasive within this area of survey research. These themes were presented with justifications for their inclusion, as well as general question types (subthemes) and suggestions for open-ended questions.

The client presented the findings to the agency's board, which approved both the themes and the preliminary items. Additional feedback included suggestions from board members for new survey items as well as kudos for founding the survey on established research findings.

Developing a Focus Group Protocol

Meanwhile, the client was running into budget concerns, and when approached by the project leader with the first draft of the focus group protocol asked the project leader to stop work on the protocol beyond the question set. Instead, the client would run informal focus groups among constituents that attended unrelated events scheduled by the agency. The budget was adjusted to reflect the reduction of hours for focus group protocol development, but a new contract was not developed.

Drafting the Survey

Buoyed by the board's kudos, the first survey draft was based on the literature search theme regulated items and items capturing the suggestions provided by the client and the agency's board. The draft was not formatted to look like a survey, instead providing the fundamental questions (including citations where appropriate) with scaling options and potential areas of concerns or issues that the team thought needed to be addressed when finalizing the items. The meeting to discuss this first draft could have gone better.

The Client: Where is the survey?

Project Leader: This the first draft. We need to nail down the specifics on which questions will be included and what response scaling options to use, as well as the inclusion of qualifying items for some of the items suggested by your board.

The Client: But this doesn't even look like a survey.

Project Leader: No. You're right. However, before we invest the time to format and fit the survey to your specifications of four pages, we need to secure the content.

The Client: Well, I guess that makes sense. But I don't think we need to worry about providing qualifying statements for any of the items, because the board members who suggested the questions didn't say that any qualifying statements were necessary.

Project Leader: I see. However, without the qualifying statements, questions asking participants to rate their satisfaction with their previous volunteer experiences, for instance, could allow them to rate an experience that happened 20 years ago, or could allow them to identify their rating with an experience you would not classify as fitting the parameters of your study.

The Client: Well, I don't think that would be a problem here, or it would have been brought up in the meeting.

Project Leader: Okay then.

The second draft of the survey incorporated the changes discussed in the first draft meeting and more new ideas gathered from another meeting with agency board members. This version of the survey had the preliminary formatting set, but was not yet formatted to fit the required four pages. The client brought some new concerns to this meeting, in the form of a text size requirement and additional survey items. That is, they were to ensure that the survey font size would be large enough to allow a sample with potentially diminished reading vision to easily read each survey item and easily identify the response option that fit them. They were also to increase the number of demographics questions included to allow for additional population segments to be fully identified. This was problematic on one level, as the survey had a page limit. The second problem rolled into sample size estimation.

The client sent the second draft of the survey to external reviewers while the team attempted to accommodate the new changes. A meeting was called by the client to discuss the comments of these external reviewers. Much to the team's dismay, the external reviewers made suggestions that echoed those made by team members in the second draft meeting, namely that the survey needed to provide qualifying items. For the third draft, the client was adamant that these changes needed to be made and was unclear as to why such provisions had not been incorporated in the survey in the first place.

Based on this dizzying conversation, the new rendition of the survey now was to include a grid that tracked past volunteer experiences and evaluated those experiences. This of course, did not fit into any of the themes that had originally been agreed upon. Furthermore, the set up would only capture a partial picture of past volunteering behavior—neither allowing for temporal indices nor time quantities.

All additional drafts followed a similar pattern. Team members would make the changes suggested; the client would come back with new ideas or repeat ideas that were previously rejected.

Stratifying the Sample

While the survey was going through its various draft renditions, the project leader and the client were working on setting the sample stratification limits. The biggest hurdle to overcome came from the client's inability to secure the demographic frequency estimations. Once this task was finally completed, the demographic variables that were required for stratification had increased. This, of course, changed the sample size estimation, which in turn caused a stir, as the client's budget could not afford to sample the number needed to achieve power. The role of power in hypothesis testing and sample size estimation was thoroughly explained to the client, with little estimated impact. The biggest frustration in this area for the firm came in the client's inability to provide hypothesis statements, rather providing vague generalities that spoke of a need for comparisons without providing the substance of what should be compared and why.

It was during the last conversation with the client on this topic that the firm began to harbor very significant concerns about its client's values. Specifically, the client was consistently concerned about budget constraints. With talk of increasing the sample size, the client began looking for additional ways to save money. Her solution, as told to the project leader, was to track constituent survey completion in order to only send out reminder cards to participants who had not yet submitted their survey. The client was reminded by the project leader that to engage in such a tracking practice would require a change in the Human Subjects Application that removed the statement guaranteeing anonymity.

Pursuing Approval From the Institutional Review Board

As is the custom of this firm, due to the academic framework within which the firm works, once the survey began to move toward completion, the team began to draft a Human Subjects Application. The client was informed of this procedure, and based on goal changes over the course of the project, was very supportive of the idea. The protocol of the Human Subjects Application was submitted to the Institutional Review Board for approval with the client's support.

Muddying the Waters

Unbeknownst to the firm, the client was consulting with other members of the university community and members of the board about the potential of expanding the application of the study to include publishing findings in a professional setting. It was from these outside sources that the client experienced a change in expectations and desires with regard to the content of the survey and the development process that was involved in creating the final product. Thus, the client began making changes to both the survey and the survey dissemination protocol without consulting with the firm.

Additionally, as the client's aspirations for the project grew, the staff in the agency was increased to include a part-time graduate assistant who was dedicated solely to working on this project. As time wore on, the client began chastising the firm for not being as efficient as the graduate assistant, acknowledging neither the difference in time constraints between the two parties nor the specific parameters for the literature search set forth within the contract.

Not until the project leader received another approval letter from the Institutional Review Board did the firm realize that the client had resubmitted the Human Subjects Application with the firm's name and credentials. Meaning, the firm had no chance to review and approve changes that could affect its reputation within the research and professional community. This prompted the project leader to call a face-to-face meeting with the client, which included the director of the firm.

The Final Straw?

The tension at the meeting was palpable. The client was agitated about what she considered to be the firm's lack of competency. The project leader was agitated about the client's implications of incompetency, as well as the secret submission of the new Human Subjects Application. The director was concerned that the client might feel outnumbered, but recognized the need to be there to support the project leader.

The discussion began with a recap of the terms of the contract. The project leader provided a copy of the signed contract and a defense of the firm's actions relative to the contract parameters. The discussion then moved to the client's submission of a new Human Subject's Application.

Project Leader: You can imagine our surprise when we received an approval letter for the new version of the Human Subjects Application.

The Client: Well, we were concerned that the process was taking too long, so we submitted the new application with our new version of the survey.

Project Leader: We certainly recognize your desire to move forward with this project. However, I feel compelled to point out that not only did you submit the new application with our firm listed as the responsible party, you also failed to remove the statement about guaranteeing anonymity to the participants and to disclose the use of tracking numbers within the procedures.

The Client: Oh, I am certain that this will be no big deal. We are only going to use the tracking numbers to reduce the cost of mailing reminders. It is anonymous enough for that.

At this point the project leader gave a brief, but thorough rundown on the ethical obligations researchers have with regards to their participants. To which the client stated. "Oh, ethics, schmethics! I'm not interested in publishing this in a high-quality, scholarly journal. We just want to publish this in one of the smaller, industry-related journals. We're not trying to do real research here."

The meeting drew quickly to a close.

Discussion Questions

1. One could say that this particular consulting relationship was heading for trouble from the start. What could the consultants have done differently in the entry stage to avoid the problems encountered once the contract was in place?

2. Due to the fact that a contract was signed by both parties, one may assume that the contracting meeting was a success. However, based on the problems encountered once the project was underway, what aspects of the contracting process (with regard to purposes of contracting) were not clearly defined?

3. Identify when and how the consultants could have employed the principles of recontracting to facilitate a more cooperative relationship with the client.

4. When the client pushed for the consultants to ignore one of the fundamental rights of participants, it became obvious to the consultants that a value conflict had reared its ugly head into this consulting project. How could the consultants have uncovered this potential conflict prior to the shocking exposure during the meeting described at the end of the case scenario?

FOR FURTHER READING

Anderson, D. L. (2010). *Organization development: The process of leading organizational change.* Thousand Oaks, CA: Sage. See particularly "Core Values and Ethics of Organization Development" (pp. 35–54), "The Organization Development Practitioner and the Consulting Process" (pp. 83–100), and "Entry and Contracting" (pp. 101–116).

Cady, S. H., & Lewis, M. J. (2002). Organization development and the bottom line: Linking soft measures and hard measures. In J. Waclawski & A. H. Church (Eds.), *Organization development: A data-driven approach to organizational change* (pp. 127–146). San Francisco: Jossey-Bass.

Rousseau, D. M. (2005). *Psychological contracts in organizations: Understanding written and unwritten agreements.* Thousand Oaks, CA: Sage.

Vaux, A., & Stockdale, M. S. (1992). Applied research consultants (ARC): A service and training model. In A. Vaux, M. S. Stockdale, & M. J. Schwerin (Eds.), *Independent consulting for evaluators* (pp. 196–211). Newbury Park, CA: Sage.

Measuring Organizational Effectiveness in the Nonprofit Sector

The Case of the Community Action Network

Matt Koschmann

Learning Objectives

- To help you understand the complicated issue of measuring organizational effectiveness in the nonprofit sector.
- To recognize the tensions in the nonprofit sector between "businesslike" approaches to organization development and more holistic approaches to service provision.
- To learn more about the role of communication and the "social construction" of organizational effectiveness.

It was a sunny Friday morning in Austin, Texas, the summer heat and humidity already making their presence felt at 9:00 a.m. I stepped into a coffee shop on Congress Avenue, welcoming the air-conditioned contrast and quickly scanning the room for an open seat. It had been a long week working with my various consulting clients, so it was nice to get out of the office for a change of scenery as I embarked on a new project. After ordering a drink, I settled into a comfortable armchair near the window and placed a manila folder full of papers on the coffee table in front of me.

The folder was given to me by Luke Sorenson,[1] an old college friend who now worked in the nonprofit community. Luke was the director of the Community Action Network (CAN), a large collaboration of nonprofit organizations and government agencies that work on social services and community development in the city of Austin. Recently I agreed to offer my consulting services to the CAN after Luke told me about their need for some organizational expertise.

Last month Luke and I met for lunch, and he explained how a lot of changes were happening in the nonprofit community in response to the economic downturn, and people were starting to get nervous. There was more demand on the system because of unemployment, but less money and services available because of budget cuts and decreased tax revenues. Many of the CAN's partner organizations had to rethink their relationships with various funding sources—like private foundations and government grants—and competition for resources was getting fierce. In particular, there was more pressure from funders for nonprofits to measure and demonstrate the effectiveness of their organizations.

Since the CAN operated as somewhat of a hub or clearinghouse for the nonprofit community, they thought it would be valuable to do some research and create a report about measuring organizational effectiveness in the nonprofit sector, something official and authoritative their partners could use to inform their decisions and that they could share with various funding agencies, Luke explained to me. But they needed someone from outside the nonprofit community for the report to be credible. That's where I came in.

After some negotiation, I agreed to work on the project. What they needed was an executive report about measuring organizational effectiveness in the nonprofit sector. They needed to know how best to think about this issue, with recommendations for both nonprofit organizations and funding agencies. I had about 4 months to work on this project. The CAN had one of their semiannual meetings of all their partner organizations coming up toward the end of the year, and we decided that would be a good time to present the report.

Yesterday, Luke had stopped by my office to drop off the folder that I was now paging through. He had done some preliminary research to help me get started, a loose collection of newspaper clippings, photocopies of articles from academic journals, and a contact list of various people in the Austin nonprofit community.

I decided to start with a little background reading to get acquainted with some of the main issues. I began with the stack of research articles Luke compiled. The first two were from a couple of professors at the University of Missouri—Kansas City, Robert Herman and David Renz. Their most recent publication was a compilation of "theses" about nonprofit organizational effectiveness they developed during the past 10 years of researching this topic.

First, they concluded, nonprofit effectiveness is always a matter of comparison, although it is important to differentiate among different types of nonprofit organizations. Effectiveness is also multidimensional—nonprofits should use many different criteria to measure their effectiveness. Additionally, nonprofit effectiveness is related to the organization's board of directors and the use of "correct" management practices, like strategic planning and financial forecasting. However, it is doubtful that there are any universally applicable best practices that are appropriate for all nonprofit managers and boards of directors. Next, nonprofit effectiveness is a "social construction," meaning that effectiveness is only "real" in the sense that people believe and act "as if" effectiveness was real;

effectiveness does not exist apart from the beliefs and actions of other people. This doesn't mean that effectiveness is arbitrary or doesn't have material consequences, but it does mean that effectiveness is best thought of as an "achievement" of organizational members and other stakeholders who convince each other that an organization is pursuing the right objectives in the right way. Also, "organizational responsiveness" is a useful way to measure effectiveness in the nonprofit sector. Finally, the level of analysis (i.e., interpersonal, group, or organizational) makes a difference when assessing nonprofit organizational effectiveness.

"Lots to consider here," I thought to myself. But at least this gave me a good foundation for thinking about organizational effectiveness in the nonprofit sector.

I paged through the rest of the folder to scan the other materials. The list of personal contacts caught my attention. The first name on the list was Dr. Laurie Lewis, a professor in the Communication Studies Department at the University of Texas. Luke's notes said she was an expert in organizational communication, with an emphasis on the nonprofit sector. Seemed like someone I should talk to. And since she was right here in Austin, I called her office and made an appointment for the following day.

I stepped off the elevator on the seventh floor of the Jesse H. Jones Communication Center and made my way down the hall to Professor Lewis' office. I was greeted warmly by Professor Lewis and settled into her office. I reiterated a few things I mentioned on the phone about my project, and then asked her to share her thoughts about organizational effectiveness in the nonprofit sector.

"The first thing you need to know is that nonprofit effectiveness is intimately connected to the mission of the organization. Missions are at the heart of a nonprofit organization's identity, and nonprofits are effective to the extent they are fulfilling their missions. But that's the challenge, because nonprofit missions are notoriously difficult to measure," she explained.

"Why is that?" I asked.

"The problem is things that are easy to measure are not always the most important things for nonprofit organizations. You can easily measure your budget or material resources; you can even measure the number of clients you help or services you provide. But for many nonprofits the concern is more about the *quality* of those services and interactions with clients. Is it more 'effective' to serve 200 clients in a month, or have very transformative and productive meetings with only a dozen clients in the same month? Probably some combination of both, but that is very difficult to measure. In the for-profit world it's pretty straightforward to focus on the financial metrics of profits or return on investment. But a lot of those concepts don't translate well to the nonprofit sector. And nonprofit organizations are interested in impacting things that are difficult to quantify, like social improvement or personal well-being. Plus, many nonprofits have ambitious missions that are difficult to measure. If a nonprofit's mission is to end racism and discrimination, have they failed if racism still exists in our society? Of course not. But it still begs the question, how do we know this organization is effective and achieving its mission?"

We talked for a while about nonprofit organizations she worked with in her research and how they measured the effectiveness of their work. It sounded like there were many divergent perspectives, so I knew I'd have to keep digging.

As we wrapped up our conversation, there was still one question on my mind.

"One more thing before I go. You're a professor of communication. How does communication relate to this concept of organizational effectiveness, especially in the nonprofit sector?"

"Oh, I'm glad you asked. Too often we think about communication as a simple process of message exchange between senders and receivers. But communication is much more dynamic than that. Communication actually plays a role in *constituting* the very relationships and organizational realities we take for granted."

"Does this have to do with the 'social construction' of organizational effectiveness?" I asked, thinking back to Herman and Renz's research.

"Absolutely. A concept like organizational effectiveness is not just some objective standard we try to live up to, but rather an understanding we create together through interactions with various stakeholders of the organization. It is through communication that organizational members develop notions of effectiveness, success, or failure, and these understandings continue to exist—or not—in our interactions with other people. So from my perspective, you can't fully understand organizational effectiveness without a good understanding of how communication creates and sustains this concept in organized systems of collective activity."

"So you're not saying that organizational effectiveness in the nonprofit sector is just about talk," I said.

"No, no . . . not at all. What I mean is that any concept, such as organizational effectiveness, exists in the ongoing negotiations and interactions of organizational members and stakeholders who are relevant to the organization. There are different perspectives and opinions about what makes a particular nonprofit effective; there aren't some obvious objective criteria that we all agree on. Therefore whatever constitutes effectiveness for a particular nonprofit organization will result from various interactions and agreements, all of which can change over time and become more (or less) stable. It doesn't mean that there aren't real material influences or consequences related to effectiveness, but only to say that any notion of effectiveness for nonprofit organizations exists within communication. That's why I think communication scholars have so much to add to our understanding of organizational effectiveness in the nonprofit sector."

This idea of organizational effectiveness being socially constructed was still a bit confusing to me, but the communicative aspect of organizational effectiveness was starting to make sense, especially as I thought back to Luke's comments about nonprofits having to establish and justify the effectiveness of their organizations in relation to various groups, like funding agencies, volunteers, individual donors, and even clients. This all happened through communication.

At this point I knew I needed to learn more about what was going on in the Community Action Network, and what their collaborative partners thought about measuring organizational effectiveness. Over the next month and a half I set up several meetings with various people who worked for the CAN's partner organizations.

One of those people was Lucinda Beckett, the director of the local United Way chapter. We met one afternoon in her office in East Austin. As a member of the executive team for the CAN, she was already familiar with the work I was doing and was anxious to talk with me.

"This is such an important topic," she began, "because it cuts to the heart of the work we do and our ability to sustain our work into the future. All nonprofits want to do good work, but we must demonstrate to others that we are actually doing good work and that our organizations are effective. Nonprofits usually don't generate their own revenue and there are many legal restrictions about how they can invest financial profits back into their operations, so they are dependent on others for the very resources they need to survive. Therefore we have to be able to measure and demonstrate our organizational effectiveness to other stakeholders, especially funding agencies. But *how* to do that is the million-dollar question. Many in the business community want us to identify objective measures and quantify our activities. You can do that with things like operations management and financial accounting, and we do. But when you try to measure the overall impact of services on someone's life, then you have a very different measurement factor than most business are used to. It's hard to quantify much of the work we do. I can tell you how many people we have in each program, how many meals or services we provide in a given week, or how many dollars we allocate per client. But that doesn't really tell you much about the quality or impact of our work. It gives us some tangible numbers that look good in a report, but it doesn't get to the heart of the issue: life transformation for people who need our help."

"So what's the alternative?" I asked.

"Well, if the business community has a tendency to be overly practical, many in the nonprofit sector have a tendency to be overly idealistic. They think we should focus on doing quality work, regardless of how the numbers play out. If we have to spend more money on a particular client, so be it. If we have to spend more time on a particular problem in a given week, then that's what we should do. We shouldn't have to answer to number crunchers who keep their hands clean from a safe distance. We're in there doing the hard work and we should be supported regardless. Now, I think the answer is somewhere in the middle. Somehow we need to be able to measure certain aspects of our work, but we also need to demonstrate the quality of our work apart from quantitative metrics. Part of me thinks that's not totally fair, that we shouldn't have to make all the adjustments and concessions. But the reality today is that the funding agencies are writing the checks that we need to operate, so the burden is on us to demonstrate our effectiveness."

"You mentioned the answer being somewhere in the middle. Do you have a sense of what that could look like?" I asked.

"Kind of. Like I said before, it's important for nonprofits to quantify and measure those things that are quantifiable: finances, material resources, personnel, certain aspects of service delivery, etc. But for other things, I think it has more to do with creating a relevant process and evaluating the overall quality of that process."

"What do you mean by that?" I asked.

"Think about it like this," she said as she reached for a little prop on her desk, one of those Newton's Cradles that has five suspended metal balls that swing back and forth. "If I swing the first ball it hits the others and makes the ball on the end move. The first ball has no contact with the last ball, but the momentum and energy of the first ball passes through the system and eventually impacts the last ball. So we can't say that the first ball has a direct influence on the last ball—they never touch. But we can say the first ball has an indirect influence, especially if the balls in the middle are lined up in such a way as to capture the energy of the first ball and transfer it to the last ball. I think a lot of things we do in the nonprofit sector work the same way. It's very difficult to measure the direct impact of many things we do. How do we know that the extra time we spend with a kid in an after-school program directly impacts his grades or relationship with his parents? How do we know that a literacy program at the homeless shelter was directly related to a client getting a job at a particular organization? We don't. But we do know many of the important factors that relate to the outcomes we're trying to influence. For example, we know that learning in school is influenced by things like parental support, nutrition, literacy, and access to technology. We don't know exactly how each one directly contributes to learning, but we do know that kids who learn well have all of these. So our job is to line up all those things—the balls—and put some energy and momentum into the system. If we are doing that, then we can make a good argument that the positive outcomes on the other end are a result of our work, or that our efforts eventually will lead to positive outcomes. So in terms of demonstrating our organizational effectiveness, our job is to explain the processes needed to influence the important outcomes, and then show how our work is facilitating and supporting those processes."

I wrapped up my conversation with Lucinda and headed back to my office to start summarizing my notes. Lucinda mentioned one key person she thought I should contact: Larry Schell, the director of the Austin Foundation, a large private foundation that supported many of the social service and community development initiatives in the Austin area. Larry was the chief financial officer at a large technology corporation for 20 years before he left to direct the Austin Foundation. I called his secretary and made an appointment for later that week.

"I always wanted to be involved in philanthropy and foundation work, and my experience and success in the business world enabled me to do that at this point in my career," Larry explained as we sat down in his office on the 21st floor of the Frost Building in downtown Austin.

"With all your experience you must have some opinions about measuring effectiveness in the nonprofit sector," I said, inviting him to share his thoughts.

"Honestly, I'd like to see the CAN and many of its partners move more toward a business model of operations. I know people pooh-pooh that and think the big bad business people are trying to take over the nonprofit sector. 'Where's the compassion? Where's the service?' they say. Well, if you're out of money and you have to close your doors, then who are you helping? I know it sounds harsh to some people to talk about nonprofit work in terms of efficiency and productivity, but the truth is at the end of the day we're talking about finances and resources, and you need to have an effective way to manage these things. I care about children and the homeless as much as the next guy, that's why I believe so strongly about the need to run a good organization—so we can serve more people. Our foundation has a limited amount of money we can devote to various projects, and we want that money to go to good use. Of course you can't quantify everything, but that doesn't mean you don't have standards and hold people accountable."

Larry explained more about his perspective, providing examples of nonprofit organizations that had to shut down because of their inability to measure their impact and secure funding from donors and foundations. He also talked about "successful" nonprofits that could show a clear "return on investment" and consistently demonstrate their ability to "move the needle" on important community indicators, like high school graduation rates or incidents of domestic violence.

"At the end of the day, these are the types of organizations we as a foundation like to support, and they are the organizations that survive in today's economic environment," Larry explained.

Larry had another meeting with a city official in a few minutes, so we finished our conversation. I quickly asked him if there was anyone else he thought I should talk to about these issues. "You really should meet with Roderick Bufkin. He runs the big homeless shelter downtown. He and I don't always see eye-to-eye on everything, but he's an important voice in this community and his perspectives should be part of your report." He offered a quick handshake as we left his office.

I stopped at a café after my meeting with Larry to grab a quick bite to eat and organize my notes from our conversation. Since I was downtown and near the homeless shelter, I thought I'd get in contact with Roderick right away and see if he was available.

"Good timing," Roderick said. "One of my afternoon appointments was cancelled, so I've got a free hour if you want to meet."

I took a final bite of my lunch, left some money on the table for the waitress and hurried off to the homeless shelter a few blocks away.

"I've been working in the nonprofit sector a long time," Roderick began after a quick introduction.

"One of the trends I'm seeing that I don't like is this continual push for nonprofits to become more 'businesslike.' It's not that I don't think we need to be financially responsible and make good use of our resources. Of course we need to; that's just common sense. But in my experience the phrase 'businesslike' is usually code for efficiency and competition, and it's used to talk about money and resources in ways that favors certain interests above others. Take for example the work we do at the homeless shelter. One of the biggest problems related to homelessness is mental illness. People who can't function at a normal mental capacity are going to have a much more difficult time holding down a job and being responsible for a place to live. But people with mental illnesses are incredibly difficult to work with. There are no easy solutions, and progress is very slow and incremental. That means we need to spend more time and resources working with people who are mentally ill. And we should; that's what our organization is all about. But we're getting more pressure from our board and some of our funders to make our dollars go further. That means we can't devote the resources we need to people with mental illnesses. Sure, it would be easier and more 'efficient' to send people with mental illnesses away from our shelter to the overcrowded state mental facility. That would certainly free up a lot more of *our* time and resources, and we could show a better 'return on investment' because our staff could spend more time with more clients. But we aren't here to just be an efficient organization; we're here to 'serve the least of these' in our society. Funders need to believe in the value of our mission and trust that we are doing good, important—and yes, sometimes inefficient—work; not hold us to 'meeting our numbers,' 'hitting our metrics,' or any other business buzz word you can think of. So the challenge for us is to continually communicate with our funders and other stakeholders about the quality of our work and our contribution to society."

Hearing that reminded me of what Professor Lewis said about communication and organizational effectiveness, that nonprofits need constant interactions with key stakeholders in order to establish and maintain perceptions about the effectiveness of their organizations. I thought this was related also to what Herman and Renz meant by the "social construction" of organizational effectiveness.

I wrapped up my conversation with Roderick, and he gave me a brief tour of the homeless shelter before I left. "What you're doing is very significant," Roderick said as we shook hands in the front lobby of the homeless shelter. "This report is going to be valuable for all the nonprofits and funding agencies in this community. Just remember the important work we're doing here at the shelter and the need to think about organizational effectiveness in a more holistic way."

Over the next couple of weeks I had many other similar conversations with various members of the CAN's partner organizations, as well as representatives from funding agencies and others supporting the nonprofit community. Definitely lots of perspectives to balance.

By now my research was starting to converge around several key ideas. The CAN partner meeting was a week away and I was excited to talk about all the interesting and valuable things I learned about organizational effectiveness in the nonprofit sector. I sat down at my computer and began writing my report.

Discussion Questions

1. If you were the consultant in this case, what five recommendations would you develop for your report about organizational effectiveness in the nonprofit sector? Consider not just explanations about what organizational effectiveness is, but specific things nonprofits and funding agencies should do as a result of your analysis.

2. What exactly does it mean for organizational effectiveness to be a "social construction"? As the consultant in this case, how would you explain this in your report? Can you think of other relevant organizational concepts that are socially constructed?

(Continued)

(Continued)

3. In general, who are the important stakeholders in the nonprofit sector? How do these stakeholders relate to understanding the concept of organizational effectiveness? What do nonprofit organizations need to do to be perceived as effective by these various stakeholders?

4. One of the biggest challenges for organizational practitioners is to develop process and outcome metrics (numerical measurements) to evaluate the success of any organizational program or intervention. What sorts of performance metrics are relevant for nonprofit organizations? If an important aspect of a nonprofit organization's work cannot be quantified, how else can this work be measured and evaluated?

5. Think of a nonprofit organization you are familiar with (maybe a homeless shelter, a religious organization, an environmental group, or a political association). If you provided financial support to this organization—as an individual or an institutional funder—what do you want to see accomplished with your money? What aspects of this organization's work should be measured and evaluated? How will you know if the processes and outcomes of this organization are successful?

NOTE

1. This case is based on research conducted by the author. Pseudonyms are used to protect anonymity, but all the organizations, events, and places are real. Some situations have been combined or adapted for educational purposes.

FOR FURTHER READING

Balser, D., & McClusky, J. (2005). Managing stakeholder relationships and nonprofit organization effectiveness. *Nonprofit Management & Leadership, 15*(3), 295–315.

Frumkin, P. (2002). *On being nonprofit: A conceptual and policy primer.* Cambridge, MA: Harvard University Press.

Herman, R., & Renz, D. (1999). Theses on nonprofit organizational effectiveness. *Nonprofit and Voluntary Sector Quarterly, 28*(2), 107–126.

Herman, R., & Renz, D. (2008). Advancing nonprofit organizational effectiveness research and theory: Nine theses. *Nonprofit Management & Leadership, 18*(4), 399–415.

Lewis, L. K. (2005). The civil society sector: A review of critical issues and research agenda for organizational communication scholars. *Management Communication Quarterly, 19*(2), 238–267.

Case 17

NOT IN WATERTIGHT COMPARTMENTS

Service Quality Improvement and Organization Development

PAOLA FALCONE

Learning Objectives

- To help you see how both analysts and consultants need to adopt a systemic approach to the case on which they are working.
- To focus your attention on the need for coherence among diagnosis, intervention design, and intervention evaluation.
- To focus your attention on the evaluation stage.

THE ORGANIZATION

Alpha Rehabilitation Services (ARS) is a private organization operating in the health care sector. It offers services of diagnosis and rehabilitation. Founded in 1996, ARS has grown over the years, increasing both number and typology of services offered. Present service offerings include the treatment of motor pathologies, as well as cognitive and language ones (e.g., patients suffering from aphasia, for whom it is difficult to remember and to speak). The organization's core values are the absolute centrality of the patient, service personalization, and a high-quality service. It is a long-term personnel-intensive activity: treatments can go on for many months, even more than a year in the most serious cases.

The age of patients asking for ARS services is heterogeneous, ranging from 2 years old of the youngest patient to 86 for the oldest patient.

In spite of being mass-market companies, those in the health care sector usually take more time to get their brand popular on the market. So, ARS took longer to grow. The organization slowly became known and visible in the market and was appreciated by the community of clinicians—doctors influence the patients' choice of private rehabilitation services—and satisfied patients started positive word of mouth. This all contributed to increasing the number of patients.

ARS has modern, well-organized headquarters: rooms and common spaces are distributed on the three large floors of a building located in a central area of the town. Adequate equipment and a hospitable, pleasant environment provide the framework for the work of the staff, which is the real strength of the organization. As the staff plays a crucial role in the quality of service delivery, the management of human resources has been particularly careful. Selective recruitment, regular professional updating, regular growth stimuli, space for personal creativity, and rewarding mechanisms are some of the tools used to increase both the motivation of the staff and the organizational quality.

THE EMERGING PROBLEM

A fall in the quality of supplied services occurred in a sudden, subtle, and casual fashion. This was really anomalous, as service quality had always been of a very high level, constituting a strength and a source of pride for ARS. The general director decided to inquire into the situation with the help of a consulting team.

THE FIRST MEETING

On the morning of April 15, consultants Paul Wilson and Valery Mead entered Dr. Harris' office. He was the general director of ARS.

As Dr. Harris clearly stated from the beginning, ARS's service quality had always been a feather in its cap. Patients and their care were absolutely of central importance. Nevertheless, recently things had not been the same. As the director explained, some complaints from the patients had focused their attention on some quality gaps. There had been occasional episodes, which may not have received such attention from other companies. But they were new to ARS and Dr. Harris feared they could be indicative of a new trend, and if so, had to be interrupted. The company had an ISO 9001 quality certification, but even more importantly, it was a benchmark in the field and its strategic positioning on the market relied on quality service. It would have been easy to lose everything they had been building over the years.

Both the consultants and Dr. Harris agreed that the organization was not so different from a patient one observes in order to formulate a diagnosis—in this case an organizational one—and to identify therapeutically effective solutions. They agreed to meet again 2 weeks later to discuss the situation. By that time the consultants would have gathered all the information and produced a written report with their observations, diagnosis, and the identification and description of some intervention proposals. At the end of the meeting, the consultants asked for some documentation in order to start studying the case: company revenues of the past 5 years; number of treated patients; organizational chart; and list of the personnel, with names, age, roles, type of contract, and seniority in the organization.

Paul and Valery spent the rest of the day analyzing these documents and planning the work for the following 2 weeks.

THE DOCUMENT ANALYSIS

ARS was a healthy organization, from both an economic and financial point of view. Revenues had grown over time in proportion to an increase in the number of patients. Costs had grown in proportion to the growth of the volume of activity, but their accounting had been careful. Profit was not so high, but this was not a problem for company owners committed to developing the organization. The number of ARS clients increased through the years almost regularly by 10% to 15% per year. But in 2009 the positive trend underwent a remarkable increase, rising 44% compared to the previous year, as clients grew from 125 to 180 per year. Also, the number of staff had progressively been growing over time, in proportion to the new volumes of patients asking for treatment (See Figure 17.1).

Figure 17.1   Staff Numbers Over the Years

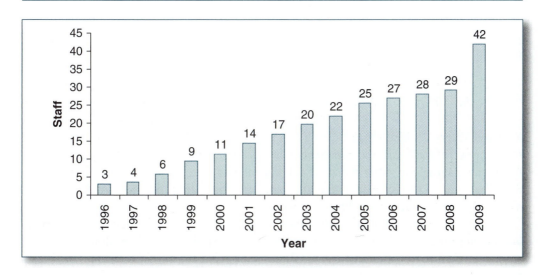

Figure 17.2 The Organizational Chart of ARS

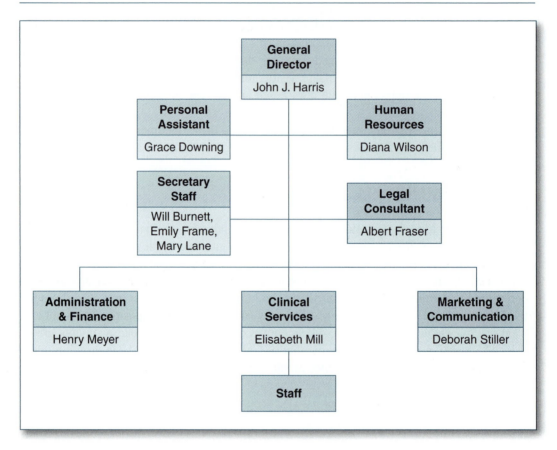

At the moment of the analysis, the staff was composed of 42 individuals, including full-time and part-time therapists and specialists.

STARTING THE INTERVIEWS

Paul and Valery decided to start with a series of interviews with the general director, the staff, the secretarial staff, those patients who had complained about some quality defections, and a sample of other patients. The consultants started from the latter, contacting them by phone. They verified that the patients' complaints did not concern clinical aspects, but organizational and relational ones.

Most of the reasons for the dissatisfaction (see Table 17.1) regarded two points: the last-minute modifications in the scheduled time for therapies and the prolonged times to receive clinical reports or certification. Both members of the clinical staff and the secretarial staff were responsible for writing them.

Table 17.1 Check Sheet for Errors and Other Causes of Client Dissatisfaction

Type of Problem	Frequency	Impact on Client Dissatisfaction
Lack of Time to Talk With the Staff	20	High
Calls to Modify Scheduled Time for Therapies	15	High
Prolonged Waiting Time for Clinical Reports and Certifications	12	High
Exchange of Clinical Records	1	Very high

In addition, relatives of the patients complained that in recent months therapists did not have enough time for consultations anymore. Those consultations regarded the patient's condition, progress, and prognosis, as well as information about their care at home. Those discussions with therapists had been informed and reassured them. Clearly the consultations were important to the relatives interviewed and their decline was seen as a lack of attention toward them.

As they met at the end of the day to assess the situation, Paul and Valery agreed that the operations performed and the structure appeared to be working well. However the negative quality dimensions had an indirect negative impact on the ARS image (see Figure 17.3).

Figure 17.3 Quality Assessment After the First Interviews of Complaining Patients

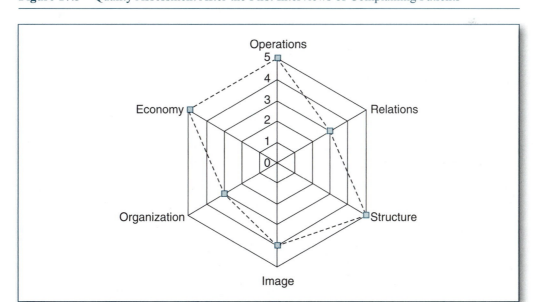

At this point, the case seemed easy to resolve. With just some very small procedural corrections everything would have been all right. But there was still something missing. Paul and Valery knew that in organizations, and most of all in service ones, things are rarely found in watertight compartments, and they elected to continue with internal interviews.

A PROBLEM OF SERVICE QUALITY DECREASE OR SOMETHING MORE?

Internal Interviews

From the internal interviews conducted in the subsequent 2 days, Paul and Valery received some more relevant information. The organization appeared to be based on two main pillars:

- The operational one: the secretarial staff
- The strategic one: Dr. Harris

The secretarial staff was the lynchpin of the process flow, being more or less involved in every organizational process. Their activity had peaks in the busiest hours of the day and during the past year had radically increased. It was a good team, manifesting team spirit, always available to satisfy both staff and patients' needs. During the interviews, the secretarial staff showed a high commitment and they were aware of the fact that they held the whole organization together. Using the clinical metaphor, the secretarial staff was the nervous system of the organization.

The other pillar was Dr. Harris, a charismatic leader. Respected and esteemed, he had a prestigious background given his qualifications and professional experience. He was fully trusted by the ARS owners and members. He was nominated general director in 2000 and, since then, he had never been the subject of any controversial episode during the management of ARS. Even though he was very busy with the direction of the organization, he always tried to find time for staff meetings, talks, and training. He was always in his office and remained informed about what was going on, as well as being the first to arrive in the morning and the last to leave at night. No one knew anything about his private life, and some doubted he really had one outside of ARS. He was directly responsible for the success of ARS as he had brought it to quality certification and introduced all the innovations that had made it a leading organization. He had personally chosen and trained all of his collaborators. For him it was important to know that he could count on his own team in every way. He promoted the values of trust, cooperation, and innovation.

As the consultants clearly realized, the staff was very satisfied and proud to work under his direction. He had a clear vision of the organization: to make ARS the first rehabilitation service provider in the country for top-quality integrated rehabilitation.

In ARS, patients could find the best answer to different associated problems concerning the motor, as well as the cognitive and neural, sphere. He knew that this would take years to accomplish, but he strongly believed in it and his vision would guide the organizational work needed. Using a clinical metaphor again, Dr. Harris was the mind and the heart of ARS.

THE ORGANIZATIONAL INTERNAL STRUCTURE: AN INNER SPLIT

From the interviews of the staff members, consultants learned something very interesting that had not been revealed from the organizational chart, nor had emerged from the interview to Dr. Harris. The 42 clinical collaborators were actually two different groups: the group of the "older" 30 and the group of the "new" 12 who had been recently hired.

The "Older" Group

This group was made up of those who had been in the organization for the longest time. Highly committed toward ARS, they felt they were the gatekeepers and guarantors both of the organization and its reputation. They felt valuable to the organization given their skills. They shared Dr. Harris' view, vision, and approach to work and had been trained under his supervision. They were fully aware of the fact that quality is a multidimensional concept and that all its dimensions are to be considered.

They complained about the need to rush all day and that they had little time to spend with both colleagues and the patients' relatives. In addition, as a result of the higher volumes of activity, Dr. Harris had not, of late, spent much time in meetings, training sessions, and informal talks with them as he had before. They missed this, as Dr. Harris was their leader. They were aware and committed, but consultants realized that daily routines, plus the overload of tasks, had somehow made them lose contact with the vision of the organization.

When asked about the episodes of low-quality service, they mostly attributed them to the high workload for both the staff and the secretaries. Some indicated the existence of a high level of internal split, referring in particular to the newly hired staff members. During the interviews they frequently labeled them "the new ones." They perceived their new colleagues to be less experienced, less committed, and adhering less to ARS's values and culture. The internal human resources policy included a well-defined entry training program (in terms both of times and contents) and tutorship of the new members by the older ones as an integration mechanism. Recently, however, this had not happened. In fact, due to the urgent need for a high number of new personnel, there had been no opportunity to train the newly hired staff in the usual methods, systems, and procedures. In effect, the organization was a two-speed one, with different performances.

To reduce this discrepancy, an older member revealed, patients with more severe pathology levels were not put under the charge of the newer staff. Consultants gained the impression that older members perceived their new colleagues as "extra hands" for the new needs of ARS. Older staff members did not know the new ones very well; during coffee breaks or lunch time each group would spend time with members of its own group. This also was facilitated by the different locations of their rooms on the first and second floors of the building.

The "New Ones"

The new members were gratified to work for such an important company. They had previously worked for minor organizations at the lowest salary rates and were satisfied with these new conditions. They felt valuable to the organization because they had been hired as a supplementary workforce helping it face an increased demand for care. However, they did not show a high level of awareness of the organization and its values. To the consultants, they really did not seem as focused as the older ones were on the multidimensional nature of quality. For them *quality* had one meaning: being therapeutically effective. Both organizational and relational factors were for them absolutely secondary with respect to the centrality of the therapeutic performance.

They knew ARS was a learning organization and they complained that they had not had the opportunity to get the same training their predecessors had before. They seldom had occasion for internal training and exchange. But they were conscious of the difficulties the organization was facing as a result of its growth. They were motivated, but showed some difficulty in identifying and describing the organizational vision. They were concentrated on the short-term vision of the daily activities.

During the interviews they seldom referred to the "old ones." As they explained, they used to come in the morning to ARS and do their job with their patients. During their coffee break the new ones preferred to spend time among themselves, as they were closer in the new rooms for the therapies, which had been created on the third floor in response to the new, additional needs.

CHECK ON THE RELATIONSHIPS WITH PATIENTS

Through the structural data and the information obtained through the interviews, Paul and Valery had acquired some information to construct a hypothesis, but they needed more to support it. They agreed that more feedback from all patients in treatment was needed. They could write a questionnaire, but decided to agree on a specific tool with the clinical staff. From the consultation, they opted for a modified version of the Helping Alliance Questionnaire (HAq-II). Helping Alliance measures the patient's level of compliance, which is directly connected to the perceived quality of services and the quality of the relation with the therapist. The questionnaire allows an assessment of patients' perceptions, feelings, and attitudes toward the therapist, and it also allows a cross comparison with the therapist's own overall perceptions.

From the administered questionnaire, an overall positive evaluation emerged, with some very positive responses to the highest score (the scale was from 1 to 6). Most of the relational items had results in the medium range (3 or 4) for statements such as: *"I feel the therapist understands me"; "a good relationship has formed with my therapist"; "at times the therapist seems distant."*

By matching the patients' questionnaires with the therapists who treated them, Paul and Valery found that most of the below average scores were given by patients of the new therapists.

THE PROPOSED INTERVENTION

At the end of the interviews and questionnaire analysis, Paul and Valery had a clearer picture of the situation. They agreed that there were several variables to work on and that the intervention had to regard the whole organization. They produced a full, detailed report, including the diagnosis, the identified solution, plus evaluation issues. Here is the list of points of the intervention they proposed, working on several variables:

- The start of the tutorship program. Each new member had to be coupled with an old one, responsible for their performance and integration.
- Mixed rehabilitation teams, joining together old and new members.
- The employment of a new secretary to join the staff and reduce the workload per member.
- The redefinition of the director's presence and communication to the staff by introducing a weekly meeting on Monday morning with the staff to discuss problems or have short training sessions.
- The promotion of intellectual honesty about errors. During these meetings the staff, especially the youngest members, had to realize that errors are possible and are something people can talk about. Only through their identification and analysis is it possible to remove their causes.
- The redefinition of space inside the building. The physical separation of old and new members on different floors was detrimental to integration and communication and had to be overcome. New and old members had to be mixed on the three floors of the building to facilitate their communication and exchange.
- The creation of a comfortable break room, with chairs and coffee and snack distributors.

- A weekend outdoor training experience for all the ARS staff to be spent on internal branding rediscovery, focusing on organizational culture, identity, vision, and team spirit. Dr. Harris would restate, refocus, and share his vision with both groups, giving them elements to build on. Paul and Valery proposed games and exercises to build the team, alternating with time to debrief the experiences.
- Posters and cards carrying inspirational quotes and the vision statement could be put in the common areas to reinforce the messages.
- A training on service delivery and therapeutic alliance, with the definition of several standards, including all new and old members of the therapeutic staff, as well as the secretarial staff members.

The consultants also presented some evaluation notes, regarding how to evaluate the effectiveness of the proposed intervention, in regards to their time-horizon (short-term changes vs. medium- or long-term ones) and possible tools to use.

Dr. Harris was surprised by the depth of the problem he had only partially identified without having actually appreciated its seriousness. He was particularly concerned by the fact that he had been totally absorbed by the organizational vision and the direction and had underestimated the importance of monitoring and guiding the organization in managing those changes. His idea of the organization (a self-sufficient, flexible learning organization, able to find its own adaptation) was not adequate. His lack of awareness, which had meant a lack of presence and action, was undermining the realization of his vision.

He appreciated the work of the consultants, agreed with their proposal, and the intervention started a month later.

Discussion Questions

1. On the basis of the information presented in this case, summarize the elements of the organizational diagnosis made by the consultants, identifying the main problems and causes.

2. What do you think about the proposed intervention? Is it appropriate? Is it coherent to the premises, as well as internally coherent for its design? Would you have suggested something different to Mr. Harris?

3. Connect each proposed solution to each problem identified in the diagnosis, indicating the variable of intervention, its level of importance, which actions were specifically meant for each problem, and evaluate the effectiveness of each in terms of contribution to solve the identified problem. Please complete Table 17.2. If you identify alternative solutions, you can briefly describe them.

Table 17.2   The Actions-Variables of Intervention Table

Variable of Intervention *(Identify each variable the OD intervention acts on.)*	Level of Importance *(Rate the relevance of each variable to the solution of the problem) scale: 1–3.)* *1: Poor influence* *2: Medium influence* *3: High influence*	Proposed Corrective Action *(Report for each variable of intervention on the left the correspondent OD intervention actions proposed by consultants.)*	Potential Rate of Effectiveness of the Proposed Solutions for the Problem They Were Meant To Solve *(Rate each proposed solution on a scale: 1–3.)* *1: Poor effectiveness* *2: Medium effectiveness* *3: High effectiveness*

1. Define which of the above identified variables (and related elements of the intervention) need to be evaluated and how this can be done, using Table 17.3.

Table 17.3   The Intervention Evaluation Table

Variable of Intervention *(Report the identified variables in the table compiled for Question 3.)*	Desired Outcome *(Describe the expected result.)*	Time Horizon of Possible Changes *(Define if possible changes in each element are short-, medium-, or long-term ones.)*	How to Evaluate Changes and Outcomes *(Define how it is possible to evaluate changes and outcomes for each variable of intervention. This way it is possible to evaluate the effectiveness of the intervention.)*

2. On the basis of your answer to Question 4 (and the information contained in column four of Table 17.3), please select some measurements (related to service quality and human resources) that can be used by consultants in the evaluation of changes and of the effectiveness of their intervention.

FOR FURTHER READING

Barney, J. B. (1986). Organizational culture: Can it be a source of sustained competitive advantage? *Academy of Management Review, 11*(3), 656–665.

Bright, K., & Cooper, C.L. (1993). Organizational culture and the management of quality. *Journal of Managerial Psychology, 8*(6), 21–27.

Normann R. (1984). *Service management, strategy and leadership in service business*. New York: Wiley.

Peters T. J., & Waterman R. H. (1982). *In search of excellence*. New York: Harper & Row.

Tague, N. R. (2004). Seven basic quality tools. *The quality toolbox*. Milwaukee, WI: American Society for Quality. Retrieved from http://www.asq.org/learn-about-quality/seven-basic-quality-tools/overview/overview.html

Part II

CASES IN ORGANIZATION DEVELOPMENT INTERVENTIONS

Case 18

GLOBAL CHAIN OF COMMAND

A Japanese Multinational Manufacturer in the United States

SACHIYO M. SHEARMAN

Learning Objectives

- To help you learn different cultural and organizational values that can be crucial in understanding a multinational organization.
- To help you understand how some cultural values are manifested in communication in a multinational organization.
- To help you explore the ways in which cultural value differences can be addressed in an organizational context.

A PHONE CALL

"May I speak with Mr. Townsman?" asks a woman with a Japanese accent.

"This is he," Ron replies.

"Hello. I hope you are well. I am a secretary of Nihon Buhin Kaisha America. I am calling you on behalf of our president, Mr. Yamada, about a possible consulting work request."[1]

Ron has been working as an independent consultant for several years. Before he began to work independently, he worked for a major consulting firm. He specializes in assisting at-risk organizations and in improving workers' morale, organizational climate, and overall company efficiency. As he listens, he recalls a former client mentioning that he had recommended Ron to his Japanese friend.

NBK America is a subsidiary of Nihon Buhin Kaisha, a Japanese multinational organization that manufactures various parts, such as fuel tanks and exhausts, for a Japanese automobile company. When the Japanese economy was going strong, a subsidiary was opened in the United States. As a small city in middle America needed more jobs for the residents back then, the city and the state offered tax relief and a land-purchase deal to actively invite Japanese companies to bring their business to the area. When the NBK America manufacturer opened, residents welcomed the company with enthusiasm.

This manufacturer had been in business for a few decades and the company had its peak production in the past as the American economy thrived. However, with the deteriorating U.S. economy in recent years, the company started to suffer. This harsh economic period, coupled with a poor organizational climate, began to create problems. Various issues that went unnoticed in good times began showing up on the surface. This particular branch was experiencing the vicious cycle of lowering efficiency in production, the loss of workers' morale, and not having resources available for employee incentives or training.

NEW PRESIDENT'S DECISION

Recently, a new president from Japan, Mr. Yamada, arrived with an assignment to turn around the company. He was told that NBK America would be closed if he was not successful in redirecting the organization and raising profits within a few years. The former president told Mr. Yamada to attempt to do things differently from the Japanese ways. The Japanese company, with upper level Japanese administrators, tended to do things in ways consistent with Japanese business practices. But it is problematic to force Japanese organizational values on American workers, and this may have contributed to the vicious cycle of problems in this subsidiary. In an attempt to take the former president's advice, Mr. Yamada decided to hire an American consultant to get American ideas for reviving the company. In fact, one of his friends had recently recommended an American consultant. Shortly after he arrived in town, Mr. Yamada had his secretary set an appointment with this consultant.

WELCOME PARTY AT KABUKI JAPANESE RESTAURANT

At a popular local Japanese restaurant, Kabuki, a dozen Japanese managers are having a dinner meeting in its party room. They are all wearing their company uniforms with the company's logo printed above their chest pockets, a customary practice for a Japanese manufacturer. As one waiter brings food, another waitress picks up some dishes from the table that is set low and where they all are seated.

"Thank you all for gathering here tonight. When I first heard that I was ordered to come here, I was surprised. I thought I would miss Japanese foods," President Yamada says as he smiles to his fellow Japanese workers. They all laugh politely. "And I also thought that I was excited for the opportunity to lead this subsidiary in the United States. You all know our ship, or this branch, has been going through some rough ocean waves recently. With all of your help, I will try my best to understand how things work here quickly so we may steer our ship to the right direction. Thank you again for this warm welcome."

The mood at this gathering was a cheerful one. In actuality, Japanese workers were concerned with the upcoming change in the leadership. They had all heard the rumor that headquarters in Tokyo gave an ultimatum to this incoming president—turn around this organization or cut some losses by closing it down. Mr. Akagi, the vice president, thinks to himself, "I wonder if he can make any changes. President Yamada might become the last president of this subsidiary. I just have to do my job and support him as much as I can. At first, I have to help him to get adjusted here. I hear that Mr. Yamada has a good idea about hiring an American consultant, but I wonder if this American person can understand what goes on in a unique multinational manufacturer like ours."

DINNER AT OH! MARIO FAMILY RESTAURANT

At around the same time, two families, the Millers and the Nestles, are having dinner in a family restaurant, "Oh! Mario." Christina Miller, Paul's wife, says, "This place has the best kids' menu and I love it that it's free for kids under 10 years old." Ann Nestle, Ken's wife, says, "That's great to know. This incentive is certainly working well." She laughs.

Ken and Paul work at NBK America. Ken is an assistant manager who manages production lines, and he has been in that position for more than a decade. In fact, Ken was one of the first American managers NBK America hired after this branch was opened. Paul joined the organization as an assistant manager for production and quality control a few years back. Since Paul started at NBK America, Ken has helped him navigate within the company. They often take breaks and lunch together at work, and now they are good friends.

Ken shares with Paul the history of the organization and how things have changed in recent years: "There was an incentive by the state to welcome a Japanese company that could bring jobs into this town in the 1980s. NBK in Japan wanted to expand and the incentives from the state got them here. Mr. Saito was one of the Japanese managers who worked hard to start it up and he's the one who hired me. He and other Japanese managers had all sorts of difficulties at first. They took some time adjusting to American ways, as they were bringing in all sorts of Japanese ways of doing things—from the uniform, the assembly line patterns, warm-up exercises in the morning, and morning meetings. They took everything so seriously and were strict about following rules and regulations. They've worked hard, and they also wanted us to work a lot. . . . They are real hardworking, but it seemed like they really had no life other than work."

Paul chuckles and says, "You make it sound like that's the past. But, that's the way they still are! You know what I mean? The Japanese managers are at work *all the time*. They stay really late at night almost every day as far as I can see. Whenever these Japanese managers request us to do overtime, they seem okay with it. I have never heard any of them complain or leave like some of our assemblers do. Hell, I heard that they even come to work on weekends at times! I don't understand it. How can they have any time at home? How do they have a life?"

"Well, right. . .that's what I thought when I started. But let me tell you, they've loosened up a lot, compared to when they started here. They needed to realize that American people value fun and friends, and spending time with our families, you know?" Ken replies.

Ken's wife interrupts, "You sound like you're a great family man. I wish you would come home earlier and to go see our kids' soccer games more often, you know."

"Well, I am doing that as much as I can, honey," Ken says. "The orders come in with last-minute deadlines. We're expected to meet demands, no matter what. We have to oversee those assembly lines. . . . Japanese managers may sound polite, but they don't flinch about their expectations whenever the *nouki,* the deadline for auto parts, is close. And you know we're constantly late, so we constantly have to do the overtime."

Paul agrees. "Yup, we surely are expected to do overtime all the darn time. I guess we've got to do what we've got to do."

Ann says, "I know; I do understand. I just hope that Ken can come home earlier and do things with the kids a bit more."

Christina agrees. "I know what you mean, Ann. It seems like they've been doing major overtime for a few months now. How do these Japanese families deal with this overwork?"

"When I got to know Saito-san back then, I asked him about it," Ken says. "He said that their way of 'taking care of their families' is to work and be successful at work. So they think that they ARE taking care of family by staying late and working hard, even though it means being absent from home."

Paul says, "Then, it seems to me that these Japanese families may separate the father's role and mother's role more clearly, as the father being a breadwinner of the family. Well, I'd tell you right now that I would not want to live like that myself. Not spending time at home or being with my kids just doesn't sound right to me."

Christina says, "Well, they've got to realize that they came here to live. They're in the United States. We are Americans and we love spending time as a family. We don't live to work, but we work to live and enjoy our life."

Ken nods. "Right, right. Other workers at the plant would all agree with you. They hope that the Japanese don't expect us to do what they do. But we have to remember: this is a Japanese manufacturer making auto parts for Japanese automobile companies. Anyway, these days we should be grateful we have jobs. And I want to get the job done. I just get stressed by trying to meet the Japanese managers' high demands and listening to our team leaders' complaints all the time."

Paul adds, "Oh, don't get me started with these team leaders. They can always find excuses for stopping the assembly lines. They don't seem to want to complete things on time. Their jobs are to motivate the assembly workers, but they don't do that. As far as I can tell, they're working against the objective of getting things done quickly. The assembly workers don't seem to care. They don't want to do overtime and they're absent as much as they can possibly be without getting fired. They are the ones getting paid for overtime!"

"Look at the bright side," Ann says. "This company has better health care benefits than others. Let's stop talking about your work already and focus on the food."

Christina says, "A brighter side for me right now is the free kid's meal." They all chuckle.

INTERNATIONAL TELECONFERENCE

It's 6:00 a.m. and the secretary, Ms. Sato, is setting up a teleconference with company headquarters in Tokyo.

Massaging the side of his head, Mr. Akagi comes in mumbling, "I drank a little too much last night and this early meeting is killing me."

Ms. Sato replies, "Sorry to hear that. May I bring a cup of tea for you, after setting up this teleconference screen?"

"Well, thank you, Sato-san. That would really help."

Mr. Watanabe, a quality coordinator and a senior engineer, comes in. "I heard you, Akagi-san. Well, I know it's a bit too early, but we cannot help it. It's our biweekly meeting with the Tokyo Honsha (headquarters). I understand that we have to adjust to their work time."

"I understand that," Mr. Akagi says, "but the summertime is over. Now it's an hour earlier than usual! I know that we cannot complain; people at the Tokyo headquarters are working late to talk with us."

Mr. Takagi, a chief sales member, comes in at the last minute. "Whew! I got here on time. I thought I'd be late."

Ms. Sato starts the teleconference software and checks the microphone. "Test, test, test, test. Can you hear me?"

Blurry faces appear on the screen. Through the reflected screen, the head of international affairs of the Tokyo headquarters replies, "Yes, we can hear you. Can you hear us?"

Ms. Sato says, "Yes, we can see you and hear you. I think we have 2 minutes till the meeting time, so let's keep this line on. A few others and the president should be here shortly. Let me bring out some tea."

Right on time at 6:30 a.m., the meeting starts.

"Ohayou gozaimasu," (*Good morning*) say the people from headquarters.

"Konbanwa," (*Good evening*) say President Yamada, Mr. Akagi, Mr. Takagi, Mr. Watanabe, Ms. Sato, and others in the meeting room.

The meeting continues for about an hour. The agenda is the usual greeting, exchanging news, and reporting on the status of major orders, inventories, and human resource–related issues. Then at the end, the headquarters shares their concern about declining profits and sales from this U.S. subsidiary.

The chief of international operations of the Tokyo headquarters states, "Well, the subsidiaries in Europe are doing well and their profits are putting us in the black. We just cannot continue like this. We know that the United States has been in recession and it has been tough. It might be hard, but you may need to make some changes. We suggest you look at ways to expand your sales teams and to explore new territories. We will continue to look at our options for the future.

"In the meantime, we really have to secure our current customers. With what we heard, your factory is having trouble keeping up with deadlines recently. We all know the impact that it has if we delay shipments to customers by one day! We need to keep the customer bases we already have. We have to keep up with the demand and meet deadlines for orders, and avoid any defects, so we can secure the customers we have now. Do you understand?"

Looking solemn, Mr. Yamada replies, "Yes, sir. We understand. Without doubt, we will do our best to keep up with the demand and secure our customers. We also will look carefully at ways to improve our production and sales figures, and ways to expand our customer basis."

Mr. Akagi sighs and thinks to himself, "Headquarters doesn't understand what's going on in this branch. It's been a vicious circle. Production cannot meet the deadlines. With this slow production, we don't have resources to add incentives or to offer employee educational benefits. The workers work late without much incentive. As the workers' morale goes down, production is slowed and increases the number of defects. Japanese headquarters would not understand the reluctance of workers to work late or their increased absenteeism that we see here. Well, at any rate, I have to relay their message to the middle managers. I have to ask all the assistant managers and team leaders to work late again. I bet they will not like this."

RELAYING THE MESSAGE

Mr. Yamada asks Mr. Akagi and Mr. Kawabe to relay the message to the workers. Mr. Kawabe speaks in broken English with Ken, Paul, and the other assistant managers about the information from the headquarters in Japan.

Ken understands that this time, they cannot be late, and for them to do that, many of the line workers will need to put in overtime to meet the deadline. Ken repeats exactly what is said by Mr. Kawabe to make sure he understands. As Ken repeats his words, Mr. Kawabe feels as though he is understood and is relieved.

Ken sighs, "Now here you go again. I have to go back and share the need for more overtime with a bunch of unhappy team leaders."

Ken relays the message right before the lunch break. "Okay, I have an important message to share. I got the word from above that they want to keep production up to meet the next deadline. We want you all to work overtime. Also, please ask all your workers to stay 3 hours overtime this week, so we can make the deadlines. Remember it's a leader's job to motivate and to make them want to be here."

All the team leaders complain among themselves, though not loudly. Team leader Denise listens but walks away frustrated, thinking to herself, "Yeah right, you can't make them want to work. Nobody can do that. Cameron has been so rebellious these days, ever since I suggested how things can be done in front of the others. So I bet Cameron won't stay and if she doesn't, the others won't either. I know half of my team would stay for sure, but that won't be enough to keep the line going."

MACHINE MALFUNCTION

Not long after that, a team leader reports to Paul that one of the machines on the line has malfunctioned. Paul examines the problem. Mr. Watanabe, who happens to be walking around the assembly lines, approaches.

"Oh, a malfunction?" Mr. Watanabe asks.

Paul replies, "Yes, I can fix it in no time. Just give me 15, 20 minutes."

Mr. Watanabe says, "Well, good, that you can fix it quickly, but that's not enough."

"Okay, then what should I do?" Paul asks.

Mr. Watanabe says, "I know you can fix it quickly, but I would like to know why this has happened. We need to know why this type of mechanical malfunction is occurring. We need to know more about this problem."

"Okay, what do you want to know?"

Mr. Watanabe hesitates. "Well, you know, the details. I want to know the situation, or the patterns about how this happened and when. I want to know how to prevent this from happening again."

Paul says, "Sure, I can report that to you as soon as I can then."

Mr. Watanabe says, "Okay. Let's figure it out so this kind of malfunction will not happen again."

"Sure. Like I said, I can fix this in no time."

They both stare at the machine.

AT LUNCH BREAK

Paul joins Ken at the dining hall.

"Hey, how are you?" Ken asks.

Paul replies sarcastically: "Well, we're off to a great start today. One of the machines broke. The assembly line has stopped."

Ken nods. "Well, that happens."

"Right. You know, I was examining the machine and figured that I could fix it in no time. Then, Mr. Watanabe jumped in and insisted on taking time to look into the problems and really examine them."

"Oh, I see," Ken says. "So, that's why line 3 was stopped earlier."

"Mr. Watanabe wants me to take some time to examine the problems and give him more details. When I tell him I can fix it in no time, he says, 'We need to know more about this problem, so this kind of thing won't happen again.' So now, though this is a minor malfunction, I have to write up a report and find out the patterns of malfunctions."

AFTER FIVE

Ken thinks to himself, "It's not like I want to be here for overtime either, but as an assistant manager, I have to. I have to go check the lines and find out how many of them actually decided to leave or stay here for overtime. Of course, all the assemblers might not want to work overtime, but they're getting paid for it!"

Ken runs into Denise.

"Hi. I'm coming to see you. Can we talk?" Denise says. Without waiting for Ken's answer, she continues, "I relayed your message. But only about half of my team is willing to stay, so the line is not going to work. The same thing happened with the other teams, so I'm going to combine my members with another line to make one assembly line. I hope that's okay."

Ken says, "Sure, I guess that's what we have to do to get the line moving. Do you have any other problems?"

Denise nods. "Actually, I promised my daughter I'd be with her this evening, and I had to ask my husband to be with her. That's okay, but many of the workers already had plans. They could have stayed for overtime if it had been announced earlier. Why can't we get notified about this earlier? Why do they expect us to work overtime all of the time?"

Ken just listens. So Denise continues, "I understand that you cannot do much. And this is nothing new; I am just communicating what I've been told. Ken, are you really communicating my complaints to the Japanese managers?"

"Of course. I just get the same response each time. They say that they'll think about it. They also say that we're having a difficult time due to the recession, which I do have to agree with."

"If you cannot get the message across to them," Denise says, "maybe I will talk to them directly!"

"No, let me handle it. They don't like people going out of the chain of command. You know that, don't you?"

Denise walks away.

BREAKING THE CHAIN OF COMMAND

Denise walks into the office to meet Mr. Akagi. "Mr. Akagi, do you have time to talk right now?"

Mr. Akagi seems surprised to see her. "Sure, fine, what can I do for you?" He seems a bit nervous.

Denise starts to explain everything: her subordinates' work attitudes, her difficulties as a team leader, her team members' dissatisfaction with the overtime, and how overtime requests are being made. At one point, she realizes she is being loud and not paying attention to his reactions.

Mr. Akagi, in a state of shock, stares at her. So Denise slows down a bit. She provides more details to back up her points. She also notes that she didn't want to come to him, that she had tried to go to Ken first, but things didn't change and she needed to bring it to his attention.

Mr. Akagi says "Yes" and "I see," nodding at times. But he also tries to cut her off. Finally, when Denise pauses, Mr. Akagi says, "Sounds to me like you have a lot to say. Please communicate to your immediate boss and he can discuss these issues further."

Denise recognizes that the conversation is over. At first she believed that Mr. Akagi was actually listening to her. But he wants her to talk with her immediate boss, which is exactly what she has been doing! "Nothing is going to change," she thinks to herself.

MEETING AT NBK AMERICA

Ron, the outside consultant, rehashes the company profile in his mind as he drives. In a few hours, he will meet with company management. He thinks, "The past few years have been rough for many companies in the United States, and this company has unique challenges. It's a multinational organization with the headquarters in Tokyo, with American middle managers and workers, and with Japanese management people mixed in. I bet there are various cultural issues to consider." He imagines meeting with the Japanese managers in just under an hour. He tells himself, "I have to bow naturally to greet Japanese businessmen."

"Hello. May I help you?" a Japanese lady at the information desk says, smiling.

"I have an appointment with Mr. Yamada at 2 p.m.," Ron tells her.

She guides him upstairs to the meeting room where five Japanese men are waiting. They all stand, bow, and greet Ron. Each man presents him with a business card, so Ron exchanges his card and shakes hands with each one of them in the order that he was greeted. He is careful to receive each business card with both hands, while attempting to remember their last names: Mr. Yamada, the president of this firm, Mr. Akagi, the vice president, Mr. Kawabe, the production manager, Mr. Watanabe, the quality-control manager, and Mr. Takahashi, a sales manager. Mr. Yamada invites Ron to sit and tells all the others to have a seat.

After a 2-hour conversation, Ron learns a lot more about NBK America. This mid-sized manufacturer has roughly 300 employees and is hierarchically structured. The top management is all Japanese. A dozen middle managers, a few dozen team leaders, and all the assembly workers are American. Japanese managers are sent in from the headquarters in Tokyo, and American middle managers and assemblers are hired locally. These Japanese managers all speak English but not very well. The sales manager, Mr. Takahashi, and the secretary, Ms. Sato, both speak English well and play the role of interpreter during the meeting.

These managers share information about the company and how it started to decline. As the demand for the auto parts declined gradually, it seemed that the company had no choice but to cut some of the training, the incentive programs, and the family events like the company picnic. When they cut these out, the managers thought it would be temporary, but that continued. The employees no longer enjoy the company picnic or receive awards for "best in production." Moreover, when things were going well, the cultural differences seemed negligible. But now they have become problematic. The organizational climate is hostile. Workers are faced with unforgiving rules and regulations, tight control, and little open communication. Some workers have expressed their dissatisfaction in the form of increased absenteeism, lowered production, and increased use of defective parts. No one at the top or middle level seems aware when the downhill cycle started. They are just trying to stay afloat in rough waves. They also thought that every business has bad times and the company would soon be headed up again. Instead, the company is caught in a vicious cycle of lower efficiency in production, poor workers' morale, and no incentives or training.

ASSESSMENT AND INTERVENTION OPTIONS

Mr. Yamada tells Ron, "So, I made a decision to hire you and ask you to assess the situation and provide me with suggestions in a prompt and timely manner." Other Japanese managers seem reluctant, but President Yamada is enthusiastic about the idea.

Ron agrees to do this task with the promise that he will receive full cooperation in the process. Ron indicates that his consulting process starts with an assessment based on interviews with key employees and observations at the firm. Ron promises that he will provide valuable suggestions for this organization to make changes, with both long-term goals and short-term goals in mind. Ron requests the list of workers and positions and is told that he will need to select a few dozen employees to interview.

Ron examines the organizational chart (Figure 18.1) and mulls over which employees he wants to interview. He plans to interview employees at different levels of the hierarchy.

Figure 18.1 NBK America Organizational Chart

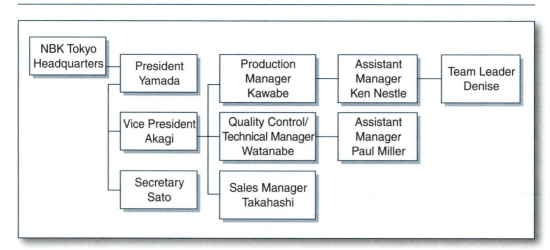

He also thinks to himself that he needs to talk to these American middle managers, as they play key roles in relaying the messages between the top management and team leaders and assemblers. He needs to move quickly.

Discussion Questions

1. If you were the consultant hired by President Yamada, what would you do from here?

2. Who would you interview? What questions would you ask as an assessment? How might the interviews with American workers and with Japanese workers be conducted differently?

3. What Japanese and American cultural values are demonstrated in the scenario? What cultural variability dimensions and organizational values do you find in this case?

4. Find examples in the case of collectivism, high-context communication, high-power distance, long-term orientation, and other cultural values that may be applicable.

5. Which interventions (individual interventions, team interventions, and whole organization interventions) would work best in this case? If you were to conduct separate interventions for Japanese managers and American managers, what program would you introduce? If you were to conduct separate interventions for different levels of the hierarchy at this organization, what program would you introduce?

6. What should an organization development consultant remember about different cultural values as the intervention strategy is developed? Which interventions might prove more or less effective in this particular multinational context?

NOTE

1. This case is based on information the author obtained from her consulting work, surveys, and interviews with actual Japanese manufacturers in the United States. Typically, there are other Japanese managers, American middle managers, several team leaders, and many assemblers in this organization. The organizational chart includes characters depicted in this case. The names of all the characters who appear in this case are fictitious.

FOR FURTHER READING

Brannen, C., & Wilen, T. (1993). *Doing business with Japanese men: A women's handbook.* Berkeley, CA: Stone Bridge.

Chanda, N. (2007). *Bound together: How traders, preachers, adventurers, and warriors shaped globalization.* New Haven, CT: Yale University Press.

Gesteland, R. R. (2002). *Cross-cultural business behavior: Marketing, negotiating, sourcing and managing across cultures.* Copenhagen, Denmark: Copenhagen Business School Press.

Morrison, T., Conaway, W. A., & Borden, G. A. (1994). *Kiss, bow, or shake hands: How to do business in 60 countries.* Holbrook, MA: Bob Adams.

Yoshimura, N., & Anderson, P. (1997). *Inside the Kaisha: Demystifying Japanese business behavior.* Boston: Harvard Business School Press.

Case 19

SAFE PASSAGE

An NGO in Guatemala City Responds to a Leadership Crisis

CANDACE A. MARTINEZ

Learning Objectives

- To help you gain an understanding of the singular vision and personal attributes required to found and operate a social purpose nongovernmental organization (NGO) in a developing country.
- To provide an illustrative example of the challenges of leading a nonprofit organization.
- To make you aware of the complexities facing an organization when it undergoes a sudden leadership transition.

Safe Passage, or Camino Seguro, is a 501(c)(3) nonprofit corporation that provides a haven in the "toxic environment of the Guatemala City garbage dump" (*http://www.safepassage.org*). Through its educational, sports, and social programs for the children and families who comprise the informal refuse collectors ("waste-pickers") and trash recyclers in the city garbage dump, it allows children a respite from the abject poverty that defines their lives, affording them a safe passage from childhood and adolescence to adulthood. As one child puts it, Safe Passage, "keeps us away from drugs and other bad things. We stay away from vices. When we grow up, we're going to be good men."[1]

Safe Passage (SP) was founded in December 1999 by Hanley Denning, an energetic and idealistic young American woman from Yarmouth, Maine. Originally planning to return to the United States after a 2-year stint in Guatemala, studying Spanish and working part time at La Asociación de Nuestros Ahijados, a nonprofit that helps marginalized children, the day before she was scheduled to leave, a friend invited her to visit the capital city's slums near the garbage dump, the largest in Central America. Almost immediately upon setting her eyes on the squalor and hopelessness of the people living off of and near the dump, Denning made the decision to do something about it. That very evening she canceled her return flight, called her family in Maine, and asked them to sell her computer and car. She was not coming home just yet. For the next 7 years Denning dedicated her life to making her dream come true. Starting with her own savings and financial support from friends and family, she established a U.S.-based nongovernmental organization (NGO) for the destitute families who subsisted on the trash they collected every day. With a generous donation of a vacant church to serve as her first "school," she daily walked the shanty town streets that lined the garbage dump, as well as visiting the dump itself, to recruit future students. She asked mothers to drop their children off at the church for a warm meal in a nurturing environment while they (the mothers) scavenged in the dump. From an initial 40 students, SP gradually grew to its size today: more than 500 of Guatemala City's poorest children and their 300 families.

On the afternoon of January 18, 2007, the 36-year-old Denning was killed in an automobile accident on the mountain road near Guatemala City. Shocked and grief stricken, Denning's family, friends, coworkers, and members of the SP community slowly internalized the fact that their leader was gone. The directors on the board, in addition to their great personal loss, were faced with an organizational challenge: how to continue fostering "hope, good health, educational achievement, self-sufficiency, self esteem, and confidence" for their constituents without the vision, passion, and love of the irreplaceable Denning? How to fill the leadership void?

SAFE PASSAGE: THE EARLY YEARS

With a population of 13 million people, Guatemala is the most populated country in Central America. More than half of its citizens live below the national poverty line (less than US$2 per day); another 15% lives in dire poverty (less than US$1 per day) (Central Intelligence Agency, 2010). The social and economic ravages of poverty that affect large numbers of the population are everywhere visible: malnourished children, subhuman living conditions, disease, illiteracy, and rampant urban crime. Illicit drug use and trafficking are also among the country's pressing challenges ("Guatemala and Organized Crime," 2010; UNICEF, 2010).

While the exact number of waste-pickers or informal recyclers in Guatemala City is unknown, it is widely accepted that theirs is one of the most unpleasant and hazardous of occupations in this sprawling metropolis of 3 million to 4 million inhabitants. Sifting through the municipal dumpsite to locate items that are edible or saleable to intermediaries, waste-pickers work long and arduous hours, ever-threatened by spontaneous methane gas explosions (Medina, 2009). Women who attend the Safe Passage Literacy Program report that 16-hour days are not uncommon as family members pick through the garbage dump at the Guatemala City landfill and then go home to sort, wash, and dry their day's goods for future resale to recycling intermediaries. On a good day, a waste-picker in the garbage dump might earn $5; on an off day, she or he might make the equivalent of about 75 cents.[2]

This was the milieu in which Hanley Denning decided in 1999 to establish a protected space where children could be children and would have the opportunity to play, laugh, and have a healthy meal. With a background in education and social work, Denning's vision for these children was a path out of poverty through education. As stated in its mission statement, the goal of this social NGO is to

> . . .empower the poorest, at-risk children of families working in the community of the Guatemala City garbage dump by creating opportunities and fostering dignity through the power of education.

With less than $5,000 of her personal savings, Safe Passage was launched. Denning calculated that a minimal amount of money, approximately $100 a year, could cover the costs of feeding and educating one child. She therefore carried out a fund-raising campaign in tandem with the recruiting of SP's children, as a revenue stream, however modest, was drastically needed to support and grow the new NGO. Denning had no plans in writing; her goal was to help those needy children and face new challenges as they appeared. She relied heavily on a close network of friends and family that she recruited to her cause to spread the word, provide her moral support, staff the growing programs, and find people who could donate their time or money.

Denning's passion to help the disenfranchised was accompanied by an equally strong commitment to keeping the NGO afloat. Having registered SP as a U.S.-based nonprofit organization in Maine, a U.S. office was set up in the same state in 2003. Denning had made numerous fund-raising and public relations trips to the United States and recognized the need for an American presence to oversee the growing number of sponsors, donors, "friends," volunteers, and outreach events held around the country with increasing frequency. As the number of children and families who attended SP rose, so did the need to have in place a physical office away from the day-to-day operations of the programs, one that could concentrate on building the donor base. Contributions increased in tandem with the efforts of the organization to systematically seek out new donors, encourage more fund-raising events across the country, and fine-tune the volunteer and service programs that organized trips to Guatemala throughout the year. Raising awareness of SP's mission paid off. The number of donors soared from two in 1999 to almost 5,000 in 2007, as can be appreciated in Table 19.1.

Logically, higher levels of donors translated into more contributions. From 2005 to 2007, revenues from operating activities (e.g., contributions, sponsorships, and other income) increased from about $1.5 million to $2 million. Under Denning's leadership, the NGO's annual budget also increased significantly, from $5,000 to about $1.6 million over a period of 8 years. Although expenditures kept pace with revenue income, the nonprofit organization was clearly in a stronger financial position in 2007 relative to previous years.

Table 19.1   Safe Passage Donors 1999–2007

Year	Number of Donors
1999	2
2000	102
2001	267
2002	451
2003	1,026
2004	1,333
2005	1,762
2006	2,889
2007	4,990

Note. Many donors contributed multiple gifts. Data provided by Safe Passage. Used with permission.

SAFE PASSAGE: ORGANIZATIONAL DESIGN

In early 2003 Denning made the executive decision that in addition to the U.S. office SP needed a board of directors in the United States to manage its myriad stakeholders and to formulate and implement a long-term strategy for its future. She chose 12 of her closest associates to become the first SP board members. In addition to the board, Denning, as executive director, worked closely with the organization's various executives in Guatemala: director of finance, director of human resources, director of development and outreach, director of marketing, director of programs, director of social development, director of operations, and director of volunteers. Figure 19.1 displays a conceptual diagram of the organizational structure of SP.

The organizational structure with Denning at the helm was informal but centralized. Like any organization with one or two founders, for the first years Denning made all major executive decisions as well as minor operational decisions (in consultation with her advisors) until the board was established. Once the board of directors was functioning, the structure became more formalized but somewhat more decentralized. While Denning continued to lead the organization in the direction she envisioned and to oversee the daily operations, mindful that its core values and mission were never compromised, the long-term strategic direction of the NGO (i.e., its ability to sustain itself

Figure 19.1   Safe Passage Organizational Chart

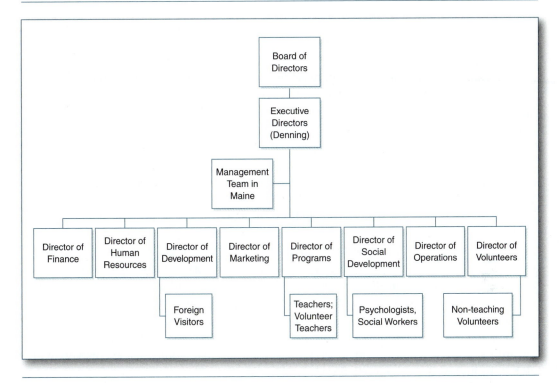

Note. Compiled from annual reports. All positions are located in Guatemala City unless otherwise noted. The board meets four times yearly, in Maine and in Guatemala.

vis-à-vis the competition from other charitable nonprofits seeking contributors' donations) was subject to more scrutiny.

With Denning's charismatic guidance and the board's support, SP continued to grow, developing new programs and refining old ones. Since the first year, Denning introduced the concept of "adopting" or "sponsoring" a child with a monthly stipend. Other NGOs such as Save the Children, the Smile Train, and WorldVision had used this model to advantage for years. After a few years, Denning introduced the possibility of sponsoring a mother, an initiative that grew out of visitors' and volunteers' being especially impressed with the mothers and wanting to do something specifically for them. The SP board later expanded donations to include not only one-off monetary contributions, but also in-kind donations and planned gifts, mechanisms for charitable giving that other NGOs had adopted. Never far from the board's mind or from the consciousness of anyone in the organization's management team was the knowledge that if donations ever dried up, so, too, would SP.

SAFE PASSAGE: THE LEADERSHIP CHALLENGE

Faced with the stark reality of a leadership void after Denning's sudden death, the board of directors in Yarmouth, Maine, went into action. No one looked forward to the searching, vetting, and hiring process as the opportunity costs it represented were steep. It would consume time that could otherwise be spent growing the organization to the next level, training new employees and volunteers, finding new contributors, and implementing new programs. Nevertheless, everyone in the 12-member board understood that finding the right person to fill Denning's shoes was vital to the present and future of SP. Donations were the lifeblood of the organization; the board could not risk their slowing down in the wake of Denning's absence. An equally dynamic, dedicated, and proactive leader would have to be found in a reasonable amount of time before potential donors' contributions were captured by other charitable organizations.

The board's first decision propelled Ed Mahoney as the interim director until Denning's replacement could be found. A retired accountant who had been living in Florida, Mahoney had been working closely with Denning in Guatemala from the early years and had set up the accounting system for SP. His interim charge was to oversee the day-to-day operations of SP's programs in Guatemala City and, basically, to be sure the organization stayed the course in the short term. Maintaining the current operation based on an acceptable level of contributions prevailed over trying to locate new sources of revenue. Designing and implementing new programs was temporarily put on hold. The board's second decision was to set up a transition team that would deal exclusively with the tasks involved in locating a new executive director.

The board was split on the attributes and strengths that the new leader of SP needed to possess. A small minority of the board preferred not to advertise for the position but rather to promote one of SP's current staff members in Guatemala City to the position of executive director. The rationale was that only an insider could fill the shoes of the late Denning and hit the ground running from day one. Another group of board members thought that the next director should be, as far as humanly possible, an exact replica of the charismatic Denning in order to ensure the new director's immediate acceptance by the organization's families, staff, and volunteers in Guatemala, as well as by SP contributors and other donors in the United States. It did not matter to this group whether the candidate came from within or outside the current SP management team. Another contingent of the board was of the opinion that hiring a Denning clone would be ideal but not likely. It believed that the position could be suitably filled by anyone familiar with the roots and mission of Safe Passage, a person who, in addition, had experience working with a social NGO in Guatemala so that the culture shock of the grass-roots organization's challenges would not be overwhelming. A final faction of the board wanted to cast a wide net and recruit the next executive director from an international pool of rising stars with at least one similar social entrepreneurship experience in a developing country.

As the spring of 2007 came to a close, Denning's family and friends, her loyal staff, and the beloved children and families at SP continued to mourn her untimely death.

The executive board and the SP staff had not allowed their grief to cripple them, however. Mike Denning, Hanley's father, summed up everyone's feelings when he said, "Hanley's only desire was to keep it going" (Hench & Maxwell, 2007). With these words as their guiding light, all of SP's stakeholders were confident that the future held promise for the organization and even brighter futures for the children whose lives it touched. Despite the tragic circumstances surrounding the leadership transition, the executive board and the transition team were optimistic the right individual would be identified and hired to fill the void that Denning's sudden death had created.

Discussion Questions

1. Given the untimely death of the NGO's charismatic founder and leader as described in the case, the board of directors at Safe Passage is seeking the advice of outside consultants as to how they should proceed. Imagine that you were called on to give your analysis of the best way for the organization to make its leadership transition. What specific recommendations would you make to the board? What do you recommend they do in the short term and in the long term? What complexities are present in this particular leadership transition? How would your suggestions differ if the urgent need for a new and effective leader were not present?

2. In your view, what specific background and qualifications are most important for Safe Passage's next leader to have? Which typologies capture the essence of a leader in general? Which ones capture the attributes that Safe Passage needs in its next hire? What types of capabilities are necessary for the next leader to possess so that the transition runs smoothly?

3. The Safe Passage transition team has been successful in its search for a new leader. You have been called on again to give your advice, this time to the new hire. What kind of coaching plan would you construct to assist the new leader upon arrival in Guatemala City? What are the key elements the new leader will need to communicate to all of the NGO stakeholders—children, mothers, waste-picker community, donors, volunteers, staff, top management team, board members—to assure them that the mission and vision of the NGO will continue in the future? What would you tell the new director?

NOTES

1. A member of Safe Passage's lacrosse team, being interviewed for the video, "Maya Lacrosse Camino Seguro" (http://www.youtube.com/watch?v=s5YxwDSWpEo&feature=related). Quotation in Spanish: "*Nos alejamos de las drogas. De las cosas malas. No andamos en vicios. Cuando seamos grandes, vamos a ser unos hombres de bien.*"

2. The national minimum wage in Guatemala is approximately 1,850 quetzales a month or about US$200.

REFERENCES

Central Intelligence Agency. (2009). *The CIA world factbook 2010.* New York: Skyhorse. Retrieved from https://www.cia.gov/library/publications/the-world-factbook/geos/gt.html

Guatemala and organized crime: Reaching the untouchables. (2010, March 11). *The Economist,* p. 39.

Hench, D., & Maxwell, T. (2007, January 20). Crash kills poor children's "angel." *Portland Press Herald,* p. A1. Retrieved from http://groups.yahoo.com/group/armysecurityagencyvets/message/176736

Medina, M. (2009). *Global recycling supply chains and waste picking in developing countries.* Helsinki: United Nations University, World Institute for Development Economics Research. Retrieved from http://www.wider.unu.edu/publications/newsletter/articles/en_GB/12-2009-wider-angle-1/

UNICEF. (2010). *At a glance: Guatemala.* New York: Author. Retrieved from http://www.unicef.org/infobycountry/guatemala.html

FOR FURTHER READING

Lewis, D. (2001). *The management of non-governmental development organizations: An introduction.* New York: Routledge. See Chapter 4.

Haily, J., & James, R. (2004). Trees die from the top: International perspectives on NGO leadership development. *Voluntas: International Journal of Voluntary and Nonprofit Organizations, 15*(4), 343–353.

Medina, M. (2007). *The world's scavengers: Salvaging for sustainable consumption and production.* Lanham, MD: AltaMira.

Shameem, S. (2001). *Who will bear the torch tomorrow? Charismatic leadership and second-line leaders in development NGOs* (International Working Paper Series, #9). London: Centre for Civil Society, London School of Economics and Political Science.

THE CASE OF JIM

A Vice President in a National Nonprofit Association

CYNTHIA ROMAN

Learning Objectives

- To identify multiple clients in an individual coaching organizational intervention.
- To successfully conduct a contracting meeting with multiple clients to determine expectations and desired results.
- To effectively feed back coaching data to motivate desired action.

The National Association of Volunteers (NAV) is a national, nonprofit organization dedicated to supporting individuals and families who need to rebuild their lives. The organization operates numerous human service programs across the country, including housing for the homeless, health care for needy families, long-term and home-based care for the elderly, addiction recovery, and disability support services. With its headquarters in Washington, DC, NAV has a large, paid, professional staff, as well as thousands of volunteers in its community-based programs.

Kathleen, Senior Vice President of Human Resources, is based at national headquarters in DC. Kathleen is relatively new with NAV, having been hired 2 years earlier to bring a breath of fresh air to an organization that has clung, some say stubbornly, to its historic traditions and values. Kathleen was previously a senior vice president (VP) for a well-known hotel chain and she recently earned her doctoral degree in human resource management. She is an active volunteer in NAV as well as a paid executive and believes strongly in the mission of the organization.

Jim, Vice President of Legislative Affairs, has been with NAV for more than 35 years. In fact, he has spent his entire career at NAV, working his way up from college intern during the Johnson administration. As might be expected, Jim is as much a part of the history of NAV as any living person could be. Jim will be the first person to tell you that he wrote the first policy and procedures manual and that he has been to several parties at the Robert and Ted Kennedy homes. He loves to talk about politics, particularly about his view that NAV's heyday was during Johnson's Great Society in the 1960s. He openly disapproves of the direction and strategies of NAV. He is also resentful that a recent reorganization put a layer between him and the CEO. For 20 years, he reported directly to the CEO. Now, he reports to a newly hired senior VP.

Kathleen has been trying coach Jim for the past year to carry out the expectations the CEO has for his position and for his department. For the most part, her efforts have met with resistance and frustration. Their meetings usually start out with friendly small talk. Usually Jim will regale Kathleen with genuinely fascinating stories of bygone days when he and the CEO lobbied the halls of Congress together or attended parties where he met important movers and shakers from the Carter or Reagan administrations. Inevitably, though, when Kathleen asked about Jim's progress in implementing the new strategic plan in his department, he started his usual litany of complaints regarding the philosophy and direction of the plan. Kathleen listened and then again pressed for his progress. His response was to make excuses for why he had not followed through and to ask for more time. After more than 6 months of this recurring dialogue, Kathleen's patience had worn thin.

MEETING THE CLIENT

Early in the fall, Kathleen called me for help. My name is Jennifer and I am an outside consultant in organization development (OD) and an executive coach. I have 5 years of experience in human resources, 2 years of experience in OD and I recently graduated from a well-known coach-training program. Earlier in the year, I left my corporate job to start my own OD consulting practice. My aunt is on the NAV board of directors and convinced Kathleen that I am highly skilled in coaching and could help Jim become motivated to accept his new role, tasks, and accountability in NAV. Kathleen was hopeful that maybe Jim would respond better to an outside coach than to an inside staff person. To be honest, Kathleen was at her wit's end with Jim and she wanted another opinion. The following is the phone conversation Kathleen had with me.

Kathleen: Hi, Jennifer. How are you?

Me: Hi, Kathleen. Fine, thanks. Nice to hear from someone at NAV, my favorite organization. My aunt told me to expect your call. What can I do for you?

Kathleen: I think you can help us with a coaching issue. I hope you can help Jim accept his new role in implementing our new strategic direction. So far, my coaching hasn't worked. I think he'll do better with a coach from the outside. He just complains and resists change with me.

Me:	Let me understand a little better. Who does he report to?
Kathleen:	Jim reports to Carlos Menlow, our new senior VP. However Carlos just came on board and is spending all day, every day with Brad [the CEO]. For many years, Jim reported to Brad and they used to be quite close. However, when we reorganized earlier this year and Carlos was hired, Brad chose to put Jim underneath Carlos. That did not go over well with Jim and it pretty much ended their friendship. In addition, we have radically changed our vision, and Jim didn't like that either. He's stuck in the past and unwilling to do what we believe is necessary to carry out our new strategic initiatives in the Legislative Division. Coaching is our last hope for Jim. If this doesn't work, . . . well, I don't know . . .
Me:	What do you mean, you don't know?
Kathleen:	Well, Brad has implied that we may not keep Jim if he doesn't come around.
Me:	Are you saying that you would terminate Jim if he doesn't change his attitude?
Kathleen:	Maybe.
Me:	This sounds like a performance improvement situation to me, Kathleen, and not a coaching goal. Why not put him on a performance improvement plan?
Kathleen:	There are a couple of reasons. First of all, Jim has a long and proud history with NAV. We recognize everything he has done for this organization and we don't want to tarnish his reputation. Second, we believe in coaching and, if this goes well, we hope to institute coaching through the organization. Accountability is a value we hope to emphasize and coaching is a leadership approach that we hope will promote accountability here and in the field. If you can get Jim to accept his accountability to change with the times, well, WOW, people will see how powerful coaching is!
Me:	So, do I understand correctly, that you want me to help him to accept his need to change his attitudes and his behavior and to perform more successfully?
Kathleen:	Yes, exactly.
Me:	That's a really tall order. What I'd like to do is work with him for six sessions and reassess how it's going. If you and I are agreed that we're not making adequate progress, then I'd like to renegotiate or terminate the coaching relationship. How does that sound? If that's agreeable to you, I'm up to it.
Kathleen:	Great! Let me tell him that we have assigned him a coach and then you can call him to set up your first appointment.

THE FIRST COACHING MEETING

During my first meeting with Jim, I found him to be pleasant and receptive to a coaching relationship. However, Jim spent most of the hour-long meeting complaining about how the problem was the strategic direction of the association and how resentful he was that his contributions were no longer valued. I found it difficult to stem the flow of his comments long enough to set up subsequent coaching sessions. Jim insisted that these sessions be outside of the office. When I suggested my office, Jim replied, "No, let's go somewhere we can relax. I have found NAV to be so stressful; it will be a relief to have someone I can relax with and talk with openly. I really like the restaurant Nick's Place down the street. I often take our clients there for dinner. Let's have our coaching meetings there at 5:30 p.m. Okay?" I agreed; glad to get a decision on something during this never-ending meeting.

Eventually, I also got Jim's agreement to interview the CEO, three of his employees, and three colleagues—the directors of Legal Affairs, Housing Services, and Finance. When I explained the role of feedback in the coaching process, Jim said, "Sure, I understand. You'll find that my working relationships are excellent. The CEO just doesn't understand how good my work really is." Because time was running short and I was eager to start scheduling the interviews, I told Jim I would develop the interview questions. As I gathered up my belongings, Jim said, "Jennifer, I think I'm going to get a lot out of this coaching relationship. Maybe you can convince Kathleen and Brad they've made a mistake in hiring that new guy and changing the strategic direction of NAV." I smiled, said my goodbyes and thought to myself, "Boy, do I have a lot of work to do!"

DATA COLLECTION AND ANALYSIS

I thought a great deal about this coaching project after my first meeting with Jim. Something about the relationship was bothering me but I couldn't put my finger on it. One factor that I knew I wanted to ask Kathleen about was the missing new senior VP, Carlos. I thought he should be more involved with Jim and his low performance. But I wasn't sure how or when to address that. Over the weekend, I drafted the following interview questions I planned to ask.

1. Does Jim involve his team in work-planning activities in a meaningful way?

2. How effectively does Jim create a work environment that encourages creative thinking and innovation?

3. How does Jim communicate his disagreements with others' opinions?

4. How effectively does Jim serve as a role model for embracing productive change?

5. How effectively does Jim think about what others are saying and give thoughtful responses?

6. How well does Jim solve problems?

7. Can Jim create a vision of the future?

8. How well does Jim actively listen to others' views and ideas?

9. How effective is Jim as a leader?

10. What could Jim do better?

I sent the draft of the interview questions to Kathleen for review. She added one additional question: "How effectively does Jim meet deadlines?" With this final set of 11 questions, I walked into the CEO's office for my first interview.

My interview with Brad proved pivotal. Brad had been CEO of NAV for 25 years. He knew Jim very well and was keenly aware that Jim was resisting just about every element of the new strategic plan and was not meeting the expectations of his position. He described Jim as a bull in a china shop of the political hallways of Washington, DC. He was angry at the way in which Jim had derailed recent initiatives he had carefully crafted as well as Jim's nonapologetic style of communication. In his long tenure at NAV, Jim and Brad had practically grown up together and at one time had shared an office together. Through the years, they had been both colleagues and friends. But recently, their friendship had soured and now they rarely saw each other at work, let alone during personal time. Brad seemed a little distant when I asked what would happen to Jim if his attitude or performance didn't improve. I pressed the question. Brad replied, "I guess we'll have to let him go. But that's why we hired you, so we won't have to let him go." I didn't say anything but swallowed audibly.

The next interview was with Ava, the head of Legal Services. As I sat down with her in her small, cluttered office, I began by telling her that the interview data would be anonymous and that I would be taking notes. Ava looked over the questions and then got up to close the door to her office. She sat down and said to me, "I assume you know about Jim's problems."

Me: I don't know what you mean.

Ava: Has anyone told you about Jim's drinking problems?

Me: No. How has that impacted his effectiveness and performance in your opinion?

Ava: A great deal. We had to call the police at the last major meeting because he drank too much and refused to let anyone drive him home. He got very loud and a couple of our board members witnessed it. It was very embarrassing.

Me: What has been said to him by management?

Ava: Not much. Brad pretty much avoids him now. He leaves Jim to Kathleen and to me.

Me: What about Carlos? Isn't he Jim's new manager?

Ava: Carlos is being groomed as Brad's successor in 2 years. Nobody wants Carlos to be associated with Jim. Jim is like the plague around here.

Me: Then, why was I hired?

Ava: I'm not too sure. But I think it's because everybody is really hopeful that you can turn him around. And we all hear great things about coaching. No pressure, huh? Oh, and one more thing. Jim has a sexual harassment complaint filed against him.

Me: What? Neither Jim nor Kathleen shared any of this with me.

Ava: Hm, I probably shouldn't have either. We have investigated and have not found any evidence to support the complaint. Jim is a loose cannon in my opinion.

Me: Okay. Thank you for your thoughts. Let's move on to the questions.

Ava and I finished the interview and I spent the rest of the day with the other interviewees. The next day I summarized all the interview data and organized it into the following themes.

Strengths

- Decision making, developing subordinates, giving positive feedback, technical expertise is strong, financial expertise is strong, knows NAV history better than anyone, well-known on Capitol Hill, speaks up often at meetings on behalf of NAV

Theme One: (Anger)

- "Can get very embarrassing to watch Jim verbally criticize NAV in a congressional office. I wouldn't tolerate it." (*subordinate*)

- "Frequently Jim will raise his voice and be insulting. This seems to happen mostly after he's been drinking. It's gotten so I try not to sit at his table at our dinner meetings." (*peer*)

- "He yells too much and I'm going to ask for a transfer." (*subordinate*)

- "Nobody understands the background and historical perspective of NAV like Jim. I respect and appreciate his contributions to the organization." (*CEO*)

- "Doesn't support the current goals of the organization and doesn't hesitate to tell anyone who will listen." (*peer*)

Theme Two: Project Management/Planning

- Subordinates are often confused about what is due and the process for going through projects. (*subordinates*)

- Doesn't follow through as he promises on tasks and projects. (*peers*)

- Gives very poor project updates and appears to not know what's going on with his own department. (*management and peers*)

- Tends to work better one-to-one than with teams. (*subordinates*)

Theme Three: Career Satisfaction

- "Jim seems to feel his career is at a standstill. Doesn't feel energized or excited about his work." (*peer*)

- "Jim resents the hiring of Carlos and the subsequent loss of his relationship with Brad. He feels isolated and rejected." (*peer*)

I e-mailed the data summary to Jim and made an appointment for 3 days later to discuss the themes with him.

DATA FEEDBACK MEETING

I was really eager to discuss the data themes with Jim. I deliberately sent him the data in advance with instructions to think about the feedback and come to our meeting in a "problem-solving" frame of mind. Unfortunately, that's not what happened. When I arrived at Nick's Place for our data feedback meeting, Jim greeted me warmly. He showed me to the table he had reserved for us where there were two glasses of wine waiting for us. He then handed me his resume. When he saw my look of surprise, he said,

"Well, Jennifer, I don't think I have any choice. It's obvious that my colleagues don't appreciate me anymore and that I have to leave. I have spent the past 3 days discussing my finances with my wife and working on my resume. I've even made a few phone calls to some contacts on the Hill. At first, I was really shocked. I've given everything I had to this association. It's been my life. It's really difficult to see how little it counts with people you thought were your friends. But life goes on. My family is what counts and I have a few more years before this ole' bull is put out to pasture. So what I'd like to do is have you take a look at my resume and give me your opinion. And since NAV is paying for your time, I wonder if you would help me brush up on my interviewing skills. And I thought maybe you could help me put together a list of other associations to contact. How does that sound? I don't want Kathleen knowing about this, okay? We have five more meetings, about 2 months. By then, maybe I'll have a new job."

Needless to say, I was unprepared for this reaction to the data and this direction in our coaching relationship. I had to respond at that moment so I told Jim that I was surprised by his reaction but that I would help him achieve his objective of finding a new job. However, I'm troubled by the entire way in which this engagement has proceeded. Please help!

Discussion Questions

1. Who is the client in this coaching engagement?

2. What are the desired results of this coaching engagement?

3. How effectively does Jennifer communicate understanding of the client's problem?

4. How effective is the contracting meeting between Jennifer and Jim? What items should be discussed and agreed upon?

5. How effectively did Jennifer plan and conduct the data collection? What, if anything could Jennifer have done differently during the data-collection phase of the engagement?

6. How did the client react to the data summary and feedback phase of the engagement? How effective was Jennifer's response? What could she have done differently?

FOR FURTHER READING

Argyris, C. (1993). *Knowledge for action: A guide to overcoming barriers to organizational change*: San Francisco: Jossey-Bass.

Bianco-Mathis, V., Nabors, L., & Roman, C. (2008). *Organizational coaching: Building relationships and programs that drive results.* Alexandria, VA: ASTD Press.

Block, P. (2000). *Flawless consulting* (2nd ed). San Francisco: Wiley.

O'Neill, M. (2007). *Executive coaching with backbone and heart: A systems approach to engaging leaders with their challenges.* San Francisco: Jossey-Bass.

Whitmore, J. (2004). *Coaching for performance.* (3rd ed.). London: Nicholas Brealey.

A SMALL WORLD AFTER ALL

RODNEY L. LOWMAN

Learning Objectives

- To explore when it is appropriate to use individual level assessments (tests) as part of an organization development (OD) effort.
- To understand contextual issues that may arise in doing OD in a company located in a rural community.
- To determine what an OD consultant should do when a planned intervention seriously misfires.

As a specialist in organization development (OD), Sam Shruggins, a short, pudgy man of 50 with a reddish face, had worked with a variety of organizations and on a wide assortment of issues in his mostly rural part of the state. Being rather isolated geographically, the companies Shruggins worked with were primarily small to medium sized, but he had built a successful practice and in time was known as being the "go-to" person when OD was needed. Over the years he had developed a favored approach that usually worked pretty well for most of the problems he was asked to address. Typically the approach included some type of testing as part of the assessment phase.

MERCURY STANDARD

The engagement with the Mercury Standard Corporation, located about 3 miles outside of the small city of Brewer on a lovely and well-manicured acreage adjacent to a golf course, at first seemed pretty routine. He had been called in to assist with what he understood to be a team development effort. Myron Morton, the vice president in charge of operations at Mercury, as most people locally called it, had heard Shruggins speak at one of the Brewer Rotary Club meetings. Sam had spoken about creating effective teams and barriers to working together effectively. The situations he had described in his brief talk included a number of examples that seemed to describe Mercury's senior management team to a T. Pleasant to one another on the outside, the team was generally conflict avoidant and was viewed by Morton as ineffective in dealing with real issues.

Concerning what Morton viewed as trivial issues (such as whether to take the Martin Luther King holiday) they could fill an hour-long meeting with lively discussion and points of view. When it came to discussing a strategy for growing the business or talking about new marketing efforts, however, Morton had to pull to get any real discussion going and rarely did anything come of it.

Morton had worked at Mercury only 4 years—still a newcomer and outsider by local standards. He came there from Capital City, the state's second largest city, to assume a vice presidency and what was for him a promotion. Morton's wife, a home maker, had been raised in a small town and had looked forward to returning to a similar place so that the couple's two soon-to-be teenaged sons could have a tamer, safer place in which to pass their adolescence. He himself had hailed from a larger city in another state and preferred a less rural location, but when the offer came in they agreed that they would give it a try and stay at least until their boys had graduated from high school.

In the third year of Morton's new job, his boss, Mr. Pettis LeMaster, the company's CEO, suffered a recurrence of prostate cancer and became increasingly absent as he traveled to the state's medical hub in Metro City, the state's largest city and commercial center. In his absence, and with the board's approval, he asked Morton to run the executive committee meetings and to continue to oversee operations. LeMaster continued to manage the work with the board, most of whom he had known for more than 40 years since he had founded the company.

Not too much was said directly to Morton about the interim arrangement he was asked to fill. However, his wife, who had become active in several women's clubs and civic groups, learned from an acquaintance that Esther Michelson, Mercury's chief financial officer (CFO) who had been at Mercury since its founding, was not too happy about this arrangement. It felt to her, it was reported, that she and her longstanding service and loyalty had been overlooked when Morton was asked to take the interim lead. On the quiet side and always the "lady" when dealing with others in a public context, Michelson never said anything to Morton about her feelings and after his wife had relayed the information about what she had said to a mutual friend, he decided to let it pass.

Most of the other members of the senior management team were locals who had worked their way up in the company to their present positions. Only three of the seven members of the executive committee (other than Morton and the CEO) had college degrees. All were considered successes in their local community. If they had had any negative reactions to Morton, they never told him about them. Although Morton would not have chosen most of the senior executive team members, he did not feel it appropriate to remove any of them in the current circumstances, but he did want to take the team to a new level of functioning. In a small town he knew you could not move too quickly or expect too much too soon without facing a lot of push back from unexpected sources.

Mercury was one of three employers in Brewer that had more than 100 employees. With 500 employees, Mercury was the second largest employer in the city, the local general hospital being the largest. Mercury was considered to be one of the best employers by many locals because they paid good wages and because their benefit package was particularly attractive with generous health, dental, and retirement benefits. Although Mercury had had its ups and downs over the years, salaries and benefits had always been protected for those who remained with the company. In fact, Pettis LeMaster was something of a local hero for what he had done with Mercury and his loyalty to the community. Several attempts at buying out the company had been made, but on each occasion LeMaster fended them off, even at a cost to his own financial well-being. Personally, LeMaster didn't really need any more money—he had no plans to leave Brewer (where the cost of living was fairly low) although he did want his wife, children, and grandchildren to have a sufficiently large inheritance that they would never have to worry about money.

THE FIRST ON-SITE OD MEETING

To someone who did not live there, Brewer was a rather uninviting town located on the Frazier River, which connected Lake Suffrage and Lake Bedrock, two of the larger lakes in the region, both of which were popular with boaters in the short chilly summers. While Mirishmar, 3 hours west of Brewer, had developed into an attractive and thriving college town, Brewer always seemed frozen in a time that was at least a century or so ago. Called a "blue-collar town," that term may have accurately described what Brewer once was but was no longer accurate since most jobs these days in Brewer had become white collar and in the service industry. Still, the self identity of being a blue-collar town lived on. As in many small towns, a small group of professionals and business leaders controlled much of the money locally, there was a moderate-sized middle class, and a larger poorer class who were still struggling to make ends meet.

Sam Shruggins had been to Brewer on many occasions; earlier in his career he had done some consulting work with the local hospital when it planned what turned out to be a successful expansion strategy. This particular wintry day for his first return visit to Mercury was one of the worst of the already long and bleak winter that year, but Shruggins was an old pro at getting around icy snowed-over roads and he took pride in never once having missed a consulting engagement due to weather. When the weather was predicted to be dangerous he came in the night before, as he had done this time. When he did so, he typically stayed at the Native Hotel and Casino, which usually had a mid-week special, and was a little nicer than the franchise motels that plentifully lined Grand Avenue, the city's main commercial street.

This morning it was slow going getting the 5 miles to the company headquarters. His four-wheel drive truck moved along fast enough but too many amateurs, as he liked to call them, were out on the road that day, slowing everyone down to their timorous pace.

Fortunately he had allowed enough plenty of time and still arrived with time to spare at the Mercury plant.

Despite the beautiful landscaping at Mercury, the company's buildings themselves were quite unattractive. An old transmission plant from the 1920s had been purchased by LeMaster and the company's other founders when they had started the Mercury Standard plant. What was distinctive, at least in the few nonsnowy months, were the lovely grounds. Trees and paths had been intermixed and the company had installed a popular walking trail that in winter was used by cross-country skiers. The sidewalks and parking lots were always (almost instantly and somewhat mysteriously) cleared of snow and what the buildings lacked in beauty the grounds made up for.

Shruggins parked his truck with no problem that day and walked up to the visitor's entrance to the company headquarters, a beige brick building with steel awnings over the windows. Inside he was greeted by a middle-aged woman with frosted hair and a huge smile. "You must be Mr. Shruggins. Cold enough for you?" she asked, a little impishly. Shruggins returned his best, most jovial smile, the one he used with company gatekeepers. He was friendly, smiling, and a little flirtatious.

"Mr. Morton is waiting for you on the fourth floor," she said. "Just put your hat and coat over there and you can take the elevator up. Mary will take care of you there." Her voice sang and made him feel warm and happy, as it did most people who were greeted by her.

The hat and coat rack were empty—a slow visitor's day he assumed. A puddle of water quickly accumulated on the floor when the steamy heat from the radiator quickly warmed his black coat to room temperature.

Miss Mary Feldenstein was just off the elevator on the fourth floor. A woman of about 60, she was expecting Shruggins and greeted him cordially if a little crisply. She'd seen a number of consultants come and go since Mr. LeMaster had turned over so much authority to Mr. Morton. There was just the slightest note of coolness in her voice when she offered him coffee and a place to sit.

His coffee had just been served when Sarah Scott, whom Morton had brought with him from his last company, opened a door and cheerfully greeted him. "Come on back, Mr. Shruggins. We're delighted you could get through to us on this snowy day." Sarah seemed like a woman who could not stop talking and she went on and on, barely stopping for him to reply. "Did you get caught in the snowstorm? I was almost late coming in today and I'm never late. I sure hope you didn't have any trouble." Shruggins just let her talk, smiling a little, and soon he was in the conference room with the long, dark, black wood table, paneling on the walls, and photographs of the current board members—all white males who appeared to be over 60. The lack of windows lent the room a sense of importance, as did the tall chairs, but the cheap wood paneling on the walls sent a mixed message.

"Mr. Morton will be right in," Sarah said. And before he could even sample his coffee, in walked Mr. Morton. At the Rotary meeting he had worn a suit and had a cordial air about him. Today, however, he was in a shirt and tie with black slacks. He greeted

Shruggins quickly, made the obligatory comments on the weather and sat at the head of the long table.

After the small talk (perhaps a minute's worth) Morton said, "I appreciate your coming. I'll be frank with you. This team needs to move faster than they are going now and I'd like your help with that. I also have some duds in the group but I feel like I'm stuck with them for now. I'd like you to get this team more aligned and at least pulling in the same direction and to perform at a higher level."

"I'll do my best," Shruggins said. Just as he was formulating how he would best ask his usual string of questions about the team and Mr. Morton's perceptions of the issues, Morton said, "I've arranged for you to meet the team now as part of our regular Monday morning meeting. You'll have a chance to get to know them and we can determine the best way to proceed."

Before he could respond to that statement, in came Sarah Scott, letting her boss know that the team was ready to join them. She noted that Mr. Appleby (the head of marketing) was not there yet because of car problems. Morton's face briefly turned red but he quickly said, "Bring the others in, please."

Shruggins was not too happy with this beginning but he concluded that if he wanted this OD job he had to go along, at least for now. For starters, his goal was to engage with the entire team, not just with Morton. The group assembled but most looked a little apprehensive and a couple of them downright anxious.

Like most first OD meetings, this one went fairly well. Participants were polite and after a while, when the purposes of the OD effort were explained by Morton, a little humor crept in. Shruggins explained that he would like to meet with each member of the team individually to get better acquainted with them all. People seemed relieved that they would have a chance to privately present their point of view. Since Morton had indicated the time for this meeting was up, they agreed to get together again in 2 weeks on the same day and time. After the group meeting, he said he would begin the individual interviews.

At the end of the meeting, Shruggins distributed an assessment for participants to complete individually and to bring back to the next meeting. It was a short form of a five-factor measure of normal personality commonly used in personnel selection (see, e.g., Rothstein & Goffin, 2006) and Shruggins had often used this test early on in OD efforts. He had found it to be a harmless measure that served as a good ice breaker and tension reliever. Although he did not train as a psychologist, Shruggins had attended a course by the test publisher, who on this basis allowed him to purchase the measure. The participants all laughed a little and made comments about the "shrink" finding out all their secrets, but no one objected to completing the measure either in the meeting or thereafter.

THE SECOND MEETING

Two weeks later the snow in Brewer had mostly melted, the roads were clear and the sun actually peeked through. People greeted him pleasantly and the management team seemed to be in a good mood. This meeting had, with some effort on Shruggins' part, been scheduled for 2 hours. The first part of the meeting was spent talking about the individual interviews that would commence that day and the general way that he liked to work to help teams grow. He applauded the group on its willingness to agree to work together and to tackle the issues before them.

The second hour of the meeting was spent reviewing the results of the assessment measure that each had completed and brought with them to the meeting. Shruggins had found from experience that having people take a short measure like this was a good way to open people up and to demonstrate that there were many differences in peoples' personality and that this had implications for how they could best work together successfully. Shruggins had used this particular test and approach dozens of times before and it had always been an effective way to get people thinking and to break down some of the barriers to beginning serious work together.

After a brief discussion of the purposes of the assessment process, and the reminder that the results were just for their own use and were confidential to them, Shruggins had the participants self-score the measure. He had given them a self-scorable form and asked the staff to pull the measure apart, which resulted in the scoring template being made visible. Within 5 minutes, all participants had their numbers, which they then plotted on a graph that assigned them to a category (e.g., high or low openness) on each of the five dimensions measured by the test. He then presented a short lecture on the five personality factors using the abbreviation OCEAN to describe the five variables of openness, conscientiousness, extroversion/introversion, agreeableness, and neuroticism (McCrae, 2009). Many in the group asked relevant and sometimes lively questions. A few were silent and Esther Michelson in particular seemed preoccupied and unengaged. When he discussed the neuroticism dimension, she seemed to be blushing. Shruggins also noted that several of the participants seemed to be sneaking peaks at their neighbor's results so he reminded the group that these results were just for one's own use, not to be shared.

IN A SMALL TOWN, THERE ARE NO SECRETS

Later that evening, Sarah Scott, who sat in on all the meetings to take notes and as the secretary to the senior management team, and who also had completed the test, called her best friend Louise Carson to discuss what had happened that day in the meeting. She talked about the measure of "normal personality" they had completed and noted that Esther Michelson, who she had sat next to, had seemed quite upset during the meeting. She told Louise in confidence that Esther had scored high on something the consultant had called "neurotic" (something like that; she remembered the names of the scales spelled out OCEAN) and the two laughed at how accurate that test was in nailing Esther's rather acerbic and sometimes brittle personality. She also stated that her boss, Mr. Morton, had told the group he had come out introverted on this test and that she had heard someone who had been in the group say after the meeting about his remark, "well that sure explains a lot of things."

After the call, Louise, who, since her retirement from Mercury, had become an active volunteer in the community, spoke to her friend Barbara Jackson and in passing mentioned the "juicy gossip" from Mercury. Barbara in turn spoke that evening to her acquaintance and bridge partner Millie Talson, who then spoke to her best friend Betty Buran, a columnist for the local newspaper, The *Brewer Morning News*. Buran's husband had formerly worked for Mercury and had been laid off in one of the cut backs that took place last year. He had not found new work and was getting by doing odd jobs.

Around town, especially among those who subscribed to larger newspapers, the local newspaper was something of a joke, snidely known as the *Morning Snooze*. It mostly consisted of birth, death, and athletic contest announcements and the arrest records from the day before, along with a few by-then stale national news stories. The writers on the paper were poorly paid and they took their solace when they could by writing opinion articles disguised as news stories that made their targets look bad. The maligned individuals usually cancelled their subscriptions, especially when the paper refused to print letters to the editor with their side of the story. The paper's editor fancied himself a muckraker and was independently wealthy, so he did what he wanted and did not much care if the circulation was declining.

Within a week, Barbara Buran's "About Town" weekly gossip column featured a short item about the personality test results of Mercury's executives. In it she opined, "Your humble columnist is no psychologist but she has learned that some of the senior executives at Mercury Standard took a test administered by a visiting consultant and that certain executives came out on the test as being neurotic and introverted. Far be it from this source to say who should be working as executives at one of our city's major employers, but might the company's recent layoffs have been avoided by—well—a better adjusted group of senior executives?"

Like most newspapers, this one was available online. Soon the comments about the Mercury executives were available on the Web. Readers could write in online comments and a number of snide comments (e.g., "They didn't need to bring in an overpriced OD consultant to find out that some of the honchos at that company weren't playing with a full deck. I could have told them that for nothing!") were posted. Some members of the board read the story and contacted LeMaster to find out what was going on with this unfavorable publicity. "Was Morton really the right person to fill in for LeMaster?" some asked.

The Monday after the item appeared, Morton had Sarah Scott call Shruggins to tell him they were not going to be pursuing the planned OD intervention at this time due to "other pressing business matters" but they would get back to him if additional help was needed. Morton declined to return Shruggins' several calls. There was no further discussion of the incident in the senior executive group and, once the dust blew over, business went on as it had done before the ill-fated OD efforts. However, whenever behind-the-scenes conflict arose among some of the senior team members someone would refer privately to the other parties as "that neurotic," "the introvert in our midst," or that "closed minded progress-blocker," depending on who was doing the talking and who wasn't around to hear.

> ### Discussion Questions
>
> 1. Should Shruggins have used the personality test in this manner? Was he qualified to use it?
>
> 2. Were there steps that Shruggins might have taken before using the assessment measure that could have minimized any misuse of the test?
>
> 3. Did Shruggins (and did Morton) have any responsibilities once the situation blew up as it did?
>
> 4. Would it have been better not to have used the assessment measure at all?

REFERENCES

McCrae, R. (2009). The five-factor model of personality traits: Consensus and controversy. In P. J. Corr & G. Matthews (Eds.), *The Cambridge handbook of personality psychology* (pp. 148–161). New York: Cambridge University Press.

Rothstein, M., & Goffin, R. (2006). The use of personality measures in personnel selection: What does current research support? *Human Resource Management Review, 16*(2), 155–180.

FOR FURTHER READING

Eyde, L., Robertson, G. J., & Krug, S. E. (2009). *Responsible test use: Case studies for assessing human behavior.* Washington, DC: American Psychological Association.

Groth-Marnat, G. (2009). *Handbook of psychological assessment* (5th ed.). New York: Wiley.

Lowman, R. L. (Ed.). (2006). *The ethical practice of psychology in organizations* (2nd ed.). Washington, DC: American Psychological Association.

ACCOUNTING TEAM PROBLEMS AT ACME MANUFACTURING

MAGGIE GLICK

Learning Objectives

- To help you understand when a team intervention is necessary.
- To practice the development of interventions when more than one group of individuals is involved.

Acme Manufacturing was recently sold to a large conglomerate manufacturing company with locations all over the world. As a small, independent manufacturer, the top management team were used to calling the shots. They are used to being lean and agile; however, the new parent organization requires more focus on cost savings than they are used to. They have always worked well together but the rules have changed and they are uncertain about the new owners' expectations. This ambiguity is causing strained relationships in the top management team.

BACKGROUND INFORMATION

The corporate management team at Acme Manufacturing is preparing for their first monthly meeting with the CEO of their new parent company. Acme is a small manufacturer of control devices with 12 manufacturing plants in six states. All the locations are in rural settings, some with proximity to larger cities. The CEO and COO have both worked their way up through the management ranks at Acme, first serving as plant managers (PMs). Both have been with the company for more than 10 years. The vice president of IT also has served in many capacities at Acme prior to his promotion to vice president (VP). The CFO is a seasoned accountant with more than 20 years of experience managing lean accounting departments.

Prior to the acquisition, management of the plants was very decentralized, including operations and accounting. Each plant had an annual budget and was held accountable for bottom-line results. Little attention was paid to the account-level detail in each plant, as long as the financial results were on track with budget. This team has struggled, like many teams do, to maintain a competitive edge in a business environment where most manufacturing has been shipped overseas. They are dedicated to each other and to being successful, but they are frustrated trying to learn the rules of the new game. This is complicated by feeling like they have lost control.

The new owners take a very different approach to reviewing the monthly financial data. Acme's general ledger accounts have been "mapped" into the parent company's accounting system without any input from the Acme staff. An income statement for the month of January has been generated by the parent company accounting staff detailing every account for every plant. The management team has never reviewed an income statement at this level of detail and numerous problems are evident, not only in the account mapping but also in the use of accounts. Some plants are missing an electricity expense, but it is quite apparent they must have an electricity bill for each month. Other plants are reporting twice as much cost for electricity as they should be for the month—indicating they probably have recorded two electricity bills in one month. It is also obvious not all accounts are being used at all locations because certain raw material expense accounts have balances in one location but not another.

DETAILS OF CURRENT ACCOUNTING TEAM FUNCTIONALITY

Bill (CEO): We are all expected to meet with Randy [parent company's CEO] next Wednesday to review January's financial results, but I have no idea how to read this income statement they provided.

Leslie (CFO): I've heard through the grapevine that Randy goes through the income statement account by account asking questions about each location. Now that I see this new income statement I understand what that could mean. I don't find this easy to read either but I can take this statement, add our old account names and descriptions to it and at least that will give us familiar accounts to dig in to. I really wish they had asked us to review the chart of accounts mapping before they did the conversion for us—it would have saved us a lot of time trying to interpret their reports.

Mark (COO): If you can provide me with that report, I'll review it, highlight the items I don't understand, and send it out to the plant manager at each facility. I'll give them 2 days to work with their accounting managers to provide answers to our questions.

Bill: Leslie, do you think you can have that done this afternoon? We're on a really short fuse here. And don't beat yourself up about what you should have or could have done. We haven't been given a whole lot of choice, but they own us now and we have to adjust to their rules.

Leslie: I'll do my best.

Later that afternoon Leslie takes the reports to Mark.

Leslie: Wow, Mark, it looks like we might have bigger problems than we thought.

Mark: I was afraid of that. What did you find?

Leslie: You know, Ted [the previous CFO] used to let each plant manage their chart of accounts, but we stopped that after I came on board. Well, it seems the accounting managers can still change the names on the accounts even though they can't set up new account numbers, so they have accounts with different names being used for different things. How in the world are we going to explain this to Randy without looking incompetent?

Mark: We just have to do our best and hope he doesn't expect too much this first month-end. It might be time to start making some of the changes we have been talking about.

Leslie: Look, Mark, I know you want to cut costs and I know Randy is putting a lot of pressure on us to show higher profit, but I already have three accounting managers running six locations and the other six managers are just not strong enough to handle more than they already have.

Mark: Well maybe we don't have the right people on the bus.

Leslie: That could be true, but I'm so busy with all the additional reporting demands that I don't have time to deal with the details at each facility.

Mark: I think it's time we bring in someone to help you who will have the time to address these issues.

Leslie: I agree, and I have some ideas about that. Let's talk about it once I get these reports figured out.

MEETING WITH THE NEW CEO

Randy: It looks to me like margins are still too low. What changes are you making to improve the margins at each location?

Mark: We're asking each PM to review their staffing levels and review cost of goods in detail each month. We're also in the process of moving some of our benefit plans onto your plan. Since you have so many more employees, your rates are better than what we can get.

Bill: Randy, we're still trying to figure out all the rules of the game here, and it's going to take some time, but we have good people in all locations and we are focused on the cost saving measures that you are pressing us on.

Randy: Okay. I have another meeting I need to get to. Keep focusing on cutting costs. Also the costs don't look very consistent from plant to plant; do you know why?

Leslie: Yes, at least we are trying to understand why and fix that problem. Each plant is used to operating independently and we are trying to standardize their accounting practices, but it's hard to find time.

Randy: Okay—well keep working on that too. We'll meet again next month. [Randy gets up and leaves the conference room.]

Bill: Whew! Well, I think that went pretty well.

Mark: Well? That went terrible! We look like a bunch of monkeys who don't know what the heck they're doing.

Bill: Whoa, wait a minute. A lot of this is not our fault.

Mark: The heck it isn't. We need to get those accounting managers working together as a team—they need to all use the same account numbers for all the same types of things. And we need to think about getting rid of the ones who don't "get it."

Leslie: I agree, and it's my fault. I just haven't had time, but it looks like I'm going to have to make time. Bob [the VP of IT] is really complaining about a few of the accounting managers or their clerks who can't use the job-costing software correctly, especially when they "push the wrong button" and he has to spend 4 hours on a Saturday night fixing messes.

Mark: Yeah, he has made the same comment to me and his team is getting ready to roll out a new version of that software—have they discussed the schedule for this with you yet?

Leslie: No, he hasn't, and I think we need to delay that until we can get some of these other problems ironed out.

Bill: Well, you had better hurry up because I promised Randy that we'd have the new software running at all locations by June 30th.

Mark: Great. Leslie, it looks like you and I need to spend some time working on a plan to help these accounting managers get their act together. These problems can't continue.

Leslie: Okay. Do you have some time tomorrow to discuss some of the ideas I have?

Mark: Sure, let's do it tomorrow afternoon.

WHAT DOES ACCOUNTING HAVE TO DO WITH HUMAN RESOURCES (HR) AND ORGANIZATION DEVELOPMENT (OD)?

The next day Leslie, the CFO, meets with Mark, the COO.

Mark: Okay, Leslie, what thoughts do you have about moving forward with your team?

Leslie: The more I think about our meeting yesterday, the more embarrassed I am. I can't believe that I haven't taken time to fix some of the problems we knew we had but that weren't priorities. The most frustrating part is that some of my accountants and managers get it right every time. But the others—they can't even find their own mistakes; they rely on me to do it for them. I made this chart to show where we have strong accounting managers and where we don't. I also went back to my notes from our last accounting meeting and the managers seemed really frustrated with me at the time, but I was so overwhelmed with the acquisition that I didn't have time to address their problems once I was back in the office. I really need to hire someone to help manage some of the day-to-day processes, but I know that won't be approved if I don't cut someplace else. My staff in this office is already overworked and I can't ask them to do more. But I don't think that's true for the plant accounting managers. If they are truly acting as managers, they should each be able to oversee two plants.

Mark: Great! Problem solved. You have four good managers and 12 locations—that's three each! I'll go start the termination process for the other five.

Leslie: Now wait a minute; it's not that simple. Plant #12 isn't within commuting distance of any of the other locations, so we have to have someone to manage that facility alone. Not only that, if we're going to expect managers to spend their time driving from location to location, we will have to compensate them in some way. In the winter some of those roads can be pretty tricky, and you know we can't always rely on electricity or phone line connections to allow the managers to work from home.

Mark: Okay, I see what you mean. Let's table this for a minute and talk about the other ideas you have in mind.

Leslie: One of the most important things we need to do is to get one consistent chart of accounts and then get the accounting managers trained to use it. We need to make sure the accounting clerks are trained in their jobs because I have a feeling the accounting managers are doing more of the clerical work than they let on. They were hired to be managers, but I don't think they know what that means. I think they need some training in how to review the work of their staff and how to provide feedback for improvement. If they were reviewing the work instead of doing it themselves, then I think they could manage three plants each. But I can't make that happen overnight. In fact, I'm not quite sure how to make it happen at all.

Mark: That's a really good start. What other things are you thinking about?

Leslie: It would be nice if they could be trained on the job-cost system and if a manual was available for trouble-shooting problems. That might solve some of the weekend phone calls to Bob. If we train them in groups, then maybe that will encourage them to share ideas about their own best practices—especially the managers that do "get it." This might help to facilitate their working as a team, instead of as individual plants. If they could rely on each other instead of competing against each other, I think everyone in the plants will benefit, not just the accounting departments.

Mark: You're right. The PMs need to function more as a team too.

Leslie: You know it was always part of our culture to try to be the best plant, but the new owners don't care about that competition anymore. They want to know what our bottom line is, who contributes, and who doesn't. They want performance so that we all win in the end, but I don't know how to get that across to the plants. They're all so competitive with each other, but it won't work anymore. I'm really worried about this new software rollout. Especially since some of our staff still doesn't know how to use the old software. I'm so tired of Bob calling them a bunch of idiots. You know part of the problem is IT—they change things and don't tell us, they roll out software without any training or user's manuals, and then they get mad when things go wrong. It's so frustrating.

Mark: Well, Bob has been with the company for a long time. He's really smart and everyone likes him, so you can forget about trying to change him.

Leslie: I know, but I still don't think that's acceptable. If everyone liked me but I couldn't do my job, I certainly wouldn't expect to keep it. All I am asking for is an organized system for rolling out the new software, along with some training on how to use it. And it would be nice if he didn't refer to my staff as a bunch of idiots.

Mark: I'll talk to Bob about that. Let's put the software rollout on the agenda for the next staff meeting. Is there anything else that you think would help your team?

Leslie: I guess the last issue bothering me is Jenny—you know, the accounting manager for plants #6 and #7. She's really bright, she's working on an advanced accounting degree, and frankly she works circles around everyone else. There's a lot of potential there, but I'm worried the others will eat her for lunch if I promote her. Some of the other managers have a lot more seniority, but no one else really performs at the same level. It won't be easy to supervise the other accounting managers, especially since some of them have been on their own for so long. The PMs really don't spend that much time with them, so they've managed the accounting clerks however they want. I don't think it is very effective to have accounting managers reporting to PMs when I'm responsible for the work they do. On the other hand, I'm not sure it's fair to put Jenny in such a difficult job, but she has indicated that she wants to move up. I'm pretty sure that with the proper mentoring she could become the controller overseeing all 12 plants. The other thing we can't do is go in and make all of these changes at the same time. We still have 12 plants to run and we have to have some kind of accounting department that is functional—I can't just make all of these changes at once. There's going to have to be an intervention plan put together with a timeline for implementation.

Mark: Okay, so let's just recap all of your ideas, and then we can talk about an intervention. If I heard you correctly, you want to streamline the chart of accounts across all plants and train the accounting managers and their staff on how to use it. Then you want to train the accounting managers to really function like managers because you think they might be doing a lot of this work themselves. Once they are trained as managers, you would like to give them oversight for three plants instead of two, and then we can weed out the underperformers. At the same time we need to work on a plan for the new software rollout and make sure that the proper training occurs.

Leslie: Yes, and that the training come with some sort of reference manual.

Mark: Right, a manual for using the software. Okay, and finally, you want to come up with some kind of development plan for Jenny. This means plants #6 and #7 will need a new accounting manager.

Leslie: Yes, or we need to decide if one of the other managers can be developed into the kind of accounting manager we need.

Mark: I understand. It sounds like this is a big project. Maybe we should consult with the OD staff of the parent company. They might have some resources that would help us out.

Leslie: That's a good idea. I need some help putting all of this together. I'm an accountant, not an HR consultant.

The following is the staffing chart Leslie referred to during her conversation with Mark.

Plants #1 and #2: Accounting manager has been with the company 20 years and the accounting staff rarely makes errors.

Plant #3: Accounting manager has been with the company 3 years but errors are common, especially with simple things like electricity bills that should be recorded every month. This plant is located within 30 miles of plants #1 and #2.

Plants #4 and #5: Accounting manager has been with the company 10 years and was trained by the accounting manager for plants #1 and #2. This accounting staff rarely makes errors.

Plants #6 and #7: Accounting manager has been with the company 5 years and is the only accounting manager with an accounting degree. The accounting staff makes frequent errors, but they are corrected before they cause problems for corporate. The accounting manager is working on an advanced degree and has indicated she would like to move up in the company.

Plant #8: Accounting manager has been with the company 2 years and the accounting staff makes frequent errors that cost the IT department countless hours to fix. This plant is located within 45 miles of plants #4 and #5.

Plant #9: Accounting manager has been with the company 8 years and the accounting staff rarely makes errors. This plant is located within 35 miles of plants #6 and #7.

Plant #10: Accounting manager has been with the company 5 years and the accounting staff makes frequent errors that cost the IT department countless hours to fix.

Plant #11: Accounting manager has been with the company 25 years and the accounting staff rarely makes errors. This plant is located within 60 miles of plant #10.

Plant #12: Accounting manager has been with the company a year and the accounting staff makes frequent errors that cost the IT department time and the accounting department time. This plant is not located within driving distance of any other location.

Discussion Questions

1. If you were the leader of the OD department for the parent company, what recommendations would you have for Leslie about how to proceed with accomplishing her goals for the team?

2. What is the best format to handle team discussions? Do you suggest a team meeting, meetings with each individual accounting manager, or another format?

3. Are there certain activities you would recommend to help the Acme team (at corporate and at the plants) adjust to the new corporate culture?

4. Are there process issues that need to be addressed by Leslie, and how would you recommend she do this?

5. Is there an overall intervention strategy that you would propose?

FOR FURTHER READING

Chermack, T. J., Bodwell, W., & Glick, M. (2010). Two strategies for leveraging teams toward organizational effectiveness: Scenario planning and organizational ambidexterity. *Advances in Developing Human Resources, 12*(1), 137–156.

Crother-Laurin, C. (2006). Effective teams: A symptom of healthy leadership. *Journal for Quality & Participation, 29*(3), 5–8.

Kozlowski, S. W. J., & Ilgen, D. R. (2006). Enhancing the effectiveness of work groups and teams. *Psychological Science in the Public Interest, 7*(3), 77–124.

Pearce, C. L., Manz, C. C., & Sims, H. P. (2009). Where do we go from here? Is shared leadership the key to team success? *Organizational Dynamics, 38*(3), 234–238.

Pina, M. I. D., Martinez, A. M. R., & Martinez, L. G. (2008). Teams in organizations: A review on team effectiveness. *Team Performance Management, 14*(1/2), 7–21.

Who's Making the Decisions at Livingston University?

Andrea M. Pampaloni

─── **Learning Objectives** ───

- To better understand the complexitites of teamwork.
- To recognize how position and power can influence group interactions.
- To demonstrate the need for effective communication in achieving group outcomes.

BACKGROUND ON LIVINGSTON UNIVERSITY

The Organization

Livingston University is a leading technological university with an emphasis on research. It has a total enrollment of 2,150 undergraduate and 3,500 graduate students with about 250 full-time faculty. Its broad-based curriculum focuses on entrepreneurialism and cross-disciplinary research, contributing to its excellent reputation for which it has been cited by several nationally recognized ranking entities. Livingston also makes considerable effort to develop collaborative partnerships, both externally between and among businesses, government, and other universities, as well as internally across departments, in an effort to enhance the learning environment of the school for students and faculty.

Decision to Redesign the Website

As a result of increasing competition among institutions of higher education to attract and retain students, Livingston decided to undertake a rebranding campaign to better position itself among its peers. One area needing immediate attention was the school website.

Even prior to the implementation of a formal Web Redesign Committee, there was consensus across multiple department and divisions of the school that the website was uninviting and ineffective, which was supported by feedback from potential students. Thus with the approval and support of the Office of the President of the university, the responsibility both for hiring a consultant and putting together a redesign committee fell to the director of communications. The director, Byron Bailyn, identified 14 departments and key individuals from throughout the university to participate on the committee to ensure participation and representation.

Although resolving the issues associated with the website was Byron's defined problem, he knew there was more at stake. Implicit in his direction from the university president, Nora Scottie, Byron understood that this group was expected to model the spirit of collaboration that Livingston considered a foundational element to its image and reputation. The outcome of this group would be closely monitored as a benchmark for future endeavors. Byron knew that he had his work cut out for him.

The Web Redesign Committee

Byron looked at the clock and saw that he had 15 minutes before his meeting with the university's president, Nora Scottie. He felt the beginning of a migraine as he wondered how it had gotten to this point. Less than a year ago, Byron was flattered and excited to be selected by President Scottie to lead a new branding initiative. The goal was to update the image of Livingston University to attract new students and faculty, and the first step was to give the website a much needed overhaul. As he gathered his notes and thought back to the energy and enthusiasm of those first few committee meetings last April, he wondered how things had gotten out of hand.

The Web Redesign Committee had started off well, with an enthusiastic group of diverse participants representing 14 different departments throughout the university. This included people from each of the three schools within the university (business, humanities, and engineering), the admissions department, library, information technology, student life, finance office, office of development, and the communications office. Byron was pleased that 25 people came to the first meeting, and although attendance dropped off a bit as the meetings continued as was expected, he thought that the core group of 15 or so people from at least 10 different departments provided a good range of representation.

With this level of support from people with such various backgrounds, Byron was eager to address the group's task and optimistic about the outcome. At the same time he was nervous about the process that lay before him. Although the group's specific task was the redesign of the website, President Scottie made it clear to Byron that more was at stake. A unique aspect of Livingston's mission was the development of a heavily interdisciplinary curriculum. The long-term goal was that students would not only take complementary courses across departments and schools within Livingston, but also benefit from workshops or other experiential learning experiences in conjunction with administrative offices such as communications, public relations, and information technology to better prepare the students for postgraduation careers. It was made clear to Byron that this committee was being viewed as an unofficial model to demonstrate the value and effectiveness of universitywide collaboration in decision making before making any drastic changes to the curriculum that might backfire. As President Scottie had said, only half-jokingly, "We want to make sure everyone can play nicely together!" It also was made clear that as the Executive Director of Communications he was expected to do everything with his power to "encourage" the committee members to work together toward a productive solution. Byron knew that there was a lot riding on the outcome of this committee's efforts, for both himself individually, as well as the university.

As an indication of its commitment to the project, the university hired an outside consultant specializing in branding and technology for higher education institutions to design the new website. Since the project was on a fast track with a target of unveiling the new website before the new semester began in September, the group got to work right away. They agreed to meet every 2 weeks to keep the momentum going and to meet the deadline. At the initial meeting Byron introduced the consultant, Martin Kelly, and gave an overview of the project. He also noted that the consultant's contract was limited in scope to 15 Web pages, including a new home page, as well as pages earmarked for university history, a message from the president, frequently asked questions, and other universal content. The intent was to establish and promote a clear brand across the general information sections of the site and to provide a foundational structure from which other departments could develop their own sites, though it would have to be at their own budgetary expense. The committee understood the limitations, and several people approached Martin after the meeting to discuss potential changes to their department's Web pages, or talked among themselves to consider possibilities that might benefit their departments.

Encouraged by the participation and collaborative spirit of the initial meeting, the next day Byron e-mailed a brief survey to committee members to get their views on the current website, both the positive aspects that they may want to retain, as well as any changes they would like to recommend. Although he was a bit disappointed by the limited number of responses he received, he was pleased to see that those who did respond provided detailed feedback. Also, there was a degree of consistency across the comments that confirmed that revisions to the website were the appropriate starting point for Livingston's branding makeover.

This informal needs assessment served as the starting point for the next meeting 2 weeks later. Byron began the second meeting by highlighting some key themes that had emerged from the survey (e.g., too much information; difficult to navigate; unappealing visuals). He then turned it over to Martin, who made a presentation to the committee highlighting his firm's experience and capabilities, and offering general ideas and examples for the committee to consider. Martin took up the discussion Byron had started, encouraging participants to elaborate on the comments they made on Byron's survey, or other issues that they thought might better identify a new direction for the website. When Martin was done, Byron took questions from the group. In answering them, he noticed that many of the comments reflected the goals of the individual's department. He had been prepared for some level of territoriality, so he encouraged them to take a more collectivistic view toward how they could best address the needs of the entire university community. He managed to shift the discussion to focus on broader issues, but Byron sensed that this would be something he would really need to stay on top of if they wanted to complete their task within the deadline. The meeting adjourned with Martin's promise to have some initial designs prepared for the committee's review at the next meeting.

Before presenting the preliminary design to the committee at the next meeting, Byron and Martin agreed that they should preview it for key senior administrators and the deans of each of the three schools to get their buy-in, and to ensure that the design was in keeping with Livingston's view of the image of the school. Byron was anxious about the comments the executive level might offer, but they were positive overall and indicated they were interested in what the committee had to say. Encouraged by this initial feedback, Martin and Byron were eager to see if the committee was in agreement. There was a buzz in the room at the third meeting as Martin unveiled three potential designs for the new home page. The new pages were drastically different from the current home page, with more white space, less print, and cleaner graphics. Everyone started talking at once, excitedly noting the contrast from the current design and commenting on the layout, colors, and design. Once everyone got beyond the initial delight at the improvement and began focusing on specifics, a more serious discussion on the merits of each design ensued. One of the three options presented was quickly ruled out as it was a distant third to the other two designs. A second was well-liked, but the inclusion of a recurring graphic image of a student put some people off, so the consensus was to work with the final design.

While the comments were positive overall, several issues arose. Dr. Allison Marks, an associate dean, noted the need for a search function as well as the inclusion of a link from the home page to various school calendars. Bridget Wright, a senior assistant to the dean of the business school, was adamant that there should be direct links to each of the university's three schools on the home page. The director of admissions, Rick Daniels, wanted to see a more prominent link to the admissions department, though he was quick to point out that he was concerned about potential students being confused. Maureen Dennehy, the vice president of information technology, pointed out that the new website would require a more advanced technological infrastructure to accommodate the "bells and whistles" of the more sophisticated design. Although significant, the group agreed that the issues were solvable, so the rollout date was identified as mid-summer and the group suggested that a great deal of fanfare announce its arrival.

Carrying the momentum forward, Martin came to the next meeting well-prepared. He revised the initial designs to incorporate comments that the committee had made, and also introduced his idea for Livingston's new "brand," including logo, colors, fonts, and usage guidelines. Further, to address the technological concerns raised by Ms. Dennehy, he had done some preliminary research and created an evaluative comparison of possible content management systems (CMSs) that could handle the features of the newly designed website. Based on his findings, Martin noted to the group that because the selection of a new CMS would directly influence other decisions about the site, the timeline for the rollout of the home page and additional contracted pages had to be pushed back to the beginning of July.

While disappointed by the delay, the committee was pleased with Martin's work. They agreed it was better to address all issues upfront, particularly since it was summer and the pace at the university was slower than usual, rather than be surprised later on. As Byron opened the meeting to discuss the revisions, comments and questions continued to focus on representation of the three schools on the home page, availability of the calendar and search function, and who should be involved in the selection of the CMS. Bridget Wright asked if each school's home page would mirror the university landing page. Byron reminded the group of the contractual parameters and that the original contract did not include development of separate images and pages for each school. Several groups again expressed interest in discussing separate contracts with Martin's company to develop their departmental websites to make them better sync with the new home page. In fact, Martin had told Byron that Rick Daniels had already approached him about the possibility of entering into a contract to update the Admissions Department website.

Despite the generally positive progress, Byron's anxiety was increasing. He was acutely aware of the subtle shifts that had taken place throughout the course of the meetings. He noticed that departments continued to stick together, figuratively and literally, based on the issues they were advocating. For example, Bridget Wright and Dr. Marks had begun sitting next to each other and supporting the ideas each other raised. Likewise, Stew and Claire, representatives for the library, typically sat next to Josh and James from student affairs, providing a supportive yet distinctly nonconfrontational cluster at one end of the table. The key players, namely those in more senior positions at the university, continued to press the agenda of their individual departments rather than focusing on the collective needs of the university. Further, in addition to their "pet" topics, they also monopolized discussions on peripheral issues. Byron recalled how during the last meeting Martin was questioned at length by both Bridget and Dr. Marks on his choice of a particular font, despite his expertise in the area and clearly stated reasoning for his selection.

On his way back to his office after the meeting, Byron was increasingly troubled by the direction the group had taken. Now closer to the end of the task than the beginning, the core group of "regulars" who attended the meetings remained involved and enthusiastic; however, the subgroups were monopolizing the direction of the meeting, and thus the development of the website. He was becoming frustrated that the equity he hoped to achieve through the formation of a "neutral" group was not coming to fruition. As he reviewed the issues the group targeted for further discussion and replayed the meetings in his head, he was hit with a sinking feeling that all the key issues that were still on the table for discussion had been identified by senior representatives within the group. In fact, as he gave it more thought he recognized that there were some people, like Stew, Claire, Josh, and James who hadn't ever spoken at a meeting! With the final decision on the website coming up soon, Byron knew he was rapidly approaching a point where it would be too late to create a more equitable climate before the project ended.

Byron decided that he needed to take a different approach at the next meeting to address the disparity. He was ever mindful of President Scottie's mandate that the different departments should "play nicely together" and that the diverse make-up of the committee should be reflected in the decision making. What sounded so good in theory, Byron was realizing, was much more difficult to translate into action. The reality was that there were not many occasions at Livingston when an assistant dean sat in the same meeting as a staff person and both were considered equal participants. If this group couldn't come together on something like a website, which was relevant to all their departments, how could they expect to be successful in forming other interdepartmental teams to address even more significant important campuswide issues? Byron snapped himself back to the matter at hand. "There's no sense worrying about that now," he thought, "when there might not be a future for me unless I can get this group to 'play nicely'!"

As a first step, Byron logged on to the restricted blog Martin had set up for the committee. He was happy to see that there was some activity by meeting participants as well as a few peripheral committee members who did not regularly attend the meetings. Dr. Marks also had made the selected design available to a group of students, who he had authorized blog access to get their feedback. Byron was encouraged that the blog was drawing some interest beyond the committee. While there were a variety of responses, they were general comments typically highlighting "wish list" items the respondents would like to see included on the redesigned website, from color suggestions to more detailed technical issues. However, as in the meetings, there were virtually no comments from the "silent minority," as Byron had come to think of those devoted committee members who attended the meetings but never went against the more prominent members or voiced their own issues or concerns. As he scrolled through the site he also noticed that Dr. Marks had posted a comment about the calendar function and a search option and was adamant about the inclusion of both. Rick Daniels had likewise made a comment about the importance of prominently featured links such as admissions and financial aid to better serve potential students. "Smart approach," thought Byron, "he's selling his own position without making it all about his department."

Since the blog confirmed a dichotomy that seemed to be based on differences in seniority, and given the shortening timeframe of the project, Byron knew that the next meeting would be his last opportunity to try to change the dynamics of the group. At that meeting, Martin would be presenting revisions to the selected design based on the committee's feedback. If the silent minority didn't speak up about issues they felt could impact their departments, the website design would be finalized with what amounted to no representation by these groups. While he recognized that some people may not be commenting because they were in full agreement with the committee's decisions, if they weren't participating because they were uncomfortable or intimidated, which Byron expected was the case, then all hopes of creating a flatter group model would fly out the window. It would take a delicate balance to encourage these participants while trying not to offend the more vocal senior members. "Oh brother!" Byron thought to himself. "I'm doing it, too! I'm more worried about maintaining the status quo than taking the risk of saying the wrong thing! If I can't do it, how can I expect the others to?"

This epiphany sparked Byron into action. He sat down at his desk with his meeting notes and the blog open on his computer. He started a list and began grouping different discussion topics from the meetings and he realized that the meetings were very much in line with the culture of Livingston, particularly when it came to observing the hierarchy. He noted that although meeting participants were intended to have equal voices in the process, those with higher status, like the deans or their representatives, more openly expressed themselves, often with little or no feedback from other members. As he continued with his lists, Byron realized that in addition to their pet topics, those in senior positions also tended to monopolize discussions on peripheral issues like font size and locations of menu bars. "No wonder the silent majority doesn't speak!" Byron said aloud. "They can't get a word in edgewise!" With the evidence staring him in the face, Byron decided on a course of action.

At the next meeting Byron started off with a different approach. He distributed to each participant a worksheet that he had created. On it was a list of issues related to the design of the website that had repeatedly been discussed but not yet resolved, along with different options for their resolution. He asked each member to identify their recommended course of action for the listed items, noting that by doing so they could better direct their time and efforts to the issues that needed it most. As the group filled out the forms Byron mentally crossed his fingers. His hope was that this method would identify issues of concern to the *whole* group, forcing a more participatory discussion. Alternately, if there was little disagreement, he could report to President Scottie that even if the idea of an equitable group that wasn't based on seniority didn't work out, the group had completed their task and arrived at a consensus regarding the final redesign of the website.

The committee members passed their completed sheets toward him and talked among themselves while he and Martin tallied the results. As they reviewed the responses they exchanged a glance. Like Byron, Martin had become frustrated with the progress (and some of the members!) of the committee. After the last meeting when he and Byron went back to Byron's office he had burst out "I've been doing this for over 20 years! I've created websites and brands for at least 15 other schools and I know what works and what doesn't work. You're paying me to tell you, but these people aren't listening! You've got some serious issues to work out and they're stuck on what shade of color to use!" Byron commiserated with Martin and they vented for a while, but the fact remained that Byron was responsible for the project and its successful completion. Now, seeing the groups' responses in front of them, they both realized that Byron's concerns about a disparity in views were valid. Although there was unanimity on several issues, the committee was split on two of the recurring recommendations: the inclusion of links to the three schools on home page, and a calendar function on the home page. Byron stood to begin the discussion.

"Thank you all for this helpful feedback. It looks like we are in agreement on a number of issues, so I recommend we focus on the two key issues that remain. There are conflicting views on what links we should include on the home page; specifically, whether links to the three schools and to a calendar function should be included." Byron had barely finished his sentence when Bridget Wright spoke up. "This is ridiculous! There are only three schools and they should be prominently displayed on the home page. I don't know why we're even having this conversation again." Byron controlled his rising anger as he reiterated the same response that Martin had repeatedly proffered since the first time this issue was raised. "Of course it's important to offer information about the schools, but visitors can easily get to that using the academic tab, which, as Martin has pointed out to us based on his vast experience in creating college websites, is more intuitive for potential students. The idea is to keep the home page crisp and free from clutter to focus on those elements that are there."

He paused for a breath and thought to himself, "It's now or never!" Picking up the copies of the worksheet he said "Based on the responses we received here today, a number of people agree. Would any of you like to weigh in on this topic?" Out of the corner of his eye Byron saw the silent minority was very still. With a quick look at Claire, Stew leaned forward like he was about to say something. Byron held his breath hoping for the breakthrough, but before Stew could speak Dr. Marks jumped in. "I'm in agreement with Bridget. How much space will it take up? Why don't we just have it in both places?"

"Well," Byron started, stalling for time to allow Stew to jump in. However, Stew had quickly leaned back in his seat and became completely absorbed in his notes. "As Martin has pointed out, students are more likely to go to the academics tab because while they may know what area they want to major in, they're not always clear on which school houses their chosen major." The debate continued, as it did when the topic shifted to the inclusion of the calendar function, with Bridget and Dr. Marks advocating for their preferences, and Byron and Martin providing a counterview.

"We're not getting anywhere," Dr. Marks said as the end of the meeting got nearer. "What do you propose, Byron?" Before Byron could answer Bridget spoke up. "When is the next review by the deans? I think they would be interested in weighing-in on the final decision" she said pointedly. Byron responded that a meeting was scheduled with the deans for later that afternoon. Before he could get back to Dr. Marks' query, however, Dr. Marks got up and said "Well then, we may as well wait for their input instead of wasting any more time here. We'll look forward to hearing your report on the meeting, Byron." Shortly thereafter the meeting ended and the committee members, usually chatty following a meeting, left in relative silence.

Now, a week later, Byron sat in his office preparing for his meeting with President Scottie. He knew she'd want a detailed report on how the redesign process was going but also on the interactions within the committee. As he gathered his notes he looked up at the e-mail she had sent to confirm the meeting: "Looking forward to your update on the project and the committee. Is everyone playing nicely together?"

Discussion Questions

1. Byron was excited about convening the website redesign because it was an opportunity to offer an equal voice to participants across various levels of the university. Where did or didn't this occur? How did this affect the direction and outcomes of the group?

2. How did power play into the decision-making process of the Web Redesign Committee? In groups with participants from various organizational roles and levels, is it possible for everyone to have an equal voice?

3. Could some kind of intervention have helped the team work together more collaboratively? What would you have done if you were in Byron's position to make this team more successful?

4. In an organization with a hierarchal culture, is it possible to have "flat" committees in which all members are equal? Based on your group experiences, what do you think could have been done differently with the Web Redesign Committee to foster more equitable participation?

5. Imagine that you are a consultant hired by the school to shadow key members of the organization, and you sat in on all the meetings of the Web Redesign Committee. You have been asked to provide constructive, critical feedback to Byron on his role in the committee. Identify the strengths and weaknesses of Byron, as well as the team, and provide a briefing of alternative steps that might have been taken to encourage a more equitable participation environment.

FOR FURTHER READING

Hirokawa, R. Y., & Poole, M. S. (1996). *Communication and group decision making.* Thousand Oaks, CA: Sage.

Krone, K. J. (1992). A comparison of organizational, structural and relationship effects on subordinates' upward influence choices. *Communication Quarterly, 40*(1), 1–15.

Orlitzky, M., & Hirokawa, R. Y. (2001). To err is human, to correct for it divine: A meta-analysis of research testing the functional theory of group decision making effectiveness. *Small Group Research, 32*(3), 314–331.

Schein, E. (1985). *Organizational culture and leadership.* San Francisco: Jossey-Bass.

Shults, C. (2008) Making the case for a positive approach to improving organizational performance in higher education institutions. *Community College Review, 36*(2), 133–159.

GREENCYCLE PUBLISHING

DONALD L. ANDERSON AND JENNIFER A. THOMPSON

Learning Objectives

- To allow you to practice identifying sources of conflict within and between teams.
- To practice outlining an intervention strategy and activities for an interteam intervention.

Greencycle Publishing is a publisher of nonfiction specialty books focusing on the environment and sustainability movement. Titles published by the company fit with the company's core lists in the areas of environmental practices and conservation, environmental resource planning, business ethics and sustainability, global environmental politics, and corporate social responsibility.

The company was founded in 2002 by David Green, who remains the CEO and publisher of the organization. He has an extensive background in publishing, having had roles as an acquisitions editor, director of sales and marketing, and managing editor for a major New York publishing house for almost 25 years prior to founding Greencycle. All books published by Greencycle are approved by David himself. He considers every proposal, signs every contract, and has a keen eye for trends in the publishing industry and the environmental movement. Observers describe him as a successful and intelligent businessman with a commanding presence and a boisterous temperament that many find intimidating. He is a "big picture" thinker and aside from initially approving them, rarely likes to get involved with the minutiae of publishing any individual title.

As one of the few remaining small publishers in a highly competitive field, Greencycle relies primarily on word of mouth advertising for its titles, which are sold only through the company's website and a few major online retailers. David once said, "We sell books, but we also sell ideas. We are only as good as our next title, and that requires us to seek out and publish the work of innovative and cutting-edge authors whose work will allow us to continue to offer groundbreaking titles that lead the industry." Greencycle's commitment to its authors and insistence on producing the highest quality books in both content and design are well-known throughout the industry.

As more consumers seek electronic publications and more authors publish content on the Internet, the publishing industry faces enormous pressure to find and promote successful books. Last year the company published 122 titles, and budget projections call for 150 titles this year—about three per work week on average. Despite the growth rate of published titles, margins and profits remain tight.

THE ORGANIZATION

David leaves the day-to-day management of the editorial and production processes to Arthur Thomas, the managing editor. Arthur's duties include overseeing the editorial aspects of the company, including book content and production. Under Arthur are two areas of work: acquisitions and production.

The roles and responsibilities of each department are described below.

Acquisitions Editors

The acquisitions editor always thinks about the future. The editor's job is to ensure that a regular pipeline of titles will be published over the coming months and years to maintain Greencycle's reputation as a leading publisher of environmental titles. To do this, the editor's main responsibility is to solicit book proposals from leading authors who specialize in topics published by Greencycle. Networking is a central component of the job and editors regularly attend major industry conferences to meet prospective authors and to promote Greencycle titles at the conference sales booth. Each editor is compensated, in part, on working with prospective authors to develop 60 to 70 books per calendar year. (This plan takes into consideration that a percentage of authors will fail to write books as committed, will not meet the agreed publishing schedule, or will fail to meet Greencycle's publishing standards). Throughout the book-writing process, the acquisitions department editors work with authors to ensure that their manuscripts meet Greencycle's requirements, such as ensuring that reprint permissions are sought for photos, art, or other graphics reprinted in a Greencycle title. Each acquisitions editor has an editorial assistant to help with administrative matters, answer author correspondence, and develop contracts.

When an author submits a final manuscript, the acquisitions editors ensure that the submitted manuscripts are complete before they are discussed in a formal launch meeting attended by the acquisitions editors, production editors, Arthur Thomas, and David Green. At this meeting, the manuscript is formally handed off to the production editors, who take it from there.

Figure 24.1   Greencycle Publishing Organizational Chart

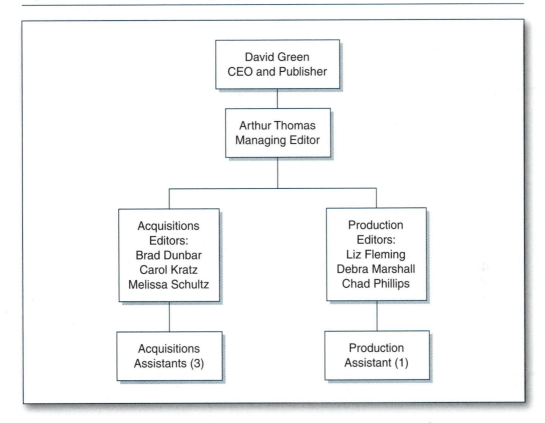

Production Editors

The production editor's work begins after the launch meeting, when the clock starts on the production process. The production editors are responsible for the painstaking work of taking submitted manuscripts and guiding them through the process until they become finished books. Production editing requires an eye for detail, as the editors read every single word and page of the book multiple times. The production editor works with a network of freelance copyeditors, layout and design specialists, proofreaders, and indexers, always monitoring each book's progress to keep it on schedule. At each stage, the manuscript is sent by the production editor to the freelancer, and after copyediting, design, and so on, the manuscript is returned to the production editor, who is always responsible for the quality of the product. The ever-present looming deadline is the top priority of the production editor, as is the quality of the finished book. A poor quality layout and typographical and grammatical errors are the enemy of the production process, and such quality faults would no doubt cause Greencycle's authors and customers to lack confidence in the content, as well as cause embarrassment to the organization's reputation. Each production editor juggles between 25 and

30 manuscripts at any given time, and the production editor is fully aware that he or she makes the final quality check of the book before it goes to press. The production editors share a production assistant who helps to check manuscripts and works with authors when questions arise.

David is proud to say that the Greencycle production process is among the fastest in the publishing industry. He considers it a central factor in Greencycle's financial success, since each day the process is delayed means another day the title cannot be sold to an eager market. His "blow ups" at schedule slips are legendary.

SCENE 1: ACQUISITIONS STAFF MEETING

The acquisitions editors try to meet weekly to accomplish several objectives. They discuss the new books each is ready to propose to David, cover any threats to the schedule for books that are in the writing process, and share the status of books ready to be handed off to production at the next launch meeting. If any editor is out of town during the launch meeting, the others can cover the book in the meeting on his or her behalf. Meeting like this weekly is a goal rarely met, however, since one of the three is almost always at a conference, on the way to a conference, or returning from a conference. When all three are in the office at the same time, however, as they are today, an in-person meeting is a luxury. The acquisitions staff meeting typically takes place in the lavish boardroom upstairs in the Greencycle Publishing building.

Brad:	Good morning, acquisitions team! Glad to see everyone in the office for once. How was the Association for Environmental Politics conference?
Carol:	Exhausting. I got in late last night after my plane was delayed. An entire box of display books got lost in shipping to the conference hotel, so I spent 3 hours on Monday night looking for it. I finally found it in the hotel manager's office, so I was up until 2 a.m. setting up the display, and back at 7:30 to run the booth.
Melissa:	That happened to me 2 weeks ago in Seattle. Then, last week I was in Austin and it wasn't books that were lost, but all of the order forms and brochures. Marketing had the wrong conference name on the box, so it got returned.
Carol:	I'm so glad to finally be home. I hadn't seen my daughter in 8 days after two back-to-back trips. Anyway, it was a good conference. I talked to one of my current authors about a second title in the corporate sustainability series, and I think David will go for it.
Brad:	That sounds promising. I haven't been that fortunate. If I don't have something come through soon, I'm not going to reach the threshold for a quarterly bonus. I'm getting really stressed about it.
Carol:	Does anyone have anything going to launch this week?

Melissa: I got an e-mail that Warner submitted his manuscript yesterday, so it's finally ready to go, after a long delay. I'll present it this week.

Brad: David will be happy to see that.

Melissa: I know. He's really been on my case about it. Sometimes these authors can be so frustrating, missing deadlines, and I can't do anything about it. Hopefully production can pull off a miracle and get it to press early.

Carol: Uh, yeah, I'm sure they can. [*everyone laughs*]

SCENE 2: PRODUCTION STAFF MEETING

The weekly production staff meeting is cancelled as often as it is held, typically because one or more of the production editors is working on a major crisis directly impacting a book's schedule. In the production staff meeting, the team typically reviews the current list of books in production with special attention to any book that threatens to slip past its schedule. In these cases, another production editor or the production assistant can sometimes share the workload, but such spare time is rare. The work can be sent to a freelancer, but the added expense generally makes this impossible. The production staff typically meets in one of the production editor's offices, as they do here when they convene at Debra's desk.

Debra: [*pulling one of several boxes off a bookshelf*] Does anyone want any cereal? I haven't had breakfast.

Liz: I think there's still leftover pizza from last night in the break room refrigerator.

Chad: I missed a pizza night? I'm sorry. I had to leave last night by 6:30 to pick up my wife from the airport.

Liz: No big deal, we all cover for each other from time to time.

Chad: We get to buy our own pizza at our desks, acquisitions gets steak dinners on an expense account. That seems fair, eh?

Debra: Don't even get me started. OK, so what's going on? Does anyone have anything in danger of remotely staying on schedule? [*laughter*]

Angela: [*walking in quickly*] Sorry I'm late.

Debra: That's OK, you haven't missed anything.

Angela: [*handing a manila envelope to Debra*] Here, these are for the Warner book.

Debra: What is it? [*opens the envelope to find a dozen color photos held together by a paperclip*] No notes or anything?

Angela: Melissa's assistant just handed them to me and said they were for Warner. I assumed you'd spoken with Melissa about it, since it's one of her authors.

Debra: I don't know anything about these. What does it say in the art log?

Angela: [*using Debra's computer, opens the electronic files to reveal a blank art log*] There's nothing. They didn't fill out the form.

Debra: How am I supposed to know where these random pictures go in the book? This book is already behind schedule, David has been fuming about it for weeks, and they didn't even fill out the art log?

Chad: They never do anymore.

Liz: Nope. Brad literally threw a manuscript on my desk the other day without a word.

Debra: And they know not to clip photos together. The clips leave marks that appear in the scans. The design guys are going to freak out.

Liz: Acquisitions thinks we can just work magic, like any problems are ours to figure out. Every time they do this, we spend another late night here with pizza.

SCENE 3: MANAGING EDITOR'S OFFICE

Debra: Arthur, I have to talk to you.

Arthur: Sure, Debra. Come in. What's up?

Debra: It's about the Warner title.

Arthur: Yes, how's it going? David is anxious to get that one to press.

Debra: Well, it's going to be late. Acquisitions just threw the pictures at us, and now I'll have to spend hours deciphering where the pictures go, whether we even have permission to print them, and what the author intended. The layout was already done, so we're going to have to pay for extra time to scan and correct photos. I don't think we're going to meet the schedule with all of this that just got thrown at me at the last minute.

Arthur: They know better than that.

Debra: I know! They're not filling out the art logs, and everything is coming late!

Arthur: Can Angela help you figure it out?

Debra: Angela is as overloaded as everyone else, Arthur. It's not just this one title, it's everything. The manuscripts are coming over to us in terrible shape; even though they get launched and we've been promised that everything is ready to go, it's not. We have books with missing chapters, incomplete table of contents files, and incomplete permissions forms. It takes hours of extra work for us just to sort through what they should have done long ago.

Arthur: I'll talk to the acquisitions editors about it. You have enough to do without doing their work, too.

Debra: It would be nice if we could get one of the acquisitions assistants to help us out, since there are three of them and we're sharing one assistant?

Arthur: I'll see what I can do.

SCENE 4: MANAGING EDITOR'S OFFICE

Melissa: Arthur, can I talk to you?

Arthur: Absolutely, Melissa, please come in. What's up?

Melissa: Production is a disaster. Debra just barged into my office and threw these pictures on my desk for Warner. She says the book is late and she's not going to work on it any longer until I fill out the art log. Arthur, I wrote the chapter title on the back of each picture. If you simply look at the photo and look at the chapter you can see exactly where the picture goes. I know it was a problem that the author clipped the photos together, but this happens all the time. Either we can get the author to send new pictures or we can fix it in editing. It's not a big deal. She just needs to send an e-mail to the author. That's it.

Arthur: It sounds like production should have had enough information to go on, even if the art form wasn't completed.

Melissa: Absolutely. Look Arthur, I know how important this book is. We've all been working hard to get it to production so it can get to press on time. Seriously, this is about filling out a form? What are the real priorities? It's always like this with them. They're constantly coming back to us in acquisitions asking questions about books we've already launched, and they're not making any effort to figure it out. She wants me to get back to the author to ask about pictures? Seriously? Please. I can't do my job and their job, too.

Arthur: I understand. I'll talk to them about it. We need you focusing on acquiring new titles, not doing production work.

SCENE 5: ARTHUR'S STAFF MEETING

The managing editor's staff meeting usually takes place in his office. Each of the acquisitions and production editors is required to attend, even if it means calling in from a hotel late at night. The meeting is often a tense one, because Arthur uses the time to focus on books that are behind schedule, knowing that David is likely to ask about these titles in particular.

Arthur: Next, I'd like to focus on MacLean. Carol, is that yours?

Carol: Yes. I spoke with him last week, because we were all wondering what the situation was. He's decided to take the final chapters of the book in a bit of a different direction and focus on the legal issues concerning water rights in the West. He promises a manuscript by the first of the month.

Arthur: [*sighing*] That's not exactly what we had agreed last time. Brad, what is the status of Marshall?

Brad: I'm not sure. I haven't had a chance to contact him. Last time I talked with him, though, he was getting close.

Arthur: Close, meaning what? Please find out and let me know. [*The production editors barely stifle their pleasure at Arthur's frustration with acquisitions.*] Turning to production. Liz, what's going on with Lopez? [*The acquisitions editors share a knowing look.*]

Liz: We will be 2 weeks late. We have to start over with design and layout. It was my understanding based on our discussions that it was going to be a title in the Environmental Policy series, but that changed at the last minute. So, we had one layout to make it consistent with that series, and now we have to go back to redesign it to make it unique. [*glares at Carol*]

Carol: [*avoiding eye contact with Liz, and looking at Arthur*] Actually, we talked about this a few weeks ago, so I'm not sure why this is just coming up now.

Liz: Yes, and what you said was that you would get back to me, but you never did.

Carol: It would have been helpful to know that you had already made a decision to send it to design.

Arthur: All right, let's just get it done as quickly as possible. That's all for today.

The group left Arthur's office. He closed his door, returned to his desk, and scanned through his notes. The list of titles behind schedule seemed to be growing each meeting. David was going to be furious at this latest round of delays. Clearly the current situation could not continue. Something needed to be done, but what?

Discussion Questions

1. Is Arthur's staff a team? Why or why not? In your view, what are the elements of an effective team? Which of these are present on Arthur's team and which are missing? Would your answers be the same if you focused on the acquisitions team and the production team independently?

2. If you were consulting with Arthur on the problems or opportunities for organization development interventions in this company, how would you describe and prioritize the main problems?

3. How would you work with the client to structure an interteam intervention? Are there other interventions you would recommend? If so, which ones?

FOR FURTHER READING

Blake, R. R., Shepard, H. A., & Mouton, J. S. (1964). *Managing intergroup conflict in industry.* Houston: Gulf.

Dyer, W. G., Dyer, W. G., Jr., & Dyer, J. H. (2007). *Team building: Proven strategies for improving team performance.* (4th ed.). San Francisco: Jossey-Bass.

Levi, D. (2010). *Group dynamics for teams* (3rd ed.). Thousand Oaks, CA: Sage.

Wheelan, S. A. (2010). *Creating effective teams: A guide for members and their leaders* (3rd ed.). Thousand Oaks, CA: Sage.

Case 25

WHEN A TEAM BREAKS IN TWO

SCOTT DICKMEYER

Learning Objectives

- To help you understand the tensions that may surface in organizational teams.
- To help you recognize how ineffective managerial communication may lead to a culture of competition rather than cooperation in an organization.
- To help you recognize the importance of understanding how a team got into a situation prior to determining the solution for the organizational problem.

As you drive through the beautiful rolling hills toward your meeting with Tim and Chuck, you find yourself wondering how today's meeting is going to unfold. Working on this project has been one of the most unique, fascinating, and difficult consulting jobs in which you have ever been involved. However, you have no idea what to expect next. You are aware that Tim and Chuck do not know everything you know and therefore are looking at the issue very differently. Unfortunately, having promised confidentiality, you cannot tell them *all that you know,* yet you are going to have to figure out a way to move this situation toward an effective and ethical resolution.

TIM'S DILEMMA

Tim is the manager of a home improvement and efficiency division for a nonprofit agency dedicated to improving the lives of impoverished people. The company Helping Hands, Heating Homes, Healthy Hearts is known in the community as Six-H. Four months ago, Tim approached you after hearing you present at a conference on effective teamwork. He told you he was committed to a team approach in the workplace and saw himself more as a coach rather than a manager. However, he was having a real problem with his team. Tim's team is comprised of assessors, crews, and inspectors. Assessors go into homes and determine what work needs to be done to improve the energy efficiency of the house and the materials necessary to do the job. Crews do the necessary work, and inspectors determine if all efficiency needs have been met and are at the appropriate standard. When all goes well, the three parts of the team work seamlessly together, providing a high-quality, energy-efficient solution for the client. According to Tim, the key to success in his business is effective communication. Communication ensures that the members of the team understand the game plan, learn from their mistakes, and continually grow and improve. Unfortunately, the members of "team Tim" do not communicate effectively. Even worse, they do not seem to see themselves as a team. In fact, the way they treat each other makes it appear that they are at war. It seems that the only time crew members talk to assessors is to yell and swear at them about how poorly they assessed the needs of the client. For example, last week one crew leader approached an assessor screaming, "You dumb a**, they needed four f***ing windows, two f***ing doors, and insulation in the attic AND basement. Get your head out of your a** and do your job right, you g**d*** moron!" It is not surprising that the assessors actively avoid the crew members, but hiding is not an effective solution to the problem and inhibits any chance of effective teamwork.

Tim tells you that he has tried to solve the communication problem in a variety of ways, but all have failed; in fact, the situation has gotten worse. Tim feels it is a no-win situation. On one hand, others he has asked for advice suggest he fire the whole bunch. On the other hand, he knows that his workers are really good at what they do and are dedicated to the mission, vision, and values of the organization. Tim was stuck; if he fired the crew members, he would lose exceptional, well-trained, and highly skilled employees. Yet, if he let the crew continue this abusive behavior, he would lose the respect of the assessors, inspectors, *and* crew members.

At this point Tim asked for your advice. You told Tim that you had a unique intervention plan you think may work in this situation. Since the main issue seemed to be with the assessors and crew members, they would be the groups to work with a facilitator. Each group would have its own facilitator as it goes through a process known as dumping, exposing, and identifying. During the "dump session," participants identify each and every bad experience they have had in the organization. The second stage involves exposing the pain that these bad experiences caused. In the third stage, participants identify how they communicated during and after these painful experiences and how others in the organization reacted to their response. The following week the two groups would get together in a meeting attended by Tim and other supervisors. At this meeting, the two groups share the results of working through the three stages and, under the guidance of you and the other facilitator, make a plan for moving forward together. Tim likes the idea and suggests you contact a facilitator named Chuck who has worked with the assessors in the past.

PLANNING THE INTERVENTION

You meet with Chuck and feel that he is definitely a competent trainer and facilitator. He has a lot of experience working with a diverse set of clients. Unfortunately, while he agrees on the plan for the intervention, he seems to have a different purpose than you do. As you explained to Tim, your purpose is to work toward understanding how the team got into this problem in the first place and use that knowledge to help them get out of the problem. Chuck's purpose for the process seems to be to "fix the problem" and he seems to see the crew as the problem that needs fixing. You are uncertain if Chuck's approach is a result of his having worked as a trainer with the assessors in the past or if he is biased by the things Tim has tried to do to address the situation. In a meeting with you and Tim, Chuck emphasized that Tim needed to address both groups together at the beginning of the intervention, telling them that if they did not change their behavior as a result of this process, they would be fired. You are concerned that such a statement may make the participants feel less comfortable disclosing during the dump session. However, Tim is enthusiastic about addressing the groups and feels that he can find a way to make everyone comfortable with the plan. He is prepared to do whatever is necessary to improve the team culture—including firing those who do not buy into the program and change their behavior.

CREW MEMBERS INTERVENTION SESSION

The location for the crew members' intervention is the basement of the local bowling alley. As you arrive, tensions are high. You attempt to set a more comfortable tone as you lay out the plan for the day. Then you introduce Tim, who is very nervous as he addresses the crew. He begins by focusing on the desire to have a workplace where good work is done in an atmosphere that is enjoyable, noting that the current situation is not enjoyable for anyone. The crew members nod their heads in agreement. Getting more comfortable with the situation, Tim describes his commitment to the intervention process. Specifically, he tells the crew that it is very important that they actively engage in the dumping session. He goes so far as to provide examples from his life of when people suffered because they held on to old hurts. He discloses that he understands that when those hurts are let go, healing begins and people move forward to a better, more fulfilling life. It is obvious to you that Tim really wants the crew to recognize his passion for improving their experiences at work and that he is sincerely looking out for their best interests. He insists that no matter what they say, there would be no negative consequences for sharing their concerns. He promises confidentiality by saying, "What is said in this room stays in this room."

Tim then explains that to move ahead, the crew members need to be willing to be part of the plan. As a team, they need to help with the plan and eventually be part of the solution. The crew seemed to be with him, looking at each other as if to say, "we can do this," while nodding and affirming that they were "on board." Tim finishes his presentation by saying that at the end of the intervention process, the crew members had four choices.

1. You embrace the plan and act in ways that help us achieve the plan.

2. You question the plan, but act in ways that help us achieve the plan.

3. You do not embrace the plan, but you are a "good soldier" and act in ways that help us achieve the plan.

4. You do not embrace the plan and do not act in ways that help us achieve the plan.

He said his goal was for the crew members to take the first choice and embrace the plan. Yet, he knew that not everyone was ready for that and if they choose number two or number three, he would respect that decision and hoped they would eventually embrace the plan. However, if a crew member took the fourth choice, that crew member will not work here anymore, and that decision would be for the good of the team.

You are proud of Tim. His presentation shows that he sincerely cares for the crew members and is committed to the process. You are happy to hear him promise no negative consequences for participation in the intervention process and his encouragement for them to talk about their concerns and hurts—even if he was pointed out as the "bad guy" in those conversations. You are especially happy to hear him promise that you will not be asked to "out" crew members by committing to confidentiality. You also feel he struck a good balance by laying out the four choices, focusing on his desire to see them buy into the plan, but willing to accept that they may not embrace the plan while remaining "good soldiers." You feel the tone for the day is set and they are ready for a difficult, but important conversation as crew members engage in the dump session.

After Tim leaves, you work diligently to get the participants to engage in the dump session, but no one is willing to open up. You put them into small groups to discuss their concerns and past hurts, but when you listen in to their conversations it is obvious that they are not on task. You try a different approach and hand out notebooks to each crew member. You put them at separate tables and ask them to write down every bad experience they had ever had in the organization. You are horrified to watch them simply look at the paper and not write anything down. You wait patiently. Finally, Tom starts writing and then slowly, one by one, each crew member begins to document their experiences.

After 20 minutes, Joe throws down his pen and says, "I need a smoke." He leaves the room but is back within 5 minutes and continues writing. After 30 minutes more you notice that several crew members seem to be done. Not wanting to cut the process short, you say, "When you are done, feel free to go outside or up to the bar. I will come and get you when everyone has finished." Eventually only Tom was left writing. You look at your watch and realize he has been writing for more than an hour and has not slowed down. Finally, after an hour and a half, Tom puts down his pen, looks at you and says, "I guess that's about all I got." You ask how he feels. "Good," he said. "I guess it is good to get it all out—I feel lighter, ya know? I guess I been holdin' in a lot of stuff." He looks back down at his notebook and all he had written. "God, I need a cigarette," he says as he gets out of his chair. Watching Tom head up the stairs you think, okay, finally we are getting somewhere.

You give Tom 15 minutes to relax and then call everyone back to the basement. You ask how everyone feels about writing down their experiences and they note it was good to get things off their chest and on to paper. Good, you think, now we can get moving on the process. But when you ask if they are ready to start listing their thoughts on the flip charts at the front of the room, there is no response. You remind them that this first step called for getting everything out. They now need to start documenting the negative consequences on their work, relationships, and personal well-being. Still, no one is ready to speak up. You wait.

Eventually Bob says, "You heard Tim this morning. He said that *we* are the problem and *he* is looking to fire us—so, I ain't gonna say anything because I need to keep my job!" It becomes clear to you that the "you will be fired" message was the only message they retained from Tim's presentation. You remind them that Tim offered three other options. They remain resistant to share their responses and you are getting nervous. Out of desperation, you remind them that Tim said everything in this session was confidential and that you will not tell him their specific examples. "So how's anything gonna change if Tim doesn't know what we talked about?" asks Bob. You explain that you are a trained professional and quite capable of explaining the problems in a way that maintains confidentiality. You then tell them that you know how much courage it takes to open up and talk about these things and you absolutely promise to do everything in your power to make the situation better. "Okay," Tom says. "You know my wife says I talk too much, that I ain't got the brains to know when to keep quiet, but I got a lot of s*** written down here and I guess I'm old enough to take social security if they fire my a**. Here ya go. . . ." Tom reads off his list, which is long and seems to take forever. Then others begin to open up. It takes almost 2 hours and when everyone is finished, you end up with a very long list of bad experiences crew members have encountered in the organization.

Once crew members start talking about their experiences, the other two stages come together easily. Several individuals describe how their experiences and hurt feelings led them to bond more tightly as a crew. As they bonded closer together, they found that they did not trust anyone outside of their group. After talking through the issues related to trust, you send the group on a break. When everyone is out of the basement, you look over what is written on the flip charts and things start to make sense. No single person or group is "at fault" for the current, very bad, situation in the home improvement and efficiency team. You begin working on an explanation on how the home improvement and efficiency team got into this problem in the first place. You are surprised at how easy it is to see the situation in a new light.

The problem comes down to three things: legitimate concerns shared by crew members, a set of four issues that led to the crew bonding closer together, and an overarching response to the situation by the crew that caused, and continues to fuel, the lack communication from the team to the assessors and Tim. You write your thoughts on a set of flip chart sheets and call the crew back to the basement. You are excited to show them your results.

When the crew returns, you validate that the experiences they shared today were difficult and painful and that they led to increased stress for the crew, auditors, inspectors, field supervisors, and Tim. While the situation is bad, it is not that surprising. The root problem is that the home improvement and efficiency team did not have a clear external enemy or a well-defined, agreed-on goal. You explain that research reveals that teams bond more closely together when they have a clear enemy. For example, a sports team may bond when preparing to face a bitter rival.

In situations with no clear enemy, such as an orchestra, theatre group, and so on, the team bonds as they prepare to achieve a well-defined goal, such as an effective performance in front of an audience. You inform the crew members that research also indicates that when a group does not have a well-defined, agreed-on goal or a clear enemy, they often find, or even create, an internal enemy. With an internal enemy, the whole team does not function well together, but each of the internal groups bond more closely together by sharing their hatred for the internal enemy. In the situation of the home improvement and efficiency team, the absence of a clear external enemy or well-defined goal has led to an internal, created enemy; the crew sees the assessors as an enemy and the assessors see the crew as an enemy.

The crew seems to feel comfortable with this explanation. Several speak out and offer examples that demonstrate their agreement with this assessment. Tom says, "So, you figured out what the problem is, but you told us we can't solve the problem until we know how we got into it in the first place. So, you heard us tell you about all the s*** we deal with. You got that big list over there—so how'd we get into the problem in the first place?"

It is time for you to lay out the three stage process you uncovered while the group was on their break. You explain how the crew group became noncommunicative, which had a negative effect on the home improvement and efficiency unit's ability to function as a three-part team (assessors, crew, and inspectors). You further state how this involved a set of crew concerns and crew issues that, over time, led to distrust. The crew then became more insulated and less likely to communicate with team members outside of the crew. The concerns led crew members to believe that management did not trust the crew to do their work, even though they were the ones who consistently saved everyone's a** by catching the mistakes of the assessors. The concerns led to confusion and uncertainty, which made the crew wonder if they could trust management. These concerns ultimately were manifested in issues that led the crew to bond more tightly in a situation that they perceived as "it's us against the world."

You turn to the easel and uncover the first sheet of your analysis and ask the crew to listen carefully to your explanation. The first sheet describes two overriding crew concerns that obstruct the crew from effectively doing their work.

Crew Concerns

Chain of Command: too many people need to provide approval prior to decisions being made or work being done—this is not a lack of appreciation for who is in management, but a concern that crew is not trusted to make decisions at the worksite.

Follow-Through: when decisions are made or policies announced, the crew expects that there will be follow-through, but often there is not—this leads to confusion about what the crew *is supposed to do,* what is really going on, and whether what management says really matters.

The second sheet describes four crew issues that led them to bond more tightly and added to the belief that "it's us against the world."

> ## Crew Issues
>
> - We do not feel respected.
> - We do not feel appreciated.
> - We do not feel trusted.
> - We do not feel like we have a voice, or we do not feel like we are in on things.

The third sheet identifies the results of the crew concerns and issues.

> **We do not trust anyone but our own team members.** As such, the crew does not communicate their concerns to management and does not confront auditors about their issues—until things have built up to a point where members of the crew "blow up" at assessors who were not aware that the crew was angry or concerned.

Looking around the room, you can tell that everyone feels good about your analysis. Their voices were really heard and you listened to them, coming up with a really good explanation of their situation. In fact, all the tension you felt throughout the day was gone. You are really proud of the work of the crew. You are also proud of your work—it was not easy to gain their trust and work them through the process, but it is obvious that it all worked out. The crew is prepared to move forward by figuring out a plan that will build a strong, effective, and committed home improvement and efficiency team. Then Bob, the crew member who talked about getting fired, speaks up. "Well I feel a lot better now because I at least got to talk about the stuff that has been going on, but I still expect that the purpose of this whole thing is to set us up for getting fired." Unfortunately, there is still a great deal of agreement about this perception. You take a deep breath and say you have confidence that management sincerely wants to improve the workplace and the experiences of all members of the organization. You also tell them that you will work hard to make sure management understands that the crew members are good, hard-working, and loyal employees whose experiences have led to a situation in which they are noncommunicative. You also promise them that the situation can get better and you have helped groups in much worse situations. Finally, you tell them that you will act as an advocate on their behalf. You wrap up for the day and crew members leave. Soon just you and Bob are left in the basement. He looks at you and says, "You know, I believe you are on our side and I like how you explained

everything, but I've been here for a long time and I have seen how they deal with s***
around here. But I believe in you. So, I guess we will see what happens. Thanks for
everything and see ya next week."

As you leave the bowling alley you wonder what transpired with Chuck and the assessors. You won't have to wait long since you have a planning meeting with Chuck and Tim
in 2 days. The three of you will determine how to facilitate next week's meeting, where
the crew and assessors will report the results of working through the three stages to each
other, the inspectors, supervisors, and Tim. After the reports, and under the guidance of
you and Chuck, the home improvement and efficiency team will make a plan for moving
forward together.

INTERVENTION FOLLOW-UP MEETING

Walking into the meeting with Tim and Chuck, you feel uneasy. You promised not to
identify the concerns and issues of the crew until the whole home improvement and efficiency team meets next week, yet you think you need to prepare Tim to hear the crew's
side of the story. How will you prepare Tim to hear the concerns and issues of the crew
while respecting your commitment to confidentiality?

As the three of you take your seats around the table, Chuck asks, "So, Tim what
have you heard from the guys about the intervention?" Tim responds that he has heard
the assessors were really happy with it. Chuck smiles and leans back in his chair. Tim
goes on to say that the crew, especially Bob, seems to think nothing is going to change
and is already resisting the process. Suddenly Chuck says, "I am telling you, next
Monday you have got to begin the day by pushing the idea that if the members of the
crew do not buy into this program and change their behaviors, their days here are
numbered!" You want to respond, but decide that you should sit back and get a feel
for Tim's perspective. As Tim is about to respond, Chuck adds, "You know the assessors are sick of all of this, they think the crew has intimidated you and that they are
really the ones who are calling all of the shots around here. They think you are afraid
of Bob and Tom and the only way things are going to change is if one or two of these
bad apples get fired and frankly, I agree. I think you need to bring out the ax and get
busy!" Tim responds that he is surprised to hear that he has lost the respect of the
assessors, but if what Chuck says is true, he may be in danger of losing the respect
of the inspectors and supervisors as well. You bite your tongue and continue to listen
as Chuck tells Tim every negative thing the assessors said about the crew. What happened to "what is said in this room stays in this room," you wonder. Tim shakes his
head and says, "Wow, this mess is even worse than I thought. I guess my only choice
is to at least fire one of the crew members, probably Bob, to send the message that
I am serious."

Tim then looks at you and says, "Well we haven't heard from you yet; what do
you think?"

Discussion Questions

1. How will you respond to Tim's question?

2. How do you think Tim and Chuck will respond to you?

3. At next Monday's meeting, how do you think those listed below will respond to the crew's concerns, issues, and lack of trust?

   a. Assessors
   b. Inspectors
   c. Tim
   d. Chuck

4. The goal of the meeting on Monday is to report out the results of crew and assessor interventions and *then* make a plan for moving forward to resolve the problem. Knowing what you know from the crew and Chuck's description of the assessors concerns, how do you recommend moving forward toward a resolution of this problem?

5. Looking back, was it a good idea to select Chuck to facilitate the assessor's intervention and cofacilitate the Monday meeting where you will work toward moving forward toward a resolution to this problem? Explain your position and provide examples from the case to back up your claims.

FOR FURTHER READING

Lencioni, P. (2002). *The five dysfunctions of a team: A leadership fable.* San Francisco: Jossey-Bass.

Pearce, C. L., & Conger, J. A. (2003). *Shared leadership: Reframing the hows and whys of leadership.* Thousand Oaks, CA: Sage.

Salas, E., Goodwin, G. F., & Burke, C. S. (2009). *Team effectiveness in complex organizations.* New York: Routledge.

DIGGINS/REINHOLDT PLASTICS, INC.

A Study in Resistance to Change in the Aftermath of a Merger

PATRICIA A. LAPOINT AND CARROL R. HAGGARD

Learning Objectives

- To help you understand potential reactions to the presence of an outside organization development team.
- To allow you to analyze a change situation, and to understand factors that produce both support for and opposition to change.
- To practice developing strategies for dealing with resistance to change.

One year ago, Diggins Tubing and Plastics, Inc., merged with Reinholdt Plastics Company, a German-based plastics manufacturer. Diggins CEO Edward Jenkins was the driving force behind the merger. His vision was a company that would be highly competitive in the international marketplace since the merged company would be able to capitalize on the resource strengths of the two individual companies. While Reinholdt Plastics was a leader in technological innovation, Diggins' strength rested in the superior quality of its production processes. Diggins had been recognized for its best practices within the industry. Jenkins knew that for the merger to be successful, it would require the creation of a new business model, one that expanded its international emphasis as well as the creation of a new organizational structure to support the new model.

The organizational structure for Diggins/Reinholdt was configured according to functions similar to the structure of Diggins. The key changes to the organizational structure

Figure 26.1   Organizational Structure for Diggins/Reinholdt, Inc.

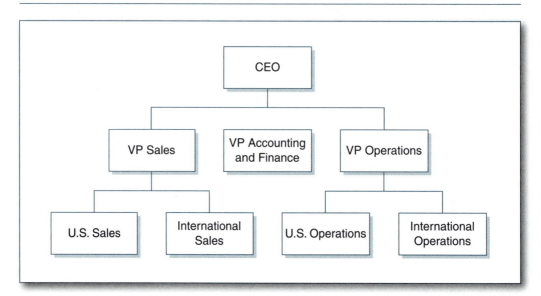

are at the business-unit level (U.S. Sales, International Sales, U.S. Operations, and International Operations). The merger with Reinholdt positioned the company as a global company with operations in the United States, Europe, and Asia, and the new organizational structure reflects this strategic change. To facilitate the realignment of the blended companies, Jenkins contracted organization development (OD) consultants Johnson, Robinson, and Kilpatrick Consulting, Inc., (JRK), which specializes in the strategic integration of merging companies to help smooth the transition.

Diggins Vice President of Operations, Rice Donnelly, was given the responsibility to oversee the merger. Approximately 1,200 employees from both companies would in some way be affected by the merger. Most employees affected are classified as nonexempt employees (clerical support, assembly line operators, technicians, and sales personnel). Some management personnel would be affected as well. While undoubtedly there would be some duplication and thus some reduction in staff, in Jenkins's view "being affected" didn't automatically mean employee termination. With the goal of international expansion, Jenkins foresaw increases in the sales staff as well as the production lines for the international products.

One year after the merger, the OD consultant team arrived at Diggins/Reinholdt and began to study personnel records and make observations, recording in great detail the workers' performances. Interviews with about 10% of randomly selected personnel from each job classification had been scheduled throughout the first and second weeks of on-site analysis. The purpose of the employee interviews was to gather information from the employees' perspectives about their performance, their attitudes toward management and the company, and their attitudes about their jobs. Rumors began to circulate throughout the organization that the OD team was there as "management hatchet people" to identify employees for termination.

As the first week unfolded, many of these scheduled employees were absent—10% on Tuesday, increasing to 35% on Friday. Several employees indicated that they were ill when they called in absent, while others stated they were under severe pressure and stress as a result of the uncertainty related to the merger. Most of the conversations with the absent employees focused on employee fears. One employee even stated that her physician suggested she take a leave of absence until the uncertainties in the working environment improved.

While the on-site interviews were not producing the amount of data that would be necessary to draw valid conclusions, the interviews that were conducted provided some very illuminating information. Christine Barclay, the JRK team leader on this project, was able to present VP Donnelly with the following data. She began her report by describing employee attitudes about the merger before the merger, which revealed a great deal of skepticism regarding the merger. (See Table 26.1.)

Table 26.1 Employee Positions on Merger (6 Months Prior)

Position on Merger (premerger)	Sales Personnel	Clerical Support Personnel	Line Operational Personnel	Technical Personnel	Management
Support	67% (216)	18% (48)	24% (79)	48% (74)	82% (103)
Opposed	33% (107)	82% (221)	76% (250)	52% (80)	18% (22)

While some employees were skeptical about the merger, others were looking forward to it. One production line manager said:

While most of my guys are complaining about the merger, I can't wait for it to occur. When we couple our technology with Diggins' production processes, we should have operations that will be the envy of the industry.

Table 26.2, which shows employee attitudes 9 months after the merger, indicates that while sales and management support the merger, the other segments of the business do not.

Table 26.2 Employee Positions on Merger (9 Months After Merger)

Position on Merger (postmerger)	Sales Personnel	Clerical Support Personnel	Line Operational Personnel	Technical Personnel	Management
Support	73% (236)	15% (40)	25% (82)	39% (60)	68% (85)
Opposed	27% (87)	85% (229)	75% (247)	61% (94)	32% (40)

The data in Tables 26.1 and 26.2 generally show the percentages of support and opposition responses for most groups to be similar in both surveys, but the management group percentages in the 15-month interval between the two surveys decreased in support of the merger.

At least part of the lack of support could be over confusion regarding how employees would "fit" into the new company. In the words of one employee:

> I was advised not to meet with you folks, but I'm desperate for information, and hope you can provide some. Before the merger, I was in charge of one of the U.S. production lines. I now am the second shift supervisor for one of the tubing lines. Before the merger, I was told that after the merger I would be given more responsibilities, but that was 18 months ago. While my new position was a demotion, I thought that it would be temporary. Yet the merger has been finalized for a year and I'm still in the same job, and I don't have a clue as to the company's plans for me. Not only is the cut in pay important, I am just as concerned about how I fit into this new structure. Can you PLEASE tell me what is going on?

Not only do some of the supervisors have negative views, most of the production line workers have very negative views regarding the results of the merger. As one worker described:

> My new boss is a jerk, plain and simple. He doesn't have a clue as to how the line should operate. While our former supervisor used to walk around to see what was going on and to say 'hey' to the guys and check if there was anything that we needed, the new guy just stays in his office—when he is here. He seems to come in late and leave early and has lots of "meetings" where he is out. But no one can really tell, as when he is here, he's in the office with the door closed. Us guys on the line feel isolated from him.

Such views are not shared by all. In the words of one member of the management group who supports the merger:

> Sally is a dream to work for; she is so open and caring, unlike George, who used to be in charge of our area. We got a REAL improvement when we got Sally as our manager.

However, employees in other areas hold a very different perspective. In general the production line workers hold a negative view of the merger (see Table 26.2). One employee provides a potential rationale for this attitude.

> Things have really changed since the merger. While he loves to talk, Jay, our new supervisor, doesn't provide much information. He tells us very little about what is going on in the company as a whole, or even our area for that matter. With Jay, we

have no idea of how our production compares to the other shifts, much less where the company is going, how the merger seems to working out, or most importantly how our area will be affected by all of this change. We feel like we are left out of seeing "the big picture." We could be in real trouble and not even know it. They could decide to close down our shift and we would have no clue that such a decision was even being considered. This has all of us worried and wondering. He is a very personable guy and seems to be well-liked, but our worst fear is that we will be blindsided by a shutdown of our line.

Table 26.3 presents the issues that have produced the greatest degree of concern among the employees.

Table 26.3 Position on Merger During 18-Month Period Premerger and Postmerger

Merger Issues	Strong Opposition	Moderate Opposition	Moderate Support	Strong Support
Adequate Information	62% (470)	18% (136)	14% (107)	6% (45)
Job Security/Redundancy of Workers	2% (15)	3% (23)	17% (129)	78% (591)
Coworker Conflicts	11% (83)	10% (76)	15% (114)	64% (485)
Conflicts With Management	2% (15)	6% (46)	24% (182)	68% (515)
Breakup of Work Group and Social Relationships	10% (76)	23% (175)	16% (121)	51% (386)
Increased Formalization/ Bureaucratization of Work Structures	59% (447)	17% (129)	13% (99)	11% (83)
Stress-Related Work Environment	3% (23)	8% (60)	10% (76)	79% (599)

Note. Based on a response rate of 63.4% (N=1,200), 761 responses; 758 usable responses.

While in general the sales staff supports the merger (see Table 26.2), some of the sales personnel show concern about a more formal, bureaucratic structure; e.g., the concern for having two bosses. (See Table 26.3 and the comments below.)

It's not clear who I report to. I now seem to have two bosses, Bob, the old one who acts as if nothing has changed and he's still in charge of the department, and the new one, Tom, who, based on his title is now in charge of the department. However, because he is so new, Tom often defers to Bob on routine matters. Yet it's clear that Tom has his own ideas as to how the department should be run and sometimes insists that we do things his way. All of this has created turmoil in the office, as no one is exactly sure of what we should be doing and who we should be listening to.

The clerical staff, which demonstrates the lowest level of support for the merger (see Table 26.2), may feel the most vulnerable to potential layoffs. One employee described her concerns this way.

From my view, in our area the merger doesn't seem to be working. We have people thrown into an office, supposedly working together, but there's no real coordination of our activities. We all still seem to be doing the same stuff that we were doing before, just now two other people are looking over your shoulder. It's so maddening to not know what is going on. We're good people and produce good work, but the lack of direction is frustrating. At least I have a job. I'm 63 and thought about leaving, but where am I going to go? I just hope to hang on until my pension kicks in.

Several informal groups of employees voiced their concerns regarding the impact the changes might have to the status quo. These comments follow.

GROUP 1: THE PLASTIC MEN BOWLING TEAM

Lee, Herb, Tim, and Carl were having a beer in the lounge of the Bowl-a-Rama following their Thursday night league play, the last match of the season. The Plastic Men was the name of the team that Diggins had sponsored for the past 10 years.

Carl, a 12-year member of the shipping staff, offered a toast: "Here's to beating our arch rivals, The Electrics, tonight. Even though we ended up 26th out of 32 in the league, we beat The Electrics."

Herb, a 15-year employee who runs a molding machine, quickly said: "Having beaten The Electrics, who finished in 27th place, means that our season was a success and we have cause to celebrate."

Lee, a 17-year employee in the advertising department, solemnly added, "Perhaps it's too soon to celebrate as this might be our final time to bowl together."

"What do you mean?" Herb asked.

Following a heavy sigh, Lee said, "Now that the season is over, so might be the company's sponsorship. I've overheard discussions among my bosses about cutting back on advertising and promotional activities. I think that's all a result of the merger."

Carl added, "Based on what's being shipped out, sales are not yet reaching the levels that the 'guys up top' expected."

The celebration quickly turned glum as the four men's speculation turned from the survival of their bowling team to wondering about their own job security; after all, each of them had been part of Diggins for such a long time.

As he sipped his third beer, Herb asked: "Hey, have you heard anything about those organization development people? They just showed up and started scheduling appointments to talk to us about our work. No one ever tells us guys on the line anything, so I was hoping that you guys might know what's going on."

Tim, a 24-year employee who is head of maintenance, said, "Oh, you mean 'The Rice-A-Roni boys. They're Rice Donnelly's 'hit squad,' brought in to do what he doesn't have the guts to do: fire folks so as to make the merger a success, or so I have heard. They have to bring in outsiders, as the 'big guys up top' have no idea of what we do or how important we are to keeping this place running."

Herb, Lee, and Carl all nodded in agreement.

Tim went on: "My staff is all in an uproar. I know of five workers in my area who are actively looking for other employment. I bet that when it's all said and done that I will lose half my staff."

The other men hang their heads and grumble.

"Back to Herb's question," Lee said. "I have an interview scheduled next week; does anyone else?" The other men all nodded yes. "Then I say that we be no shows."

Carl raised his glass. "Yes, while the Plastic Men may go down, we won't go down without a fight. We'll show them, no Rice-A-Roni for us!" They all raised their glasses to clink in agreement.

GROUP 2: THE LUNCH BUNCH

As is typical on Fridays, Kelly, Maria, Beth, Alexa, and Lydia all left their respective offices at Diggins/Reinholdt to meet for lunch at a nearby restaurant. Although they all worked in different offices, these five ladies had become close friends through their association at Diggins, now Diggins/Reinholdt.

As usual, Lydia, a 22-year purchasing employee, started the conversation by complaining about her week: "I had to babysit the grandkids while watching my youngest mare fold and had to deal with the aftereffects of an eagle swooping in and snatching up one of my favorite cats."

Alexa, a 17-year employee who processed sales orders, interrupted, partially as a means of shutting Lydia up: "Has anyone heard about Bennett? I heard from Clarice, who works in the mailroom and always has the latest scoop, that Bennett, who was the head of promotions, was being terminated. The story that Bennett is moving to California to take care of his elderly parents has to be a cover up; after all, he just met with those JeRK consultants 2 days before the word of his leaving leaked out. They just don't want anyone to know the real reason."

Maria, an administrative assistant in the marketing department where Bennett worked, knew that Bennett was concerned about his parents, but she chose not to say anything to dispute Alexa's story as, after all, it sounded like something that "they" would do.

Beth, who worked in accounting, quickly chimed in. "I'm not at all surprised, as ever since the merger, and especially after the Hatchet Men arrived, no one is safe, no matter how long they've been here or how good a job they're doing."

Kelly, office manager in operations for 19 years, added, "I heard that they want to eliminate 1,200 jobs in order to make the merger successful."

"I heard that it was 1,500 jobs," Lydia said.

"The whole situation makes me very, very nervous," Kelly said. "There's just too much uncertainty and I feel particularly vulnerable. I'm so upset I can't sleep at night. I'm the sole wage earner in my family and I'm missing several hours of work each week to take my mother to the doctor for postsurgical treatments. I don't even know how much longer I can afford these weekly lunch meetings, much less if I will have a job once the JeRKs finish their work. I felt very nervous during my meeting with Connie, one of these so-called OD specialists. She looked like she was barely out of college, someone that could well be my daughter. How do I describe what I do to someone who has no clue of what real work is? While there are some basic tasks that repeat, no 2 days are alike as each day presents its own unique problems related to operations. How can I describe what I do? I'm terribly afraid that Connie will neither fully understand nor appreciate what I do. Add to that the time I'm missing from work and I can see where Connie will think that my position isn't necessary. A kid gets to decide if I can keep my job," she exclaimed in frustration.

"I got a very similar feeling in my interview," Lydia said.

Kelly added: "Well then, based on our experience, I would advise the three of you to skip your interviews if at all possible."

As each woman returned to her office, she spread the word about Bennett's impending departure.

GROUP 3: TENNIS ANYONE?

Four members of the sales department, Deb, Cindy, Larry, and Paul, meet on Mondays to play tennis during the noon hour. After playing for 45 minutes and grabbing a quick shower, they headed to the cafeteria to get a sandwich before heading back to the office. As he sat, Larry said loudly, "These fries are as soggy as some of the women in the office."

Clearly offended, Deb asked, "What do you mean by that crack?"

Paul, who frequently had to act as a shield for Larry's often inappropriate and sometimes sexist remarks, said, "I think what Larry means is that some of the staff in the office appear to be very upset. For instance, last Friday, when she returned from lunch, Alexa was crying. When I asked her what was bothering her, she said she was upset about Bennett being fired. I tried to console her and assured her that Bennett wasn't fired but was leaving to take care of his elderly parents. She said that the story was a cover up by 'those JeRK consultants.'"

Larry burst out with, "I'm sick of all this negativism. Don't they get it? The merger is the best thing that ever happened to this company. Just look at the four of us; my sales have increased, as have all of yours. Collectively our commissions are up 40% and we're making more money than ever. By expanding the international markets, sales will only be getting better in the future."

The other three nodded in agreement.

Larry added, "Big Ed [the CEO] hired JRK as a means of smoothing the ruffled feathers of those who just don't understand how business works. They're just too stupid to realize that JRK is just doing the job they were hired to do. If they don't get it, then I say good riddance."

"Larry, sometimes you can be such a butthead," Deb said. "No doubt you're right in that the merger benefited us personally, as our sales have increased and I can see the potential for significant growth. But put yourself in Alexa's position and maybe you can understand why she would be upset. As we have all complained, with increasing use of technology, we're doing more and more of the work to process sales orders that Alexa and her cohorts did before. While someone still needs to process and code the orders to send them to the appropriate production facility, between our tablet computers and smartphones we seem to be doing more of the basic clerical work in writing up our sales orders. While I'm certainly no expert in the area, it seems to me that there doesn't seem to be the need for as many sales order processors as in the past. Thus I can understand Alexa's concern, as the loss of any position could be seen as a threat to her position."

CONCLUSION

The comments of the employees, both those made in the interviews and as reflected in the group conversations, undoubtedly reflect that there is both support for and concern about the success of the merger. Employee behaviors are also an obvious indication of their attitudes either in support of or opposition to the merger. Clearly, the employees are taking the merger very personally, as it directly affects both their income and job security.

Even with the data she presented, Christine Barclay, the OD team leader, informed VP Donnelly that with so many employees absent she had concerns about their ability to conduct a valid study at this time. Barclay said that she had witnessed similar types of behaviors of employees in other companies experiencing postmerger activities. In her experience, such reactions were common when there had been inadequate preparation for the merger, thus the employees were not ready for changes. She added that those companies that moved forward too quickly in postmerger integration activities generally took significantly longer to transition.

As VP Donnelly processed the information from the OD consultant, he was perplexed. He thought that he had developed a strong merger plan, yet the data collected thus far seemed to raise questions as to how well the process of implementation of the plan was executed. Not willing to admit defeat, VP Donnelly asked Barclay, "OK, you have given me some data and seem to be suggesting that more data is necessary. What do you recommend that we do?"

Discussion Questions

1. Did the company plan the merger integration activities effectively? What data do you have to support your answer?

2. Are the employees sufficiently ready to be interviewed by the JRK consultants?

3. What can management do to facilitate the employees' transition, or is it too late?

4. What are the key issues of resistance to change behaviors in this case (what are they and what led to their occurring)?

5. Develop a content plan and an execution plan to deal with the resistance to change issues.

FOR FURTHER READING

Creasy, T., Stull, M., & Peck, S. (2009). Understanding employee-level dynamics within the merger and acquisition process. *Journal of General Management, 35*(2), 21–42.

Lotz, T., & Donald, F. (2006). Stress and communication across job levels after an acquisition. *South African Journal of Business Management, 37*(1), 1–37.

Schraeder, M. (2001, December). Identifying employee resistance during the threat of a merger: An analysis of employee perceptions and commitment to an organization in a pre-merger context. *Mid-Atlantic Journal of Business.* Retrieved from http://www.allbusiness.com/north-america/united-states/837987-1.html

WHOLE ORGANIZATIONAL DESIGN INTERVENTION

JULIE WILLIAMSON AND RACHAEL THOMAS

Learning Objectives

- To support your learning about how organizational design issues arise in complex business situations, with ambiguous goals and conflicting agendas between groups.
- To learn how to apply the STAR model to understand these types of situations from an organizational design perspective, and to use the model to structure thinking about possible solutions.

GenLife, Inc. was an established multinational insurance company, was well-known in the area, and employed approximately 3,000 people, many locally. They had grown through an acquisition strategy over the past 10 to 15 years. They tended to acquire and absorb rather than leave businesses to run independently, but they often struggled to integrate systems and operations. In a recent effort to "get smaller to grow bigger," GenLife had sold off a part of its business that dealt specifically with executive life insurance (ELI) and approximately a third of its employees either joined the acquiring company, ExecuLife, or were let go, depending on their job functions. Most of these jobs were sales related, directly tied to the ELI business. Approximately a third of GenLife's revenue went to ExecuLife with the sale, and it was anticipated GenLife expenses would reduce by approximately a third as well.

However, just 3 months after the sale, GenLife CEO Ryan Bind was finding that very little had changed in the cost structure of GenLife. Apparently ELI hadn't used corporate shared services very much, so there were still high support needs postsale. The remaining business of GenLife was left supporting the company, and it was simply too expensive to run. The estimates for how much cost would be eliminated at divestiture were off by as much as 30%. Many of the shared processes to support the remaining business were done through convoluted spreadsheets with arcane links that were understood only in parts by certain individuals and processes were largely undocumented. The company had invested significantly in a centralized system to assist in enterprise management processes, but very few people used it, preferring their manual processes.

In summary, the sale of ELI had reduced revenue for GenLife with little reduction in overall costs. So the CEO called in consultants Lisa Mendez and Joe Henderson to address the situation. Drastic measures were required in the next 6 months to avoid serious financial damage. Six months was a hard date—at that point, GenLife would be running at a deficit if costs weren't reduced.

The company's infrastructure was provided via a shared services structure for internal operations, including Human Resources (HR), Legal, Facilities, Finance and Accounting (F&A), Real Estate (RE), Actuary, and Information Technology (IT). These seven groups had supported both the remaining and the sold businesses, and costs had been allocated evenly across all areas. With the divestiture out of ELI, a third of the revenue had been reduced, but the shared services organization had not shrunk in a similar way. In fact, of about 450 people, only 14 shared services resources had gone to ExecuLife.

THE CHIEF EXECUTIVE OFFICER'S PERSPECTIVE

As the CEO, Ryan had approved the sale of the ELI business, and during the due diligence period had been convinced by his team that the business case was solid; however, that was proving to be incorrect. He knew now that the remaining business was too expensive to run without the ELI revenue.

Ryan presented the financial situation to Lisa and Joe as both fact and history—as he put it, "There's nothing to be done about the mistakes that were made—we were wrong about how much of the shared infrastructure would move over, so now we need to reduce our costs. But we have to be able to run our business! So we can't just cut across the board and hope for the best. Plus, no one really knows how things get done around here. There is little documentation, mostly just people who have been doing their jobs for a long time. If we lose them, we'll go off the rails. So we need to do this thoughtfully and take advantage of the opportunity to put some things to right."

Ryan explained his suspicion that the organization, which had grown haphazardly over the years, was not serving the real needs of the business. According to him, at an executive and senior level, some groups had been created just to give people something to manage as they got promoted, not necessarily because it made good sense. Some of the managers were better at lobbying for staff and funding and were providing "Cadillac" levels of service while others were bare-bones for no logical reason. The processes being used within the groups were, he felt, convoluted and based on legacy assumptions about what was necessary. There was no clear definition of what was minimally required versus what was "above and beyond" for running the business. Finally, he was convinced his executive team wasn't working well.

"Look," he said, "I don't like this one bit. I've been with this company 35 years, and all these guys came up through the ranks with me. We just assume we are all doing our jobs well and don't check up on each other. But, things feel a little out of control if this is what it really costs to run our business. We're going to have to let people go, but I want to make sure we let the right people go, and we're going to have to change what we're doing, but I want to make sure we make the right changes. If it's going to be bad, let's get it all out there over the next 6 months and have an end date for the pain."

Ryan also explained that if GenLife was going to be successful, the strategy of growth via acquisition would need to be supported by a lean and flexible shared service organization. "We need to be able to acquire and integrate new businesses without an equal increase in costs," He sighed. "But we can't seem to manage the business costs we have today." Ryan was concerned not only for the short-term future of GenLife, but its long-term viability in an increasingly cost competitive market.

Ryan laid out a few guiding principles for Lisa and Joe. He wanted to:

1. Look everywhere for cost containment in addition to letting people go.

2. Take advantage of the situation to "get a handle" on processes.

3. Treat people fairly and be honest about the hard decisions that would have to be made—at a minimum, approximately 30% of the staff, or about 120 people, would have to be let go. There would be no option to reassign people from one group to another (a common avoidance technique among managers during a layoff).

4. Redesign the remaining groups to work better together—fast, efficient, and able to scale. He felt they were operating ineffectively as silos, and the management structure was "heavy" and did not support the strategy of getting small to grow big.

5. Be more thoughtful than the traditional management approach of simply telling each group to cut 30% of the staff and 30% of their expenses—data-supported recommendations were important.

Ryan had some data that supported his perspective that the teams were not working well. He routinely found errors in accounting reports and had to proofread board slides and financial reports regularly to ensure accuracy. For a CEO of a mid- to large-sized corporation, this level of detailed review was a signal of a real problem further down in the organization. He also made the following points.

- Most of the teams were led by people who had been in the company a very long time—the current CFO had been with the company for 35 years, for example. However, at entry levels in the organization, turnover was very high—higher than industry standards. Further, the middle management layer had expanded significantly over time.

- The organization tended to reward firefighters. In exit interviews, younger employees in particular cited people "making their own fires so they could be heroes" as reasons why they left. Exiting employees also referred to the lack of career opportunity at GenLife.

- Many people considered their work "nonnegotiable" due to their understanding of regulatory and reporting needs both internal and external to the organization, but Ryan wasn't convinced it was all necessary.

- Only certain people in the organization understand the convoluted accounting structures, which are largely undocumented.

At the end of the conversation, Lisa and Joe looked at each other. Joe spoke up first. "You've given us a good overview of what you want out of this and where you have concerns. But we're going to need some information from your people to really understand the breadth and depth of the issues and what it will take to solve them."

The CEO wasn't thrilled. "Haven't you done this before?"

"Sure," said Lisa, "and experience tells us there's more to this story than just your perspective. If you want us to give you a workable approach together with an accurate time and cost estimate for something that has a shot of working in the timeframe you've presented, we need more information."

Ryan paused, and agreed to give them a week of access to his team, and any other information they deemed necessary. "But," he said emphatically, "I'm not paying you to tell me how much you are going to charge me! I know how consultants work. And don't forget, the clock is ticking—you are taking 1 week out of the 24 we have before time runs out."

Lisa and Joe readily agreed to take on the investigation as a part of their business development effort, and got Ryan's commitment to send a note to his team to expect a call and to make time for an interview.

INTERVIEW DEBRIEF AND DOCUMENT REVIEW

That night, Lisa and Joe looked through the documentation Ryan had given them. It contained current organizational charts and staff numbers. There were also spreadsheets showing the department cost allocations, broken out into rough groupings to provide an understanding of how the groups are weighted. See Figure 27.1 for the current organizational structure, Figure 27.2 for the cost allocations, and Figure 27.3 for the current headcount.

The next day, Lisa and Joe set up time with the CFO, the CIO, and the CHRO, who were available on short notice, although they could only get a few minutes with each. As they headed over to the building, they discussed what they should ask to get the information they needed to create their approach, thinking through how they would structure the interviews and what information they required.

Figure 27.1   Current State Organization Structure

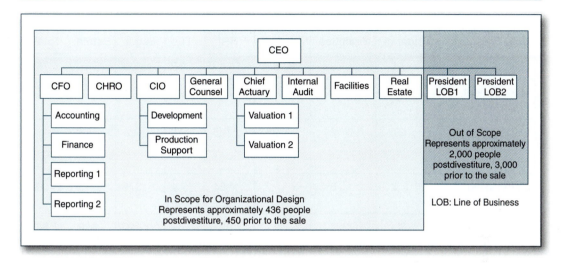

Figure 27.2   Cost Allocation by Functional Area

Cost Category	Actuarial	Facilities	Finance	HR	IT	Legal	Real Estate	Total
Auditors Fees	17	–	1,832	170	–	6	–	2,025
Books, Journals, Magazines	310	1	16	4	2	82	0	415
Community Donations	2	–	2	405	2	–	–	411
Computers and Peripherals	14	172	1,745	1,150	230	200	72	3,583
Corp Sponsorship	–	–	–	1,815	–	8	–	1,823
Depreciation	–	98	3	14	0	2	48	165
Emp. Benefits and Other Costs	1,402	580	1,814	1,326	687	1,365	177	7,351
General Administration	802	–	–	26	–	–	–	828
Insurance	–	402	–	144	–	98	124	768

(Continued)

Figure 27.2 (Continued)

Cost Category	Actuarial	Facilities	Finance	HR	IT	Legal	Real Estate	Total
Legal Expenses	1	3	92	–	73	4,590	–	4,759
Management, Consulting Fees	52	170	54	520	1,300	8	12	2,116
Marketing, Communication, Advertising	29	2	98	186	12	25	62	413
Membership Dues	1	6	7	64	4	575	3	660
Office Furniture, Supplies, Printing	32	375	117	925	49	40	110	1,648
Other	920	230	820	70	–	200	130	2,370
Packaging and Mailing	1	28	9	32	3	29	14	116
Rent	–	320	–	64	10	–	2,780	3,174
Salaries	4,672	1,934	6,047	4,420	2,290	4,551	590	24,504
Staff Development/ Training	31	14	32	50	–	–	6	133
Telephone and Internet	30	54	97	80	14	52	15	342
Temp/ Employment Fees	1	41	77	82	47	2	14	264
Travel and Entertainment	92	14	74	145	26	102	3	456
Total	8,408	4,444	12,936	11,692	4,749	11,934	4,160	58,324

Note. Figures represent thousands. So, for example, Finance spends approximately $1.832 million on auditor fees, while Legal spends approximately $6,000 on auditor fees. Numbers may not add up due to rounding.

Businesses often look at what different groups are spending in expense areas. This helps for leveling across areas in spending on training, development, and equipment, and brings to the surface area-specific spending in certain areas, like auditors or insurance.

Figure 27.3   Current Shared Services Organization Headcount

Function	FTE
Finance and Accounting	119
Human Resources	62
IT	70
Legal	83
Actuarial	50
Facilities	61
Real Estate	5
Total	450

THE CHIEF FINANCIAL OFFICER'S PERSPECTIVE

At the CFO's office, Lisa and Joe were greeted by his assistant, who asked them to have a seat, explaining that Gary was working on "putting out a fire." After a few minutes, Gary came out and escorted them into his office, apologizing for the delay. "There are still questions about the divestiture that we're all-hands-on-deck to answer. Seems like we just can't get it all done in the time we have. Plus, we're trying to get ready for the quarter close, and we have extra work this time around for the regulators, since we have to restate everything in terms of the new company financial structure. Like we need more work!"

Lisa and Joe gave a brief overview of why they were there. They could be candid with Gary, who clearly knew the financial situation. "Yes," he said, "it's tough. Our shared services teams have been with us a long time—I came up through F&A, been here 32 years. Ryan and I went to grad school together."

Lisa got straight to the point and asked Gary to talk about his current structure within F&A, as well as the impacts of the sale. Specifically, she asked about how F&A interacted with other teams and what kinds of dependencies existed. He gave two main responses.

"You know, for dependencies, one problem we always have is that our HR group doesn't understand what we do. We end up recruiting for ourselves, we just tell HR when we have someone we want to bring in. I don't even bother sending job requirements over to them anymore. We've actually brought in our own HR person to help us out, only we call her an administrative assistant. But she does all of our recruiting and on-boarding. Only thing she can't do is hire. But she does everything up to and after that.

"Something I don't understand is why IT can't seem to do what we need. We always ask for things and they come back and say 'our project list is 2 years long, we can't help you today.' Seems to me we invested in this new system, but it can't do half of what we can do by ourselves. I'd rather have Kerry (one of his leads) run a spreadsheet for me than trust those guys over in IT to get something done. They always say we need to change because they can't help us with the system."

Joe asked about team structures and how people move between teams—the kinds of growth and development opportunities available. Gary responded: "We can't afford to move people around for growth and development. The reward for figuring out how to do something is that you get to do it for the rest of your life. I still have to make the final adjustments for our quarterly board reports—it's too complicated for someone else to learn. As far as rewards, well, we incent people to find creative solutions to problems."

As Lisa and Joe thanked him for his time, Gary reiterated, "I'm running a complex business here; we're not like anyone else. Whatever you come up with, it really needs to meet our unique processes and structure."

THE CHIEF INFORMATION OFFICER'S PERSPECTIVE

Lisa and Joe headed over to IT. Their documentation review had highlighted that the IT systems were mostly "old school," meaning COBOL programs running on mainframes. The new F&A system that had been implemented was vendor supported, and there were very few internal resources in the IT group who knew how to work with it effectively.

The CIO, Ken, was expecting them, and he seemed on edge during the conversation. He started off saying "You know I don't really understand why we even sold ELI. Seems like it was doing pretty well, and it was easy enough to support. What kind of strategy is it to sell off a money-making, easy-to-run business?" Ken continued on this vein for a few minutes.

Lisa and Joe realized from their document review that the IT organization was one of groups that had much of its costs allocated to ELI, but which had not had a meaningful cost reduction associated with the sale. When asked, Ken admitted that they really didn't have a good idea of how much time anyone spent on any given system, and the work done for the divestiture was mostly "guesstimates." At that point, his pager went off, and he abruptly ended the meeting.

THE CHIEF HUMAN RESOURCE OFFICER'S PERSPECTIVE

The next stop was Human Resources. They wandered around the maze of cubes and offices, finally locating the CHRO, Henry. He was still wrapping up a meeting. "Come in," he called, as the person at the desk leaned forward and shouted, "But we need people on this—yesterday!" Lisa and Joe felt a little embarrassed and hovered at the door as the person finally gathered his paperwork and left the office in a huff. Henry just smiled and explained that GenLife executives were kicking off the assessment phase of an acquisition and resources were urgently needed to staff the team. "This happens at least a few times a year so we're pretty used to it," he said. "It's always a fire drill, but we get through it. Our folks are really dedicated and we reward them for the long days and weekends they put in." Lisa mentioned that the CFO seemed very busy. Henry laughed "They like to be heroes as much as we do!"

As they sat, Henry filled Lisa and Joe in on the role of HR and its evolution over the past few years. "When Bill, the previous CHRO, left, it was a huge loss to GenLife," he said, "but culturally we needed to change to a more professional, dynamic organization, so it was probably for the best. Bill was pretty old-school when it came to HR." Henry admitted that he didn't have a strong HR background. He'd moved through the ranks of Finance and then later in Real Estate, but he had faith in the strength and size of his team, all 62 of them. "This year the team has been working on a new competency model, new executive training, succession planning, plus of course there's our future leaders program, skills training, our recognition program, wellness program, and the local community action program," he said, proudly showing a large wall chart of activities with hundreds of line items. "We're building a world-class HR department!" he exclaimed. "At GenLife we have over 200 people who have been with us for over 25 years—that says something about us."

The biggest challenge Henry saw for the group was the existence of multiple systems being used to manage employee information, benefits, and compensation, with business units and acquired companies operating on different human resource information systems (HRIS). "We spend a lot of time transferring information and working on spreadsheets. Our HR generalists each support an area of the business and when we try to look across the business units, or even across Shared Services, we spend a lot of time reconfiguring and reformatting data just to get a picture of what's going on. Most of our employee files are actual physical files," he explained. "You can imagine with all our staff, we're thinking of renting an aircraft hanger!"

Lisa smiled and asked, "Reporting must take up quite some time then?"

Henry jumped up and went to grab some files, which he waved around as he responded. "Oh yes, we get new requests all the time from the business unit leads asking What's my loaded cost for each employee? Why am I spending so much on training? When can I get my open positions filled? But our generalists are amazing and very flexible, we pride ourselves on the range of things our HR generalists can pull out of their hats—heck we've even had generalists running SOX audits at a pinch!"

As Lisa and Joe started to collect their notes, Henry confided, "To be honest, I'm not sure what this initiative is really going to achieve. We're already working overtime just to get through what needs to be done. I don't know how Ryan thinks we're going to be able to provide the same level of service with fewer people."

SUMMARY

Lisa and Joe returned to their office and sat down to categorize what they had learned. There were serious concerns about understanding the work being done in the organization and how the CEO's desires could be addressed through organizational design while also downsizing the staff. Process work would have to be done during the project, adding to the complexity. They had 3 days left to put together a pitch, and a lot of work ahead of them.

Based on what they knew, they created an outline of a proposal. They decided to leverage the STAR model (Kates & Galbraith, 2007) to evaluate what they know of the current situation and then plan out the rest of their week.

Discussion Questions

1. Summarize the situation as you see it, based on the information presented, making interpretations where necessary. Using Galbraith's STAR model, evaluate what you know about the current organizational design. The STAR model is a common approach to understanding what is happening in an organization and to organize thoughts about design concerns. Within this case, there are many "pieces" that you might pick up. Use the STAR model (Figure 27.4) to bring them together and consider their implications.

Figure 27.4 STAR Model Application

	What do you know?	What do you assume?	What do you conclude?
Strategy			
Structure			
Process and Lateral Capability			
Reward Systems			
People Practices			

- Given your analysis of these dimensions, what are the key problems that need to be solved?
- What type of approach would you take to the organizational design process? Discuss how you would approach documenting the current state and creating a future state.
- What are the pros and cons of that approach?

2. Given the situation described, what information would you want or need to get during the week you have available, and what obstacles might you anticipate in getting that information? Consider what information you would look for in each interview.

3. What organizational design approach would you recommend to the CEO that would meet the needs and satisfy the constraints presented?

4. How would you construct your own team to execute on the approach you selected? How many people, what kinds of skills and experiences, and how long would you anticipate them working on the design?

REFERENCE

Kates, A., & Galbraith, J. (2007). *Designing your organization: Using the STAR model to solve 5 critical design challenges*. San Francisco: Jossey-Bass.

FOR FURTHER READING

Galbraith, J. R. (2002). *Designing organizations: An executive guide to strategy, structure, and process*. San Francisco: Jossey-Bass.

Galbraith, J. R., Downey, D., & Kates, A. (2002). *Designing dynamic organizations*. New York: AMACOM.

Simmons, R. (2005). *Levers of organization design: How managers use accountability systems for greater performance and commitment*. Cambridge, MA: Harvard Business Press.

Sharp, A., & McDermott, P. (2008). *Workflow modeling: Tools for process improvement and application development*. Norwood, MA: Artech House.

THE CHANGE STORY OF YELLOW AUTO COMPANY

ALEV KATRINLI, GULEM ATABAY, GONCA GUNAY AND
BURCU GUNERI CANGARLI

Learning Objectives

- To help you define the internal forces for change.
- To explain the benefits of working with external change agents during the change process.
- To discuss possible organizational interventions for wide-ranging problems.
- To discuss what it might take to make change happen successfully.

Yellow Auto is a car dealer of a well-known global brand: Renault. The firm was established in 1989 by Deniz Sale in Bergama, a small town near Izmir, which is the third largest city in Turkey. It was a very small firm with few employees, and they attempted to meet demand in Bergama. Due to the small population of Bergama, the company had low sales volume that, although sufficient to cover the cost of operation, provided modest profit.

After a while, Deniz Sale's sons, Can and Caner Sale, took over the management from their father. Can Sale, the older brother, had a university degree in geological engineering while Caner Sale had a master's degree in mechanical engineering. Both were fluent in English. Although they had no educational background in retail or management, they and their father believed they were ready to take over the management of the dealer since they had many years experience in the company. On taking up the reins, they recognized that to grow the company, it should be moved to Izmir, where there was a considerable demand for automobiles. Using the family assets, they moved Yellow Auto to Izmir in

1998. First, they purchased old premises in the district of Camdibi, where a variety of automobile dealers and spare-parts sellers could be found. In this new location, they started to offer three main types of service: automobile sales, spare-parts sales, and after-sale repair service. They benefited from considerable support from Renault, which determined and dictated national marketing activities, pricing, contents of catalogs, and similar issues according to Turkish market expectations.

After the 1994 economic crisis, the demand for automobiles increased steadily. Yellow Auto was affected by this positive trend, and its market share grew with the support of Renault and the positive effect of relocation of the premises. To meet the growing demand, Can and Caner Sale decided to recruit more staff. Thus, by the end of the 1990s, there were 52 employees.

Among these, only three were family members. The younger brother, Caner Sale, was appointed as a general manager. He made decisions regarding all the operations done within the company. However, the older brother, Can Sale, preferred not to intervene too much, and his young brother only consulted him on the important decisions, such as making investments. His position was similar to a top management consultant, but he also had a right to make decisions. The third member of the family, Asli Sale, was the daughter of Can Sale. She joined the company immediately after graduating from university in food engineering. As she had no experience related to the automobile industry, Can and Caner Sale decided to offer her a secretary position. After a while, she proved that she was willing to work and could deal with "people" problems, so she was transferred to the sales team. A year later, she was appointed as a sales director. Apart from the family members, the company employed a number of staff, including a secretary, an after-sales service director, two employees responsible for insurance (one was head of insurance), four responsible for spare-parts supply, three for accounts, and one for operating logistics and general administration.

A team of eight worked in the sales department under Asli Sale. Two were assigned to in-store sales, responsible for sales in the company's own premises, the plaza. The active-sales team consisted of five people with driving licenses. They were responsible for organizing out-store activities and customer visits. Also, they completed procedural works for car licenses and license plates under the supervision of the manager. In addition to these two teams, there was a further employee, responsible for second-hand automobile sales.

Thirty members of staff were employed under the after-sales service director, in two subunits. One provided all after-sale services, including insurance services and auto repair. The other was responsible for providing spare-parts to the auto repair unit in a timely manner. Coordination between two subunits was attained through the manager.

Although authority and responsibilities allocation seemed to have been allocated, the lack of documentation or an organizational chart related to this may have been the reasons for Caner Sale's frequent intervention in the decisions and problems.

PROBLEMS AROSE

As stated above, Turkey offered a great market for automobile companies due to its population. Especially large cities like Izmir can be considered as important markets for automobile companies. Yellow Auto started to grow, with the advantage of selling a popular brand, Renault, to such a large market. However, the owners of the company could not fully benefit from this growth as the company started to face the typical problems that many small but growing firms face in Turkey (Ceren, 2004). These problems mainly concerned issues that emerged in different areas of coordination and control of employee activities.

First of all, problems of coordination and communication within the company became more visible. In the company there were many rules, but most were unwritten and existed in the mind of Can Sale. Employees had little autonomy while making decisions and they were expected to consult managers even on minor details. However, managers were also uncertain about their authority limits and frequently had to consult Can Sale. The head of insurance services said, "Mr. Sale believes that he knows the best. He never takes notice of our opinions and he always wants us to do exactly what he says." As a result, employees preferred to work directly with Can Sale, bypassing their managers. Regarding this, the salesperson responsible for the secondhand automobiles stated that, "Can knows the job better than Asli. That's why I prefer to bypass her and work with Can." However, this situation increased the workload of Can Sale, and sometimes created confusion in information flow and slowed the work. Moreover, managers were discontent with the situation since they felt that their authority was not accepted by their own subordinates. From the subordinates' perspective, they complained about lack of sufficient support from their managers.

In addition to communication and coordination problems, employees also were discontent with their jobs and the company conditions. Almost all complained about the inappropriate physical conditions: the age of the building, lack of facilities, and provision for social activities.

Apart from the companywide problems, specific problems within each department could be observed. For example, in the sales department, the in-store sales team seemed to be operating ineffectively due to a lack of appropriately qualified personnel. The majority of the salespeople were not educated for their jobs, and most did not even have a university degree. Hence, they could not behave in a professional manner when communicating with potential customers who visited the store. Moreover, there was almost no systematic activity to attract potential customers. Although regular phone calls to customers were one of the major duties of the team, these calls were not effective because the customer database was outdated and there was lack of monitoring of calls.

In the active sales team, different problems could be observed. Due to the nature of their work, active sales personnel spent much time outside the company. Their work involved visiting potential customers and inviting them to the plaza. However, they had no specific work schedule and did not work under a control mechanism. Due to this situation, in-store sales people believed that the active sales team sometimes engaged in personal rather than company business while absent from the premises. As it can be understood from this situation, the relationship between the two teams had deteriorated to the extent that each believed the other team was ineffective and given redundant attention from the top management. Sometimes, the level of conflict increased to the extent where they attempted to affect the sales of the other team in a negative way, which in return affected the whole company's sales performance negatively. Unfortunately, dysfunctional conflict was not limited to the conflict between teams. Within the teams, sales staff tended to see each other as rivals, and rather than cooperating they competed with each other due to the effect of the individual performance-based appraisal system. Thus, team spirit was lacking in the sales department, which was sometimes obvious from the viewpoint of the customers.

Similar to the sales department, there were significant problems in the after-sale services and spare-parts departments. First of all, the physical conditions of the after-sale services unit were not appropriate, with an unhygienic environment that was inadequately heated and ventilated. Moreover, there was no computerized system for inventory control. Spare parts personnel had imprecise information on the numbers of spare parts in the warehouse. Hence, in the periodic inventory counts there were always missing parts that had been lost or stolen. Lack of a systematic computerized inventory control system might create another problem. As spare parts personnel could not know the exact inventory levels, a spare part might be purchased from the supplier even if it existed in the warehouse, or a repair procedure may have been delayed due to mislaid spare parts.

As expected, such problems began to affect the company's relationship with Renault itself. Yellow Auto faced difficulties in following the rules and standards dictated by Renault in terms of financial reporting, customer satisfaction, and achieving target sales volume. Owners were aware that without a radical solution, their relationship with Renault would be seriously damaged. Unfortunately, it would not be the only relationship in danger of being damaged; its relationship with the customers was being harmed as well. Existing customers complained about the unprofessional behavior of the sales personnel and delayed delivery time. Also, they were unhappy with the insufficient facilities, the unappealing appearance of the premises, and the unsatisfactory level of cleanliness. Moreover, Yellow Auto was losing its ability to attract customers. The owners believed that to attract and satisfy a wide range of customers, Yellow Auto should have implemented different strategies based on customers' age, education, and income level. However, due to lack of qualifications, staff could not understand different customer groups' expectations and were unable to develop different strategies based on the various customer groups. Instead, they focused on short-term promotion activities whose target market was not well-identified. As the owners were aware of this situation, they made considerable personal effort to communicate with customers and understand their problems and expectations. However, this meant close involvement with sales activity, and therefore, insufficient time to monitor the other activities in the company. Moreover, their involvement in sales was perceived as "excessive intervention" by the salesforce, and the salespeople complained about a lack of flexibility and decision-making rights, which decreased their motivation as stated above.

As the aforementioned problems heavily affecting the relationships with Renault and customers, Can and Caner Sale decided to focus on the potential solutions. They were aware that without radical solutions, they would lose their market share to other automobile brand dealers or other regional Renault dealers.

CHANGE STARTED IN 2001

In 2001, the top managers of Yellow Auto determined a goal of capturing 50% of the market share in the region. They knew that achieving this goal required a radical change that would provide solutions to the aforementioned problems. They were also aware that the change should address many issues, including physical conditions to company culture. As with every decision made in the company, this decision also was made by top managers without the participation of the directors or employees. However, top managers were aware that change carried risks and that it might create further significant problems if it was not well-managed. Hence, they decided to seek the support of management experts, and they began to work with academicians from Izmir University of Economics. A team of academicians working as external consultants accepted responsibility for initiating and managing the change process in the company.

Consultants started by analyzing the existing situation in the company and attempting to understand the expectations of the owners. At this stage, different analysis methods were employed. First, a search conference, which identified the strengths, weaknesses, opportunities, and threats (SWOT) for Yellow Auto, was conducted with the participation of all employees. Results of the SWOT analysis are shown in Table 28.1.

After the conference, consultants decided to use different questionnaires regarding job requirements, information flow, organizational culture, and leadership styles of the top managers in order to determine more clearly the existing state of the company.

Table 28.1   Results of SWOT Analysis

Strengths	Weaknesses
Strong financial structure	Confusion about authority and responsibility allocation
In-depth knowledge and experience of Can Sale regarding automotive industry	Insufficient facility and age of the premises
Good reputation in Izmir automobile market	Lack of team spirit
	Conflict among the departments
Opportunities	**Threats**
New but related markets can be available (e.g., it is possible to enter car accessories market)	New rivals
Increasing demand for automobiles	Increasing demand of Renault regarding documentation, customer relations, etc.

In the job analysis survey, employees were asked four main questions regarding their job descriptions. In the first question, they listed the tasks they were performing in their current position. In the second question, they identified the tasks that should be done by them but currently were executed by other employees. In the third question, they determined the tasks that were performed by them that should be executed by others. Finally, they were asked whether they had sufficient authority to perform their tasks. Results of the first three questions indicated that there was no agreement or unity regarding their job requirements since there were many redundant tasks, as well as tasks not listed by any of the employees that were left out. In addition, answers of the last question showed that nobody believed they had sufficient authority to perform their tasks. Hence, results of the job analysis survey showed some critical problems with the authority and responsibility distribution due to lack of clarity in job descriptions. Also, with the help of additional questions, it was found that the active sales team had problems such as not having sufficient information to allow them to respond to customers' complaints. They did not believe that, under current methods, it would be possible to meet customers' expectations within a reasonable time if they achieved the target of 50% of market share.

In the job satisfaction survey, employees were asked to indicate their level of expectations and satisfactions related to different aspects of their jobs. The comparison of the level of their expectations and satisfactions showed that significant gaps existed in terms of financial benefits, psychical conditions, and relationships with peers.

Results of the organizational culture questionnaire indicated that employees perceived that organizational culture had a power-and-authority focus rather than a system, purpose, or relationship focus, as they identified their main values as competition, assertiveness, achievement, and power. Regarding the leadership style of Can Sale, results of the leadership style questionnaire showed that his style was perceived as autocratic but also charismatic. These results seemed to be consistent with the results of the organizational culture questionnaire.

To provide a deeper understanding of the problems identified by the questionnaires and discuss the results of the search conference, in-depth interviews with employees and managers were conducted. In these interviews, questions regarding job requirements, company culture, and problems and potential solutions were discussed. Through these processes, the consultants intended to create an atmosphere of mutual trust by allowing employees the opportunity to express themselves freely on almost every aspect of the company, including the behaviors of the top management, especially that of Can Sale. For example, an employee from accounting stated that, "Without informing Can Sale, nothing can be done in the company. He is a very smart manager. He likes to intervene too much if he thinks that he knows about the subject. He can easily decrease employee morale, but also easily makes us happy."

Based on the results of the aforementioned analyses, consultants and owners came together to decide on how change was to be initiated, as well as the priorities. Guided by the organizational behavior iceberg (Robins & Coulter, 2009, p. 299), consultants emphasized the importance of values, social norms, and attitudes that affected behaviors and performance for achieving a successful change. Although the managing owners had previously adopted an autocratic management style, they showed a willingness to cooperate with the consultants and an openness to development efforts. Therefore, the consultants and top managers worked in an atmosphere of open communication and trust.

Based on this, they began to target different issues, from physical conditions to organizational climate, human resources policies to organization structure. This process took 3 months. At the end, surveys that were implemented at the beginning were repeated to assess the degree of change in attitudes of employees toward their job and the organization.

Discussion Questions

1. How do you evaluate the change efforts in terms of being transactional or transformational?

2. Why might the employees show almost no resistance to change in the company?

3. What are the benefits of working with consultants as external change agents?

4. Consider the job satisfaction, organizational culture, and leadership style surveys that were repeated at the end of the change process to assess the degree of change in employee attitudes. Do you expect significant change in employee attitudes? Why or why not?

5. Assume that you were one of the consultants working with the owners of Yellow Auto. For the client, please prepare a proposal that explains activities that should be done during the change process.

REFERENCES

Ceren, F. (2004). *Küçük işletmelerde büyüme ve örgütsel sorunlar* (Organizational and growth-related problems in SMEs). Retrieved from http://kalkinma.org/?goster.asp?sayfa=makale&id=19

Robins, S. P., & Coulter, M. (2009). *Management.* Upper Saddle River, NJ: Pearson Education.

FOR FURTHER READING

Ford, J. D., & Ford, L. W. (2009). Decoding resistance to change. *Harvard Business Review, 87*(4), 99–103.

Greiner, L. E. (1967). Patterns of organizational design change. *Harvard Business Review, 45*(3), 119–130.

Robbins, S. P., & Judge, T. A. (2010). *Organizational behavior* (13th ed.). Upper Saddle River, NJ: Prentice Hall.

WE *MUST* LEARN TO INNOVATE!

Culture Change (and Shock) in a Consumer Packaged Goods Company

JEREMY P. FYKE AND G. ALAN FYKE

───────────── **Learning Objectives** ─────────────

- To understand the cultural implications of large-scale organizational change.
- To understand common employee reactions to large-scale organizational change.
- To understand intervention strategies used by change agents in the field.

Larry's head was spinning as he left the initial meeting of the newly formed Newton Innovation Team. The goals of the team seemed clear and the intentions good, but Larry had no idea how the team could accomplish them. Walking back to his office, he saw Lars Rogen, the lead consultant from Lars Group, talking with Richard, his CEO. Richard motioned him over. "Tell me how the meeting went," Richard said anxiously to Larry.

When Richard hired Larry as Director of Strategic Accounts and Business Development just 1 year prior, he made it clear he demanded honesty, so Larry knew not to pull any punches. "You know what? I'm excited about the concept of the innovation team and I get what you want to do. I just have a hard time seeing us as ever being an innovative company. I mean, the meeting went great, but I just don't see how it's possible for us to pull this off."

"I appreciate your candor. I know you will keep an open mind as we continue to work through this," Richard said, patting Larry on the shoulder.

"That's the key," interjected Lars. "Give us some time to add more of the pieces and I believe we can clear it up for you, okay?"

"Oh, sure," said Larry. "Don't get the wrong impression, Lars. Richard knows he can count on me."

"Thanks Larry. Let's plan to catch up next week," Lars added as he left the room.

"You got it," Larry said. As he headed back to his office he was worried. Richard had "that look" and everyone knew that meant trouble.

Over the weekend, Larry had plenty of time to reflect on his comments. Although he knew he was accurate in describing his feelings, he wondered if Richard really understood his concern and confusion. "It's hard to know where you need to go without knowing where you've been," thought Larry. He needed to be more precise in voicing his concerns next time. So, to prepare for his meeting with Richard, Larry sat down at his computer to type notes and recall Newton's history, culture, structure, and business model.

Larry wrote in big bold letters, center-aligned at the top of the page:

WHO ARE WE?

He figured he had to start somewhere.

Newton manufactures commodity consumer packaged products for consumers in the mass market, including pharmacies, food chains, and chain drug stores. Newton's success as a manufacturer of high-volume, low-profit items requires a business model focused on operational efficiencies and the elimination of production downtime and errors. Operational efficiency requires a hierarchical personnel structure. This focus and structure creates a "Newton-centric" company culture, where decisions are put through a "what is best for Newton" filter. Within this type of culture, there is little room for personal creativity and innovation.

As Larry reviewed his summary, the conflict that caused his concern and confusion was becoming clear. Larry's next heading read:

WHY CHANGE WILL BE *HARD!*

Newton has a 133-year history of doing everything to eliminate outside distractions and reduce friction; Newton is a "well-oiled machine." Innovation, the way Lars described it, means making fast decisions, looking for new ideas, shaking things up, being creative, and doing things Newton has NEVER done before! They would have to shake up the inner workings of the machine: the people! Beyond that, innovation means listening to what customers want and finding a way to make that happen.

When thinking about a dramatic change in company culture, Larry had many more questions than answers. He would make sure he brought them up at the next meeting. His next heading was:

QUESTIONS FOR LARS

How are we going to take this old-school, hierarchically structured company and turn it into an innovative, fast, new-ideas company with the consumer and customers at the center?

How would people with more than 20 years of experience doing the exact same thing every day react to learning new things and being open to all new ideas?

Will my friends even *try* to learn?

Will any of this work?

Larry thought, "Change scares a lot of people. Actually, just about everybody I know, especially when not much has changed in a *long* time." Not only had not much changed, but Newton had built systems to eliminate changes and increase sameness. "What is driving all this change anyway? Something must be going on," mused Larry. The more he thought about it, the more he wondered if he could adjust. Was he too old and set in his ways to be innovative? After all, he wasn't a creative or innovative person. Maybe he was among those included just for appearances but not expected to be around after all the changes. "Seriously," Larry thought, "how often does a company bring in a consultant and *not* end up losing or laying off a bunch of people?" Scenes from the movie *Office Space* began to flood his mind. Was the initial meeting with Lars only the first of many that would result in a meeting with "The Bobs" and ultimately lead to layoffs? Larry did not have the answers, in fact, he was downright worried, but at least now he understood his questions. As he clicked "print" on his computer to get his notes, he felt a little better about the impending meeting.

Monday morning at the weekly meeting of the senior executive team, Richard made the official announcement and introduced the members of the Innovation Team. Richard paced back and forth at the front of the conference room like a caged lion. Abruptly, Richard said, "Working with consultants from the Lars Group, the innovation team is an important component of our future as we work together in transforming our company." Then Richard made an announcement that surprised everyone. "Over the weekend, the board and I closed on an agreement-in-principle with Benson Company to sell our high-volume commodity businesses." After a pause that seemed to last an hour, he continued, "I know this announcement comes as a surprise and may even shock some. I recognize that as much as we share information around here, this is different. I hope you can appreciate our need to keep the negotiations on something like this very close to the vest."

Larry looked around the room and shock was a good word for it. His boss, David, Vice President of Marketing, was sitting in stunned silence, facing away from everyone. Just as Richard started to speak again, David interrupted, spinning around rapidly in his chair to face Richard. "You're selling the high-volume commodity business? What does that leave us? How will we survive on what's left?" With that, Larry knew David had truly been caught off guard by the announcement.

Richard smiled. "Great question, David, and I appreciate you getting it out there because I imagine everyone else is thinking it. Before we get to what's left, let me start with the 'why' of this deal. I think that will help." Richard laid out for the team the background market conditions that led to his decisions. Over the next hour he went through the details of why the deal had to be done. "As I looked at the market and the changes in customer dynamics, I realized we needed a new vision for the future if we are to thrive. With the deal we are doing with Benson, with the proceeds from the sale, we are going to invest in innovation. We will develop and launch branded items that consumers have a need for. What this means for us is quite a shift. . .um, no, a complete overhaul of our company. We have to be faster, smarter, and most importantly do things with a sense of urgency. Innovation is only valuable to those at the front of the line, or better yet, those selling the tickets others line up for!"

Everyone laughed and Richard continued, "I'm not telling you anything new when I say this is different than how we have been doing things, right? Hopefully, that explains the 'why' of the deal. Now, David, to your question of 'what will we have left and how will we survive?' We will still have the balance of our items. We sold ten items, about 52% of our sales dollars, so we have 48% of the business left."

"Right," said Lisa, the controller, "but those items do about 75 to 80% of the units! How will we ever pay the bills with what we have left?"

The group grumbled in agreement with Lisa, waiting for Richard's response. "No question, Lisa. You're right on the money. Let's go down that road. Larry, put this up on the board so we can all get a firm grasp of the numbers, will you?" Richard asked. As Larry wrote the figures on the whiteboard, Richard carefully explained how Newton, although different, would not only survive but thrive.

"Ladies and gentlemen, the biggest change we are going to go through is NOT in what we make and sell, or even how we make stuff. No, the biggest change is going to be to our culture." WE WILL NOT CONDUCT WHOLESALE LAYOFFS Richard wrote in large letters on the whiteboard, right above all of the numbers Larry had recorded. I think you all know this company is a family to me. We treat people fairly here. I don't want to lose our family culture. It's our heritage and the lifeblood of this company. I've made this point clear to Lars and his group. At the same time, we have some difficult decisions to make."

After a moment's pause for the group to gather their thoughts, Richard continued, "The key for this transformation is a couple of things." Richard now took a seat, eye level with the team. "First, we, this group, no, this *team,* have to catch this vision of transforming the company into 'The New Newton.' Richard jumped from his seat and wrote it on the white board. He returned to his seat and continued, "This means *big* culture changes, keeping the best part of our family heritage. Second, we must become an innovative company from what we do to how we do it. That's what the Innovation Team is all about. Lars and his group will lead the 'I team' through a process and they will lead us. As they do, all of us are going to be involved. I know some of you will grab hold of this and be excited. For others, it may take a little while to sink in. My expectation is that everyone will be on board and fully supportive."

At this comment, Larry looked around the room. Faces were filled with anxiety. There were no smiles and most heads were down. Most noticeably, David was once again spun around in his chair, facing away from everyone.

"It is important that this be an open process and that you ask questions as we go along," Richard said. "Also, be patient. We're all going through this. With change, any change, there will be some bumps along the way. Be patient with the process, with yourself, with others, and with me. This is an exciting time. Welcome to The New Newton, and with that, I'll turn this meeting over to Lars and his team."

"Thank you, Richard," said Lars. "OK. You have all had a *lot* piled on your plate. Let's take a break, take a few minutes to check your messages. Let's come back together in 20 minutes. When you come back, I'd like each of you to be prepared to fill in the blank in this statement." Lars rushed to the white board and wrote: When I hear the word *change,* I feel _____. "No right or wrong answers, just tell us what you think of."

"Oh," Larry thought, "I don't need 20 minutes; I can tell you right now. How about: Scared! Terrified! Confused! Worried!"

Richard chuckled nervously as Lars dismissed the meeting for their 20-minute break.

At 10:20 sharp, Lars called the group back together. He was not totally surprised that David, the VP of marketing, was not in the room. "Let's give the rest of our group a few minutes and then we'll begin," said Lars.

With that, Lars went to check on David. He found him in his office, his feet up on his credenza, talking on his phone. Lars knocked just loud enough to let David know he was there and David turned around. Lars waited as a red-faced David said with a hushed voice, "Call you later honey," and hung up the phone.

"Everything OK? We are ready to start," Lars said.

David answered, "Oh, you guys go ahead with your meeting. I'll get the notes from someone. I've got too much going on."

Lars closed David's door and said, "David I appreciate that the announcement Richard made this morning caught you by surprise, so I understand, to some extent, you feeling like you are too busy to be part of this. Let me ask you something though. Do you think pulling back and not contributing is the best, not only for you but for your team? I mean, what message is that going to send to Richard? I can't force you to join us of course, but I will tell you that Richard asked me to provide him with feedback this afternoon on the contributions of his leadership team. I am heading back to the meeting and hope you will join us. We can use your input." With that, Lars walked down the hall and back into the conference room and resumed the meeting.

"All right, let's see what you came up with on what you think of when you hear the word *change,*" Lars began.

The door opened and David said, "Sorry I'm late guys. My wife called and I forgot the time."

Lars said, "Not a problem. We are just getting started. OK, who wants to go first with what they think of regarding change."

Mary in accounts payable spoke first saying, "Change doesn't bother me. In fact it's kind of exciting. It's something new to learn."

One of Lars's consultants, Jim, said, "I'm going to write the themes we come up with up here so we can remember them as we go along." The first thing Jim wrote on the white board was EXCITING OPPORTUNITY.

"That's a fair way to put it, Jim," Mary said.

Scott, the director of manufacturing, said "I wish I could be as positive as Mary, but to me, change is just scary. I mean, we've spent lots of time getting all of our policies and procedures put into writing and approved. Then we trained all of the employees so they know exactly what to do. Change just means we have to start all over again. It's lots of work if you ask me."

Jim summarized Scott's comments with the words SCARY HAVING TO START OVER. Scott sarcastically commented "Yeah, and that's putting it nicely." The team chuckled, adding in some much-needed comedic relief.

Lars then asked "How many of you can relate to Scott's comments?" When no one raised their hand, Lars said, "Oh, come on. None of you see change as scary? You can be more honest than that." With that, 11 of the 15 people in the room raised their hand. "That's what I thought," Lars said. "That's pretty common. A great majority of people, if they are honest, admit that change is scary or not something they like very much. The rest are usually just too scared to admit it." Lars laughed and the group laughed with him, again breaking the tension in the room. Lars continued, "Listen, to be successful, one thing we have to agree on is we need to be transparent, be honest with each other. If you like something, say so, and if you don't like something, say that as well. Richard's vision is for a big change. We won't sugarcoat that. The culture will change. He told you that. The good news is that his vision is for a better, more secure Newton. The key is to embrace the future rather than focus on the past."

"I've got another thought about change for you," David interjected. "How about 'impossible.'" Everyone in the room turned toward Lars, shocked that David had been so blunt, and not sure how Lars would respond.

Lars looked toward David and very calmly said, "Now that's more like it! That's probably closer to what most of you think anyway. If so, that's OK! Folks, if we don't start communicating like this with each other, we ARE NOT going to be successful." As Jim captured the word IMPOSSIBLE on the white board, the team, now laughing even more, was starting to feel relieved that they could be honest.

Over the rest of that day, Lars and his group of consultants took the senior executives and the Innovation Team members through a series of training exercises to equip the group to understand change so they could lead their teams over the coming months. For example, in one exercise the consultants put the employees in teams of four and assigned each team one of six stages of the change cycle. Lars went to the white board and wrote down the stages: LOSS-DOUBT-DISCOMFORT-DISCOVERY-UNDERSTANDING-INTEGRATION. Lars then instructed, "Each group has 20 minutes to brainstorm and put together a presentation to teach the rest of the groups about their assigned stage." Larry's group was assigned Stage 2: Doubt.

Larry kicked off the presentation by saying, "In this stage one experiences feelings of resentment, thoughts are skeptical, and behavior is resistant." Then, Larry's team chose to role play these various feelings for the group. For example, Larry and Cathy role played feelings of resentment by acting out a meeting between Lars and David. In the role play, David vented his frustrations about how the change would be impossible by saying, "You can't just come in here and expect us to change what we've been doing for all these years. I feel offended that we weren't consulted about this prior to you coming in." This resonated with rest of the team since most of them felt they were in the earliest stages of understanding all the changes that were going on.

"Resentment. Skepticism. Resistance. Yep, those pretty much sum it up," David said after seeing Larry's group's role play of himself. The group chuckled, including Lars and Richard.

After the meetings and training exercises were over, Lars met with Richard to update him. "Give me the bottom line first, Lars. How does it look?"

"I am very pleased with the overall contribution and attitude of the group. We knew there would be some resistance, but it will go well. For the first group of meetings, I'm pleased," Lars replied.

"OK, now give me the rest of it. What concerns you?" Richard asked.

Lars looked at his notes before responding. "It's early, but David is not on board. I think he was really caught off guard by the announcement. I don't know if he will buy in."

Richard frowned. "The bus has left the station on this, Lars. There are just so many seats on the bus and some may decide they don't want to go on this trip. In other cases, we may decide they aren't going with us. David is a key player on our team. If he's not on board, there's a good chance others aren't as well. If we lose buy-in from key members of this team, it could kill our culture. I want to give everyone an opportunity to accept what we're doing and contribute to the process. *But* I won't have a lot of patience because this deal is getting done quickly. When the bus gets rolling, those who are not on the bus, or not actively on board and participating, will be allowed to go somewhere else. Let's talk about timing. How long do you need to complete the innovation team training and put the culture, purpose, and guiding principles modules in place?"

Lars passed paperwork across the desk to Richard. "Here's the timeline from the agreement we signed a couple of weeks ago. It has points we can—"

Richard interrupted. "No, no, I know what the timeline says, Lars. It says 2 years to get all this in place. What I'm asking is, what can you do to get it done *now?* Surely it doesn't take 2 years to sit down and write a purpose statement and guiding principles! I can't wait 2 years to have the new culture, the speed-to-market, the innovation, and product development in place."

Lars sighed. "Richard, I understand, but ask for your patience. The thing you don't want is to talk about change, about a new vision, but not do it properly. My team prepared a very thorough plan to ensure that doesn't happen. I'm confident we will lead you and Newton through this change, but you have to commit to the timeframe we proposed. I have been through lots of these with companies and experience will not let me shortcut this change process. It's not fair to you because it won't be successful and in the end; it will hurt your company and mine."

Richard paused to reflect, reading through the agreement timeline, and then said, "No, I know you're right. I just am so anxious to get this going. Please agree just to be flexible on it and if you find, as we get into it, that there are any opportunities to prioritize the training or shorten the timeframe, let's discuss it, OK?"

Lars smiled in relief, extended his hand in agreement, and said, "We are in agreement on that, Richard."

With a satisfied, yet skeptical look, Richard said, "Good deal. Well, let's start loading the bus!"

Discussion Questions

1. As the CEO of the company, what has Richard done well with respect to the changes Newton is trying to implement?

2. Based on what we know about Newton from Larry's summary, how would these changes affect the company culture?

3. What were some of the challenges Newton faced with the prospect of change?

4. As a consultant, what would you do differently if you were in charge of the changes at Newton? What would be your next steps?

5. As an employee, how would you react to the tactics used by Lars (e.g., the 20-minute role play of the different change stages)?

FOR FURTHER READING

CCMC, Inc. (2009). Lorton, VA: Author. *The change cycle model.* Retrieved from http://www .changecycle.com/changecycle.htm

Eisenberg, E. M., & Riley, P. (2001). Organizational culture. In F. M. Jablin & L. L. Putnam (Eds.), *The new handbook of organizational communication: Advances in theory, research, and methods* (pp. 291–322). Thousand Oaks, CA: Sage.

Kegan, R. (2009). *Immunity to change: How to overcome it and unlock the potential in yourself and your organization.* Boston: Harvard Business School Press.

Larson, G. S., & Tompkins, P. K. (2005). Ambivalence and resistance: A study of management in a concertive control system. *Communication Monographs, 72,* 1–21. doi: 10.1080/036377505 2000342508

Westley, F. R. (1990). The eye of the needle: Cultural and personal transformation in a traditional organization. *Human Relations, 43,* 273–293. doi: 10.1177/001872679004300305

Case 30

STICKER SHOCK IN AN ORGANIZATION THAT WILL NOT STICK TOGETHER

BARBARA A. RITTER

Learning Objectives

- To help you understand the interconnectedness of organizational systems, including organizational strategy, culture, structure, and human resource management policies and procedures.
- To help you visualize and practice dealing with difficult people in a supervisory setting.

Judy Thorson, the executive director of a local not-for-profit organization called Helping Hands, sat in her office pondering the events that she expected to occur at the management meeting that afternoon. Recently, she had brought in an external consulting team to get a fresh perspective on some ongoing organizational problems regarding the internal conflicts at Helping Hands. The consulting team had indeed identified several underlying issues in specific departments, and Judy dreaded confronting her managers with the results of the report.

Helping Hands was established in the 1980s to assist people in poverty to manage their finances and work their way toward home ownership. The growing organization consisted of about 30 employees in six functional divisions (finance, resource development, community relations, volunteer coordination, client services, and thrift shop) (see Figure 30.1). Recently, Erin Moore, an employee at Helping Hands for 3 years as volunteer director, had been promoted to the job of assistant executive director in charge of four of these divisions (community relations, volunteer coordination, client services, and thrift store).

Figure 30.1   Helping Hands Organizational Chart

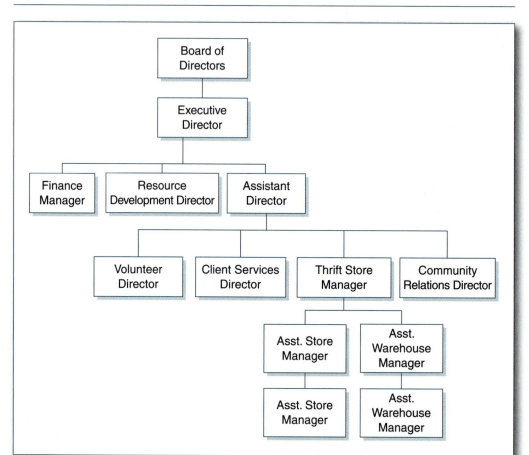

Although Judy was technically in charge of the financial health of the organization (finance and resource development), she was still dealing with people issues on a daily basis. In fact, Judy felt that too much of her time was taken up with dealing with internal conflicts and interpersonal politics, which was why she hired an external consultant to examine the organizational dynamics.

The consulting team spent many months observing, surveying, and interviewing the employees at Helping Hands. At the end of this period, they provided a report to Judy with observations and recommendations with which she was largely in agreement. The report noted that most of the departments at Helping Hands operated according to a clan culture, in an environment that is friendly and familylike, and held together by loyalty. In fact, the culture operated so informally, based on the small size of the organization and principles of mutual trust, that no standard policies or procedures (e.g., discipline) existed regarding employees.

The thrift shop employees, however, noted a culture that was based on fear, pressure, and a focus on short-term results. The consulting report showed that the cultural divide between the thrift shop and the rest of the organization was noted in every interview conducted at Helping Hands, with the exception of the thrift shop employees. When shown a picture of the organizational chart, for example, several employees drew a box around the thrift store employees to indicate that they are separate from the rest of the organization. Employees in the thrift store seemed to recognize a divide; however, they saw it as less important or impactful than the other employees. Further distinctions between the thrift store and other facets of the organization were noted in the report. That is, as most employees of Helping Hands indicated a greater preference for the Helping Hands culture to be based on innovation and long-term planning, thrift shop employees indicated a lower preference for movement toward this type of culture (relative to their current standing).

The consulting report noted that a complacency regarding the differences between the thrift shop and other facets of the organization had developed over time, as well as a resentment toward parts of the organization that differ (i.e., an in-group–out-group orientation). Employees seemed to recognize the thrift shop as separate and not a member of "the team," but did not know how to bridge the gap and begin working toward a common purpose or mind-set.

Judy knew that there were several factors contributing to the recognized divide between the thrift shop and the rest of the organization. The thrift shop, for example, had operated in a separate physical location from the other departments until 5 years ago. Not only was the store in a separate location, but it also operated largely independently of the rest of the organization. The current store manager, Chris Williams, had run the store since its inception decades ago. Chris was asked to engage with the overall organization to a greater extent when the store's physical location moved, but in reality, little change had occurred. Chris still managed the store largely independently from the rest of the organization and had little supervision from above. This was the way it had always been run and Chris did not respond well to suggestions from Judy or Erin. The situation was especially unfortunate given the importance of the thrift store to the organization as a whole. The thrift shop historically had been the main source of revenue for Helping Hands. Without the revenue generated by the store, Helping Hands could not serve so many members of the community. Judy knew the problems identified in the report were ongoing and had to be addressed. This was the main reason why she had called in an external consultant. If Chris would not listen to Judy or Erin, perhaps he would listen to an "expert."

As Judy prepared for the afternoon meeting, she remembered some of the interpersonal conflicts that had arisen over the years between Chris and the other employees, from the board of directors above him, all the way down to the store volunteers below him. For example, several years ago, it had come to the attention of the board that there were a multitude of customer complaints regarding the pricing of items on the sales floor. Chris was of the mind that items should be marked at full retail sales price regardless of condition, but he often ran 50% or 70% off sales. Regardless, it seemed customers suffered from "sticker shock" at the sight of such high prices on used items. The board asked Chris to price items taking into account the condition of the item and to lower the prices in general. At the board meeting the next month, Chris reported that he had indeed lowered prices and overall sales fell dramatically that month, so he had gone back to the high pricing with the same percentage off pricing philosophy he had used previously. The board, although not happy to be usurped, let Chris go back to his old pricing strategy.

Other incidences also had come up for Judy to deal with in regards to Chris's behavior. Recently, another employee with a rank equal in the hierarchy to Chris had asked to negotiate on an item that had been on the sales floor for an extended time. Chris refused to negotiate with the employee, but later sold the item at a reduced price to an outside customer. This, of course, was met with feelings of unfairness and resentment on behalf of the employee involved, but the negative feelings also seemed to spread to other employees who were not directly involved in this incident.

The effects of this type of behavior were not limited to those outside of the thrift shop. Just that week, an employee below Chris had come to Judy complaining that she had been disciplined for selling a plastic plant off of the sales floor that Chris had deemed decoration and not for sale. Seemingly, this policy was not explained to the employee until after the sale. So Judy had been handling issues regarding the thrift store from all levels and had done nothing directly to deal with Chris. She had not even spoken to Chris about her feelings on these issues. Instead, Judy hoped that the meeting that day would clear up a lot of these problems.

Before the meeting, Judy e-mailed the consulting report to Chris and Erin. She also asked the consultant to be present to explain the recommendations to this small group before Judy presented any changes to the rest of the organization. Her thought was that a small meeting of four people would be less threatening to Chris than a larger meeting. As the meeting began, Judy sat quietly and waited for the consultant to begin. She hoped Chris would listen to the consultant and see the problems spurning from the thrift shop. As the consultant began, Chris immediately interrupted with, "I didn't get this report. I have never seen it. No one has ever sent it to me." Although Judy knew she sent the report out by e-mail earlier in the week, she apologized and provided Chris with an extra copy.

The others waited while Chris finished reading. Finally, the meeting commenced with a discussion of the culture divide between the thrift shop and the rest of the organization. Erin responded that she agreed with the conclusions in the report and thought that they should work toward reconciling the divide. Chris, on the other hand, responded politely, "Well, this used to be a problem, but we have handled that since the store moved to this location." Although the consultant cited current examples and the issue was pressed by Erin, Chris would not agree that this was a current problem.

Judy brought up one example that she thought was quite pertinent to the discussion related to how the store was run differently from the rest of the organization. The last time that Chris took a vacation day, his employees created a sign that informed thrift shop customers how many clients Helping Hands had assisted. Judy thought the sign was a great addition to the store when it was hung behind the register, but when she walked by on her way out that evening, the sign was gone. The assistant store manager suggested to Judy that the employees had removed the sign before Chris came back the next day for fear of reprisal. Although Judy thought this was odd, she didn't say anything about it at the time. It seemed to her, however, to be indicative of the fear felt by the thrift shop employees; a fear generated by Chris (Judy did not suggest this out loud, however). In response to the sign issue, Chris suggested that, "I just don't know why they would feel like that. I asked, but no one told me." Chris continued to go on about his employees, "I let the assistant managers make decisions when I am gone, unless it's about something really important. The problem is, they never tell me about the important stuff, even if I ask them about it."

As Judy was afraid of being too brash and did not see how she could make Chris understand, she moved on to discuss the short-term focus in the store that sometimes worked in opposition to the long-term organizational goals. In the forefront of Judy's mind was the situation with the board of directors in which Chris would not consider the long-term, strategic pricing strategy suggested. Chris responded, "Things happen faster in the store. I have to make changes every day, but I do have a long-term focus." When Erin questioned Chris about the pricing issue, Chris replied, "Why am I always singled out and everyone else thinks they know best how to run my department?"

Recognizing that the meeting had already lasted several hours and Chris was getting more and more defensive, Judy changed tactics and suggested that the consulting report could be shared with the rest of the organization and they would come to a group consensus about the challenges faced and the best solutions to those challenges. Chris, now clearly angered, demanded, "This report is not to be shared. The majority of this report is about the thrift shop and it should stay in the thrift shop. I will decide what to do about it. There's no other department in this organization where all other people think they should have a say in how it's run. I don't tell Becky how to run client services. Why? Because I know nothing about it and it isn't my department to run. This is *my* department and I will decide how to run it. I don't know why everyone always singles me out."

In the end, the only agreement reached during the meeting was to try a new pricing strategy as suggested by the consulting report. The pricing strategy involved a percentage off of the original price depending on how long it had been on the sales floor (e.g., original price, 25% off, 50% off, and 75% off), based on the first-in, first-out (FIFO) pricing strategy. Judy committed several of the other employees to go change the sales tags on the current items the following Monday. Chris promised to look over the rest of the report and decide for himself if he thought anything else was necessary. Although disheartened at the end of the meeting, Judy was happy that they had at least managed to agree on a pricing strategy that seemed reasonable.

The following Monday, several employees (including Erin) did report to the thrift shop to help change tags. As Chris was explaining the new pricing strategy and how the tags would need to be changed, Erin was shocked to hear him say that they were going to take 50% off all listed prices and leave it at that. This was a small organization and it was not only Erin, but all of the employees, who knew that Chris had decided to implement his own policy once again.

Discussion Questions

1. What is the main problem in this situation?

2. To what extent is the cultural divide problematic? Is it something that needs to be addressed? Why or why not? What recommendations would you make to Judy to decrease the cultural divide between departments?

3. What role does Chris play in the organizational problems? What role does Judy play in the organizational problems? If you were Judy, how would you handle the situation now?

4. What are the underlying organizational issues that allow these problems to persist?
   a. To what extent is the lack of overall strategic goals a problem at Helping Hands?
   b. How do recent structural changes (e.g., creating a new position for Erin) affect this situation? Does the organizational structure play a role in exacerbating this situation?
   c. To what extent do organizational policies or procedures (HRM) play a role in exacerbating this situation? How does the lack of overall human resource policies effect this situation?

5. Taking into account the interconnectedness of organizational strategy, culture, structure, and human resource policies and procedures, what changes would you make in each area?

FOR FURTHER READING

Galbraith, J. R. (2002). *Designing organizations: An executive guide to strategy, structure, and process.* San Francisco: Jossey-Bass.

Harrison, M. I. (2005). *Diagnosing organizations: Methods, models, and processes.* Thousand Oaks, CA: Sage.

Seijts, G. H. (2006). *Cases in organizational behavior.* Thousand Oaks, CA: Sage.

Velga, J. F. (1988). Face your problem subordinates now! *Academy of Management Executive, 2*(2), 145–152.

Watkins, M. (2003). *The first 90 days: Critical success strategies for new leaders at all levels.* Boston: Harvard Business School Press.

Part III

Exercises in Organization Development and Change

In this part, you will find exercises designed to complement and enhance your understanding of organization development concepts and the cases provided in this book. The following exercises are included here.

1. Contracting With a Client
2. Organization Development Practitioner Skills
3. Data Gathering
4. Giving Feedback
5. Resistance to Change
6. Resistance to Change Scale
7. Cynicism About Organizational Change
8. Myers-Briggs Type Indicator
9. Coaching and Individual Instruments
10. Team Values
11. Team Diagnosis and Intervention
12. Team Facilitation
13. Identifying and Changing Organizational Culture
14. Perceived Organizational Innovativeness Scale
15. Designing and Redesigning Organizations

The chart below demonstrates how these exercises can be used in conjunction with the cases found in the book.

Topic	Relevant Cases	Relevant Exercises
Entry and Contracting	Cases 1–2	Exercise 1: Contracting With a Client Exercise 2: Organization Development Practitioner Skills
Data Gathering	Cases 3–5	Exercise 3: Data Gathering
Diagnosis	Cases 6–9	Exercise 11: Team Diagnosis and Intervention
Feedback	Cases 9–10	Exercise 4: Giving Feedback
Resistance to Change	Cases 11–12	Exercise 5: Resistance to Change Exercise 6: Resistance to Change Scale Exercise 7: Cynicism About Organizational Change
Individual Interventions	Cases 19–21	Exercise 8: Myers-Briggs Type Indicator Exercise 9: Coaching and Individual Instruments
Team Interventions	Cases 22–25	Exercise 10: Team Values Exercise 11: Team Diagnosis and Intervention Exercise 12: Team Facilitation
Whole Organization Interventions	Cases 26–30	Exercise 13: Identifying and Changing Organizational Culture Exercise 14: Perceived Organizational Innovativeness Scale Exercise 15: Designing and Redesigning Organizations

Exercise 1

CONTRACTING WITH A CLIENT

In the contracting meeting, the practitioner and client meet to determine what work the client would like to have performed. The problem is explored in more detail, and the client and practitioner jointly agree on the next steps. Good contracting meetings enhance the client-practitioner relationship, clarify expectations, and add to the practitioner's understanding of the problem. In summary, the purpose of the contracting meeting is to:

1. Further explore the problem.

2. Clarify the client's goals and objectives for the request.

3. Allow the client and the practitioner to get to know each other, and to validate that the practitioner has the knowledge and skills to accept the project.

4. Understand the organization's commitment to change.

5. Agree on mutual roles and needs.

6. Clarify time pressures and expectations.

7. Clarify how the client and consultant will interact.

8. Clarify confidentiality needs.

9. Plan the next steps.

INSTRUCTIONS

For this exercise, you and two of your classmates will role play a contracting meeting with a client. Return to either Case 1 or Case 2 (the case studies on contracting) and read the case again to refresh your memory of it.

In a 15 to 20 minute discussion, role play a contracting meeting between the OD practitioner and client in the case. At the end of the dialogue, use the discussion questions below as a guide to evaluate your meeting. If time allows, change roles and select a different case study, and try the role play again.

Decide which of you will assume each of the following roles.

1. The OD Practitioner or Change Agent

As the OD practitioner, your goal during the contracting meeting will be to learn more about the presenting problem the client wants to discuss. You will have the opportunity to ask questions of the client, clarify your own role and needs, and reach the nine objectives listed above of a good contracting meeting.

2. The Client or Manager/Executive

As the client, your role is to describe and represent the problem you would like the practitioner to address. You should answer the practitioner's questions as you would if you were the client in the case. For the purpose of this exercise, you will not be an expert in the field of organization development, so you will need to assume the role of a client who is considering working with an OD practitioner. Pay attention to how you feel about the questions that are asked and share your reactions at the end of the exercise.

3. Observer

As the observer, your role is to listen carefully to the dialogue, but not to participate. Make notes about the quantity and quality of the questions that the practitioner asks, how the practitioner probes for additional detail, whether the questions are nonjudgmental, and so on. Use the following questions and checklist to guide your observations.

1. Who spent more time talking?
   - ☐ Client
   - ☐ Practitioner

2. Who spent more time listening?
   - ☐ Client
   - ☐ Practitioner

3. Who asked more questions?
   - ☐ Client
   - ☐ Practitioner

4. How did the practitioner initiate the discussion?

5. What questions were asked?

6. What was expressed nonverbally (e.g., via eye contact or body language)?

7. How did the practitioner and client negotiate their needs and wants?

8. How did the practitioner address the nine objectives of a contracting meeting?

9. What else did you notice?

Discussion Questions

1. Which questions were particularly helpful? Which questions were not as helpful? How could the questions have been rephrased to be more helpful?

2. For the practitioner and observer: Did you learn more about the problem being described? What did you learn? What additional questions would help probe for additional information? Is there a question you wanted to ask, but did not? Why?

3. For the client and observer: Did any questions cause you discomfort? Which ones? Why? Is there anything you held back or were reluctant to say? Why or why not? What questions would you have wanted to answer, but weren't asked? Did you feel that the practitioner understood your problem? Why or why not? Do you feel confident that this practitioner could help you? Why or why not?

4. What did the practitioner and client commit to doing? For each of you, do you feel a genuine commitment and motivation to take that action? Why or why not? Is there anything you committed to doing that you regret? Why? Was there a turning point to the discussion when the meeting started to go badly or where commitment was enhanced?

5. Do you think this meeting enhanced the likelihood of a successful engagement? Why or why not? What would you do differently next time? What lessons should we take from this interaction about conducting successful contracting meetings?

Exercise 2

ORGANIZATION DEVELOPMENT PRACTITIONER SKILLS

Y ou are the leader of a management team about to hire an organization development practitioner to conduct a team-building exercise with your staff. The staff generally get along well, though you feel that the team's performance could be better. You would like the OD practitioner to propose an intervention to help the team improve.

In small groups of three to five members, identify the top eight to ten skills or knowledge areas you would want your practitioner to possess. You may add to the list if you think of a different skill or knowledge area that does not appear below. Compare your list with that of your team members and discuss the following questions.

Discussion Questions

1. How would you find the consultant that matched your skill or knowledge needs? Would any of these skills or knowledge needs be the same even if you had a different problem to address?

2. Would you select an internal or external consultant? Why?

3. How would you know if a consultant held the skills you seek? If you were the practitioner, how would you show that you held these skills?

4. From a practitioner's viewpoint, would you select different skills to be important to this engagement? Why or why not?

SKILLS

Interpersonal Skills and Personal Characteristics

Self-Awareness and Self-Management

Objectivity/Neutrality

Imagination

Flexibility, Dealing With Ambiguity

Honesty/Integrity

Consistency

Building Trust and Rapport

Open-Mindedness

Listening

Sense of Humor

Risk Taking

Political Awareness

Persuasiveness

Collaboration

Tact and Diplomacy

Role Modeling

Rational-Emotional Balance

Negotiation

Managing Stress

Organizational Behavior

Organizational Theory

Strategy

Open Systems

Motivation and Rewards

Change Theory

Organization Design

Power

Leadership

Conflict

Organizational Culture

Mergers and Acquisitions

Group Development

Change Management

Change Resistance and Stakeholder Engagement

Communication (e.g., use of metaphors, stories)

Consulting Skills

Entry and Contracting

Design of Data-Gathering Program

Diagnosis

Designing Interventions

Giving and Receiving Feedback

Evaluating Results of Interventions

Data Collection and Analysis

Research Design

Interviewing Skills

Survey Preparation

(Continued)

(Continued)

Data Analysis (quantitative and qualitative)

Statistical Analysis

Participant Observation

Interpreting and Reporting Results

Measurement and Testing

Interventions

Strategic Planning

Vision/Mission Development

Goal Setting

Process Analysis and Redesign

Role Development and Clarification

Restructuring

Coaching and Mentoring

Team Building

Future Search Conferences

Appreciative Inquiry

Quality Approaches (Six Sigma, Total Quality Management)

Conflict Resolution

Facilitation Skills

Training and Development

Adult Learning

Instructional Design

Training Delivery Skills

Assessment of Learning

Performance Management

Technology and Learning

Business and Management Knowledge Areas

Finance and Accounting

Human Resources Management

Sales and Marketing

Information Systems and Technology

Operations and Production

Legal Issues

General Professional Skills

Public Speaking

Written Communication

Translate Theory Into Practice

Project Management

Ethical Issues for OD Consultants

Cross-Cultural Knowledge

Exercise 3

DATA GATHERING

Gathering data effectively is a critical skill for OD practitioners. In this exercise, you will have the opportunity to practice gathering data through individual interviews.

PART I: DESIGN THE QUESTIONS

Pair up with a peer and choose Case 3, 4, or 5. Imagine that the two of you are the consulting team preparing to interview members of the organization to better understand the situation. Working with your partner, design a list of interview questions that you would plan to ask. Your interview questions should:

- Be nonjudgmental. That is, they should not presume a particular response or make assumptions in the question, leading the interviewee to a desired position.

- Be phrased as open ended, allowing the respondent maximum flexibility in answering what is important to him or her.

- Follow up to seek additional detail where necessary, asking the interviewee to reflect on a particular experience if he or she shares general observations, for example.

Once you have designed a list of 6 to 10 interview questions, proceed to Part II of this exercise.

PART II: CONDUCT THE INTERVIEW

Now, form groups of three. Each person in the new group will assume one of the following roles.

1. *Interviewer:* Your role is to manage the conversation. You will create rapport with the interviewee, explain the purpose and format of the interview, introduce your note taker and explain his or her role, and ask questions. Be sure to keep the interview on track to manage your time and gather the data you need.

2. *Interviewee:* Your role is to play the part of an organizational member in the case. Answer the questions as best as you can given what you think the organizational member in the case would think and feel about the organization and being interviewed by these OD practitioners.

3. *Note taker:* Your role is to document the interview. You may intervene with questions when necessary to follow up or ensure that you understand the interviewee's answers. Make sure that your notes are detailed enough that you will remember what was said later, including exact quotes where possible.

Conduct a 15 to 20 minute interview. You may be unable to ask all of your questions during this time. At the conclusion of the interview, the note taker should spend 5 minutes reviewing the notes, paraphrasing them to the interviewer and interviewee aloud, and explaining what the note taker saw as the top themes or feedback coming from the interview. Finally, debrief your interview experience using the discussion questions below.

Discussion Questions

1. Reflect on your experience designing interview questions. Did your questions elicit the data you had hoped to gather? In retrospect, were there questions you wish you had asked?

2. As the interviewee, how did you feel about the experience? Did the interviewer put you at ease at the start of the interview? Did the interviewer seem genuinely interested in your responses? Could you express what you had hoped to get across? Was there additional information that you wanted to share but could not? Why?

3. For the interviewer: How did it feel to conduct this interview? How did you set the interviewee at ease and explain the purpose of the interview? Which of your interview questions did you find to be the most effective? Ineffective? With what you know now, which questions would you want to rephrase?

4. For the note taker: Reflect on the note-taking process. Did you accurately capture the interview in your notes? What would you do differently next time? As an observer, what additional questions would you suggest for the next interview?

5. What lessons are there to be learned from this experience about how to conduct interviews successfully?

Exercise 4

GIVING FEEDBACK

Jasmine, the leader of a team of 11 customer service specialists, has asked you to help her grow and develop as a leader. You agreed to conduct individual interviews of each member of the team and to return to Jasmine with their feedback. You specified that team members would remain anonymous in the data you presented, known only to you. In your initial meeting, you sensed that Jasmine would have a difficult time accepting negative feedback from team members and that she might get defensive. After the interviews, you summarized the data into the following themes, with quotes from team members to illustrate each.

- **Team members believe access to Jasmine is too limited.**
  - *"Whenever I have an angry customer or need Jasmine to make a decision, it seems like I never get a response from her."*
  - *"She has cancelled my last three meetings with her."*
  - *"Except for staff meetings, she's never around."*

- **Team members appreciate being included in decision making.**
  - *"I like how she always gives us notice of what's happening from the corporate office and asks for our input."*
  - *"I was glad that she asked for volunteers to participate on the system redesign team rather than making the decision on her own."*

- **Jasmine's use of humor and sarcasm hurts team members' feelings.**
  - *"She's very childish. I don't appreciate being made fun of in front of my peers."*
  - *"She has a biting sense of humor that sometimes turns other people off."*

- **Team members would like Jasmine to be more direct.**
  - *"I like that she involves us, but everything on this team becomes a debate. Sometimes she just needs to make a decision and tell us what to do."*
  - *"She asks me 'what do you think we should do?' when I have no idea. She's the leader; she should tell us."*

INSTRUCTIONS

1. Working with a peer, plan your feedback meeting with Jasmine. What do you hope to accomplish? Create a brief agenda of your time with her.

2. Next, decide who will play the role of the consultant and who will play the role of Jasmine. Conduct a 15 to 20 minute feedback meeting.

Discussion Questions

1. For the consultant: How did Jasmine respond to the feedback? Did you accomplish with Jasmine what you had hoped to accomplish? What did you do to start the meeting and set it up successfully?

2. For Jasmine: How did it feel to hear the feedback from the consultant? Knowing what you know about the data above, do you feel you heard what should have been presented?

3. How well did the feedback (a) describe rather than evaluate the behavior, (b) give specific instances rather than generalities where possible, (c) balance positive and negative feedback, (d) help rather than punish, (e) address behaviors the recipient can control, (f) stay true to the data and avoid collusion, and (g) motivate action?

4. What lessons should we take from this role play about how to conduct feedback meetings successfully?

Exercise 5

RESISTANCE TO CHANGE

Recognizing a client's resistance is an important skill, and the ability to work with it is an even more advanced skill. One of the most comprehensive descriptions of client resistance is found in Block (2000, pp. 141–148), who describes 14 ways that it may be expressed by clients.

For this exercise, carefully read Block's 14 forms of resistance as outlined below. Imagine that you are conducting a feedback meeting with a client, and you hear the client express the form of resistance indicated. As the OD practitioner, what would you say in response? List your response on the following chart, and share your thoughts with your classmates.

1. *Give me more detail.* The client continually asks for more data, more descriptions, more information. Even when presented with the extra facts, it is not enough and even more is desired.

2. *Flood you with detail.* The client spends most of the meeting talking, providing history, background, and commentary on not only the immediate situation, but tangential issues, too.

3. *Time.* Resistance is expressed as a complaint about not having enough time to complete the project, to gather data, to meet to discuss the diagnosis and feedback, or to plan the intervention.

4. *Impracticality.* The client complains that the solutions are not practical or feasible in this group, this division, this company, this industry, and so on. This may be expressed as a complaint about what works "in theory" versus what will work "here."

5. *I'm not surprised.* The client accepts the feedback and diagnosis with agreement, nodding that it makes perfect sense. "Of course that is what is happening, it is what I knew all along," the client seems to be saying, avoiding the discomfort that can arise by being confronted with new information.

6. *Attack.* A direct attack is a clear form of resistance, when the client expresses anger, frustration, and irritation through a raised voice and angry words. It is among the easiest to recognize because it is the most explicit.

7. *Confusion.* Much like a desire for more information, the client wants another explanation, expressed in a different way. Then this explanation seems unclear and another is requested.

8. *Silence.* The client remains silent during the entire presentation and the consultant may be tempted to keep pressing forward until the client speaks up. If confronted, the client may say that the presentation is "fine," or "good," or that "nothing occurs to me to say at the moment, but keep going."

9. *Intellectualizing.* The client asks about underlying theory, perhaps desiring models or articles that apply to this situation. Instead of planning or discussing action, the client prefers to philosophize about the organization and its theoretical patterns.

10. *Moralizing.* The client wants to blame others, often as a group, stating what they should be doing or what they do not understand. Moralizing shifts the focus away from the client's own actions and sets up a hierarchical and noncooperative situation.

11. *Compliance.* Compliance with the consultant's proposal may be the most challenging for a consultant to see. After all, it is validating to work with a willing client who apparently sees the value in the change agent's proposed solutions. Underneath the agreement, however, lie doubts and reservations. When the time comes to take action, the client finds a reason to delay. If no doubts are expressed and everything seems perfect, the client may be compliant on the surface, but simmering underneath.

12. *Methodology.* As Block (2000, p. 146) puts it, "questions about method represent legitimate needs for information for the first ten minutes." Beyond that, a barrage of methods questions may represent an attempt to invalidate the feedback and avoid taking action.

13. *Flight into health.* When the time comes to accept the feedback and take action as a result of it, the issue that the client noted in the first meeting has mysteriously vanished. It becomes easier to ignore the problem or change one's opinion of it than it is to take a risk in trying to address it.

14. *Pressing for solutions.* The client expresses frustration at any additional explanation about the problem—where it came from, who is involved, what problems underlie the presenting problem, and so on—pressing the practitioner to get to the point where solutions are described.

Form of Resistance	What I Would Say If I Heard It Expressed
Give me more detail	
Flood you with detail	
Time	
Impracticality	
I'm not surprised	
Attack	
Confusion	
Silence	
Intellectualizing	
Moralizing	
Compliance	
Methodology	
Flight into health	
Pressing for solutions	

REFERENCE

Block, P. (2000). *Flawless consulting: A guide to getting your expertise used* (2nd ed.). New York: Jossey-Bass.

Exercise 6

RESISTANCE TO CHANGE SCALE

Whether in the data-gathering, feedback, or implementation phases of an engagement, an OD practitioner is likely to find clients or organizational members that resist change. The following resistance to change scale was "designed to tap an individual's tendency to resist or avoid making changes, to devalue change generally, and to find change averse across diverse contexts and types of change" (Oreg, 2003, p. 680). Complete the scale yourself, then answer the discussion questions at the end.

INSTRUCTIONS

Listed below are several statements regarding one's general beliefs and attitudes about change. Please indicate the degree to which you agree or disagree with each statement by selecting the appropriate number on the scale next to it. Describe yourself as you generally are now, not as you wish to be in the future. Describe yourself as you honestly see yourself, in relation to other people you know of the same sex as you are, and roughly your same age.

Statement	Strongly Disagree	Disagree	Inclined to Disagree	Inclined to Agree	Agree	Strongly Agree
1. I generally consider changes to be a negative thing.	1	2	3	4	5	6
2. I'll take a routine day over a day full of unexpected events any time.	1	2	3	4	5	6
3. I like to do the same old things rather than try new and different ones.	1	2	3	4	5	6

Statement	Strongly Disagree	Disagree	Inclined to Disagree	Inclined to Agree	Agree	Strongly Agree
4. Whenever my life forms a stable routine, I look for ways to change it.	1	2	3	4	5	6
5. I'd rather be bored than surprised.	1	2	3	4	5	6
6. If I were to be informed that there's going to be a significant change regarding the way things are done at work, I would probably feel stressed.	1	2	3	4	5	6
7. When I am informed of a change of plans, I tense up a bit.	1	2	3	4	5	6
8. When things don't go according to plans, it stresses me out.	1	2	3	4	5	6
9. If my boss changed the performance evaluation criteria, it would probably make me feel uncomfortable even if I thought I'd do just as well without having to do extra work.	1	2	3	4	5	6
10. Changing plans seems like a real hassle to me.	1	2	3	4	5	6
11. Often, I feel a bit uncomfortable even about changes that may potentially improve my life.	1	2	3	4	5	6

(Continued)

(Continued)

Statement	Strongly Disagree	Disagree	Inclined to Disagree	Inclined to Agree	Agree	Strongly Agree
12. When someone pressures me to change something, I tend to resist it even if I think the change may ultimately benefit me.	1	2	3	4	5	6
13. I sometimes find myself avoiding changes that I know will be good for me.	1	2	3	4	5	6
14. I often change my mind.	1	2	3	4	5	6
15. I don't change my mind easily.	1	2	3	4	5	6
16. Once I've come to a conclusion, I'm not likely to change my mind.	1	2	3	4	5	6
17. My views are very consistent over time.	1	2	3	4	5	6

Note. From "Resistance to Change: Developing an Individual Differences Measure," by S. Oreg, 2003, *Journal of Applied Psychology, 88*(4), pp. 680–693. Copyright 2003 by Shaul Oreg. Reprinted with permission.

SCORING INSTRUCTIONS

Items 4 and 14 need to be reverse coded (i.e., strongly disagree will score a 6 on these items, and strongly agree will score a 1). The resistance to change score is the mean of the 17 items (after reversing the scores of items 4 and 14). The scale also comprises the following four subscales.

Routine Seeking: Items 1–5. This factor describes the degree to which the participant incorporates routines into life.

Emotional Reaction: Items 6–9. These items describe "emotional reactions to imposed change" (Oreg, 2003, p. 681).

Short-Term Focus: Items 10–13. This factor describes "the immediate inconvenience or adverse effects of the change," which illustrates "resistance that arises in spite of one's awareness of the potential long-term benefits involved in the change" (Oreg, 2003, p. 682).

Cognitive Rigidity: Items 14–17. This subscale "contains items that address the ease and frequency with which individuals change their minds" (Oreg, 2003, p. 682).

Discussion Questions

1. What is your resistance to change score?

2. To what degree do you prefer routine over change? Can you think of a time when your routine was interrupted? How did you react?

3. How would you describe your emotional reaction to change?

4. Have you had a negative response to the short-term impact of a change, even though you could see the long-term benefit? What did you do?

5. How easy is it for you to change your mind? Why?

6. As an OD practitioner, do you think that your resistance to change score is higher, lower, or about the same as your clients' would be? How about the organizational members impacted by changes that you help to implement? What does that mean for how you would work with clients?

7. How might you use this information in an OD engagement?

REFERENCE

Oreg, S. (2003). Resistance to change: Developing an individual differences measure. *Journal of Applied Psychology, 88*(4), 680–693.

Exercise 7

CYNICISM ABOUT ORGANIZATIONAL CHANGE

The cynicism about organizational change (CAOC) scale measures the degree to which organizational members hold "a pessimistic viewpoint about change efforts being successful because those responsible for making change are blamed for being unmotivated, incompetent, or both" (Wanous, Reichers, & Austin, 2000, p. 133). When such cynicism is widespread, change is less likely to occur, since organizational members who are highly cynical are less likely to be committed to the organizational change project.

How cynical are you about organizational change? Consider a current or past organizational experience and indicate your level of agreement with the following questions.

	1 Strongly Disagree	2 Disagree	3 Neither Agree nor Disagree	4 Agree	5 Strongly Agree
1. Most of the programs that are supposed to solve problems around here will not do much good.					
2. Attempts to make things better around here will not produce good results.					
3. Suggestions on how to solve problems will not produce much real change.					

	1 **Strongly Disagree**	2 **Disagree**	3 **Neither Agree nor Disagree**	4 **Agree**	5 **Strongly Agree**
4. Plans for future improvement will not amount to much.					
5. The people responsible for solving problems around here do not try hard enough to solve them.					
6. The people responsible for making things better around here do not care enough about their jobs.					
7. The people responsible for making improvements do not know enough about what they are doing.					
8. The people responsible for making changes around here do not have the skills needed to do their jobs.					

Note. From "Understanding and Managing Cynicism About Organizational Change," by A. E. Reichers, J. P. Wanous, and J. T. Austin, 1997, *Academy of Management Executive, 11*(1), pp. 48–59. Copyright 1997 by Sage. Reprinted with permission.

SCORING INSTRUCTIONS

The cynicism about organizational change score is the mean of the eight items.

Items 1–4 represent pessimism, or a negative outlook on the ability to achieve successful change.

Items 5–8 represent dispositional attribution, or how individuals assess and attribute causes to the behavior of others.

Discussion Questions

1. To what extent are you cynical about organizational change? Does that affect how willing you are to engage in attempts at change in your own organization? Why or why not?

2. In their article reviewing the concept of cynicism about change, Reichers, Wanous, and Austin (1997) write, "People do not deliberately decide to become cynical, pessimistic, and blaming. Rather, these attitudes result from experience, and are sustained because they serve useful purposes. Cynicism persists because it is selectively validated by the organizations' mixed record of successful change, and by other people in the organization who hold and express similar views" (pp. 50–51). Have you experienced cynicism about organizational change? What "useful purposes" do you think cynicism serves an organization?

3. Can cynicism be overcome? How? If you were to conduct an OD engagement in an organization where cynicism is high, what would you do differently during the change project? Would your approach differ if pessimism scores were high or if dispositional attribution scores were high?

4. How would a high level of cynicism in the organization affect you as the OD practitioner?

REFERENCES

Reichers, A. E., Wanous, J. P., & Austin, J. T. (1997). Understanding and managing cynicism about organizational change. *Academy of Management Executive, 11*(1), 48–59.

Wanous, J. P., Reichers, A. E., & Austin, J. T. (2000). Cynicism about organizational change. *Group & Organization Management, 25*(2), 132–153.

Exercise 8

MYERS-BRIGGS TYPE INDICATOR (MBTI)

KENT D. FAIRFIELD

One of the most widely use psychological instruments is the Myers-Briggs Type Indicator (MBTI). Originated by Katherine Briggs and her daughter Isabel Briggs-Myers, the MBTI is built on the work of the early Swiss psychologist Carl Jung regarding how people perceive the world and process information. The MBTI describes four dimensions about how people tend to have a preferred way of behaving. Each dimension describes a continuum, so the extent of one's tendencies may be quite pronounced or more moderate.

Extroversion/Introversion. *Extroversion* and *introversion* describe how people get energy. Those who prefer extroversion (abbreviated E) process data by talking out loud and thinking while they are speaking. They derive energy from being with other people. Those preferring introversion (I), on the other hand, consider more what they think before they speak it. As a result, when they speak they are typically more crisp and articulate in what they say, having inwardly already processed their thoughts. Those inclined to introversion tend to be more contemplative and derive energy from being alone. Spending much time with others can sap their energy, which can be restored by solitude.

Sensing/Intuition. Those oriented to sensing (S) take in data from the world through their five senses, with acute attention to the detail of what they see, hear, feel, smell, and touch. They tend to focus on the present and the factual. Those preferring intuition (N), on the other hand, take in the world with less detail. They are more able to perceive patterns rather than individual items—seeing the forest more than the trees—and are oriented to possibilities and the future.

Thinking/Feeling. This dimension describes how people make decisions. Those oriented to thinking (T) depend on facts and logic to reach decisions. They are guided by their head through objective analysis. Those who prefer feeling (F) relate more to emotions and the possible impact of decisions on self and others. Values and a more subjective approach characterize feelers' decision making.

Judging/Perceiving. People oriented to judging (J) prefer structure and order. They seek closure and a systematic approach. Those inclined to perceiving, on the other hand, are more flexible and willing to work things out as time goes on. Perceivers may put off making a decision in order to leave their options open. As events unfold, perceivers can be more adaptable and unperturbed by the unexpected.

The results of a person's MBTI scores are summarized with one letter from each dimension, such as ENTJ or ISFP. Each designation can occur in combination with any other, so there are 16 possible personality types. Descriptions of each can give an indication of how one may tend to behave, though these are only preferences. People often act in ways not predicted by their type, but it can still be a useful predictor of behavior. There are no right or wrong types, as each one has its strengths in different situations. It can be useful to appreciate the virtues of dimensions the opposite of one's own, and over time one may become more adept at exhibiting behavior from both ends of the continuum. The tendencies do seem relatively unchanged over time, however.

One of the most important aspects of using the MBTI is to appreciate that other people may be different from oneself, but they can contribute thoughts, feelings, and actions that complement one's own. In other words, it is wise to value the differences.

EXERCISES

Extroversion vs. Introversion

After taking the MBTI (or an equivalent instrument), discover who in the room was rated for preferring extroversion and who for introversion. Form small groups with others of your type. Write down the group's ideas in response to these questions:

1. What do we, as extroverts/introverts, like about being extroverts/introverts?

2. What do we like about the others (introverts/extroverts)?

3. What do we *not* like about the others (introverts/extroverts)?

When you're finished, each group should report on its ideas. Listen carefully to what the group of the opposite type to your own says about what they like and don't like about people of your type.

---

1. To what extent do you agree? Can you see how they arrived at these observations?

2. What does this imply about the challenges of working together with people of both types?

3. If you tend toward extroversion, what might you do to benefit most from the introverts on your team? If an introvert, what does this imply about how you can be most useful to a group?

Judging vs. Perceiving

Group yourselves by type according to whether you were rated as judging or perceiving. In your group, respond to these instructions: "I am happy to report that you've just been given an unlimited budget to plan a vacation for your group. In the next 5 minutes write on the sheets what would be the group's idea of a perfect vacation."

When finished, share with the whole room the profile of your perfect vacation. In hearing from groups with the opposite orientation, listen for the kind of detail that they report.

Is their plan much more explicit than yours? Much less so?

- In what ways might the judgers' plan be much more structured? How is the plan of the perceivers more an example of keeping their options open?

- What if you were on a project team with mostly judgers and few if any perceivers? How might you disagree? How might your operations be frustrating to a perceiver? What might be the deficiency in the quality of work the team produces?

- What if you were on a team with mostly perceivers? What could be the drawback of that team makeup? What would cause discomfort for the few judgers?

- What is the potential benefit of having a team made up of both people with a judging preference and those with a perceiving preference?

FOR FURTHER READING

Keirsey, D., & Bates, M. (1978). *Please understand me: Character and temperament types.* Del Mar, CA: Prometheus Nemesis Books.

Kroeger, O., & Thuesen J. M. (1988). *Type talk: The 16 personality types that determine how we live, love, and work.* New York: Delta Books.

Lawrence, G. (1993). *People types and tiger stripes* (3rd ed.). Gainsville, FL: Center for Applications of Psychological Type.

Myers, I. B., & Myers, P. B. (1980). *Gifts differing: Understanding personality type.* Palo Alto, CA: Consulting Psychologists Press.

Exercise 9

COACHING AND INDIVIDUAL INSTRUMENTS

Instruments are especially effective when individuals can be coached and guided through the interpretation of their own data. In this exercise, you will practice the role of a coach and also experience being coached by a partner.

INSTRUCTIONS

1. Pair up with a partner. Each of you will take both of the following instruments (on pages 315 and 318) and score them according to the instructions provided. Completing the instrument is necessary for the exercise, but *how* it is completed is voluntary. If you prefer, you do not need to express your own thoughts but can mark answers according to a pattern or even randomly; your true answers are less important for this exercise. If you choose to mark the scores randomly, you will need to "act" when working with your coach or facilitator.

2. One person will be the coach or facilitator, and the other will be the coachee. Select one of the instruments to use for your coaching conversation. Coaches have the responsibility of helping their partner understand the instrument and what it means. Take time to understand both instruments and practice explaining the purpose of the instrument, what the participant will learn from it, how the participant should take it, and how it should be scored.

3. Before starting your coaching conversation, spend a few moments reflecting on the instrument and the kinds of questions you might ask to help your partner understand his or her scores. Here are some sample questions to get you started:

a) Did the results match or differ from what you would have expected? How so? Why do you think that is?

b) What strengths do you find in your results? What are you satisfied to see?

c) What opportunities for growth or development do you see?

4. After 15 or 20 minutes, change roles and change instruments. The new coach now will help her or his partner understand and interpret the scores on the new instrument.

Discussion Questions

1. What questions did your coach ask? Are there any especially effective questions you can each borrow for the future?

2. Were there questions your coach asked that you found unpleasant or would have preferred not to be asked? Were there questions you think your coach could have asked but did not?

3. What did it feel like to be coached? What did it feel like to be the coach? What did you do as a coach that you found effective, and what did you find to be ineffective?

4. If you were to repeat the exercise, what would you do again? What would you do differently?

5. In your view, what skills make a good coach? What lessons can be learned from this exercise for the coaching role?

COACHING INSTRUMENT #1: SCALE FOR THE MEASUREMENT OF INNOVATIVENESS

Directions: The individual innovativeness scale was designed to measure individuals' orientations toward change. Please indicate the degree to which each statement applies to you by marking the box indicated.

	1 Strongly Disagree	2 Disagree	3 Neutral	4 Agree	5 Strongly Agree
1. My peers often ask me for advice or information.					
2. I enjoy trying out new ideas.					
3. I seek out new ways to do things.					
4. I am generally cautious about accepting new ideas.					
5. I frequently improvise methods for solving a problem when an answer is not apparent.					
6. I am suspicious of new inventions and new ways of thinking.					
7. I rarely trust new ideas until I can see whether the vast majority of people around me accept them.					
8. I feel that I am an influential member of my peer group.					
9. I consider myself to be creative and original in my thinking and behavior.					
10. I am aware that I am usually one of the last people in my group to accept something new.					

(Continued)

(Continued)

	1 Strongly Disagree	2 Disagree	3 Neutral	4 Agree	5 Strongly Agree
11. I am an inventive kind of person.					
12. I enjoy taking part in the leadership responsibilities of the groups I belong to.					
13. I am reluctant about adopting new ways of doing things until I see them working for people around me.					
14. I find it stimulating to be original in my thinking and behavior.					
15. I tend to feel that the old way of living and doing things is the best way.					
16. I am challenged by ambiguities and unsolved problems.					
17. I must see other people using new innovations before I will consider them.					
18. I am receptive to new ideas.					
19. I am challenged by unanswered questions.					
20. I often find myself skeptical of new ideas.					

Note. From "Scales for the Measurement of Innovativeness," by H. T. Hurt, K. Joseph, and C. D. Cook, 1977, *Human Communication Research, 4*(1), pp. 58–65. Items copyright 1977 by Wiley-Blackwell; directions and scoring copyright 1977 by James McCroskey. Reprinted with permission.

SCORING

Step 1: Add the scores for items 4, 6, 7, 10, 13, 15, 17, and 20.

Step 2: Add the scores for items 1, 2, 3, 5, 8, 9, 11, 12, 14, 16, 18, and 19.

Step 3: Complete the following formula: 42 + total score for Step 2 − total score for Step 1.

- Scores above 80 are classified as "innovators."
- Scores between 69 and 80 are classified as "early adopters."
- Scores between 57 and 68 are classified as "early majority."
- Scores between 46 and 56 are classified as "late majority."
- Scores below 46 are classified as "laggards or traditionalists."

In general, people who score above 68 are considered highly innovative, while people who score below 64 are considered low in innovativeness.

The 20-item scale for the measurement of innovativeness was developed by Hurt, Joseph, and Cook (1977), who write that "the innovativeness scale is designed to measure an individual's willingness to change" (p. 63) and that results could be used to "predict the adoption behavior of individuals within a social system" (p. 64).

COACHING INSTRUMENT #2: ORGANIZATIONAL COMMUNICATION CONFLICT INSTRUMENT

Directions: Think of disagreements you have encountered in a particular task situation with your immediate supervisor. Then indicate below how frequently you engage in each of the described behaviors. For each item, select the number that represents the behavior you are most likely to exhibit. There are no right or wrong answers. Please respond to all items on the scale. The alternative responses are:

1	2	3	4	5	6	7
Always	Very Often	Often	Sometimes	Seldom	Very Seldom	Never

Cl	1. I blend my ideas with my supervisor to create new alternatives for resolving a disagreement.	1 2 3 4 5 6 7
N	2. I shy away from topics that are sources of disputes with my supervisor.	1 2 3 4 5 6 7
Co	3. I make my opinion known in a disagreement with my supervisor.	1 2 3 4 5 6 7
Cl	4. I suggest solutions which combine a variety of viewpoints.	1 2 3 4 5 6 7
N	5. I steer clear of disagreeable situations.	1 2 3 4 5 6 7
Cm	6. I give in a little on my ideas when my supervisor also gives in.	1 2 3 4 5 6 7
N	7. I avoid my supervisor when I suspect that he or she wants to discuss a disagreement.	1 2 3 4 5 6 7
Cl	8. I integrate arguments into a new solution from the issues raised in a dispute with my supervisor.	1 2 3 4 5 6 7
Cm	9. I will go 50-50 to reach a settlement with my supervisor.	1 2 3 4 5 6 7
Co	10. I raise my voice when I'm trying to get my supervisor to accept my position.	1 2 3 4 5 6 7
Cl	11. I offer creative solutions in discussions of disagreements.	1 2 3 4 5 6 7
N	12. I keep quiet about my view in order to avoid disagreements.	1 2 3 4 5 6 7
Cm	13. I give in if my supervisor will meet me halfway.	1 2 3 4 5 6 7
N	14. I downplay the importance of a disagreement.	1 2 3 4 5 6 7

N	15. I reduce disagreements by making them seem insignificant.	1 2 3 4 5 6 7
Cm	16. I meet my supervisor at a midpoint in our differences.	1 2 3 4 5 6 7
Co	17. I assert my opinion forcefully.	1 2 3 4 5 6 7
Co	18. I dominate arguments until my supervisor understands my position.	1 2 3 4 5 6 7
Cl	19. I suggest we work together to create solutions to disagreements.	1 2 3 4 5 6 7
Cl	20. I try to use my supervisor's ideas to generate solutions to problems.	1 2 3 4 5 6 7
Cm	21. I offer trade-offs to reach solutions in a disagreement.	1 2 3 4 5 6 7
Co	22. I argue insistently for my stance.	1 2 3 4 5 6 7
N	23. I withdraw when my supervisor confronts me about a controversial issue.	1 2 3 4 5 6 7
N	24. I side step disagreements when they arise.	1 2 3 4 5 6 7
N	25. I try to smooth over disagreements by making them appear unimportant.	1 2 3 4 5 6 7
Co	26. I insist my position be accepted during a disagreement with my supervisor.	1 2 3 4 5 6 7
N	27. I make our differences seem less serious.	1 2 3 4 5 6 7
N	28. I hold my tongue rather than argue with my supervisor.	1 2 3 4 5 6 7
N	29. I ease conflict by claiming our differences are trivial.	1 2 3 4 5 6 7
Co	30. I stand firm in expressing my viewpoints during a disagreement with my supervisor.	1 2 3 4 5 6 7

Note. From "Assessing the Putnam-Wilson Organizational Communication Conflict Instrument (OCCI)" by S. R. Wilson and M. S. Waltman, 1988, *Management Communication Quarterly, 1*(3), pp. 367–388. Copyright 1988 by Sage. Reprinted with permission.

SCORING

Calculate the mean score for all categories. Lower scores represent a predilection for that conflict style.

N = Nonconfrontation

Cl + Cm: Solution Orientation (Cl = Collaboration, Cm = Compromise)

Co = Control

The three conflict styles are defined as follows.

Nonconfrontation: Avoidance and smoothing as indirect strategies for dealing with conflict

Solution Orientation: Direct confrontation, open discussion of alternatives, and acceptance of compromises

Control: Direct confrontation that leads to persistent argument and nonverbal forcing (Putnam & Wilson, 1982, p. 638)

REFERENCES

Hurt, H. T., Joseph, K., & Cook, C. D. (1977). Scales for the measurement of innovativeness. *Human Communication Research, 4*(1), 58–65.

Putnam, L. L., & Wilson, C. (1982). Communicative strategies in organizational conflict: Reliability and validity of a measurement scale. In M. Burgoon (Ed.), *Communication yearbook 6* (pp. 629–652). Newbury Park, CA: Sage.

Wilson, S. R., & Waltman, M. S. (1988). Assessing the Putnam-Wilson organizational communication conflict instrument (OCCI). *Management Communication Quarterly, 1*(3), 367–388.

Exercise 10

TEAM VALUES

FRANZISKA MACUR AND KENNETH M. MACUR

INSTRUCTIONS

1. Read the list of values below. In group settings, discourage communication, because each participant's selections should be made independently of the group. The list is not intended to include all values, but enough suggestions to guide the discussion and ultimate decision making. If you wish, you may add additional words or phrases.

2. Take 5 minutes and identify 10 of the items that are most important to you. Do not prioritize or order the items at this point, but simply put a checkmark next to your top 10.

3. Once the 10 are selected, narrow your selection down to five.

4. Then narrow your selection of five to three.

5. Order the remaining three, with the most important being ranked 1.

6. Create one bar chart for each participant's top selection (ordering the chart from most popular to least). Create a second bar chart for each participant's second selection.

7. Discuss the results.

   a. Where is there agreement and where is there disagreement on team values? Do any terms need to be defined? Some discussion may be necessary to operationally define selected items.
   b. If your team has an existing values statement, do the results support this?
   c. Are there conflicting top choices, such as working alone vs. working with others?
   d. Complete the exercise to create the top three to five for the team. Because the list is intentionally incomplete, very often different words will be selected in the final version. For example *relationships* and *working with others* might give rise to the value of *partnership*.

☐ Achievement

☐ Advancement and Promotion

☐ Adventure

☐ Affection (love and caring)

☐ Arts

☐ Challenging Problems

☐ Change and Variety

☐ Close Relationships

☐ Community

☐ Competence

☐ Competition

☐ Cooperation

☐ Country

☐ Creativity

☐ Decisiveness

☐ Democracy

☐ Ecological Awareness

☐ Economic Security

☐ Effectiveness

☐ Efficiency

☐ Ethical Practice

☐ Excellence

☐ Excitement

☐ Expertise

☐ Fame

☐ Fast Living

☐ Fast-Paced Work

☐ Financial Gain

☐ Freedom

☐ Friendships

☐ Growth

☐ Having a Family

☐ Helping Other People

☐ Helping Society

☐ Honesty

☐ Independence

☐ Influencing Others

☐ Inner Harmony

☐ Integrity

☐ Intellectual Status

☐ Involvement

☐ Job Tranquility

☐ Knowledge

☐ Leadership

☐ Location

☐ Loyalty

☐ Market Position

☐ Meaningful Work

☐ Merit

☐ Money

☐ Nature

☐ (Being around people who are) Open and Honest

☐ Order (tranquility, stability, conformity)

- ☐ Personal Development (living up to the fullest use of my potential)
- ☐ Physical Challenge
- ☐ Pleasure
- ☐ Power and Authority
- ☐ Privacy
- ☐ Public Service
- ☐ Purity
- ☐ Quality of What I Take Part In
- ☐ Quality of Relationships
- ☐ Recognition (respect from others, status)
- ☐ Religion
- ☐ Reputation
- ☐ Responsibility and Accountability

- ☐ Security
- ☐ Self-Respect
- ☐ Serenity
- ☐ Sophistication
- ☐ Stability
- ☐ Status
- ☐ Supervising Others
- ☐ Time Freedom
- ☐ Truth
- ☐ Wealth
- ☐ Wisdom
- ☐ Work Under Pressure
- ☐ Work With Others
- ☐ Working Alone

Exercise 11

TEAM DIAGNOSIS AND INTERVENTION

Below you will find a summary of a team's average response on a short team diagnostic survey. Working with a peer, answer the following questions.

1. What do you believe to be happening on this team? What do team members say are the team's strengths? What do team members say are the team's areas of improvement? How would you prioritize the opportunities for improvement?

2. How would you present this data in a team feedback session?

3. What team development intervention(s) would you recommend? Design an intervention plan, including an agenda, timeline, and any activities you would suggest.

TEAM SURVEY (QUANTITATIVE AND QUALITATIVE RESPONSES)

The numbers in each column reflect the number of people on the team who checked each box.

	1 Strongly Disagree	2 Disagree	3 Neither Agree nor Disagree	4 Agree	5 Strongly Agree	Average
1. The mission of this team is clear.	0	2	2	4	4	3.8
2. I have a clear understanding of my role on this team.	0	1	2	5	4	4.0

	1 Strongly Disagree	2 Disagree	3 Neither Agree nor Disagree	4 Agree	5 Strongly Agree	Average
3. I know how my team contributes to the organization's goals.	0	0	0	8	4	4.3
4. Considering everything, I am satisfied with my job.	1	2	3	4	2	3.3
5. I am proud to be a member of this team.	2	2	1	4	1	3.0
6. Our team meetings are effective.	1	0	5	4	2	3.5
7. Our team decision-making practices are effective.	0	1	3	4	4	3.9
8. The goals for our team are clear.	0	0	3	5	4	4.1
9. Team members handle conflicts openly.	2	3	5	1	1	2.7
10. Team members share important information with each other when necessary.	0	3	3	4	2	3.4
11. Team members encourage each other to do their best.	3	3	4	2	0	2.4

The following are written responses to the open-ended question, "Anything else you would like to add?"

- *"I would say that we are a high-performing team. We consistently achieve our team goals and are always at the top."*

- *"This is a fine team to be on if you are a member of John's inner circle. Otherwise you will be ignored."*

- *"We don't support each other as a team. I don't think anyone here has my back if I'm struggling. To be honest, I don't trust a single one of them."*

- *"We wait until John makes decisions and announces them rather than taking the initiative. I would like to see us make more decisions by consensus."*

- *"John has been a great leader of this team. I think we have great potential, but some negative members of the team bring us down in meetings with pessimistic attitudes."*

- *"I wish I knew more about what other members of the team were doing. We have some updates in staff meetings, but they are too brief to get much detail."*

- *"This team is cliquish. There is a core group of them that excludes the rest of us."*

Exercise 12

TEAM FACILITATION

Advanced Device Company has shown a decrease in customer satisfaction for the last 2 years. Specifically, the quarterly customer survey reveals that customers are not pleased with the shipping timelines of their orders or the quality of their orders. Orders are being sent after the committed shipping date, and more than 35% of orders contain some error (e.g., incorrect products being sent, shipments missing one or more items). The order entry and shipping process is presented below

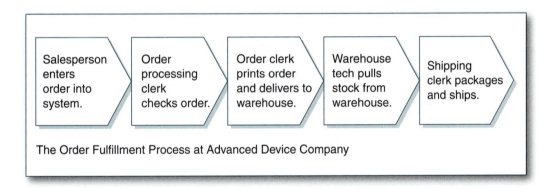

The Order Fulfillment Process at Advanced Device Company

For this exercise, you will need to form a project team of four members to conduct a "workout," or a problem-solving session in which you will have the responsibility to redesign the process to improve customer satisfaction. Your organization also has hired a facilitator to help you conduct your process redesign. You have 20 minutes to hold this discussion. Each of you should determine which role you will enact and who will be the facilitator. (If your team has more or fewer members than roles, you can have some roles filled more than once, or not at all). Read the role descriptions that follow, and begin your conversation. Remember that senior management will arrive in the conference room in 20 minutes to hear your recommended solution.

Facilitator. Your role is to help this team (a) understand the root cause of the customer satisfaction problem, (b) discuss possible alternative solutions, and (c) select an alternative. The team will need to make its decision and describe the advantages of this approach over the alternatives discussed to senior management when they enter the room. You should not take on the role of presenter.

Salesperson. You have been in sales for your entire career and have worked at Advanced Device Company for the past 6 years. This has been the most disorganized company you have ever seen. In the past you had sales support assistance to help with things like order entry, but not here. The order entry system is a mess, and it usually crashes on you when you are trying to enter orders, causing you to have to input multiple orders on the same account. The last order you entered took the entire morning, making you late for a client lunch. You should advocate solutions that put more of the responsibility on an order processing person, who has the time to devote to the system, so you can return to doing the sales job you were hired to do.

Order Processing Clerk. You have worked at Advanced Devices for 16 years, always in order processing. This is your area of expertise. No one knows how to work the entry system as well as you do, though you quietly fear that increased automation soon will mean the elimination of your job. The only real solution is to go back to the old way before the computer system was put into place. Even so, the system works fine if you take the time to learn how to use it, and there is plenty of training. Salespeople in particular need to learn how to use the system correctly and stop creating multiple orders for the same account. You enjoy your daily walk to the warehouse to deliver orders as it gives you a break from sitting in front of a computer screen all day. You don't know what is causing the customer satisfaction problems, but you do know that each order leaves your desk in perfect condition. Lately it seems that a lot of people around here are blaming order processing for all of the problems, but you know that it's not your department's fault.

Warehouse Tech. You've worked at Advanced Devices for the past 18 months, and it's a pretty good job. You're still getting up to speed on where everything is in the warehouse, and you don't get a lot of assistance. Your job entails grabbing a stack of 30 to 40 hard-copy, paper orders (this is not an environmentally friendly company) from the basket by the warehouse door and trying to fill them all (walking throughout the warehouse to find the ordered item, bringing it up front to shipping, and so on). The sales and order people are nice, but you wonder why this can't be more automated. Why couldn't customers simply place orders online and the system could sort the items by where they are in the warehouse? It would be great if the order form itself had the warehouse location, like "Row E15" next to the product code. That would save you so much time.

Shipping Clerk. In the 2 years you've worked here, one thing is consistent. Your daily wish is that you had another job, and you have little feeling other than contempt for your colleagues. Every day your warehouse tech colleague runs around crazy trying to fill boxes with orders. Your job is to enter the shipping information manually into the shipment system and put on the label. You can see that half of the boxes don't contain what they're supposed to, and you can easily see that you end up sending multiple shipments to the same place, but at least it fills the day, and the pay is the same whether or not you correct the mistakes. Most of the time your colleagues just argue and blame each other for every error, while you just sit back and watch.

Discussion Questions

1. What were the results of your discussion? Did the team come to an agreement on the causes of the customer satisfaction problem? What agreement did the team reach?

2. What techniques did the facilitator use to try to encourage the team to reach an agreement? What was effective and what was less effective? From the perspective of the participants, did these techniques help you to shed some of the "baggage" of your role and to participate in coming up with a solution?

3. What techniques would you use as a facilitator of a group like this to structure discussion, encourage participation, and reach agreement?

Exercise 13

IDENTIFYING AND CHANGING ORGANIZATIONAL CULTURE

"Organizational culture has a powerful effect on the performance and long-term effectiveness of organizations," write Cameron and Quinn (2006, p. 5). The authors report on studies showing that organizations that had implemented quality initiatives were most successful when they also addressed a major culture change at the same time. Increasingly, major organizational initiatives require attention to culture change if the organization is to support the new values, attitudes, and behaviors, and to avoid returning to the status quo. For the change agent, the task is to identify which elements of culture are congruent or incongruent with the new initiative and develop mechanisms to address them.

When we speak of organizational culture, we are considering elements such as the following.

- Architecture and Office Layout
- Styles of Dress
- Structure and Patterns of Meetings
- Language and Jargon
- Decision-Making Styles
- Explicitly Articulated Values and Beliefs
- Underlying Philosophies and Preferences
- Hidden Assumptions and Values

Note that the elements of culture at the top of the list are relatively easy to notice as an outsider, and they tend to be more easily changed. As the list continues, however, cultural practices and preferences become more implicit than explicit, are more difficult to see and readily identify, and are thus more challenging to change.

Cameron and Quinn (2006) describe four culture types.

Clan: People strongly identify with the group, as in a family, placing a strong emphasis on the team and teamwork. Organizational members are loyal and friendly. A commonly held set of values is important to members.

Adhocracy: Innovation is prized, with organizational members having a large amount of independence and autonomy. The organization emphasizes developing cutting-edge products and services and leading the market. Flexibility, adaptability, and risk taking are key values.

Hierarchy: Tradition and formality are dominant values. The emphasis is on stability, rules, and efficient processes. Decision-making authority is clear and predictability is prized.

Market: Organizational members are competitive, hard working, and demanding. Productivity and beating the competition are emphasized. The emphasis is on financial results, profits, margins, and the delivery of value to customers.

EXERCISE 1

Using YouTube or another online video site, find a brief video from a real organization that displays its cultural beliefs (try to avoid television shows, advertisements, or movie clips). You might locate an employee orientation video, training video, or advertisement for job seekers.

Discussion Questions

1. What organizational culture type or types do you believe the video depicts? What evidence do you have for this view?

2. Do you think this culture type is appropriate for this organization? What do you believe are its advantages and disadvantages?

3. Imagine that you were trying to change this culture to another one of the culture types listed above. What actions do you think the organization could take to undertake such a transformation? How do you think the video you found would be different if it were to display this new culture type?

EXERCISE 2

Part 1: Form a group of three or four colleagues. Imagine that you meet in the company break room and begin discussing one of the company's new products. Choose one of the culture types above and role play a discussion that illustrates that culture type. As you hold your discussion, consider the following.

- How do you imagine the break room layout to look? What would be displayed on the walls?
- How would members be dressed?
- What kind of language do you imagine members would use?

- How would they make decisions?
- How would they handle conflict?
- What nonwork topics might come up, if any?

Part 2: After a brief conversation, include a new member in the discussion who will display a different culture type of his or her choosing (e.g., if you had chosen hierarchy, the new member can display clan). Continue the discussion.

Discussion Questions

1. What were the results of the first discussion? How did it feel to be a member of this culture? What do you think were the advantages or disadvantages of this culture type, given this discussion?

2. What happened when the new member joined? How did the existing culture look and feel when confronted by the "new" culture? Did the new culture appear to have any advantages to the existing culture? How did the new member feel when confronted by the expectations and assumptions of the existing culture?

3. What implications does this exercise have for changing organizational culture?

REFERENCE

Cameron, K. S., & Quinn, R. E. (2006). *Diagnosing and changing organizational culture: Based on the competing values framework* (Rev. ed.). Reading MA: Addison-Wesley.

Exercise 14

PERCEIVED ORGANIZATIONAL INNOVATIVENESS SCALE

Directions: People and organizations vary a great deal in their innovativeness. Innovativeness has to do with how early in the process of adoption of new ideas, practices, and the like that the individual or organization is likely to accept a change. The statements below refer to some of the ways members of organizations perceive their organizations to be. Please indicate in the box below the degree to which you agree that the statement describes your organization.

My organization:	1 Strongly Disagree	2 Disagree	3 Neutral	4 Agree	5 Strongly Agree
is cautious about accepting new ideas.					
is a leader among other organizations.					
is suspicious of new ways of thinking.					
is very inventive.					
often is consulted by other organizations for advice and information.					

(Continued)

(Continued)

My organization:	1 Strongly Disagree	2 Disagree	3 Neutral	4 Agree	5 Strongly Agree
is skeptical of new ideas.					
is creative in its method of operation.					
usually is one of the last of its kind to change to a new method of operation.					
is considered one of the leaders of its type.					
is receptive to new ideas.					
is challenged by unsolved problems.					
follows the belief that "the old way of doing things is the best."					
is very original in its operational procedures.					
does not respond quickly enough to necessary changes.					
is reluctant to adopt new ways of doing things until other organizations have used them successfully.					
frequently initiates new methods of operation					
is slow to change.					
rarely involves employees in the decision-making process.					
maintains good communication between supervisors and employees.					
is influential with other organizations.					

My organization:	1 Strongly Disagree	2 Disagree	3 Neutral	4 Agree	5 Strongly Agree
seeks out new ways to do things.					
rarely trusts new ideas and ways of functioning.					
never satisfactorily explains to employees the reasons for procedural changes.					
frequently tries out new ideas.					
is willing and ready to accept outside help when necessary.					

Note. From "The Development of a Measure of Perceived Organizational Innovativeness," by H. T. Hurt and C. W. Teigen, in *Communication Yearbook, 1* (pp. 377–385) edited by B. R. Ruben, 1977, New Brunswick, NJ: Transaction Books. Items copyright 1977 by the International Communication Association; directions and scoring copyright 1977 by James McCroskey. Reprinted with permission.

SCORING

Step 1: Add the scores for the following items: 1, 3, 6, 8, 12, 14, 15, 17, 18, 22, 23.

Step 2: Add the scores for the following items: 2, 4, 5, 7, 9, 10, 11, 13, 16, 19, 20, 21, 24, 25.

Step 3: Complete the following formula: 66 + total from Step 2 − total from Step 1.

Scores will range between 25 and 125.

Scores above 110 indicate the organization can be classified as "innovative."

Scores between 91 and 109 indicate the organization is an "early adopter."

Scores between 71 and 90 indicate the organization is in the "early majority."

Scores between 50 and 70 indicate the organization is in the "late majority."

Scores below 50 indicate the organization can be classified as a "laggard or traditionalist."

Generally, organizations that score above 90 are high in innovativeness. Those scoring below 50 are low in innovativeness. Those scoring between 50 and 90 are moderate in innovativeness.

Discussion Questions

1. How satisfied are you with your organization's innovativeness? What relationship does organizational innovativeness and individual innovativeness have for you?

2. The authors of the study note a positive relationship between perceived organizational innovativeness and (a) employee participation in the innovation decision-making process and (b) employee satisfaction with supervisors, opportunity for promotion, coworkers, and pay. To what extent are these additional relationships true for you?

3. As an OD practitioner, how might you use this scale in a data-gathering project for a whole organization intervention?

DESIGNING AND REDESIGNING ORGANIZATIONS

Jay Galbraith, a leading author in the field, defines organization design as "a decision process to bring about a coherence between the goals or purposes for which the organization exists, the patterns of division of labor and interunit coordination and the people who will do the work" (1977, p. 5). Many people confuse organization design with organizational structure, or the boxes and pictures drawn in organizational charts. Design, however, reflects broader concerns. Galbraith defines design as having five components, which he refers to as the STAR model (see Galbraith, 2002; Galbraith, Downey, & Kates, 2002).

- **Strategy:** The organization's direction and long-term vision
- **Structure:** Roles, responsibilities, and relationships among functions
- **Processes and Lateral Capability:** Decision-making processes, integrative roles, and cross-functional collaboration mechanisms
- **Reward Systems:** Compensation and recognition, goals and measurement systems
- **People Practices:** Hiring, performance reviews, and training and development

INSTRUCTIONS

In this exercise, you will gain practice designing and redesigning an organization. Your task will be to design an organization using the five categories above that fit the profile your management team is given.

PART I: ORGANIZATION DESIGN

For this exercise you will need a single six-sided die (such as that used in a board game; alternately, you can draw slips of paper numbered 1 through 6 from a hat).

1. First, form a management team of three to five other members.

2. Next, roll the die or randomly select a number for each of the following categories. These will represent your organization's profile.

   1. Cash
   2. People
   3. Product Development Capability (research, engineering)
   4. Operations Capability (supplier relationships, manufacturing, shipping, logistics)
   5. Marketing Capability
   6. Global Reach

For example, if you roll a 6 for cash, it means that you have earned the top amount for cash. If you roll a 1 for operations capability, it means you have a low capability for the operations function for your organization.

3. Using your organization's profile numbers, your management team now will create a fictional organization and design a strategy appropriate to this organizational profile. What does your organization do? What does it produce, if anything, and what market(s) does the organization participate in? Where is the organization located? What will be your organization's strategy?

4. Next, create an organizational structure to fit this strategy. Consider the three remaining elements of the STAR model as well: processes and lateral capability, reward systems, and people practices. How will these elements help ensure that all elements of the design are consistent?

Discussion Questions

1. Galbraith notes that no design is perfect, but that all designs have flaws that need to be discussed and addressed. What are the strengths of your organization design? What are your design's weak points? How have you compensated for the flaws in your design using other mechanisms addressed in the STAR model?

2. What might cause you to reevaluate your design? As a management team, how would you know that your design needed to be changed?

PART II: ORGANIZATION REDESIGN

1. Roll the die again or draw another number. Match your selected number to the corresponding capability in the organization profile list above (1 = cash, 2 = people, and so on). Now *double* your previous score for that profile characteristic (for example, if you roll a 1 and previously had a 3 profile for cash, you now have a 6 profile).

2. Roll the die again or select another number (select again if you draw the same number you just drew). Matching your selected number to the list above, now cut your organizational profile score for that characteristic in *half* (for example, if you select a 6 and previously had a 4 for global reach, you now have a 2 profile).

3. Using your new profile and the organization design you created in Part I of this exercise, discuss whether the organization needs to be redesigned based on the changes that have now occurred. Make any design changes you feel are necessary to any elements of the STAR model.

4. As a management team, decide how you will implement your redesign. Create a rollout and change management plan to help the organization make the changes needed to adopt the redesign.

Discussion Questions

1. What changes, if any, did you decide to make to your organization's design? Why? What are the new strengths and flaws in your organization's design? Which elements of the STAR needed to be changed to address the changes that occurred to your organization?

2. What will be the challenges you face in transitioning the organization to the new design?

REFERENCES

Galbraith, J. R. (1977). *Organization design.* Reading, MA: Addison-Wesley.

Galbraith, J. R. (2002). *Designing organizations: An executive guide to strategy, structure, and process.* San Francisco: Jossey-Bass.

Galbraith, J., Downey, D., & Kates, A. (2002). *Designing dynamic organizations: A hands-on guide for leaders at all levels.* New York: AMACOM.

About the Editor

Donald L. Anderson, PhD, University of Colorado, is the author of *Organization Development: The Process of Leading Organizational Change,* now in its second edition (Sage Publications, 2012). He teaches at the University of Denver and is a practicing organization development consultant who has consulted internally and externally with Fortune 500 corporations, small businesses, and educational institutions. His studies of organizational discourse and change have been published in journals such as the *Journal of Organizational Change Management, Gestion,* and the *Journal of Business and Technical Communication.* He is a member of the Academy of Management.

About the Contributors

Gulem Atabay is an assistant professor of organizational behavior. She received her doctorate in the field of business administration with management major in 1998. She focuses on employee attitudes and emotions and their effects on employee behaviors and performance. She conducts her research mainly in health care settings, especially with nurses. She has published many book chapters and articles in reputable international and national journals. Since 2004, she has been teaching introduction to business, management, organizational behavior, organization development, and current issues in management courses at Izmir University of Economics.

Lize A. E. Booysen is full professor of leadership and organizational behavior at Antioch University on the PhD program in Leadership and Change. She is an internationally recognized scholar in the field of diversity, race, gender, and leadership and a management consultant. She holds a doctorate in business leadership from the University of South Africa, as well as masters' degrees in clinical psychology, research psychology, and criminology, all with distinction. She has been involved in the 12 nation Leadership Across Differences (LAD) research project steered by the CCL, 2001–2008. She participated in the GLOBE 65-nations research project on leadership, national culture, and organizational practices during 1994 to 2003, steered by Wharton Business School. Prior to joining Antioch in 2009, she was full professor at the Graduate School of Business Leadership, University of South Africa since 1992. She was also the editor of the *South African Journal of Labour Relations*.

Matthew J. Borneman is an assistant professor at Southern Illinois University Carbondale and the Director of Applied Research Consultants. His research interests span several areas of personnel selection, including the use of standardized tests (and their alternatives) in educational and organizational selection, faking and response distortion on noncognitive measures, and applied research methodology. His graduate work was completed at the University of Minnesota in the Industrial/Organizational Psychology program.

Burcu Guneri Cangarli is an assistant professor of organizational behavior. She received her doctorate in 2009 in the field of business administration with a management major. For her doctoral thesis, "Bullying Behaviors as Organizational Politics," she worked at Hanken University for 3 months as a TUBITAK scholar. Her research areas of interest include health care management, innovation, and bullying. On these issues, she has published many book chapters and articles in reputable international and national journals.

She has been teaching management, leadership, organizational behavior, and organization theory courses at Izmir University of Economics since 2007. She also works as an administrative assistant to rector.

Christopher J. L. Cunningham, PhD, is a UC Foundation Assistant Professor of Psychology at the University of Tennessee (UT) at Chattanooga. He teaches undergraduate and graduate research methods, statistics, organizational and occupational health psychology (OHP), and organization development. His current research involves individual differences in equity sensitivity and recovery from work-related stress. He is also the primary consultant for measurement services at The Solution Group, a human resources technology firm, and an adjunct assistant professor of internal medicine at the UT College of Medicine Chattanooga, where he works to improve the health of work efficiency of health care providers.

Laurie K. Cure is the president of Innovative Connections, Inc., a consulting company working with organizations to expand human capacity to achieve stronger organizational results. She holds a doctorate in industrial and organizational psychology and a master's in business administration. With a commitment to organizational success through the releasing of human potential, she assists organizations with strategic planning, organizational assessment, team development, change management, restructuring, leadership development and coaching, talent management, and culture development. She teaches at the university level and also delivers seminars and lectures on topics of organizational psychology. She has been recognized as an expert on the topic of fear in the workplace and seeks to support organizations in building cultures of trust and support. As an executive coach, she is committed to personal development and supports others on their journey toward growth.

Scott Dickmeyer, PhD, is an Associate Professor of Communication Studies at the University of Wisconsin—La Crosse. His research interests are in organizational culture and communication practices in companies that make the list of the 100 best companies to work for in America. He has served as the chair of the National Communication Association's Training and Development Division and the Central States Communication Association's Organizational and Professional Communication Division. In addition to his university responsibilities, he is actively engaged in consulting and training and development.

Margaret DiCocco is ABD from Southern Illinois University Carbondale's (SIUC) Applied Psychology Program. She is currently an assistant professor for the Physician Assistant Program, also at SIUC, where she teaches research methods, statistics, and the process of evidence-based medicine.

Kent D. Fairfield is Assistant Professor of Management at the Silberman College of Business at Fairleigh Dickinson University. Formerly a vice president at the Chase Manhattan Bank, he founded Kent Fairfield Associates, consulting on teams, leadership development, and change management. His current research concerns the factors underlying sustainability management and interdependence between employees and managers. He has written about adult development and emphasizes learning from experience in his teaching, including requiring students to conduct community service projects and carry on mentor relationships with executives. His publications have appeared in the *Journal of Applied Social Psychology, Human Resource Planning, Nonprofit Management and Leadership, Journal of Healthcare Management,* and *Journal of Management Education.* He has made presentations at scores of academic and professional conferences in the United States and abroad. He earned a master's and doctorate in organizational psychology from Columbia University and an MBA in finance from the Harvard Business School.

Paola Falcone received a doctorate in marketing from the University of Rome "La Sapienza," where she is currently Lecturer of Marketing (Marketing Lab for Public Sector institutions and private organizations at the Faculty of Communication Sciences) and Lecturer of Research and Health Communication (at the Faculty of Medicine). Her research interests include brand identity, internet marketing and communication through the new media, service marketing, and marketing for not-for-profit organizations.

Mary K. Foster received her doctorate in management from the Earl G. Graves School of Business and Management at Morgan State University. Prior to that she was a business executive holding senior positions at firms such as General Electric Co., Mars, Inc., and Sylvan Learning, Inc. Her research interests include team effectiveness, virtual teams, organizational effectiveness, and change management.

Jeremy P. Fyke is a doctoral candidate in organizational communication and graduate lecturer in the Department of Communication at Purdue University. His research interests include spirituality in organizations, courage in organizations, critical and feminist theory, and stress and support in pharmacy settings. His most recent work explores discursive perspectives on change management and consulting. He has presented numerous papers for professional organizations, including the National Communication Association and Central States Communication Association conferences, and published work in *The International Journal of Pharmaceutical Compounding, Indiana Pharmacist,* and *Place Branding and Public Diplomacy.* He enjoys a great life while currently living in Indiana with his beautiful wife, Brooke, and dog, Cooper.

G. Alan Fyke serves as Vice President, Sales and Marketing, for Humco Holding Group, Inc., of Texas. He is a Certified Pharmacy Technician, member of the American Pharmacists Association, Texas Pharmacy Association, and co-owner of IGA Pharmacy, Inc. His background includes 39 years of experience in wholesale club retailing, retail pharmacy, pharmaceutical distribution, and consumer packaged-goods branding and manufacturing. In his current role, he develops and conducts sales and communication training classes for company retail and physician sales representatives and customer service staff. He lives in Texas with his wife, Bonita, and is father to three sons and has six grandchildren.

Cerise L. Glenn, PhD, is an assistant professor in the Department of Communication Studies at the University of North Carolina at Greensboro. Her research and teaching areas include communication and culture, as well as organizational communication. Her research interests center on social constructions of difference (diversity), particularly identity negotiation and representations of underrepresented groups in organizational, intercultural/international, and popular culture. Her work often utilizes intersectional approaches to identity construction, such as the intersections of gender, race/ethnicity, and socioeconomic status. She also enjoys conducting workshops and seminars related to her research areas.

Maggie Glick retired from her job as CFO for one of the world's largest cattle feeding companies in August, 2009. After a 27-year career in accounting, she is a doctoral student at Colorado State University in Organizational Performance and Change (School of Education–Human Resource Studies). Maggie holds a BA in dietetics and an MS in financial accounting, and she is a licensed CPA in the State of Colorado. Maggie is a member of the Academy of Human Resource Development, the American Institute of Certified Public Accountants, and the Colorado Society of CPAs.

Gonca Gunay is an assistant professor of organizational behavior. She received her doctorate in the field of business administration in 2004. Her research areas of interest include innovation, entrepreneurship, and justice. On these issues, she has published books, book chapters, and articles in reputable national and international journals. Since 2004, she has been teaching management, organizational behavior, organization development, and current issues in management courses at Izmir University of Economics. In 2007, she studied at Columbia University as a visiting scholar, and in 2010 she studied at Harvard University for 6 months as a Fulbright Scholar. She is the Vice Dean of the Faculty of Economics and Administrative Sciences and the Director of the Center for Innovative Entrepreneurship.

Carrol R. Haggard is an associate professor of communication studies at Fort Hays State University in Hays, Kansas, where he teaches a variety of both undergraduate and graduate communication courses, including Organizational Communication and Leadership. He is a frequent contributor to the *Journal of the International Academy of Case Studies* and has been recognized by the International Academy of Case Studies as a five-time recipient of the Distinguished Research Award; three of those awards were shared with Dr. Lapoint. In addition, his research has been published in the *Journal of Organizational Culture, Communication, and Conflict, Communication Education, Communication Quarterly,* and the *Western States Communication Journal.* His research also is presented regularly at the Central States Communication Association, National Communication Association, and International Communication Association annual conventions.

Matthew G. Isbell is a Detroit native who received his bachelor's degree from Michigan State University, master's from the University of Montana, and doctorate from the University of Texas at Austin. His research examines how organizations can more effectively collaborate. His work has been published in *Communication Monographs* and the *Case Research Journal*. He also does organizational implementation and communication consulting. He is currently an assistant professor at Merrimack College in Massachusetts.

Alev Katrinli is a professor of organizational behavior. She received her doctorate in the field of business administration with a management major in 1983. Her main research area of interest is the effect of employee attitudes on their behaviors and performance. Related to these topics, she has published book chapters and articles in various reputable national and international journals. She has been teaching courses in the field of management, such as organizational behavior, organization development, organization theory, and management and leadership, at Izmir University of Economics. She has been the head of the Department of Business Administration since 2002, and Dean of the Faculty of Economics and Administrative Sciences since 2008.

Matt Koschmann, PhD, is an assistant professor in the Department of Communication at the University of Colorado at Boulder. His research focuses on organizational communication, with a particular emphasis on collaboration and stakeholder relationships in the nonprofit sector. He also teaches classes on organizational leadership and collaborative decision making.

Patricia A. Lapoint, PhD, is a professor of management at McMurry University in Abilene, Texas. She teaches a wide variety of management courses including Strategic Management, Operations Management, Human Resources Management, Organizational Behavior, and Quality Management. She is a frequent contributor to the *Journal of International Academy of Case Studies* with her coauthor, Dr. Haggard. She has been recognized by the International Academy of Case Studies as a three-time recipient of the Distinguished Research Award with her coauthor, Dr. Haggard. In addition, she has published in the *Journal of Organizational Culture, Communications, and Conflict.*

Nicole M. Laster, PhD, is an assistant professor at Kansas State University. She teaches courses in organizational communication, communication theory, and qualitative research methods. Her research has been published in *Business Communication Quarterly* and *Western Journal of Communication.* She works with leaders in business and other organizations to manage change through adaptive communication strategies. She has 8 years of industry experience spanning the marketing, public relations, and training and development sectors.

Shawn D. Long, PhD, is chair of the Department of Communication Studies and former Director of the Communication Graduate Program at the University of North Carolina at Charlotte. He is an associate professor of communication studies and associate professor of the Interdisciplinary Organizational Science Doctoral Program at the University of North Carolina at Charlotte. His teaching and research interests include organizational communication, organizational dialogue, virtual work, diversity communication, virtual- team assimilation and socialization, health communication, and interpretive methods associated with the study of organizational culture and symbolism. His primary research methods have employed interpretative phenomenology, case study approach, and grounded theory.

Rodney L. Lowman is currently Distinguished Professor of Organizational Psychology at Alliant International University in San Diego. He also has served as program director, dean, provost/VPAA and acting president at Alliant and as president at another university. Widely published on assessment, work dysfunctions, and ethics, he has practiced organizational consulting psychology throughout his professional career. His books include *Handbook of Organizational Consulting Psychology, The Ethical Practice of Psychology in Organizations* (2nd ed.), and *Counseling and Psychotherapy of Work Dysfunctions.* Currently he serves as editor of *Consulting Psychology Journal: Practice and Research.*

Bruce O. Mabee has been an OD consultant and OD instructor for more than 30 years. He is managing partner of Milestone Partners, LLC, in a practice serving corporate, government, and not-for-profit clients in the United States, Europe, Asia, and Latin America. He has created a variety of tools and training, including the Strategic Action System and The Consulting Workshops, which develop both consulting skills and consulting culture that pull together professionals and managers. He has taught leadership and consulting in seven graduate schools, including the University of Chicago, the Chicago School of Professional Psychology, and Benedictine University. He is former president of the OD Network of Chicago. He holds a master's in management and organizational behavior from George Williams Graduate School of Management and a BFA in industrial design from the University of Illinois at Urbana.

Franziska Macur is an assistant professor for communication studies at Edgewood College in Madison, Wisconsin. She received her master's in media and communication studies and her doctorate in communication studies from the University of Bonn, Germany. She teaches organizational communication and research methods classes, and her research centers on organizational communication with a specific focus on group dynamics and facilitation. She has worked with clients using conversation analysis to study the effects of facilitated organization development and employee development; i.e., continuing professional education, on-group conversation dynamics, and group decision-making processes.

Kenneth M. Macur, CPA, is the Associate Academic Dean and Professor of Accounting and Information Systems at Edgewood College in Madison, Wisconsin. He received his bachelor's in accountancy, MBA in finance, and doctorate in accountancy from the University of Illinois at Urbana-Champaign. He has taught at the University of Illinois, the University of Wisconsin—Whitewater, and the University of Wisconsin—Milwaukee. He has worked with clients in manufacturing, service, wholesale distribution, not-for-profit, and government, advising them in organization development, strategic planning, product costing, process improvement, and technology. He is a frequent lecturer on generational differences in the workplace, as well as understanding motivation and demotivation, and has received more than a dozen awards for teaching and research. He has authored numerous articles on innovation, generational differences, finance, accounting, and curriculum development.

Candace A. Martinez is an assistant professor of international business at Saint Louis University. She received her doctorate in strategic management from the University of Illinois at Urbana-Champaign. Her research examines the influence of formal and informal norms in institutional environments across countries (e.g., political hazards and risk of expropriation, corruption, culture, government regulation of entrepreneurs) on multinational firms' strategic choices in developing economies (e.g., ownership structure, FDI). One of her current research streams explores institutional change and entrepreneurship in the informal waste collection and recycling sector in Latin America and the role of business, government, and civil society in achieving sustainability objectives. Fluent in Spanish, she has conducted field research in Cuba and Guatemala City.

Alexandra Michel is an assistant professor in Work & Organisational Psychology at Heidelberg University, Germany. Her research focuses on change and human resource management, coaching, and occupational health. Besides working in academia she is also a practitioner. After graduating in psychology, she worked in a managing position in the human resources department of a big German health insurance company. At the time she started to work as an academic in business psychology, she also worked as a change manager in higher education. She is a trained and certified systemic and solution-focused therapist, counselor, and consultant and she has full memberships in national and international scientific associations. She is the author of several book chapters and journal articles and regularly presents her work at national and international conferences. Putting her research to practice, she consults with different profit and nonprofit organizations.

Stella M. Nkomo is full professor in the Department of Human Resource Management at the University of Pretoria, South Africa. Her internationally recognized research and work on race and gender and diversity in organizations appears in numerous journals, edited volumes, and books. She serves on the editorial board of a number of international and South African journals. She is listed in the *Who's Who in the Management Sciences* and received the 2009 Academy of Management Sage Scholarly Contributions Award for her research on gender and diversity in organizations. She is a former chair of the Department of Management in the Belk College of Business Administration at the University of North Carolina Charlotte and was full professor on the faculty of the Graduate School of Business Leadership at the University of South Africa between 2000 and 2009.

Katrin Noefer studied psychology at the University of Osnabrück, Germany, the Karl-Franzens University of Graz, Austria, and the University of Victoria, Canada. She wrote her master's thesis about intercultural leadership styles during change projects. She continued her academic career at the University of Heidelberg, Germany, where she received her doctorate. Demographic changes, personnel development, e-learning, change and innovation, as well as health promotion in organizations, are her key research interests. She is also a theatre therapist interested in transferring theatrical techniques into business to raise employees' satisfaction and performance levels. She is currently working as a consultant for 4a-SIDE consultancy. In her work, she focuses on evaluating training and change projects. She also analyses team interactions and competencies and helps improving teamwork.

Brian J. O'Leary is an associate professor of industrial-organizational psychology at the University of Tennessee at Chattanooga (UTC). He completed his doctorate in organizational behavior at the A. B. Freeman School of Business at Tulane University in 2005. Before seeking his PhD in 1996, he worked for 14 years in various management positions at Western Electric, AT&T, and Lucent Technologies, primarily in government contracting and accounting. He teaches numerous graduate and undergraduate courses at UTC, including Groups and Teams in Organizations, Training and Development, Employment Discrimination Law and Introduction to I-O Psychology. He also has provided consulting services for a variety of local, regional, and international organizations, primarily in the areas of job analysis and training.

Andrea M. Pampaloni, PhD, is an assistant professor in the Communication Department at La Salle University. Her research interests focus on organizational and interpersonal communication issues, and the relationship between the two. She also has extensive work experience in corporate, government, and nonprofit sectors in the areas of marketing, research, budget development and maintenance, and proposal writing. Her current research looks at organizational image, specifically the effectiveness of open houses at colleges and universities in appealing to their targeted audiences. She has been published in the *Journal for Marketing of Higher Education* and *Teaching Ideas for the Basic Communication Course,* and she holds membership with National Communication Association, Eastern Communication Association, and Pennsylvania Communication Association.

Barbara A. Ritter is an associate professor of management in the E. Craig Wall Sr. College of Business Administration at Coastal Carolina University and she holds the James P. and Elizabeth R. Blanton Endowed Professorship. She earned her doctorate from the University of Akron and joined the Wall College in 2004. Her teaching responsibilities include undergraduate and MBA courses in human resource management, organizational behavior, and international management. Her research interests include perceptions and legitimacy of organizational leaders, justice perceptions, and sexual harassment. She has been teaching and studying these and other diversity-related issues for more than 10 years and has led training exercises for MBA students, local organizations, and national and international conferences, including the Academy of Management and Organizational Behavior Teaching Conference. Her recent publications appear in *The Journal of Applied Psychology, The Journal of Business Ethics,* and *Human Relations.*

Aruna Fernandes Rodrigues, MBA/MOD, has been an OD practitioner for more than 15 years. She has extensive experience in the areas of change strategy, organization development, organization design, business process improvement, training, and communication strategy. Her expertise is in the design and implementation of change programs for large-scale business transformations. She has supported large-scale technology implementations for organizations ranging from 6,000 to 300,000 plus employees. She has served on the board of the Cleveland chapter of the OD Network and was one of the founding members of a youth leadership program conducted in the Cleveland Public School system inspired by Kathie Dannemiller's whole systems change work.

Pravin A. Rodrigues, PhD, is an associate professor in the Communication Arts Department at Ashland University in Ohio. He has taught graduate and undergraduate courses in organizational communication, small group discussion, and leadership communication. His consulting and organizational experiences have focused on best communication practices and diversity initiatives in organizations.

Cynthia Roman is Director of Human Resource Programs and Assistant Professor of Management and Human Resources at Marymount University in Arlington, Virginia. She teaches courses in executive coaching, organization development, and consulting, as well as other courses in the School of Business Administration. She is also an executive coach and registered organization development professional who coaches, trains, and consults in a variety of organizations, including federal, nonprofit, higher education, and professional services sectors. She is certified by the International Coach Federation at the level of Professional Certified Coach (PCC). She has assisted organizations with critical management and leadership issues such as coaching, mentoring, executive presence, leadership development, communication, conflict management, team development, and change management. She is coauthor of *Organizational Coaching: Relationships and Programs That Drive Results* (ASTD Press, 2008) and of *Leading From the Inside Out: A Coaching Model* (Sage Publications, 2002).

Marilyn Schock is currently the CEO at McKee Medical Center in Loveland, Colorado. While originally from Cody, Wyoming, northern Colorado has been her home since 1986. She holds a bachelor's of science in occupational therapy and a master's in business administration from Colorado State University. Throughout her career, she has assumed various roles in the medical community, including leadership roles in rehabilitation services, managed care operations, and hospital administration. As a leader, she inspires visionary commitment and excellence through passion and purpose. She is currently a member of ACHE, a Registered Occupational Therapist, chair for the Loveland Chamber of Commerce, and active in many community activities. In her spare time she enjoys travel, outdoor activities, and gardening.

Sachiyo M. Shearman, PhD, is an assistant professor of the School of Communication at East Carolina University. She teaches courses such as Conflict and Communication, Communication Research Methods, and Intercultural Communication both at the undergraduate and the graduate level. Her research interests include cross-cultural comparative studies in communication styles and preferences, individual differences (such as dogmatism and lack of perspective-taking) and cognitive processing in negotiation, conflict resolution, and intercultural communication. Her research has been published in journals such as *Human Communication Research, Communication Quarterly, Journal of Intercultural Communication Research, Language and Communication,* and *Asian Journal of Social Psychology.*

Vicki F. Taylor is associate professor of management in the John L. Grove College of Business at Shippensburg University. She received her doctorate in human resources from Temple University's Fox School of Business and Management. Prior to that she was a human resources manager for UPMC. Her research interests include organization development, organizational cultures, change management, and human resources.

Rachael Thomas is a management consultant specializing in organization assessment, design, and transition. She has worked across a variety of industries from consumer goods and software, to industrial manufacturing, mining, and utilities in the United States, United Kingdom, and Canada. Her experiences with organizational design include moving to shared services models, managing downsizing efforts, creating designs to support future growth, and updating team structures to improve customer service. She has led both large and small design efforts, and favors an approach that encourages conceptual thinking about structure as well as detailed analysis of job functions. As a practitioner, she has had the opportunity to apply a variety of approaches and models and believes that high collaboration with the client is the best way to be successful in organizational design projects.

Jennifer A. Thompson recently earned a doctorate from the Morgridge College of Education at the University of Denver. Her dissertation research focused on the history of the curriculum at Colorado Women's College. She has published in *Frontiers: A Journal of Women Studies* and contributed a book chapter on the work of gender and multicultural theorist Peggy McIntosh. She has taught courses in women's studies and the history of women's education. Her current research interests include the history of education, women's college curricula, women in the American West, and gender issues in education. She also holds a bachelor's degree in international relations from the University of California, Davis, and a master's degree in U.S. history from the University of Colorado, Boulder. She has worked in the fields of publishing, archives management, and higher education.

Maria Vakola is an organizational psychologist and she is currently an assistant professor at the Athens University of Economics and Business, Greece. She earned her postgraduate and doctoral qualifications from the University of Manchester and the University of Salford, U.K. She has published in the field of organizational behaviour and change in academic journals such as the *Journal of Applied Psychology, Journal of Organizational Change Management, Journal of Change Management,* and *Communications of the ACM.* Her research interests focus on change recipients' reactions to change, the role of change agency in change success, and the role of organizational silence in change.

Julie Williamson is a management consultant responsible for leading teams in a variety of industries to deliver on strategic objectives. Her primary areas of professional interest include strategy definition, market entry and exit, and change management. Julie is a doctoral candidate affiliated with the University of Colorado, School of Communication. Academically, Julie's interests include the ways in which organizational knowledge is constituted through collaboration, leading to innovation and acceleration of improvements within a corporate environment. Julie is primarily a qualitative researcher, and takes a constitutive position in her work, believing that organizations are primarily created through the communication that takes place within them.

SAGE Research Methods Online

The essential tool for researchers

Sign up now at www.sagepub.com/srmo for more information.

An expert research tool

- An **expertly designed taxonomy** with more than 1,400 unique terms for social and behavioral science research methods

- **Visual and hierarchical search tools** to help you discover material and link to related methods

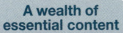

- Easy-to-use navigation tools
- Content organized by complexity
- Tools for citing, printing, and downloading content with ease
- Regularly updated content and features

A wealth of essential content

- The most comprehensive picture of quantitative, qualitative, and mixed methods available today

- More than **100,000 pages of SAGE book and reference material** on research methods as well as editorially selected material from SAGE journals

- More than **600 books** available in their entirety online

Launching 2011!

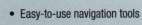

$SAGE research methods online